EXECUTIVE DE
AUTHORITY

When presidents or prime ministers make law by decree, are we witnessing the usurpation of legislative authority? The increased frequency of policy making by decree, in older democracies as well as in the newer regimes of Latin America and the post-communist world, has generated concern that legislatures are being marginalized and thus that democratic institutions are not functioning. Professors Carey and Shugart suggest which elements of constitutional design should (and should not) foster reliance on decree authority. Individual chapters then bring the experiences of Argentina, Brazil, France, Italy, Peru, Russia, the United States, and Venezuela to bear on the theory. The book combines broadly comparative analysis with intensive case studies to provide a more thorough understanding of the scope of executive authority across countries.

EXECUTIVE DECREE AUTHORITY

Edited by

JOHN M. CAREY
MATTHEW SOBERG SHUGART

CAMBRIDGE
UNIVERSITY PRESS

PUBLISHED BY THE PRESS SYNDICATE OF THE UNIVERSITY OF CAMBRIDGE
The Pitt Building, Trumpington Street, Cambridge CB2 1RP, United Kingdom

CAMBRIDGE UNIVERSITY PRESS
The Edinburgh Building, Cambridge CB2 2RU, UK   http://www.cup.cam.ac.uk
40 West 20th Street, New York, NY 10011-4211, USA   http://www.cup.org
10 Stamford Road, Oakleigh, Melbourne 3166, Australia

First published 1998

Printed in the United States of America

Typeset in Garamond #3, Penta [RF]

Library of Congress Cataloging-in-Publication Data

Executive decree authority/edited by John M. Carey, Matthew Soberg
    Shugart.
        p.   cm.
    Includes bibliographical references and index.
    ISBN 0–521–59255–0 (hb). – ISBN 0–521–59722–6 (pbk.)
    1. Executive orders. I. Carey, John M. II. Shugart, Matthew
    Soberg, 1960–   .
    K3350.E98   1998
    342'.06'02636 – dc21   97-50077
                                                                  CIP

*A catalog record for this book is available from
the British Library*

ISBN 0 521 59255 0 hardback
ISBN 0 521 59722 6 paperback

CONTENTS

CONTRIBUTORS

John M. Carey is assistant professor of political science at Washington University in St. Louis. His research focuses on how the rules of competition and procedure affect political representation. He is author of *Term Limits and Legislative Representation* (Cambridge, 1996) and co-author of *Presidents and Assemblies: Constitutional Design and Electoral Dynamics* (Cambridge, 1992). Future research will include a comparative study of campaign finance.

Brian F. Crisp is assistant professor of political science at the University of Arizona. He has published several articles and book chapters on interest group participation, presidentialism, and economic development. His most recent articles appeared in the *Latin American Research Review* and *Studies in Comparative International Development*. His most recently published book is entitled *Control Institucional de la Participación en la Democracia Venezolana* (Editorial Jurídica Venezolana, 1997).

Vincent Della Sala is associate professor of political science at Carleton University in Ottawa, Canada. He has published numerous articles on legislative and constitutional politics, and he is currently working on a project that examines changes to state structures in an increasingly interdependent global economy.

Delia Matilde Ferreira Rubio is co-chair of the Center for Studies in Applied Public Policy (CEPPA) in Buenos Aires, Argentina. She is the author of several articles on government, electoral systems, and political institutions. Currently, she is working with Matteo Goretti on a book entitled *Government Without Congress: The "Decretazo" During Menem's Administration*.

Matteo Goretti is co-chair of the Center for Studies in Applied Public Policy (CEPPA) in Buenos Aires, Argentina. He is the author of several articles on government, electoral systems, and political institutions. Currently, he is working with Delia Ferreira Rubio on a book entitled *Government Without Congress: The "Decretazo" During Menem's Administration.*

John Huber is assistant professor of political science at the University of Michigan. His research has focused primarily on understanding how institutional arrangements influence legislative–executive relations in parliamentary systems. Professor Huber's recent book, entitled *Rationalizing Parliament* (Cambridge, 1996), is a study of how constitutional arrangements in the French Fifth Republic influence interparty bargaining processes.

Amie Kreppel is currently completing her Ph.D. at the University of California, Los Angeles. Her studies focus on the political parties, party systems, and parliaments of Western Europe. Her dissertation is on the development of the Euron Parliament and the Supranational Party system. Publications include "The Impact of Parties on Legislative Output in Italy" and "The History of Conditional Agenda Setting in European Institutions"; both appeared in the *European Journal of Political Research.*

Scott D. Parrish is a postdoctoral research fellow at the Center for Nonproliferation Studies at the Monterey Institute of International Studies. Since completing his Ph.D. in political science at Columbia University, he has been a lecturer at the University of Texas at Austin and a senior research analyst at the Open Media Research Institute (OMRI) in Prague. His articles on Russian and Soviet politics have appeared in *Problems of Post-Communism* and *Transition.*

Timothy J. Power is assistant professor of political science at Louisiana State University. He has published several articles on democratic consolidation, the institutional design of new democracies, and Brazilian politics. He is currently completing a book manuscript entitled *Elites, Institutions, and Democratization: The Political Right in Postauthoritarian Brazil.* With Peter Kingstone, he is also co-editing the forthcoming volume *Democratic Brazil* (University of Pittsburgh Press).

Brian R. Sala is assistant professor of political science at the University of Illinois at Urbana-Champaign. He received his Ph.D. in 1994 from the University of California at San Diego. Professor Sala has published a number of articles on how members of the U.S. Congress respond to electoral incentives and how ideology affects roll-call voting in legislatures and executive–legislative relations; these articles have appeared in such journals as the *American Political Science Review,* the *American Journal of Political Science,* and the *Journal of Politics.*

Gregory D. Schmidt is associate professor of political science at Northern Illinois University in DeKalb, Illinois. He received his Ph.D. in 1984 from Cornell University. Professor Schmidt has published over a dozen journal articles, book chapters, and monographs on political institutions in Peru; he has served as a consultant to the United States Agency for International Development, and he has taught at several Peruvian universities. He is the author of *Donors and Decentralization in Developing Countries* (Westview Press, 1989) and a forthcoming book on the Peruvian electoral system to be published by the University Press of Florida.

Matthew Soberg Shugart is associate professor of political science at the Graduate School of International Relations and Pacific Studies at the University of California, San Diego. He is co-author of *Seats and Votes: The Effects and Determinants of Electoral Systems* (Yale, 1989) and *Presidents and Assemblies: Constitutional Design and Electoral Dynamics* (Cambridge, 1992); co-editor of *Presidentialism and Democracy in Latin America* (Cambridge, 1997); and the author of several journal articles on electoral institutions and their relationships with other phenomena, including economic reform and settlement of guerrilla conflict.

PREFACE

"Don't do edited volumes." This might be the most common piece of advice passed down from more experienced to less experienced political scientists. The reasons offered are, first, that coordinating a group of contributors inevitably entails more aggravation than simply conducting the research oneself; and second, that edited volumes tend to end up as collections of loosely related essays, not coherent and unified research projects.

With respect to the first point, we have been blessed with a group of contributors who combine intelligence, creativity, and an impressive respect for deadlines. If there was any surplus aggravation generated by this project, it was certainly our gift to them, rather than vice versa. With respect to the second point, we believe this book defies the "loosely related essays" label. Indeed, we undertook this as an edited volume because we had a clearly specified research project that we could not feasibly pursue any other way. We initially produced an essay (now Chapter 1) establishing a set of hypotheses regarding the use of executive decree authority. To test these hypotheses required more empirical knowledge of politics across a diverse set of countries than we could ever hope to acquire ourselves. The solution was to draw on specialists on politics in these countries who are committed to producing broadly comparative work and to testing theoretical propositions empirically. All the case study essays were written with the hypotheses in hand, and all address a common theoretical agenda.

Our greatest thanks, then, go to the contributors for sharing with us their enormous knowledge of politics on the ground in the various countries discussed here in this volume, for showing us how the nuts and bolts of such politics relate to our hypotheses, for their insights, and for their suggestions as to the direction of the overall project. We are also indebted to Alex Holzman for prescient editorial advice, and to Cambridge's three anonymous reviewers, whose suggestions with regard to previous drafts we have tried to embrace and whose criticisms we have tried to address.

By now we have circulated enough drafts and queries related to this project that any list of personal thanks is certain to be radically incomplete. At the risk of offending by omission, we thank Mark Jones, Scott Mainwaring, Scott Morgenstern, Terry Moe, Peter Ordeshook, Sunita Parikh, and Richard Rose. We also thank the participants in the political economy seminar series at Princeton and Columbia for their comments on earlier drafts and presentations of this work. We are also grateful to our colleagues at the University of California in San Diego, University of Rochester, and Washington University in St. Louis for specific criticisms, suggestions, and answers, and for creating intellectual environments that challenge and encourage research.

Finally, we thank our families, who have now endured our collaborative research on executives and legislatures for eight successive years. Perhaps it is they who should be allowed to comment on the aggravation associated with producing edited volumes. As is so common in these endeavors, however, space constraints do not allow us to pursue that line of analysis.

John M. Carey and Matthew Soberg Shugart

CALLING OUT THE TANKS OR FILLING OUT THE FORMS?

John M. Carey and Matthew Soberg Shugart

This power to act according to discretion for the public good, without the pre-scription of the law and sometimes even against it, is that which is called prerogative; for since in some governments the law-making power is not always in being and is usually too numerous, and so too slow for the dispatch requisite to execution, and because, also, it is impossible to foresee and so by laws to provide for all accidents and necessities that may concern the public . . . there-fore there is a latitude left to the executive power to do many things of choice which the laws do not prescribe.

JOHN LOCKE (1986: CH. XIV)

Hear me! I am your new President. From this day on, the official language of San Marcos will be . . . Swedish. {Murmurs in the crowd.} Silence! In addi-tion to that, all citizens will be required to change their underwear every half hour. Underwear will be worn on the outside – so we can check. Furthermore, all children under sixteen years old are now . . . sixteen years old.

COMANDANTE ESPÓSITO, UPON SEIZING THE PRESIDENCY OF THE
TINY LATIN AMERICAN REPUBLIC OF SAN MARCOS,
IN WOODY ALLEN'S 1971 FILM, *BANANAS*

INTRODUCTION

Locke's case for prerogative would surely be received favorably by Russian Pres-ident Boris Yeltsin or Argentine President Carlos Menem in defense of their use of executive decree. Students of democratic political institutions, however, are circumspect, equating decree with the capricious usurpation and abuse of au-thority depicted in Woody Allen's parody. The importance of legislatures as forums for deliberation and compromise among diverse political forces is widely acknowledged (Lijphart 1984; Przeworski 1991). Authority within executives, on the other hand, is usually more centralized. In presidential systems executives tend to be controlled by single parties – and sometimes even by individuals with weak or no connections to political parties (Jones 1995; Linz 1994; Mainwaring 1994). On these grounds it has become commonplace to argue that executive decree is evidence that legislatures are being marginalized and that democratic institutions are ineffectual.

Before this conclusion can be reached, however, we need to evaluate more carefully some important issues. One is whether legislative majorities might sometimes want policy to be made by executive decree rather than by the standard legislative process. Another is whether there are significant procedural differences among the various types of executive policy initiatives that are commonly referred to as decree authority. A third is whether the existence and types of decree authority that we observe are systematically associated with other institutional characteristics of political systems.

We concur with the conventional wisdom that many recent instances of executive decree – particularly in systems with elected presidents – have entailed usurpation of legislative powers. On the other hand, this is far from universally true, and the usurpation argument has frequently been overstated or derived from spurious evidence. We suggest that more frequently than is commonly acknowledged, executive decree is tolerated – or even preferred – by legislative majorities. This does not necessarily make executive decree a "good" thing, but it should redirect our attention away from an interpretation of decree based on usurpation and toward the question of why a legislature might favor decree. Moreover, we suggest three general factors that are critical when observing executive decree and interpreting its implications for legislative–executive relations: First is the severity of bargaining problems among legislators; second is the extent to which legislative majorities can expect to suffer agency losses[1] to executives with decree authority; and third is the extent to which the executive controls the process of writing and amending the constitution.

This chapter proceeds as follows. First we present the conventional interpretation of executive decree in the current political science literature – namely, that decree represents both the concentration of power in the executive and the marginalization of legislatures. Then we offer a more precise definition of executive decree, distinguishing first among various types of executive powers over legislation generally and then among types of decree authority specifically. Next we posit a set of motivations on the parts of executives and legislatures to prefer policy making by executive decree rather than by standard legislative procedures. Drawing from our new typology of decree and the possible motivations for relying on it, we offer nine explicit hypotheses for when we expect to observe decree, for the sort of decree we expect to observe, and for the reasons we expect to observe it. Finally, we lay out the plan of the rest of the volume, introducing the case studies that provide the extensive information about the use of decree in specific countries which will allow us, in the concluding chapter, to evaluate our original hypotheses in light of empirical evidence.

OBSERVING DECREE

On observing an executive implementing policy by decree, one might conclude that the executive is setting policy – and this might indeed be the case. But it could also be the case that the executive is anticipating the preferences of some other political actor – the legislature, for example. Simply by observing the action, there is no way to evaluate the relative merits of these two interpretations. Empirical studies of executive decree authority, however, have overwhelmingly favored the former interpretation, and frequently such studies have reached dire conclusions as a result. In considering economic reform packages implemented by decree by many Latin American governments during the 1980s, Przeworski concluded,

> Democracy is thus weakened. The political process is reduced to elections, executive decrees, and sporadic outbursts of protest. The government rules by decree, in an authoritarian fashion but often without much repression. All the power in the state is concentrated in the executive, which is nevertheless ineffectual in managing the economy. People get a regular chance to vote, but not to choose. (1991:186–7)

This has been the consensus interpretation of decree in the presidential systems of Latin America (Conaghan and Malloy 1994). It also is resonant more recently among observers of post-Soviet systems with elected presidents. One can even find charges that executives dependent on exclusive parliamentary confidence are able to use decree authority to act against assembly preferences (for a review, see Huber 1992). However, many accounts have not even entertained the possibility that decree could mean something other than usurpation. In a review of economic reforms undertaken in the Andean countries, for example, Conaghan, Malloy, and Abugattas (1990) note – but only in passing – that the Peruvian Constitution "allowed the Congress to delegate legislative functions to the executive for any period of time designated by the legislature" (20), and that in Bolivia and Ecuador, as well as in Peru, executives "all made political deals to stave off legislative opposition" to policies implemented by decree (21). Yet Conaghan, Malloy, and Abugattas never investigate whether decrees in Peru were products of legislative delegation (they frequently were, as Schmidt's chapter shows), nor whether the "political deals" involved substantive policy concessions to legislative actors whose opposition was "staved off." In the Bolivian case at least, the neoliberal economic policies decreed by President Paz Estenssoro in 1985 more closely resembled the platform of the plurality party in Congress, the National Democratic Alliance (ADN), than the platform of Paz's own party, the National Revolutionary Movement (MNR). Indeed, Paz's selection as president was due directly to ADN support in Congress,[2] in exchange for which he included ADN members in his cabinet. Moreover, he relied consistently on ADN support as well as on MNR support in the legislature throughout his term (Gamarra 1997). Still, Conaghan, Malloy, and Abugattas (1990) attribute reliance on executive decree to a "mental intransigence" within the executive that generated a "triumphal style" and "a highly exclusionary process" of policy making (27). Their conclusions echo Przeworski's:

> Executives [were] capable of acting in a decidedly authoritarian mode, despite the formal democratic frameworks within which executive power was formulated and legitimated. In short, in all three cases [Peru, Bolivia, and Ecuador] we see the outlines of a hybrid form of government in which a formal democratic facade masks a real authoritarian bent. (Conaghan, Malloy, & Abugattas 1990:27)

In its most sweeping form, the usurpation interpretation characterizes policy making by executive decree as *delegative democracy*: regimes in which "whoever wins election to the presidency is thereby entitled to govern as he or she sees fit, constrained only by the hard facts of existing power relations and by a constitutionally limited term of office" (O'Donnell 1994:59).[3] Kubicek (1994) extends the idea of delegative democracy to the post-Soviet states, presenting as evidence a host of economic and political reforms implemented by presidential decree in Russia and Ukraine in the early 1990s.

Much of Kubicek's evidence for presidential usurpation, especially in Russia, is compelling. The same is true for some of the Latin American cases. When a Yeltsin (in Russia) or a Fujimori (in Peru) calls out the tanks to surround the legislature and decrees that the institution is shut down, it would be senseless to argue, on the basis of constitutional texts, that we are not observing executive usurpation of power. On the other hand, presidential decree authority is far more often exercised under less dramatic circumstances – that is, when legislatures are in session and frequently according to guidelines formally established either by constitution or by statute. We argue that too frequently, these more mundane incarnations of executive decree are lumped together with "calling out the tanks," and as a result, the phenomenon of executive decree as a whole is misinterpreted. *We do not argue* that executive decree is never used by executives as a tool to implement policies for which they lack legislative support. Indeed, some of the chapters in this volume contain detailed case studies of executives who established policies opposed by a majority of the assembly. We do argue that there is a wide variety of phenomena that have commonly been described uniformly as executive decree, but we also maintain that there are important institutional differences among them. And we argue that specific institutional characteristics of political systems can largely explain the presence or absence of various types of executive decree.

POLICY AUTHORITY OF EXECUTIVES

One of the fundamental obstacles to a common understanding of executive decree is that the term is used to describe a number of different practices. In other work we note that executive rule making in the implementation of legislation, decree authority delegated by legislatures, decree authority established in constitutions, and powers allotted to presidents under constitutional states of emergency or exception are all referred to in various places as presidential decree authority (Shugart and Carey 1992). Moreover, the expression *rule by decree* is often used to describe situations of martial law. If everything from an act detailing the procedures under which an agency hires contractors to a dramatic suspension of the constitution and the jailing of the opposition can be called a decree, we obviously risk terminological confusion. Thus, in this chapter we offer a typology that directs attention to the procedural differences among decrees and the implications of those differences for the scope of executive power. Although most critics of decree have focused on its use by presidents, executive decree is quite common in parliamentary and hybrid systems as well. We offer hypotheses about decree that apply generally across regime types. We situate this typology within a larger typology of policy authority that executives may hold. Starting with the broad and moving to the narrow, this section first takes up the issue of the varying forms of executive policy authority, of which decree is but a subcategory.

There is a wide range of constitutional authorities that executives might have over legislation. Legislative powers may be conveniently broken down into two categories: reactive and proactive. The distinction centers on the relationship between the executive authority and the reversionary outcome. The reversionary outcome – frequently the status quo – is the state of the world that obtains if the executive does not exercise authority. Reactive powers are those by which the executive can maintain policy at the reversionary outcome even in the face of legislative preferences for a different outcome – in the case, for example, in which the executive blocks an attempt by the legislative majority to authorize a new class of welfare entitlements or to cut funding from a previously authorized level of appropriations. Reactive powers are thus "conservative" in the sense that they permit the executive to prevent a change that would otherwise take place. Proactive powers, on the other hand, are powers that enable the executive to effect changes in the reversionary outcome that the legislature would not have *initiated* on its own.

The most common reactive power is the veto. For instance, by exercising a veto, the U.S. president can prevent policy change unless Congress musters the two-thirds vote in each house to override. More importantly, the legislature must anticipate the veto – and many of the bills that it passes will reflect presidential preferences to some degree – in an effort to obtain presidential assent. There are other variants of reactive powers, but they are easily mistaken for proactive powers, so we discuss them later.

In the category of proactive powers, we distinguish between decree powers and agenda powers. The fundamental characteristic of decree authority is that policy decisions taken by the executive are implemented in lieu of any legislative action. This does not necessarily mean that policies made by decree cannot subsequently be retracted or altered by legislative action, but it does mean that the policy status quo can be changed – at least provisionally – even though the legislature has not consented to the change before it takes place. Agenda power, by contrast, is the authority to constrain either the set of policy alternatives from which the assembly may choose or the timetable according to which these choices must be made – or both. Thus, a first step in understanding practices that give the executive procedural advantage in implementing new policy is to clarify the distinction between decree power and agenda power.

Agenda powers are common to executives across regime types. For example, many executives can present policies under a closed rule (package vote), forcing assemblies to choose between a single policy alternative and the status quo. Such a power gives the executive a strong tool for influencing policy outcomes, provided that the legislative majority and the executive agree that change away from the status quo is desirable and that their preferences regarding the direction of change are not perfectly antithetical. In such a case the executive can make a proposal, and even if it is not the proposal that the assembly would have made on its own, the assembly may approve it rather than stick with a status quo that a majority of its members does not want to prevail. Related to this power, but giving the executive somewhat less leverage, are provisions for restricted amendment. In Chile, for instance, the executive submits appropriations legislation, to which the legislature is limited to one of two responses: (a) accept the proposal or (b) amend the proposal by spending less. Because a third option – amend the proposal by spending more – is constitutionally precluded, the executive can obtain its preferred option even if the assembly would prefer to spend much more than the executive proposes (Baldez and Carey 1997).

These forms of agenda power should not be confused with certain variants of reactive powers that on their face look quite similar. For instance, many constitutions, especially in Latin America, grant the executive *gatekeeping* authority. This term implies that there are certain policy jurisdictions in which new policy proposals may be considered only if the executive chooses to initiate a bill. Note that if the assembly is not restricted in amending a proposal once initiated, then a bill may be amended in such a way as to make it vastly different from the original proposal. If the executive does not also have a veto, then the executive with gatekeeping power is forced into a choice of either (a) the status quo or (b) what the assembly majority would prefer. For this reason we regard gatekeeping to be a type of reactive authority. Executives can block change desired by the assembly majority by not opening the matter up for consideration, but they cannot determine the specifics of policy changes once the gate is open.

In Figure 1.1 we depict a stylized policy game in a single dimension, one defined as the amount of money to be spent on any given policy area. Policy is some outcome of bargaining between the executive (E) and the assembly (A). For sim-

Figure 1.1 Bargaining between an executive and an assembly in one dimension

plicity we consider both to be unitary actors, although this assumption is obviously unrealistic in most cases, especially for the assembly.[4] Each actor is assumed both to have a preference for outcomes closer to its ideal point than to a farther point and to derive declining utility monotonically in either direction as an outcome deviates from the ideal point.[5]

Consider first the case in which the assembly wants to spend more than the executive does; the assembly's ideal point is represented by A1. According to the location of the ideal points in this example, the executive would prefer the reversionary outcome R to A1, so he or she would veto A1 if he or she had the authority to do so. If the assembly lacks the votes (or the authority) to override a veto, the best it can do is to locate policy at a point at which the executive is indifferent to the assembly's proposal and the status quo – in this case at I(E).

If the executive, instead of having a veto, has gatekeeping authority, the outcome is R. The reason is that gatekeeping authority only prevents the assembly from initiating policy change; it does not give executives any additional authority in the event they have decided to initiate a proposal. Because the executive in our example prefers R to A1, the assembly's ideal point, and because the executive in this game lacks an ex post veto, the only influence the executive can have over the outcome is simply to keep the gate closed. Hence gatekeeping is a reactive power – an authority to maintain the status quo. Now suppose that in addition to gatekeeping authority, the executive can impose restrictions on an amendment. If the executive can introduce legislation under a closed rule (i.e., in a take-it-or-leave-it fashion), the executive in this instance can attain his or her ideal point because the assembly prefers E to R and hence will pass the executive proposal.[6] Thus the package vote is proactive, in the sense that the executive can use it to introduce and obtain an outcome different from what the assembly would pass if it were the initiator of policy change.[7]

It is worth considering briefly what happens if we shift the relative positions of the actors' ideal points. Suppose that instead of a profligate assembly, we have one that is more stingy than the executive – in this case, A2. Then the veto is not effective. The executive cannot induce more spending, because a veto would actually lead to less R than the assembly had proposed. For the same reason gatekeeping powers are similarly ineffective in this case: The assembly wants to spend less than the executive. The executive could propose E, only to see the assembly amend it to A2; however, this outcome is preferable to the executive than what would obtain if he or she kept the gate closed (R). The package vote (with gatekeeping), on the other hand, would allow the executive to attain an outcome closer to his or her own preferences. Because the assembly prefers to spend more than R, the executive can submit a proposal at the point at which the assembly is indifferent between the executive proposal and R. That point in Figure 1.1 is I(A2). Thus, this proactive power allows the executive to move policy in his or her direction – that is, farther than the assembly would do if left to its own devices.

Any of the panoply of reactive powers and proactive powers allow the executive to influence the policy process, but they do so in different ways. Reactive powers are useful when the executive prefers the status quo to the ideal of the assembly majority. Proactive powers, through the advantage conferred on policy initiators, allow executives to secure policy changes that they could not have obtained with strictly reactive powers. Nevertheless, the agenda powers we have discussed thus far still require that new policy proposals be ratified by the legislature. Here is where decree powers are different. Decree means that executive decisions become the policy status quo even without legislative action. When thinking about how much leverage decree powers give the executive, one must place them within the context of other executive powers and the nature of the legislature, as well as within the context of agencies such as courts and controllers general. The empirical chapters in this volume discuss these sorts of interactions among different institutions in practice. For now, if we return to Figure 1.1 and recall our assumptions of unitary actors, we find that decree power in isolation is really quite ineffective; so too is agenda power. If the assembly has a clear ideal point – whether A1 or A2 – and is not restricted in any way from enacting it, no decree at point E will stand. The assembly will overturn it and replace it with its own preferred point by passing new legislation. Of course, the executive can always respond with yet another decree, suggesting that outcomes in the decree game might be unstable. Generalizing, we may say that any proactive power in isolation is vulnerable to assembly counteraction. Even in the package vote example discussed earlier, if the assembly has full authority to initiate policy and if the executive lacks a veto, the outcome of the use of the package-vote procedure can also be overturned. Where proactive powers are valuable, then, is where one of two conditions holds: Either (a) the executive has some reactive power in addition to his or her proactive power, or (b) the assembly, for internal reasons, is unable to identify or enact its ideal point.

Proactive powers can be formidable if the executive also has reactive powers in the same policy areas. With a veto, executives can prevent a legislature from overturning their decrees or policies (those that were passed under package vote) as long as they have the support in the assembly of whatever share of seats is needed to sustain vetoes (often just one-third). With gatekeeping power, executives can prevent any attempt by the assembly to change the new status quo that has been established through the use of proactive executive authority. In many of the cases discussed in this book, there is some combination of reactive and proactive powers. The most prominent example is Russia, where the president may issue decrees with the force of law in almost any policy area where there is no existing law. The president also has a veto that requires a two-thirds vote to override. As Parrish's chapter shows, there have been several specific policy battles in which the president has prevailed over the manifest objections of a majority of both houses of the assembly.

The second condition under which proactive powers can be effective in allowing the executive to obtain outcomes that are distinct from assembly preferences is when those assembly preferences themselves are ill-defined. That is, we must relax either our unitary actor assumption or the assumption that policy choices are unidimensional – or both. Some assemblies may be controlled by disciplined majority parties, in which case the unitary actor assumption does not grossly obscure reality. However, most of the time there is either a coalition of parties needed to pass legislation or there is a majority party that is internally divided. Under either scenario there may be many possible outcomes, even in one dimension. If coalition partners or intraparty factions are at odds over policy, the executive can use proactive powers to exploit bargaining problems within the assembly and obtain an outcome that is on his or her preferred side of (for example) point A2 in Figure 1.1.

Some important lessons of these spatial-modeling exercises can be summarized. First, the effectiveness of reactive and proactive powers often depends not only on the nature of the authority itself (i.e., on whether the executive acts to alter or protect the reversionary outcome) but also on the distribution of preferences and the extent of disorganization in the assembly. Second, we note that in the presence of cohesive assembly majorities, decree authority, which on its face would seem to imply executive dominance of policy making, will not allow executives to make their policy preferences stick unless decree is combined with reactive powers. Finally, we have suggested conditions under which executives may have influence even when they lack reactive powers to go along with decree powers: when the assembly is internally divided, when it lacks information, or when time is of the essence. In the sections that follow, we elaborate on these preliminary observations and cite some specific hypotheses about when executives or legislatures will prefer policy making by decree. But first we must clarify variations within the class of decree power. All of the discussion that has preceded is applicable to these different types of decree power, but it is important to understand differences among types.

DEFINING DECREE AUTHORITY

We define decree as the authority of the executive to establish law in lieu of action by the assembly.[8] Thus, decree does not refer to executive actions governing the administration of law that has been set by the assembly. On the other hand, executive policy initiatives are considered decree even if they eventually require ratification by the assembly, as long as the initiatives go into effect with-

Table 1.1 *Variants of constitutional decree authority*

		Decree becomes permanent law?	
		YES	NO
		Russia (Art. 90)	Brazil '88 (Art. 62)
	YES	Peru '93 (Art. 118:19)	Italy (Art. 77)
		Colombia '91 (Art. 215)	Colombia '91 (Art. 213)
Decree in effect		Chile '89 (Art. 32: 22)	Argentina '94 (Art. 99:3)
immediately?			France (Art. 16)
		Ecuador (Art. 65)	
	NO	France (Art. 49:3)	N.A.

out prior legislative action. Even our seemingly straightforward definition of decree encompasses significant empirical complexity. We observe variance in particular on two components of it:

1. that executive proposals are immediately effective as policy (yes/no)
2. that executive proposals become permanent law even without legislative action (yes/no).

The four possible combinations of these components form a two-by-two matrix, as shown as Table 1.1. (Empirical examples appear in each "box.") Both of these variations are important. The first – whether measures are permanent or not – tells us whether the assembly must take explicit action to rescind the decree or not. The second tells us whether or not there is any opportunity for debate of the measure before it becomes law.

At the top left is the prototypical decree authority, whereby the executive issues a proposal that becomes permanent law immediately and without any legislative action. In these cases the assembly may not even have had an opportunity to debate the measure before it was brought to its attention by an executive action that made a policy change a fait accompli. Moreover, cases in this cell indicate that only through the passage of new legislation (or a new decree) can the policy change. Apart from regimes in which the executive is not selected through democratic means,[9] we know of only four constitutions that grant their executives such power. The Russian president is constrained only insofar as decrees "cannot contradict the Constitution of the Russian Federation or Federal Law" (Art. 90). The Colombian president may declare a State of Economic Emergency and issue decrees to restore "economic order" (Art. 215). The Peruvian president can exercise constitutional decree authority (CDA) "on economic and financial matters, when so required by the national interest" (Art. 118). The Chilean president may decree expenditures not provided for in the budget and totaling up to one percent of the total funds appropriated in the annual budget to meet unforeseen contingencies (Art. 32:22).

At the top right is decree authority in which executive proposals take effect immediately; but in this case, such proposals lapse after some designated period unless ratified by the legislature. This describes decree in the current Italian (Art. 77) and Brazilian (Art. 62) systems, where the time periods are sixty and thirty days, respectively, as well in the Colombian (Art. 213) system, where the time period is ninety days (although it can be extended unilaterally by the executive to 180 days). As with the upper-left cell, decrees in this cell may be issued even without any prior opportunity for the assembly to debate the matter at hand. However, the executive cannot ensure that the new status quo will remain intact after the period of the decree's effectiveness has ended. Whether such a provision is effective for instituting long-term changes against assembly preferences depends to a large degree on whether the reiteration of decrees at the end of the period is permissible. The reiteration of decrees has been a matter of constitutional controversy in both Brazil and Italy, as chapters in this volume by Power and by Della Sala and Kreppel show. This form of decree may be termed *provisional* decree authority.

At bottom left, executive proposals do not take effect immediately, but they become law even in lieu of legislative action. This describes the situation in Ecuador, where the president can propose legislation, declaring it "urgent," but if Congress fails to act within fifteen days, the proposal becomes law. It also describes a procedure in France (Art. 49.3) that is sometimes termed the *guillotine*, whereby if Parliament rejects the government's proposal, then the government falls; but if Parliament takes no action, the proposal becomes law. In both cases there is an opportunity for the assembly to debate the measure before it takes effect. This is a potentially important distinction: If debate reveals a feature of the proposal that is embarrassing to the executive, he or she can withdraw the proposal before it becomes effective. There is also time to reach a mutually acceptable compromise before the end of the review period. However, in common with other forms of decree, a determined executive can allow a proposal to become law even in the face of assembly opposition. Members of the assembly can also duck the issue if they choose, letting the measure "passively" become law without ever having to vote for it – and perhaps having to explain the vote later on.

Even without the *guillotine* procedure, confidence votes – by which the executive makes survival of the government contingent on acceptance by the assembly of a specific policy – resemble our notion of decree authority but should be kept distinct. The confidence vote forces a choice between new alternatives (a new policy or a new government) and precludes maintenance of the status quo (current government, current policy) (Diermeier and Feddersen 1995; Huber 1996b). Because the confidence vote mechanism in most parliamentary systems does not impose the new policy automatically as a result of executive decision, we distinguish it from decree power. What makes the French procedure a variant of decree authority, then, is that non-action by the assembly after the executive has invoked Article 49.3 leads to a situation in which a policy takes effect despite the fact that a vote has not been held in the assembly. Finally, we know of no cases that would fall in the lower right box. Any such (hypothetical) cases would be executive policy initiatives that did not gain legal force until after a specified discussion period and that would lapse if not converted into law by the end of a given time after taking effect.

The distinction in Table 1.1 between the timing aspect of decree authority (immediately effective or not) and the degree to which decree is a tool for making provisional versus permanent policy is important because the two conditions have different implications for executive power. Where proposals are effective immediately, even if they lapse without legislative approval, executives can credibly threaten legislatures with having to bear the "clean-up costs" of *not* ratifying executive decrees. That is, once a policy is set, it may be extremely costly to back away from it, thus making it difficult for the legislature to let a decree lapse even if no majority favored it in the first place.[10] Where executive proposals are not effective immediately but do become effective in lieu of legislative action, on the other hand, the importance of decree authority results from the extent to which it constrains legislative choices over future policy alternatives. Thus, to move from the top to the bottom row of Table 1.1 is to move from pure decree in the direction of agenda power.[11]

Apart from the issues of timing and ex post legislative approval, the other important definitional issue is whether executive decree authority is delegated by the legislature or is claimed by the executive as constitutional. Four distinct phenomena are commonly described as executive decree; the first two are characterized by the statutory delegation of authority by legislatures, and the second two imply executive initiative in the absence of specific delegation.

DELEGATED AUTHORITY

Rule making. Virtually any legislation implies some level of discretion in implementation for the executive. An assembly might write explicit instructions into legislation about how a law is to be executed, or it might simply establish general goals by statute and charge the executive with establishing the specific methods by which those goals are to be met. Part of the current confusion over the extent of the use of presidential decree is probably semantic. For instance, the Spanish word *decreto* and the Russian word *ukaz* translate to "decree," but both describe other actions besides executive-imposed policy changes. What would be referred to in the United States as executive orders, as well as rule making (administrative orders) within executive departments and independent regulatory agencies, are all denoted as *decretos* in Latin American government registers and as *ukazy* in Russia. The great majority of the actions so designated represents executive decisions taken in the course of implementing existing laws or exercising what are typically inherent executive prerogatives, such as establishing interagency task forces, commuting sentences of convicted felons, or pinning medals on veterans. Only a small fraction of these actions actually imply presidential initiatives to change policy as established by statute. Thus, it is important to establish at the outset that the volume of so-called decrees does not accurately reflect the frequency with which presidents initiate new policies by decree.

Of more substantive policy significance are executive decisions governing the administration of broad laws passed by assemblies. In his chapter in this volume, Sala argues that in the United States the discretion exercised through executive orders is of limited scope. In France, on the other hand, the Constitution reserves substantial regulative and administrative functions to the executive, limiting assembly involvement in rule making.[12] In several Latin American countries, many laws only spell out the basic framework of policy, leaving important details to be completed by executive decree. In some cases – as in France – the reasons for this practice may be found in the constitutional division of legislative and administrative domains. In other cases the reasons may be more political than legal. For example, the president may be the leader of a legislative majority party that allows its leader wide discretion, or legislators may have other reasons for preferring not to undertake the task of writing detailed statutes in the first place. Later in this chapter, we discuss these political motivations for the delegation of policy-making authority, whether through rule making or by decree, in more detail.

Most rule-making orders would be of the type found in the upper-left cell of Table 1.1, although various requirements that the executive or regulatory agency "give notice" before promulgating rules would place them in the lower-left cell. However, there is a very important caveat. These decrees are not law; they are subordinate to the law. The distinction may not always be crystal clear in practice, but it is made in every legal order of which we are aware. Typically courts, administrative tribunals, or controllers general[13] are empowered to overturn rule making acts that, in their judgment, exceed the scope of statutory authority.

Delegated Decree Authority (DDA). Rather than writing legislation which allows the executive to make decisions on the rules for implementation, assemblies sometimes pass legislation giving the executive the authority to make new laws by decree – and thus to change policies explicitly set by (or outside the bounds of) existing statutes. The scope of DDA might be broad – for example, in the case where an assembly delegates without limiting the policy areas in which the executive can initiate changes. More often, however, when assemblies approve DDA, they do so in specific policy areas and for limited time periods. Of the two forms of delegated authority, it is DDA – the ability of the executive to change statute – with which we are most concerned in this book.

EXECUTIVE INITIATIVE

Constitutional Decree Authority (CDA). Some executives are endowed by constitutions with the authority to initiate policies by decree, and they are given this authority apart from any delegation of authority by statute. Two types of

CDA should be distinguished: emergency powers and standard decree authority. Many constitutions establish emergency powers by which executives can suspend civil liberties and take control of local government agencies in times of unrest. These powers, however, are usually subject to explicit legislative approval, either before they can be exercised or within a short time (perhaps a week) after their assumption, and they are usually limited to actions taken to restore order rather than to set broad policy.[14] Although these powers can be enormously important – at the extreme, they entail martial law – we feel that it is important to keep them conceptually distinct from the authority to change policy by decree in some area. Where it is an uncontested fact of constitutional law that the executive can take policy initiatives without prior legislative consent – whatever conflicts may crop up over specific policies – we have a case of CDA in its most straightforward sense; it may occur in any of the variations shown in Table 1.1. On the other hand, when executives push the limits of emergency powers that are meant to be limited to curtailing some liberties in the event of civil disturbances and instead use these powers to set new policy, or when they assert authority to take actions in spite of a seeming lack of any decree authority in the constitution, we step into the realm of what we term "paraconstitutional" initiative.

Paraconstitutional Initiative. Finally, there are decrees that represent pure presidential initiative but that are not clearly constitutionally delineated. We choose the word *paraconstitutional* to describe these decrees (rather than *unconstitutional*) out of a determination to suspend judgment – and to avoid drifting into waters (adjudicating constitutionality) that we are unprepared to navigate. Thus, we consider executive decrees whose constitutionality is disputed by legislatures or courts on procedural, but not on substantive, grounds to be paraconstitutional. Included here are the initiatives by Yeltsin and Fujimori, those backed by tanks, of course, but also many of Argentine President Menem's decrees of urgent necessity, Brazilian President Collor's attempts to reissue decrees that had previously been rejected by Congress, and Venezuelan President Caldera's reiteration in 1994 of a decreee suspending civil and property rights in spite of congressional action to reestablish those rights.

At any rate, there are important similarities between CDA and paraconstitutional decree. The boundaries of executive discretion, if any, are established by the constitution. If these boundaries are subject to dispute, they cannot simply be rewritten by statute, such as with rule-making authority or DDA. Thus, in redefining the boundaries of executive initiative decree authority, we find that elements of the standard legislative game, such as veto gates, are not relevant (as they are with delegated authority). Rather, the prospects for resolving conflicts over executive initiative decrees will depend on judicial review, on constitutional amendment procedures, and possibly on impeachment, government censure, and assembly dissolution procedures. At the extreme such conflicts may prove irresolvable short of democratic breakdown.

MOTIVATIONS FOR DECREE AUTHORITY

EXECUTIVE PREFERENCES

The next step in determining when we expect to see decree authority exercised is to establish systematically why political actors would prefer to rely on decree rather than on standard legislative procedures. Throughout the rest of the chapter, we focus on the phenomena of DDA and CDA. The most obvious preference for decree pertains to executives, who should prefer decree authority that is constitutionally guaranteed rather than subject to delegation by the legislature. Thus, we expect greater CDA the more control that executives – or actors who expect to hold executive office in the future – have over the process of writing constitutions.

The fact that so many constitutions have been written and rewritten over the past ten years in countries where executive decree is prominent allows us the opportunity to evaluate the extent to which this condition holds. Although executives have frequently been prominent advocates of constitutional reform, the modal pattern has been for constituent assemblies either to have final discretion over the content of constitutions or for assemblies to draft documents that are presented to voters for ratification by plebiscite. Members of constituent assemblies, moreover, are frequently current legislators – or at least were elected in a manner similar to legislative elections and are likely to aspire to legislative office. Not surprisingly, therefore, assemblies tend to guard the institutional prerogatives of legislatures when drafting constitutions. One indicator of this is that once constitutions are in place, it is extremely rare for executives to be granted any role in subsequent constitutional amendment procedures. Among the cases we have examined, only the Chilean, Ecuadorian, and Russian presidents are provided any formal role in constitutional amendment procedures.[15] Not surprisingly, these are among the rare cases in which constitutions drafted exclusively by executives were submitted to voters for approval by plebiscite without any consideration by an assembly. And all three provide the executives with some substantial CDA as well as reactive powers with which to defend their decrees from legislative reversal.

Another indicator that assemblies moderate executive preferences is that when assemblies modify executive draft constitutions, they constrain CDA. In Peru, for example, after President Fujimori closed Congress by decree in 1992, he allowed for the election of a new Constituent Congress, which would draft a new constitution that would be submitted to referendum in 1993.[16] Although much of Fujimori's opposition boycotted the elections for the new assembly and even though the body was dominated by delegates from his party, the Congress wrote a number of explicit constraints on the CDA that Fujimori had exercised under the previous (1979) constitution; as a result of these constraints, that decrees must be ratified by the cabinet (which is subject to congressional as well as presidential confidence [Art. 125:2]), Congress can revoke or amend decrees (Arts. 118:19), and decrees can be challenged before the Tribunal of Constitutional

Guarantees (Arts. 200, 202). Likewise in Argentina, although President Menem originally pushed the idea of a Constituent Assembly in 1993 (threatening to hold a paraconstitutional plebiscite on the matter) in order to do away with the constitutional prohibition on presidential reelection, the Assembly itself provided that any presidential decree under CDA would be subject to mandatory action by Congress within ten days (Art. 99.3).

LEGISLATIVE PREFERENCES

Given that assemblies generally exercise great discretion in drafting constitutions[17] and that assembly members more frequently and feasibly anticipate legislative as opposed to executive careers, it is imperative to consider in more detail why legislators might prefer to make policy by executive decree. We suggest two general factors that determine the attractiveness of decree: The first is the severity of bargaining problems faced by legislators when making policy, and the second is the extent of agency loss which results from endowing the executive with decree authority. A number of institutional factors accounts for much of the variance in bargaining and agency problems across systems.

At this point it is important to acknowledge that if we begin from the point of constitutional formation, most of the other institutional factors that, in our view, drive decree authority are endogenous. For example, when we claim (as we shall) that assemblies will not prefer to give decree authority to executives who hold legislative vetoes, a natural response would be to point out that if assemblies control constitutional design, they could just as well deny executives a veto as deny them decree authority – or deny them both. We do not dispute this. With regard to constitutional design, we generally make claims about the appeal to assemblies of certain combinations of institutional characteristics – such as a strong veto without CDA or CDA without a strong veto – but not about which specific combination will be chosen. On the other hand, one element of institutional design in particular – the electoral system for the legislature – frequently does serve as an exogenous constraint, and it does so even on those who design constitutions. This is because members of constituent assemblies are most often chosen by electoral rules that will remain in place for the selection of subsequent legislatures; or, put another way, those who win election to a constituent assembly under a given set of electoral rules generally are not inclined to change the rules of competition under which they are already winning (Geddes 1995). This being the case, the extent to which electoral rules are expected to contribute to bargaining problems among legislators can be an important factor in determining assembly preferences over both CDA and delegated authority. Finally, once a constitution is in place – and once changing it requires something more than standard legislative procedure – other institutional factors, such as the veto, can serve as exogenous constraints on legislative preferences over whether to confer delegated authority to executives by statute.

Bargaining problems. The more difficult it is for legislators to build and maintain coalitions capable of passing legislation, the more attractive will be the alternative of providing the executive with decree authority, either delegated or constitutional. We identify four factors that shape the bargaining problems faced by legislators: levels of party discipline, the number of legislative chambers, information about the effects of policy choices, and urgency.

Party discipline refers to the extent to which legislative party leaders can compel legislators to vote as a bloc, even if individual legislators would prefer to vote against their party on specific issues. Elsewhere, we provided a general model for rank-ordering electoral systems using a measure quite similar to party discipline – namely, the incentives for legislators to cultivate collective partisan, as opposed to individual, reputations (Carey and Shugart 1995). Here we point to a single variable in that model as central to determining levels of party discipline: the control that party leaders exercise over individual candidates' access to and position on the legislative ballot. If party leaders exercise ballot control,[18] then, ceteris paribus, we expect party discipline to be strong, mitigating bargaining problems.

The number of legislative chambers is straightforward. If the standard legislative procedure requires majority votes in more than one chamber of the legislature, then the standard procedure is more cumbersome, bargaining is more costly, and executive decree should be more attractive to legislators than in unicameral systems.

Lack of policy expertise relative to executives is another reason legislators might prefer executive decree to standard legislative procedures. Krehbiel (1992) argues that information about the connections between policy choices and policy outcomes is in chronic short supply in legislatures because of a free rider problem in developing policy expertise. That is, better information is a "public good" in the sense of Olson (1965) for all legislators; for that reason, individual legislators lack the incentive to contribute to the provision of information. In Krehbiel's model, information shortages are a motivation to delegate agenda power to legislative committees, which specialize in and are delegated jurisdiction over specific policy areas.[19] The same logic could suggest the delegation of procedural authority (decree or agenda powers) to executives, especially if the costs of gathering information about outcomes is lower for executives than for legislatures. Of course, a legislature that delegates decree authority for informational reasons still faces the prospect of agency loss to an executive that reveals information strategically. Thus, the attractiveness of decree to overcome informational problems in legislatures will depend on the composition of the executive as well as on the other factors to be discussed shortly with regard to agency loss.

Finally, time constraints might impel legislators to prefer executive decree to standard legislative procedure. Legislative procedures are frequently slow, whereas the need to implement new policies might be pressing.[20] Along the lines of the model developed by Baron and Ferejohn (1989), we find that the total value to legislators of an agreement on policy might decline the longer that that agreement is delayed. Rather than delegate proposal power to a member of the legislature or to a committee, however, legislators might prefer to rely on executive decree. Again, the attractiveness of this solution will depend on the prospects for agency loss.

Agency loss. For any type of decree, the potential for executive action to damage legislators' interests will depend first on the degree to which the executive's policy preferences converge with those of a legislative majority, and second on the other institutional resources available to legislators to control the executive. On the first count, we regard partisan support for the executive as the best indicator (across various systems) of whether preferences converge. In systems where the executive is dependent on parliamentary support, we distinguish between minority governments, majority coalition governments, and single-party majority governments. Other things being equal, we expect more decree authority in the second kind of government than in the first, and more still in the last kind. In pure presidential systems, because the "glue" that holds coalitions supporting executives together is weaker, we distinguish simply between situations in which the president's party holds a majority in all chambers of the legislature and those in which this condition does not hold. We expect more decree authority in the former case than in the latter.

The existence of an executive veto is critical to whether we expect decree authority to be attractive to legislators. If the executive has no effective veto,[21] then policies implemented by executive decree that are objectionable to legislative majorities can be overturned by legislatures through the standard legislative procedure. If, on the other hand, the executive has a veto, then decree authority – whether delegated or CDA – implies that the executive can implement policy by decree and then block any effort to change the policy that does not have sufficient legislative support (usually two-thirds) to override the veto. Clearly, executive decree combined with a veto establishes the potential for executives to act contrary to the preferences of assembly majorities.

The procedural requirements for amending the constitution should affect whether we observe CDA. In short, if an assembly writes a constitution with the interests of legislators in mind, it may choose to provide the executive with CDA, but if it does so, it should also prefer to endow future legislatures with the ability to easily alter the constitutional powers of the executive if those powers are used contrary to legislative interests.[22] In this sense, where constitutions can be easily manipulated by legislatures, even CDA can be thought of as delegated power.

Finally, the existence of an independent judiciary with the authority to rule on the legality and constitutionality of executive decrees should contribute to whether decree is attractive to legislators. Courts, or similar arbitrating agencies, such as controllers, constitutional councils, or administrative tribunals, typically are empowered to decide if executives have exceeded the scope of the authority they have been delegated. Both the procedures for appointing judges and the length of their terms on the bench should be instrumental in determining the degree of independence of the judiciary, and there is significant variation on both these factors across systems.[23] Our basic insight is that assemblies should be reluctant to delegate to an executive when they expect that in instances of dispute between assembly and executive, the court will necessarily follow executive preferences. Conversely, assemblies should be more likely to delegate the less the court is beholden to the executive.

HYPOTHESES

With this background on rationales for executive decree authority, we can offer a number of hypotheses with regard to when we expect to observe the phenomenon and why. The first hypothesis pertains to the attractiveness of decree to executives who influence the design of constitutions.

> H1: The greater the influence of the executive (or of those who expect to hold executive office) over constitutional design, the greater the CDA.

All the hypotheses that follow pertain to motivations for legislators to prefer executive decree. In all cases the "Other things being equal . . ." condition applies. With respect to CDA, we expect these conditions to pertain to the extent that those who design constitutions aspire to legislative office. With respect to DDA, of course, they describe the attractiveness of decree to incumbent legislators.

> Bargaining problems hypotheses
> H2: The greater the level of party discipline, the less likely is either CDA or DDA.
> H3: Both CDA and DDA are more likely in bicameral than in unicameral systems.
> H4: The greater the urgency of a policy issue, the more likely is DDA on that issue.

> Agency problems hypotheses
> H5: When the executive has partisan majority support in the legislature, DDA is more likely than when the executive does not.
> H6: The stronger the executive veto, the less likely is either CDA or DDA.
> H7: The more difficult it is for legislators to change the constitution, the less likely is CDA.
> H8: The greater the independence from the executive of the court that adjudicates executive–assembly disputes, the more likely is DDA.

The last hypothesis combines the logic of both bargaining and agency problems.

> H9a: When the executive has partisan majority support in the legislature, DDA is more likely as the informational advantages of the executive relative to the legislature increases.
>
> H9b: When the executive does not have partisan majority support in the legislature, DDA is less likely as the information advantages of the executive relative to the legislature increases.

The rationales behind most of the hypotheses have been explained above. H9 requires a little more elaboration, because it is based on a combination of bargaining and agency problems. The basic idea – namely, that a scarcity of information could motivate legislators to delegate authority – is straightforward, but only so long as the agent to which authority is delegated can be expected to act in the interests of the legislative majority (H9a). The greater the difference between the policy interests of the executive and the legislative majority (H9b), the greater the damage that can be done to legislative interests as a result of delegated authority to an executive with informational advantages. In this latter case, the effects of information in motivating DDA are expected to be reversed, depending on partisan support for the executive.

In Chapter 10, the conclusion to this volume, we assess these hypotheses, drawing on constitutional texts, electoral laws, and most heavily on the empirical work provided by the authors who contributed the intervening chapters to this volume. We find strong evidence both that executives will assert decree authority whenever there are institutional mechanisms that allow them to do so and that when assemblies provide decree authority to executives, they do so in ways that mitigate the authority of the executive to hurt assembly interests. We have only moderate success in identifying the specific conditions under which executive decree authority should be more attractive than standard legislative procedure in the first place.

PLAN OF THE BOOK

We are fortunate to have been able to gather a strong set of chapters on specific cases that cover a diverse array of countries. We have four Latin American cases (Argentina, Brazil, Peru, and Venezuela), a post-communist case (Russia), and three advanced industrial states (France, Italy, the United States). Some of our cases are countries with thirty or more years of continuous democracy (Venezuela, in addition to the three advanced industrial cases), whereas others are new and uncertain democracies. Additionally, this set of countries gives us a mix of regime types, with one that is often considered the prototype of a parliamentary system (Italy), another that has been the paradigmatic case for developing models of legislative behavior (the United States), and several with elected presidents who have varying degrees of formal powers over government formation and legislation. What the cases have in common is that the relative balance of executive and assembly authority over policy outcomes has been the subject of intense political conflict and equally intense academic debate. Apart from that characteristic, the cases are strikingly diverse historically, culturally, economically, geopolitically, and institutionally. We regard this as a major strength of this volume. To the extent that we can detect regular patterns in the use of executive decree across such a diverse set of cases, we increase our confidence that our understanding of the phenomenon is not the product of a region-specific quirk or a unique property of young democracies, but rather that our general hypotheses about delegation and bargaining among politicians have some bite.

The chapters are broken down into three groups, as follows. Part I includes case studies of decree in Argentina, Russia, Peru, and Venezuela. In all these countries, the central issue has been the transformation of decree from a delegated to a constitutional authority. In each case we observe initial delegations of significant legislative authority from assemblies to executives (in each of these cases, presidents), and subsequent battles over both the scope of authority entailed in the delegation and the extent of executive authority in the absence of delegation. In each case courts have played critical roles in mediating conflicts between the branches over the constitutional authorities of the executive. But the specific grounds of the disputes have varied enormously, as have the outcomes. In the first three countries legislative–executive conflict was central to crises that resulted in the creation of entirely new constitutions. In Argentina a pact negotiated in 1993 between the leaders of the country's two largest parties (the incumbent president and a former president) provided for the election of a Constituent Assembly that produced a new governmental charter in 1994. Russia and Peru are the prototypical cases of "calling out the tanks." In both countries interbranch conflict prompted presidents to shut down assemblies forcibly and to initiate the construction of new constitutional orders that restructured the relationship between legislature and executive. In Venezuela the formal constitutional division of authorities has remained intact since 1961, during which time there have been five instances of delegated legislative authority. However, presidents have consistently challenged the extent to which the constitution limits their ability to impose substantive policy changes outside the bounds of explicit delegation.

Delia Ferreira Rubio and Matteo Goretti offer an account of the transformation of executive authority in Argentina under President Carlos Menem. Menem's first term in office began with a massive delegation of economic and administrative authority by a lame duck Congress. Even before the term of the delegation had expired, however, Menem's expansive interpretation of his authority generated resistance both in Congress and the courts. The president's reliance on "need and urgency decrees" that were not based on formal delegation forced an explicit debate over the extent of executive authority in the Congress, the media, the courts, and ultimately in a constitutional assembly. Ferreira and Goretti provide exhaustive data on Menem's decrees, documenting his expansion of presidential authority both over time and across issues. They recount Menem's attempts to manipulate of the Supreme Court to support a radically broadened reading of his constitutional authority. And they account for the compromise by which executive decree authority was enshrined – but also subjected to procedural limitations – under the new Argentine Constitution.

Scott Parrish's chapter details the central role of presidential decree authority in the establishment of Russia's new political order. Parrish's distinction between the First Russian Republic (1991–93) and the Second (1993–present) parallels the progression from delegated to constitutionally enshrined decree authority under President Yeltsin. Parrish reviews the complex relationships among the legislative, executive, and judicial branches under both regimes. He explains why the Congress of People's Deputies opted to delegate massive legislative authority to Yeltsin, despite the president's lack of reliable majority support in the fragmented assembly, and he describes the intervention of the Constitutional Court under Chief Judge Valerii Zorkin who mediated – but did not resolve – the disputes that ensued over Yeltsin's use of this power. Parrish's treatment of the Second Republic documents the initially vast scope of decree authority with which Yeltsin was endowed by the 1993 Constitution, but the author is careful to note that even this authority has been challenged with some success, and he offers reasons to expect that the scope of decree authority in Russia could be increasingly narrowed by legislative and court actions, particularly under Yeltsin's successors.

Gregory Schmidt's chapter reviews the evolution of decree authority in Peru. Schmidt traces what he calls the "volcanic" nature of legislative–executive relations in Peru back more than half a century, focusing on the importance of partisan support for presidents in Congress in shaping both the extent of authority delegated to presidents and the levels of interbranch conflict. He provides comprehensive data on the use of decree under the three administrations that governed under the 1979 Constitution, employing the taxonomy of decree authority from this chapter to disentangle the complex set of delegated, constitutional, and emergency powers wielded by Peruvian presidents. Schmidt also reviews President Alberto Fujimori's expansive interpretation of delegated authority in the early 1990s and the extensive efforts of the Peruvian Congress to curtail that authority both through legislation and appeals to the courts. The ensuing standoff culminated in Fujimori's *autogolpe* (self-coup) against Congress and the election of a new Constituent Assembly; the Assembly's overhaul of Peru's institutional order largely paralleled Fujimori's suggestions, but it also included new provisions for legislative and judicial review of presidential decrees.

Brian Crisp's review of decree in Venezuela does not include constitutional breakdown and revision, but his analysis of the nature of conflict over decree use is consistent with that in the other cases in Part I. Crisp contrasts the limited formal constitutional authorities of Venezuelan presidents with the conventional assessment of their enormous power over policy, emphasizing that it is the position of Venezuelan presidents as national leaders of their political parties, rather than the formal endowments of the presidency, that accounts for this apparent paradox. This account is supported by the historical pattern of delegation to Venezuelan presidents. Until the massive fragmentation and realignment of Venezuela's traditional party system in the early 1990s, legislative decree authority had been delegated exclusively to presidents with majority partisan support in both chambers of Congress. Beyond the issue of delegated authority, however, Crisp surveys the efforts of Venezuelan presidents to interpret vague emergency powers granted under the 1961 Constitution as endowments of extensive policy making authority. Although he provides evidence that such power has traditionally been exercised only to the extent that it was tolerated by partisan legislative majorities, he also accounts for recent challenges to legislative prerogatives by President Rafael Caldera, whose election as a partisan outsider in 1993 marked the end of the dominance of Venezuelan politics by the traditional social democratic and Christian democratic parties. Crisp's chapter suggests a correspondence between Venezuelan presidential challenges to the status of emergency powers and the effects of presidents in other countries to expand decree authority, which led to a pushing for a transformation from delegated authority to a recognition of constitutional authority. Thus far, the impetus has not upset constitutional stability, as in Argentina, Russia, and Peru; but neither has there been any clarification of the precise scope of constitutional discretion.

Part II of the volume includes chapters on executive decree in Italy and Brazil. An especially close comparison of these cases is useful for a number of reasons. First, both cases exhibit exclusively constitutional decree authority and no delegated authority, but in both cases reliance on decree has been prompted by legislative deadlock between assemblies and executives. Second, the procedural design of decree in the two countries shares common roots. Beyond this, the disputes over the exercise of decree have been parallel. The critical procedural issues are reiteration of decrees and the status of lapsed decrees. Moreover, any analysis of the effects of decree on the balance of power between assemblies and executives must address the question of whether executive preferences can be imposed simply because the clean-up costs of overturning policies implemented by decree prohibit restoring the status quo or any alternative preferred by legislative majorities. Both the Italian and Brazilian cases supply illustrations of this problem.

Vince Della Sala and Amie Kreppel provide an account of executive decree in Italy that calls into question much of the conventional interpretation of the relationship between decree and executive power. They review the institutional context of decree as established under the 1948 Constitution and the evolution of the Italian party system through the early 1990s, arguing that the fragmentation and indisicpline of the party system generated governments that could not rely on support for policy initiatives even of the legislative majority that brought them to office. Thus, in the Italian case, they argue, reliance on decree is a manifestation of executive weakness rather than strength. Della Sala and Kreppel support this interpretation with data demonstrating that the frequency of decree has skyrocketed since the 1970s, precisely as the rate of support for government initiatives in Parliament has plummeted. The authors argue that the increase in decree use in Italy, rather than demonstrating executive capacity, has been prompted by procedural rule changes within the Parliament that have denied the government the capacity to control the parliamentary agenda. But as a means of implementing substantive policy changes, decree has proven to be far less effective for governments than standard legislative action, because policies implemented by decree – even when they are sustained indefinitely by reiteration of decrees that have lapsed – do not establish sufficiently stable expectations of permanence to elicit compliance by social and economic actors.

Timothy Power shows that the constitutional provisions for decree in Brazil were effectively borrowed from the Italian Constitution. Thus, constitutional decree authority in Brazil is virtually a procedural replica of the Italian version grafted onto a pure presidential system of government. Moreover, the open list and highly proportional systems of assembly election for Brazil and Italy (prior to 1994) have generated similarly fragmented and undisciplined legislative parties in the two countries; one result of this situation is that executives have had difficulty in holding together stable policy coalitions and have relied extensively on decree. In Brazil, in the absence of any requirement of parliamentary confidence, interbranch conflict has been even more pronounced than in Italy, particularly in the case of President Fernando Collor, who ran for office and governed as a partisan outsider. Not surprisingly, Collor relied extensively on decree authority early in his presidency, and he drew resistance from outside the executive. Power reviews both the judicial action that proscribed presidents from pursuing policies by decree over explicit legislative opposition and the narrow failure of a fragmented Congress to set formal restraints on presidential use of decree power through legislation. Power goes on to argue, however, that the ability of presidents to establish new policy that is effective *immediately* and that may be costly to overturn is as much a source of executive power in Brazil as the ability to *reiterate* decrees. Moreover, Power argues that vesting the legislative initiative in the executive has undermined the development of effective policy-making coalitions in the Brazilian Congress.

Part III includes chapters on France and the United States, our only two cases in which neither the existence nor exercise of decree authority has been subject to ongoing interbranch dispute. In France this situation is likely because the most salient constitutional decree procedures do not altogether disenfranchise assembly majorities from policy decisions prior to implementation. Even when authority is not explicitly delegated, decree in France allows for the assembly to express either tacit approval or outright rejection of executive initiatives *before* implementation. The procedural format of decree in France, therefore, allows both executives and parliamentarians to signal their policy positions and responsibility clearly to constituents and to hold together legislative coalitions. In the United

States the lack of contestation is likely due to both the clear absence of decree authority in the written constitution and the Supreme Court's insistence that any delegation of legislative authority outside Congress violates the constitutional principle of separation of powers.

John Huber's chapter reviews the institutional context of decree authority in France, distinguishing between authorities that allow the executive to initiate policy changes and the explicit allowance of delegated legislative authority. Huber argues that the most important decree authorities in the Constitution of the Fifth Republic are vested in the cabinet, which is dependent on parliamentary confidence. Thus, he directs attention away from the grant of emergency authority to the president in Article 16 and toward several other articles, including Article 34, which establishes specific policy jurisdictions in which the government is granted discretionary authority in implementing legislation; Article 38, which allows parliament to transfer legislative authority to the government by enabling statute; and Articles 44 and 49, which respectively allow the government to propose legislative packages to votes without the possibility of amendment (Art. 44), and to impose new legislation as a matter of confidence in the government (Art. 49), legislation which becomes law even in the absence of parliamentary action (the *guillotine*). Of these last two, Article 44 falls under our definition of an agenda power rather than a decree power, but the relationship between these types of powers is underscored by Huber's account. That is, we have suggested that reliance on executive agenda powers should result from conditions that are similar to those that prompt reliance on executive decree. Huber provides data on both phenomena, showing that they are used more heavily by French executives that head slim or unstable partisan coalitions in the assembly than by those with solid majorities. But Huber goes on to offer a more refined distinction between the types of governments most reliant on the package vote (slim majority coalitions) and those most reliant on the confidence vote (minority governments), and he bases this distinction on the specific procedural advantages of the former in holding together unstable coalitions and of the latter in preventing legislative gridlock while simultaneously allowing parliamentarians to communicate to their constituents their support or nonsupport of government policies.

Brian Sala's chapter on the United States likewise focuses on the potential for executives to influence policy outcomes in an environment in which these basic procedural questions are not fundamentally subjects of contention. Sala's account, moreover, is interesting when seen in relief against the other cases in this volume, because it evaluates how executive initiative can be used to shape policy in the absence of either delegated or constitutional decree authority. Sala examines the use of executive orders by U.S. presidents when they tell bureaucratic agencies how to interpret legislative intent. Positing that agencies, as well as Congress and the president, should have preferences over policy, he establishes the conditions under which executive orders should have any impact on the manner in which legislation is finally implemented. Ironically, Sala concludes that presidential "persuasion" through executive order should affect agency actions only when this persuasion is explicitly endorsed – or at least not challenged – by Congress. Only under these conditions, Sala argues, will agencies find presidential threats to punish noncompliance credible.

The last chapter of the volume draws general conclusions based on the extensive evidence presented in the previous chapters. Specifically, we use data provided in the case studies, as well as data we have gathered independently on a number of other countries, to evaluate the hypotheses presented in the first chapter. First, we develop a set of variables that serve as indicators of institutional characteristics identified as relevant to decree authority in the hypotheses. After assigning values to these variables for twenty political regimes, we evaluate the correspondence between the existence of decree authority and institutional factors such as the existence of an executive veto, bicameralism, electoral incentives for party discipline, the respective roles of executives and legislatures in drafting and amending constitutions, and levels of partisan support for executives. We find varying levels of support for our original nine hypotheses. In short we find evidence that the conventional interpretation by which decree is regarded as tantamount to executive usurpation of legislative authority has frequently been overstated. Executive decree is not always – or usually – analogous to "calling out the tanks." Decree authority is frequently authorized by legislative or constituent assemblies; and when assemblies provide decree authority, they generally build into that decree authority – and into constitutions – procedural constraints that protect the interests of legislative majorities.

NOTES

1 "Agency loss" refers to an inherent problem in principal–agent relationships. Principals delegate tasks to agents and, in the process, agents inevitably have the opportunity to take actions that violate the preferences of the principal. The question for analysts of agency relationships is: "To what extent can these losses be mitigated?" Under some circumstances the executive might be a fairly faithful agent of legislative preferences; in other cases the executive might run roughshod over legislative preferences.

2 Bolivia's Constitution calls for the selection of the president by a joint session of Congress in the event that no candidate receives a majority of the popular vote. Since Bolivia's return to civilian government in 1982, none has. Thus, selection of the chief executive by the assembly gives the Bolivian system an element of parliamentarism. The system is not parliamentary, however, because once selected, the president has exclusive authority to appoint and remove cabinet ministers and the president's tenure is not subject to parliamentary confidence.

3 It is ironic that the most extreme statements of the usurpation interpretation refer to "delegative" democracy, given that the distinction we emphasize here is particularly that between usurpation and delegation. Our point is that delegation of authority can be arranged to mitigate agency loss from legislative majorities to executives. But those who write about delegative democracy use the term

delegation in an unusual way, asserting massive agency loss by definition. They claim, "Representation . . . entails the idea of accountability, that the 'delegate' is held responsible for the ways in which s/he acts . . . Delegative democracy does not *per se* deny the notion of accountability, but it does not possess the level of institutionalization that facilitates it" (Kubicek 1994:424).

4 There are conditions, however, under which it is not wildly unrealistic – for example, in the case when a disciplined majority party controls the assembly. In such a case, the party is not unitary – there is an internal decision-making process that takes into account differences of opinion within the party – but once the party arrives at its positions, the assembly preference follows as the preference of the (now united) majority party.

5 In more technical terms, actors have single-peaked preferences.

6 However, note the importance of assuming that the executive also has gatekeeping authority. Without it, the assembly would reject the proposal E, keeping policy at R. Then, given its freedom to initiate new proposals, it would immediately pass A^1 instead. In other words there would effectively be no restrictions on amendments after all. This caveat on agenda powers applies to decree powers as well, as we argue later.

7 Note the implication of the difference between the veto and agenda control if the assembly's ideal point were between E and I(E). Under the veto the assembly could simply propose its ideal, which the executive would accept. Under the package vote the executive proposes E, which is accepted. Reactive powers are thus useful to executives when they prefer the reversion to the assembly's ideal. Proactive powers may be useful in moving policy closer to the executive's ideal even when the assembly's ideal is more attractive than the reversion.

Restricted amendment procedures may also allow executives to obtain more favorable outcomes than assemblies would initiate. The extent of advantage such procedures provide depends on the relative positions of executive and assembly ideal points and on the reversionary policy. In the example in Figure 1.1 if the assembly can amend spending proposals only downward, the outcome is still E, because the assembly prefers to spend more than less. If the assembly preferred A^2, on the other hand, such a restrictive amendment procedure would allow the assembly to attain its ideal point once the executive initiated a bill, which is the same outcome we would expect if the assembly were the initiator of policy change and the executive were endowed only with a reactive power, such as the veto.

8 In other work (Shugart and Carey 1992), we provide an extensive discussion of the nature of executive authority over legislation.

9 Either by election, or indirectly through a democratically elected body, such as a parliament or electoral college.

10 Consider, for example, the example of establishing a new currency by decree, as has been done in both Brazil (twice) and Argentina.

11 For the purposes of this chapter, we distinguish decree authority from agenda powers, primarily to keep the empirical scope of the project manageable. Although we do not attempt a comprehensive empirical analysis of agenda powers here, (1) we note that both decree and agenda powers are proactive tools available to some executives and are distinct from reactive legislative powers of executives (such as vetoes) because they provide executives with a form of first-mover ad-

vantage (relative to legislatures) in policy making; and (2) we expect the conditions under which legislatures might prefer to tolerate executive agenda powers should be similar to those we suggest here for preferring decree powers.

12 Although Huber's chapter notes that the scope of executive discretion in the realm of regulation may be less broad than the Constitution suggests.

13 The office of the controller general is a vastly understudied agency in Latin America – and perhaps elsewhere. For instance, Chile's constitutions since 1945 have provided for a Controller General with lifetime tenure, someone who is empowered to rule on the constitutional and statutory validity of executive decrees. Colombia before 1991 had a Controller General with similar wide-ranging authority, who was elected by Congress with no formal role for the president. In 1991 the new Constitution provided for an appointment procedure that is relatively more insulated from congressional influence, although it is still shielded from the executive. These bodies are an overlooked source of oversight of executive acts.

14 For example, Costa Rica requires a two-thirds legislative vote to approve emergency power. Chile requires a vote of the National Security Council, which includes representatives from Congress. In Peru, Congress must approve any extensions of a state-of-siege after forty-five days. All other Latin American countries except Colombia require majority approval by legislatures. France differs from the Latin American norm because Article 16 grants broad emergency authority to the president that is not subject to assembly approval. Nevertheless, Huber in Chapter 8 of this volume convincingly argues that France's impeachment procedure is intended as – and effectively provides – a parliamentary check on presidential abuse of emergency power. Emergency powers in Russia and many of the post-Soviet states appear to be far more broad and less constrained than in these other cited cases.

15 Both the Russian (Art. 134) and Chilean (Art. 117) presidents are enfranchised to propose amendments to the legislature. The Chilean president's disapproval of amendments, moreover, raises the requirement from three-fifths support in each chamber of the legislature to two-thirds, effectively giving the Chilean president a veto (albeit, not absolute) on constitutional changes. In Ecuador the president may submit to a plebiscite any amendments that Congress proposes but to which he or she objects – or that he or she proposes but Congress rejects (Art. 143).

16 International pressure was probably Fujimori's main motivation for allowing discretion over the new Constitution to an elected assembly.

17 Examples include the U.S.A. (1787); Italy (1948); Costa Rica (1949); Venezuela (1961); and Brazil (1988).

18 BALLOT=0, in Carey and Shugart (1995).

19 Although Krehbiel explicitly leaves parties out of his model, one can imagine similar assumptions about information as a public good being applied to models of majority party or coalition organization, with the "public" being defined as members of a given party or coalition rather than as all legislators.

20 This case has been made frequently with regard to executive decree, both by academics and by practitioners. See Power's chapter, especially his interview with ex-President Collor of Brazil.

21 This includes cases where executives hold "suspensory" vetoes, which force legislatures to reconsider legislation but which can be overridden by simple majority.

22 For example, in 1961, upon the resignation of President Jânio Quadros, Vice-President João Goulart ascended to the presidency of Brazil. Goulart's policy preferences were considerably to the left of both Quadros' and the majority of the Brazilian legislators. Constitutional amendment in Brazil at the time required only absolute majorities in each chamber. Congress promptly amended the constitution, and its changes required parliamentary confidence of cabinet ministers, weakened the president's veto, and established new procedures for choosing future presidents (that is, they would be selected by Congress rather than by election). The Brazilian presidency at the time was not endowed with CDA, but if it were, it is reasonable to expect that this authority would have been stripped as well.

23 As examples, consider some Latin American cases. A few countries use a procedure like that of the United States, where the president proposes justices, who are then subject to approval by one or both legislative chambers either by majority vote (e.g., Brazil) or by two-thirds vote (e.g., Argentina). In others (e.g., Costa Rica, El Salvador) the legislature elects the members of the highest court, with no role for the president. In Colombia vacancies are filled by a vote of the remaining judges. Terms also vary, from life in Argentina, Brazil, and Colombia (prior to 1991), to double that of the president and legislature (Colombia since 1991, Costa Rica, and Venezuela), to concurrent with the terms of the elected branches (the Dominican Republic).

PART I

FROM DELEGATED TO CONSTITUTIONAL DECREE AUTHORITY

WHEN THE PRESIDENT GOVERNS ALONE

THE DECRETAZO IN ARGENTINA, 1989–93

Delia Ferreira Rubio and Matteo Goretti

INTRODUCTION

President Carlos Saul Menem's tenure, which began in 1989 and is characterized by an increasing concentration of power in the executive branch, consummated in the adoption of a new constitution in 1994. Presidential expansion has not been effectively opposed by Congress, the judiciary, or other institutions. In some instances Congress itself has contributed to the concentration of power in the executive, by delegating legislative authority, for example, and by reorganizing the Supreme Court. The dominance of the Argentine president has been described as *decretazo*, or government by decree. What actually gave birth to the expression was the noteworthy increase in the president's use of so-called *decretos de necesidad y urgencia* (Need and Urgency Decrees, or NUDs).[1] By this means the executive "passes" laws, usurping congressional law-making authority without consent. NUDs were not unknown in Argentina before Menem's presidency. Between 1853 and July 1989, approximately twenty-five NUDs were issued. Between July 1989 and August 1994, however, President Menem issued 336 NUDs. He created taxes, repealed congressional laws, and modified private contractual relations.

According to Argentine law until the constitutional reform of 1994, the president could issue three types of decrees:

1. rule-making decrees in the course of implementing legislation
2. autonomous decrees based on constitutionally endowed presidential powers
3. legislative decrees based on authority delegated by Congress[2]

The first two types of decrees correspond to what Carey and Shugart call "rule making," and the third one corresponds to "delegated decree authority." The Argentine Constitution also granted the president emergency powers in the case of *estado de sitio*. *Estado de sitio* (State of Siege) is declared either by Congress or the president when interior unrest or external attacks put in the danger either the effectiveness of the Constitution or the power of constitutional authorities. In such a case civil liberties are restricted, and the executive can arrest persons without judicial order, but presidential authority in such cases do not include law-making authority.

Neither the Constitution nor the laws granted the president the authority to issue NUDs. Formally, law-making authority was reserved to Congress. In this respect NUDs were temporary exceptions to the principle of separation of powers incorporated in the Argentine Constitution. The *decretazo* has been characterized by the intensive use of NUDs as a policy-making device, whereby the executive presents legislative faits accomplis that circumvent the principles of checks and balances, replacing the rule of law with presidential fiat.

This paper deals mainly with those decrees issued by President Menem with neither constitutional nor legal authority. Until 1994, these decrees were what Carey and Shugart call "paraconstitutional initiatives." The constitutional reform of 1994 modified this standard, giving NUDs the status of constitutional initiatives.

POLITICAL BACKGROUND TO THE DECRETAZO

PRESIDENT MENEM AND THE CONGRESS

President Menem was elected in May 1989, but according to Argentina's Constitution he was not scheduled to be inaugurated until December. The administration of outgoing President Raul Alfonsin, however, was in serious trouble; hyperinflation had become acute since the beginning of that year, and after the elections there was significant social unrest in the largest cities. Under these conditions Alfonsin agreed to resign early to allow the new administration the opportunity to address the economic crisis. For this reason President Menem took office in July 1989, almost six months earlier than the date established by the Constitution.

Menem's Justicialist Party (JP) not only had won the presidential election but also had secured a plurality of seats in the Chamber of Deputies, Argentina's lower house. Tables 2.1 and 2.2 show the distribution of legislative seats in each chamber for each electoral period (1989–95).[3] Nevertheless, Alfonsin's agreement to resign early did not extend to Congress, so Menem had to wait until December for the new deputies to take office. In the lame duck Congress, the two main parties, the JP and the Radical Party (known by its Spanish acronym,

Table 2.1 *Distribution of Chamber of Deputies seats between the two major parties,* *1989–95*

Period[a]	Total Seats	Justicialist Party	Radical Party
July '89–Dec. '89	254	106 (42%)	114 (45%)
Dec. '89–Dec. '91	254	112 (44.5%)	90 (35.5%)
Dec. '91–Dec. '93	257[b]	117 (46%)	84 (33%)
Dec. '93–Dec. '95	257	128 (49.8%)	83 (32.5%)

[a]Half of the seats in the Chamber are renewed every two years.
[b]The increase in the number of seats was due to the creation of a new province: Tierra del Fuego.

Table 2.2 *Distribution of Senate seats between the two major parties, 1989–95*

Period[a]	Total Seats	Justicialist Party	Radical Party
July '89–Dec. '89	46	20 (44%)	19 (42%)
Dec. '89–Dec. '92	46	26 (57%)	14 (31%)
Dec. '92–Dec. '95	48[b]	30 (63%)	11 (23%)

[a]Under the Constitution of 1853 (which remained in place until 1994), one-third of the Senate's seats were renewed every three years.
[b]The increase in seats was due to the creation of the new province: Tierra del Fuego.

UCR, for *Unión Cívica Radical*), reached an agreement to pass those bills that the new administration thought necessary to address the situation.

The relationship between the president and Congress from July 1989 to December 1993 had not been as easy as the composition of that Congress might have suggested. In the crisis atmosphere that existed when President Menem took office, Menem sent to Congress two bills that provided for an emergency plan of government. The UCR did not oppose these bills, and the Administrative Emergency Act and the Economic Emergency Act were soon passed by Congress. At the same time that these laws declaring a state of emergency were enacted, the number of NUDs issued unilaterally by the president, exercising congressional law-making authority, greatly increased. In justifying this development, the government emphasized the slowness of Congress and the fact that emergency would not wait for the passage of laws. These declarations worsened the already difficult relationship between the two branches.

President Menem also used the threat of NUDs to expand other powers constitutionally granted to the Argentine presidency. For example, the executive, which according to the Argentine Constitution has the right to introduce government bills, sent several legislative initiatives to Congress, asking for the legislature's quick approval. Government officials, including ministers and the president, publicly stated that if Congress did not pass these bills, the executive would implement them by NUD and that if Congress introduced modifications into the texts, the executive would veto them.[4]

The veto power, too, was expanded in a controversial manner. According to the 1853 Constitution, either the president's veto could be inclusive or it could be aimed against only a portion of a bill passed by Congress; but in either case, the executive was required to send back the whole bill for congressional reconsideration. A number of Argentine presidents have challenged this interpretation, partially promulgating vetoed legislation, and Menem was no exception. Of 625 bills passed by Congress from July 1989 through 1993, the executive wholly vetoed thirty-seven bills while partially vetoing forty-one. In the cases of partial vetoes, however, the president systematically used partial promulgation. By putting the noncontested parts of the bill into effect, Menem was effectively appropriating for himself the power of a partial – or line item – veto. The constitutional reform of 1994 included partial promulgation as a formal constitutional power (Art. 80).

The increasing use of NUDs since Menem took office has been a continual source of conflict between Congress and the president. At the beginning of 1991, when Domingo Cavallo took office as Minister of the Economy, this conflict briefly seemed to diminish because of Cavallo's public attitude of respect toward Congress and because of his expressed desire to avoid overstepping executive powers (Goretti 1991). During this period the Congress passed the Currency Conversion Act, a key element of Cavallo's plan and one of the most important bases of economic stability.[5] Minister Cavallo published an article in October 1991 in which he stated, "To pass bills is rather more difficult than to issue NUDs. But ruling through laws produces greater legal stability because it creates a sense of more sound and permanent solutions that brings about the necessary conditions to foster investment and consequently economic growth" (*La Nación* 10/2/91). Notwithstanding Cavallo's deferential statements, however, the number and importance of the policies initiated by NUDs have not diminished during his tenure, but rather they have remained consistent with the previous period. In 1993 Cavallo acknowledged that without Menem's NUDs, only 20 percent of the policies involved in the economic reform would have been implemented (*La Nación* 8/31/93; *Página 12* 9/1/93).

PACKING THE SUPREME COURT

When Menem took office, he immediately sought greater influence over the Supreme Court, whose members had been appointed by former President Alfonsin. At first, the government tried to get some of the justices to resign (Verbitsky 1993). This strategy was not successful, so the executive presented a government bill to expand the size of the Court from five to nine justices – a "packing plan" similar to the one tried by U.S. President Franklin D. Roosevelt in 1937. The

Supreme Court questioned Menem's justification for the move.[6] The arguments used by both parties – the executive and the Supreme Court – were strikingly similar to those expressed by Roosevelt and the U.S. Supreme Court in 1937.[7] The story had a different ending in Argentina, however.

In September 1989 the Senate passed Menem's court-packing bill and sent it to the Chamber of Deputies. Meanwhile, there was widespread uncertainty over what the Court's attitude would be once it had to face the legal problems implied by Menem's NUDs. In a 1986 dispute over then-President Raul Alfonsin's attempt to restrict pension payments, the Court had ruled that emergency measures required prior recognition by Congress of the emergency.[8] In January 1990 Menem issued NUD 36/90, which ruled that bank term deposits would be paid back not in cash but in Treasury Bills. The government's need for a sympathetic Court grew with the increasing number of suits against the Central Bank as a result of NUD 36/90 (*Página 12* 2/1/90). It would have been a setback for the executive's economic plan if the Court ruled NUD 36/90 invalid.

Finally, on April 5, 1990, the Chamber of Deputies passed Law 23,774, a government bill expanding the Court from five to nine members (Baglini, D'Ambrosio, and Orlandi 1993:41). The opposition protested alleged procedural irregularities in the study, floor debate, and approval of the bill with no success. The most serious charge was that when the vote took place, the Chamber of Deputies lacked a legal quorum. Radical Party representatives had decided not to stay on the floor. According to some reports electronic control devices that determine the existence of a quorum were turned on not by representatives but by imposters. There was no article-by-article vote on the bill, as Chamber rules required, and the bill was approved in its final form in only forty-two seconds (Baglini, D'Ambrosio, and Orlandi 1993:53).

By the time Law 23,774 passed, one of the court's five incumbent justices had already resigned, and shortly thereafter, there was another resignation. Between April and May 1990, President Menem appointed, with the Senate's consent, six out of nine members of the Court.

THE ECONOMIC EMERGENCY

During Argentina's transition to democracy in 1983, there was a high demand for the transformation of the state from a restrictive one to a more democratic and inclusive organization. Increasing citizen participation and the free action of public institutions contributed to the process of democratic consolidation. The discussion about the role of the state within the economy was not part of the agenda, at least during the first years of the Alfonsin administration. At that time government intervention in the economic process was regarded as an inherent mission of the state. The political agenda was characterized by demands for greater democratization and participation, because of the democratic "ethos" at the beginning of transition.

Beginning with the second half of the Alfonsin administration and during

Menem's presidency, the role of the economy in the democratization process as well as the role of the state in the economy were reintroduced into the agenda. This was the result of the failure of Alfonsín's two major economic initiatives, the Plan Austral and the Plan Primavera, which showed clearly that the state could not solve the economic crisis. Citizen demands shifted from democratization to economic stability and no inflation. The state was perceived as responsible for the economic crisis, and consequently, demands were centered on the reduction of state intervention. Market principles began to be considered as the solution. The Menem administration pursued market policies to resolve two main problems. The first was overregulation. To solve this problem, the government initiated sweeping privatization and deregulation policies. The second problem was fiscal. Menem's policies in this respect aimed at the reduction of public expenditure and improvements in tax collection.

From the outset President Menem realized that emergency management of the economy would demand concentration of power in the executive. He sought this enlarged authority simultaneously by congressional delegation and by the use of NUDs. Concentration of power was favored by two conditions. On the one hand, the JP was the largest party in both chambers of Congress (after December 1989), and the JP controlled the majority of provincial administrations as well as the Supreme Court and audit agencies. On the other hand, public opinion demanded efficient government and centered its demands in the executive, which was better prepared than Congress to react quickly to economic crises (Bresser Pereira, Maravall, and Przeworski 1993; O'Donnell 1993; Przeworski 1991; Torre 1993).

DELEGATION OF POWER: EMERGENCY ACTS 23,696 AND 23,697

In July 1989, the executive sent to Congress two bills that the government believed to be necessary to handle the emergency and to put into practice its political plan. The opposition UCR agreed on passing the bills. In August 1989, Congress passed the Administrative Emergency Act (23,696) and then, on September 1, the Economic Emergency Act (23,697). The Administrative Emergency Act declared a national emergency regarding both public services managed by the state and the fulfillment and execution of public contracts and agreements. The declared emergency would be valid for one year and the executive would be able to extend this period for one additional year. The main topics that this act dealt with were:

- intervention in public agencies and public corporations;[9]
- change in the legal structure of public corporations;
- rules and proceedings for the privatization of public corporations;
- the "participative property program," which involved rules for special shareholding by employees of, and suppliers to, public corporations that were privatized;

- executive powers and rights regarding privatization, such as the power to establish tax exemptions for privatized corporations, the power to determine that the state would take upon itself the debts of those corporations while privatizing only the assets, and the power to repeal those laws that created monopolistic privileges that hindered privatization;
- rules for public emergency agreements and contracts;
- rules for the annulment or renegotiation of public contracts;
- a two-year suspension of enforcement of court judgments against the state; and
- a labor emergency plan.

The Economic Emergency Act (23,697) allowed the use of "emergency regulatory power in order to overcome the present situation of collective risk caused by the serious economic and social circumstances the nation is undergoing." "Emergency regulatory power" was defined as the power to rule and limit civil rights in times of emergency. During emergencies, regulatory powers are more far-reaching than in ordinary circumstances, which is to say measures may be issued in emergency situations that would be considered illegal in normal times. The Economic Emergency Act dealt with the following policies:

- the suspension of public subsidies and benefits;
- the suspension of industrial incentives through tax exemptions;
- the suspension of incentive programs for mining activities;
- a modification of the rules for foreign investment;
- the use of Credit Bills to pay tax drawbacks;
- a tax on fuel;
- gas and oil royalties;
- compensation for public debts;
- reform of stock market rules;
- labor dismissal and compensation policies for the public sector; and
- the sale of unnecessary public real estate.

Following traditional doctrines concerning emergency authority, both emergency acts established time limits for the emergency powers and rules. In the case of the Administrative Emergency Act, the term was one year, but the executive was granted the right to extend it for another year. The Economic Emergency Act applied other criteria establishing different terms for each rule. For instance, public benefits were suspended for 180 days, whereas industrial promotion laws were suspended for six months. The difference was important, because the executive was given the authority to extend the term for another period only in those cases where existing provisions had been suspended for 180 days. As it turned out, once the terms expired, the executive issued NUD 1930/90, which extended the emergency period for one additional year.

Through these emergency acts, Congress delegated to the president an important set of economic, tax imposition, and organizing powers, and the executive accordingly issued many decrees under this authority. The Administrative Emergency Act delegated to the executive, among other things, the power to exempt privatized corporations from taxes, the power to authorize reductions in and term extensions for the collection of debts by privatized corporations, and the power to repeal laws hindering privatization. The Economic Emergency Act further delegated to the executive the power to establish exceptions to the provisions of that same law, the power to authorize the import of goods whenever local market prices were not reasonable or when such goods were not available, and the power to exonerate the accused from penalties in cases of the infringement of tax laws. As Law 23,697 stated: "This power can be exercised by the executive even if there are prohibitions established by specific laws."

The real magnitude of delegated authority becomes clear when one analyzes the policies that the government implemented. The privatization of public corporations such as Entel (the national phone company) and Aerolíneas Argentinas (the national airline) were implemented fully by the executive. Congress received a mere notification of what was being implemented through a special committee composed of some senators and deputies (*Comisión Bicameral de Seguimiento de las Privatizaciones*). The same thing happened regarding important aspects of deregulation policy that were within the scope of the delegated authority.

These delegated decrees correspond to what Carey and Shugart call DDA (Delegated Decree Authority) and are not the same as NUDs. The difference is not related to the kind of policies initiated but to the origin of the authority to issue them. When the president issues delegated decrees, he or she is acting on the basis of congressionally delegated authority. In the case of NUDs, the executive asserts his or her authority to make new law without delegation or previous consent. Although Argentina's 1853 Constitution did not explicitly mention DDA, congressional delegation of law-making authority has been a common practice in that country. The Supreme Court declared in 1927 (*in re* Delfino) that Congress could delegate to the president the authority to make the rules regarding the details of the implementation of a law. Quoting the U.S. Supreme Court, the Argentine Court stated that "to deny the Congress the right to delegate the authority to determine certain facts, situations, or circumstances which are relevant to the implementation of the law, would stop governmental action."

Although the law-making authority delegated by Congress through the emergency acts of 1989 was broad enough for President Menem to initiate key elements of his economic program, the delegation was nevertheless clearly limited in time and scope. Menem transgressed these limitations by issuing NUDs in addition to delegated decrees. For example, Congress delegated the authority to modify laws governing public corporations that were to be privatized, but the delegation was specific to particular industries and purposes and did not give blanket authority to regulate economic activity. In order to repeal the laws that, according to the executive, were hindering free trade, President Menem relied on NUDs. The emergency acts also delegated to the executive the authority to modify public contractual relations (those in which the State was a party) but not the power to interfere with private contractual relations. When Menem decided that bank term deposits would be paid back with Treasury Bills, therefore, he had to issued a new NUD.

President Menem made intensive use of the authority that Congress had delegated. This did not generate much opposition because it was a regular practice of Argentine constitutional history and because under delegated authority there are solid expectations about what policies can be changed – and how much. That was not the case with NUDs. In contrast to previous presidents, Menem has used NUDs to initiate policies on which he had no rule-making or delegated authority, regardless of the urgency of the issue. The rest of this chapter focuses on this phenomenon.

GOVERNMENT BY DECREE

NUDs: JUSTIFICATION AND PRECEDENT

NUDs are decrees issued by the executive that regulate matters or adopt policies that usually are the responsibility of Congress. When the president issues a new NUD, he or she "makes law," taking to him- or herself the congressional authority to repeal and modify laws. Historically, NUDs have been justified by extraordinary crises or emergency situations. During the 1989–94 period, there was more disagreement than agreement regarding the constitutional status of NUDs. Those who asserted that NUDs were constitutionally invalid argued that the Argentine Constitution structured the nation's political system on the basis of a separation of powers and checks and balances. They argued that the principle of "Everything that is not forbidden is legal" does not apply to government authority. They added that the only branch that had implicit prerogatives was Congress. From this point of view, there was no justification for violating constitutional rules, even in emergency situations (Badeni 1990: 138–926; Bidart Campos 1988 II:230; Ruiz Moreno 1990:B–1029). Some authors asserted that NUDs were valid on the condition that they were issued during congressional recess (Cassagne 1991; Marienhoff 1988:263–8; Sagues 1991:97; Villegas Basavilbaso 1949: 292). Nevertheless, even then, the president would have had the option of summoning Congress at any time for an extraordinary session.

All those who accepted the lawfulness of NUDs at all shared consensus on two points: that NUDs could be issued only in emergency situations and that they should be submitted for congressional consideration. According to the first condition, in order to be considered constitutionally valid, NUDs had to be immediate responses to crises that threatened the survival of the state, and they also had to serve an end that could not be accomplished through the regular lawmaking process. From this point of view, an emergency gave birth to an "emergency law." There was also general agreement that the legal status of NUDs depended on their being sent to Congress for ratification or repeal. According to

Menem's counsel on legal and technical issues, Felix Borgonovo, "Parliament can always reject [NUDs]. They are necessary because sometimes the executive has urgent matters and Congress has another schedule" (Florit 1996). Some authors assert that NUDs could only be operative if Congress ratified them, and that without congressional ratification they had no legal basis (Gonzalez 1983:538). Other authors thought that NUDs were operative on the basis of "emergency law" (*status necesitatis*) and that ratification was not a condition for NUDs to be valid. If Congress did not pass an act repealing the NUD, then it was valid. In any case there was consensus that NUDs at least had to be sent to Congress to allow it the opportunity for ratification or rejection. Many of Menem's NUDs, however, were not sent to Congress at all.

Menem relied on another theory. In the preambles of some of his NUDs, he asserted that the lawfulness of the NUD did not require the decree to be communicated to Congress. It was enough that the executive had the "expressed intention" to communicate it (NUDs 240/92; 879/92; 964/92; 2632/92; 1684/93; 1848/93 and 2509/93). This reasoning explains why in 1991 for instance, the executive sent to Congress only 25 percent of the NUDs issued. The president could argue that in the case of the other 75 percent he at least had the expressed intention of communicating them.

Until the reform of 1994, the Argentine Constitution did not mention NUDs. Similar powers are regulated in the constitutions of many other nations. For instance, France (Art. 16), Spain (Art. 86), and Italy (Art. 77) grant the executive the power to issue emergency decrees. Some presidential constitutions also expressly grant the president the authority to issue NUDs, as a number of the other chapters in this volume make clear. The constitutions of several Argentine provinces endow their governors with the authority to issue NUDs as well. The common character of these constitutional rules consistently points to the fact that NUDs are exceptional and consequently need to fulfill certain requisites, such as previous consultation or communication to the legislature for ratification. The time periods for legislative ratification vary from thirty to ninety days. All these Argentine provincial constitutions establish that once the time period for legislative ratification has expired, NUDs will be considered constitutionally valid, whether the legislature has acted on them yet or not.[10]

For most of Argentine history, the use of NUDs as policy-making devices by constitutional governments was extremely uncommon.[11] From 1853 to 1983, constitutional governments in Argentina issued only about twenty NUDs. These NUDs were issued in times of extremely dangerous situations, such as political and economic emergencies (especially during the crisis of the 1930s).[12] President Alfonsin issued approximately ten NUDs from December 1983 to July 1989. In general these NUDs were issued on the basis of economic emergency and financial crisis, as well as in support of administrative reform policies. Some examples are:

- NUD 1096/85, known as the Plan Austral, established a new currency. One year later this NUD was ratified by Congress. The president argued that "the policy would not be effective unless it was implemented without previous announcement."

- NUD 2192/86 repealed a series of laws setting salaries for public sector employees.
- NUD 2196/86 declared a pension system emergency and suspended pension judicial claims against the state. The executive justified this NUD on the grounds that Congress was in recess.
- NUD 632/87 declared an emergency in agriculture and cattle breeding economic activities.
- NUD 1411/87 suspended the intervention of the State Audit Court in the execution of administrative acts during a strike.

PRESIDENT MENEM'S USE AND MISUSE OF NUDs

From July 1989 to August 1994, President Menem issued 336 NUDs – a figure all the more striking if we keep in mind that between 1853 and 1989, constitutional governments issued fewer than thirty NUDs. Not all of these 336 NUDs were acknowledged as such by the government. In 166 cases (49 percent), the preambles of the decrees explicitly recognized them as NUDs. In another 170 cases (51 percent), the executive did not acknowledge that they were NUDs, although careful analysis indicates that they effectively were. In order to identify these 170 NUDs, it was necessary to check all decrees (more than 13,500) issued by the president during the period under consideration. It was also necessary to analyze whether the president had been endowed with the authority to issue each decree either by the Constitution or by congressional delegation. The NUDs included in the group of 170 nonrecognized NUDs are those that modified or repealed laws or involved law-making without legal delegation. They are cases in which the executive overstepped its authority.[13] Figure 2.1 shows Menem's use of NUDs over time.

In 1989, out of a total of 30 NUDs, the executive recognized 18. In 1990, it recognized 32 of 63; in 1991, 59 of 85; in 1992, 36 of 69; in 1993, 15 of 62; and from January to August 1994, 6 of 27.[14] Figure 2.1 shows a consistent pattern of the use of NUDs throughout the period – the only exception being 1991, when there was a significant increase in their use, from a little more than 60 NUDs per year to 85. The year 1989 is near the average for the period because we considered only half of that year, from July, when Menem took office, to December.

POLICIES COVERED BY NUDs

We have identified sixteen groups of policies covered by NUDs that were issued by President Menem, as follows:

1. *Taxation:* taxes, other duties, exemptions, tax benefits, and so on
2. *Salaries:* salaries, labor hours, salary negotiations, and pensions

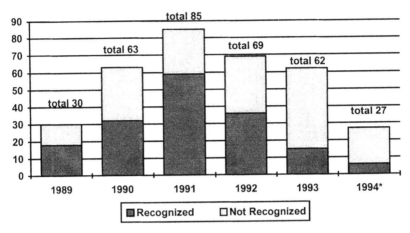

Figure 2.1 NUDs recognized and not recognized, January–August 1994 (Source: All data collected by the authors)

3. *Public Debt:* creation, redefinition of the terms of Treasury Bills
4. *Trade:* trade, marketing, import and export regulation
5. *Transport:* deregulation; land, sea, river, and air transport rules; labor conditions; and ship registration
6. *Nation/Provinces:* relationship between the nation and the provinces, tax distribution, and public services transfers
7. *Real Estate Privatization:* sale of unnecessary public real estate
8. *Civil and Political Rights*
9. *Public Agencies:* restructuring of public corporations, labor rules, and dismissal compensation
10. *Proceedings Against the State:* suspension of litigation against the state
11. *Electric Energy:* emergency, benefits, and price policy
12. *Promotion of Industry:* tax and regulatory incentives
13. *Mega-NUD 435/90 and those related to it*
14. *Mega-NUD 1930/90 and those related to it*
15. *Mega-NUD 2284/91 and those related to it*
16. *Others.*

The first twelve categories correspond to specific policy areas; the next three to the so-called "mega" NUDs – 435/90, 1930/90, and 2284/91 – which encompassed many different policy initiatives; and the last is a residual category.

The largest number of NUDs (21 percent) pertain to tax policy. Moreover, in addition to the seventy-two NUDs that Figure 2.2 and Table 2.3 show as wholly

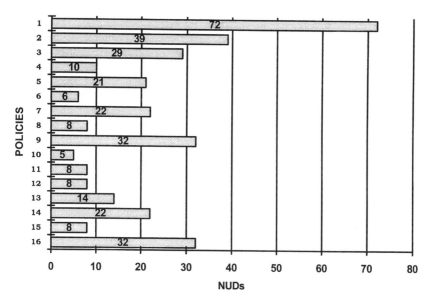

Figure 2.2 Policies covered by NUDs (Source: *All data collected by the authors*)

devoted to taxes, the mega-NUDs all initiated significant changes in tax policy among their many provisions.

If we analyze the policies covered by NUDs per year, it is possible to document the evolution of the issues that attracted the executive's interest.

The first part of the period (the second half of 1989 and the first months of 1990) was characterized by hyperinflation, which damaged salaries noticeably. The government reacted by modifying salaries both in public and private labor contracts. In 1989, eighteen NUDs were issued to regulate salaries – that is, 60 percent of all the NUDs issued that year.

During 1990 attention was centered on problems of public debt. In January 1990 President Menem issued NUD 36/90, which established that term deposits would be remitted in Treasury Bills instead of currency notes. Other NUDs were issued that consolidated public debt. Nearly a quarter of the total number of NUDs issued in 1990 were related to this issue. Public agency reorganization was also important that year: 18 percent of 1990 NUDs initiated or implemented policies to reduce public expenditure and to restructure and rationalize public agencies. Over the following three years, taxation was the main policy area affected by NUDs: 27 percent of the NUDs, in 1991, 25 percent in 1992, and 33 percent in 1993. During this time the government used taxation by NUDs as a means to redirect economic policy fundamentally. During the first half of 1994, NUDs focused largely on the option between public and private pension systems.[15]

Table 2.3 *Policies covered by NUDs, by year*

Policy Area	1989	1990	1991	1992	1993	1994	Total
1. Taxes	2	7	23	17	21	2	72
2. Salaries	18	9	3	—	2	7	39
3. Public debt	5	14	5	3	1	1	29
4. Trade	—	—	—	5	3	2	10
5. Transport	—	—	3	8	7	3	21
6. Nation/Provinces	—	—	—	4	1	1	6
7. Real estate privatization	—	3	6	3	7	3	22
8. Civil and political rights	2	—	2	1	—	3	8
9. Public agencies	1	11	7	5	5	3	32
10. Proceedings against state	—	—	5	—	—	—	5
11. Electric energy	—	4	1	2	1	—	8
12. Promotion of industry	—	3	3	1	1	—	8
13. Mega-NUD 435/90	—	7	5	—	2	—	14
14. Mega-NUD 1930/90	—	5	11	6	—	—	22
15. Mega-NUD 2284/91	—	—	4	3	1	—	8
16. Others	2	—	7	11	10	2	32
Total	30	63	85	69	62	27	336

CASE STUDIES

The following examples are some illustrative case studies of NUDs. All of the cases refer to recognized NUDs – what Carey and Shugart (Chapter 1) consider "paraconstitutional initiatives" – not to delegated decrees.

The forced government loan: The payment of term deposits with Treasury Bills (NUD 36/90). After some days of no banking activity over the New Year holiday, on January 3, 1990, the executive issued NUD 36/90, which established that term deposits would be remitted not in cash but in Treasury Bills.[16] This meant that one could not freely use one's own money. The government had created a forced public loan system for those having term deposits. The preambles of NUD 36/90 stated that "both in war and in crisis, the power to fight grants the right to fight successfully." In this "war" the government chose a "weapon" that seriously and directly impinged on private legal relationships, contracts, and property rights.

On January 23, the executive communicated the NUD to Congress, where it was ratified only by the Senate. The Chambers of Deputies did not pass the ratification bill. Consequently, there was no act. Several subsequent NUDs established general or personal exceptions regarding the forced public loan.[17] Increasing the confusion and uncertainty, some of the exceptions were established not by acts or NUDs, and not by presidential or ministerial resolution, but by simple "communications" of the Assistant Manager of the Central Bank. As late as 1993, the executive ratified by decree a resolution of the Central Bank originally issued in 1990, which established one of the exceptions to NUD 36/90 (NUD 1984/93).

NUD 435/90: the first "Mega-NUD." Apart from those NUDs devoted to specific policy items, President Menem issued several NUDs that involved numerous policies and modified or repealed a great number of acts of Congress. The first mega-NUD was 435/90. In its seventy sections this NUD dealt with more than thirty different policy issues. For instance, it:

- prohibited the Central Bank from covering the Treasury's operating deficit.
- suspended public contractual relationships and auctions.
- suspended payments to public contractors.
- extended the term of the Economic Emergency Act.
- established public policy regarding salaries.
- regulated industrial promotion.
- provided for the management of public corporations.

NUD 435/90 also established several rules related to taxation policy. For example, it:

- modified the tax on capital.
- changed the act that governed duties imposed on stamps.
- modified the rules for the indexation of taxes and duties.
- set rules related to export taxes and duties.
- modified the Value Added Tax Act.
- repealed benefits and incentives to promote exports.
- established regulations on fiscal and taxation policies.

NUD 435/90 became one of the key tools in the government's effort to "rationalize" public administration and reduce expenditures. This NUD was modified on several occasions by other NUDs (e.g., 612/90, 1757/90, and 2154/90). Furthermore, the president issued more than 249 decrees establishing exceptions to NUD 435/90, although only eight of them were recognized by the executive as NUDs.[18] Among those NUDs that modified 435/90, we can mention NUD 1757/90, a mega-NUD that contained more than 120 sections and implemented new policies over a range of issues such as taxation, privatization, public expenditure, and consolidation of public debt.

Deregulation of the economy: Mega-NUD 2284/91. One of the central aspects of Minister of the Economy Cavallo's economic program was deregulation. This policy aimed at making the market free from limits, restrictions, taxes, and duties that affected the natural performance of supply and demand forces. NUD 2284/ 91 was the key tool for this initiative. Among the main issues dealt with by NUD 2284/91 were the following:

- the repeal of those rules that hindered free supply and demand, or that distorted market prices
- the deregulation of the transport of goods
- the deregulation of professional practices
- the deregulation of the sale of medicines
- the authorization of medical imports
- the closing of ten regulatory and audit agencies
- taxation reform
- the reform of the stock market
- the creation of a unified system of social security

NUD 2284/91 repealed or directly and substantially changed more than forty-three laws. It also included a general repealing clause that stated, "All rules that oppose the rules issued in this decree are repealed." That clause implies that the NUD had effectively repealed all rules that involved market intervention. Nevertheless, in apparent contradiction to its own precedent, the executive issued a decree creating an import duty on sugar cane. The preamble of that decree stated that the executive acted on the basis of the Customs Code, by which Congress, in order to protect national production, had granted the president the authority to "charge a tax for price leveling" on the import of goods. In the wake of NUD 2284/91, then, the status of all economic regulatory law remained ambiguous. Apart from repealing existing regulations, what NUD 2284/91 really did was to change the regulatory authority. Since then, regulations come neither from Congress nor directly from the president, but from the Minister of the Economy and of Labor (Ferreira Rubio 1991).

Taxation without representation: The cinema tax. The Argentine Constitution, following the classic principle of "No taxation without representation," states that only Congress may impose taxes. However, from 1989 to 1993, the executive issued more than sixty-nine NUDs implementing taxation policies. To the number of tax-related NUDs listed in Table 2.3 and Figure 2.2, it is necessary to add other NUDs that involved some policy decisions on taxation, including the mega-NUDs. Through NUDs the president created, for instance, the following new taxes: taxes on financial assets (NUD 560/89), taxes on fuel (NUD 2733/ 90), and a tax on the exhibition of films through video and TV (NUD 2736/91). In addition, through NUDs the president modified the Value Added Tax multiple times (e.g., NUDs 2596/90, 501/91, 707/91, 171/92, 879/92, 180/93, 1684/93, and 2501/93). The following acts were also modified by NUDs: the Income Tax Act (NUDs 779/91 and 1684/93), the Fuel Taxation Act (NUD

2198/91), and the Inner Taxes Act (NUD 2753/91). The tax-free zone at La Plata Port was also created by NUD (1159/92).

The reactions elicited by these NUDs have been based on personal or group interests. The creation of new taxes naturally causes criticism on the part of those who would have to pay them, whereas the reduction of taxes was considered to be good policy by others. The case of the tax on film exhibition in TV and video, known as the cinema tax, is particularly significant. NUD 2736/91 established that the tax already applied to cinema tickets would be applied also to film exhibition on TV and by video cassettes. Associations and other organizations that represented video clubs and TV channels were sharply critical of this policy (*La Nación* 7/08/92). Their criticism was not related to the use of NUDs per se, but to this particular NUD, which obviously affected them directly.[19]

Several claims were presented to the courts. Some lower courts ruled that the NUD was unconstitutional and ordered the suspension of the tax (La Ley 1992–E–382). In June 1995 the Court declared that NUD 2736/91 was not valid according to the Constitution (CSJN 1995). It is important to keep in mind that according to the Argentine civil law system, even court decisions that explicitly rule on the unconstitutionality of an act or a decree apply only to the plaintiff; in contrast to judicial review by the U.S. Supreme Court, for example, they do not overturn the act or decree. In Argentina, court decisions – even those of the Supreme Court – have *intra partes* effects and not *erga omnes* effects.

The National Identification Cards. In April 1991, the executive issued NUD 603/91, which established that National Identification Cards would be made by a French public corporation (SOFREMI). Through this contract SOFREMI would receive approximately U.S. $200 million. The NUD also benefited the French corporation by giving it a series of important exemptions to taxes and duties. The president recognized this as a new NUD, but he did not include the clause, "Give notice to Congress," and he never sent the decree for congressional ratification.

News of NUD 603/91 was made public in the press (*Página 12* 5/4/91). In response to a series of newspaper stories, several drafts and bills were presented to repeal NUD 603/91. The chronological sequence of institutional reactions first led the State Audit Court to declare the NUD illegal (Resolution 213/91, June 5, 1991; *Clarín* 6/12/91). Then a judge ordered the executive to suspend this contract's fulfillment (*Clarín* 6/17/91), and the French Embassy in Argentina declared that the contract had been signed in secret because of the "character of the technology" (*La Nación* 6/25/91). In July a court declared NUD 603/191 unconstitutional (*Página 12* 7/30/91). Finally, the opposition in Congress moved to interpellate the Minister of the Interior, but the JP plurality in the Chamber prevented this move (*La Nación* 8/08/91). In the face of this pressure, however, the Minister of the Interior resigned and the incoming Minister announced that NUD 603/91 would be repealed (*La Nación* 8/14/91; *Página 12* 8/15/91; *La*

Nación 8/31/91). The repealing NUD was issued in September 1991; like NUD 603/91, it was never communicated to Congress. This case suggests that the most effective action against misuse of NUDs has come from the press. It was the press that uncovered the existence of the NUD and brought about the institutional reactions mentioned above.

"Tomatitas." The dominant opinion among legal scholars, one supported even by a Supreme Court sympathetic to President Menem, has been that in order to be valid, NUDs should be the consequence of extraordinary circumstances, those that are dangerous to the survival of the state or to the maintenance of social peace. Nevertheless, Menem has issued NUDs simply in order to avoid legal, formal, or institutional constraints. In 1991, for instance, he issued NUD 1809/91 to give asphalt to the Bolivian government to be used to pave an airport runway and a road between the outlying towns of Tomatitas, San Lorenso, and El Picacho. The presumed urgency in this case, according to presidential counsel Borgonovo, was the need to improve road conditions for an impending visit to the area by the president of Bolivia (Florit 1996). The NUD was not communicated to Congress and congressmen did not present any draft or bill regarding it.

TV transmission of soccer games. Another case of disputable emergency is that of NUD 1563/93. This NUD established that there would be no exclusive transmission rights for soccer games in which the national team played. NUD 1563/93 required persons and corporations that had bought those rights to renegotiate them without "exclusivity." The emergency, again according to Borgonovo, was that the preliminary matches for the 1994 World Cup were already underway and that to wait for congressional action on their broadcast rights would have risked depriving viewers of their right to follow the national team's progress (Florit 1996). According to Menem's critics, however, more effective opposition to this initiative was driven by groups who initially held exclusive broadcast rights (*Página 12* 7/23/93). The NUD was repealed by another NUD (1747/93) a month later.

Some comments on the cases. The analyzed cases show one of the characteristics of Menem's government style. NUDs have been used not only to initiate policy but also to resolve unimportant issues. In terms of policy importance, we cannot seriously compare the deregulation NUD (2284/91) to Tomatitas NUD (1809/91). Nevertheless, from a procedural standpoint, all of the 336 NUDs show the same decision to govern unilaterally, without limits or constraints. It is evident that secrecy was a vital element for the success of Plan Bonex, which was implemented by NUD 36/90. But what was the urgency in the case of the National Identification Cards? What would have been the consequences of a public debate? From the point of view of their political significance, these cases are completely different. From the institutional point of view, they both show the same essential character: the politics of fait accompli.

NUDs have been used and misused. In some cases the emergency was real; in others there were only particularistic needs, and in others the putative emergency was merely a vehicle for Menem to exercise personal discretion. In 1993, for instance, the president planned to attend the National Cattle Show. The adverse economic situation in the rural sector was expected to generate a hostile atmosphere toward the president. Some days before the presidential visit, some taxation policies favorable to cattle interests were implemented by NUD 1684/93. Tension diminished, and the president read his speech at the cattle show. Later, when the Official Bulletin eventually published the NUD, it became clear that the relevant taxes would be eliminated only by June 1995! What was the urgency then? Why did the president not present the bill to Congress? The answer, clearly, is that reliance on NUDs was politically convenient for the president. In this case there was serious public criticism of Menem's actions. Two weeks later, the president issued another decree (1802/93), which accelerated the implementation of the promised tax breaks to September 1993.

THE *DECRETAZO* AND THE OTHER BRANCHES OF GOVERNMENT

CONGRESS' INCAPACITY TO RESPOND

One of the standard justifications for the use of NUDs is congressional recess. This rationale is viable at least in those cases when it might be argued that it is impossible to convene the legislature and wait for regular law-making action. President Menem emphasized this argument – the impracticality of waiting for Congress – despite the fact that the Argentine Congress has been in session (whether ordinary or extraordinary) almost constantly since July 1989. Thirty-eight percent of all NUDs were issued while Congress was in ordinary legislative session, and a great part of the other 62 percent were issued when Congress was meeting in extraordinary session, not during congressional recess. It is also important to keep in mind that the Constitution allows the president to summon the Congress for extended or extraordinary session whenever he or she considers it necessary.

As we have noted, there is a general consensus among constitutional scholars on the requirement of communicating NUDs to Congress as a condition for their legal validity. Some of Menem's NUDs included in their preambles the assertion that their validity was related to the "expressed intention" to notify the Congress (NUDs 240/92, 879/92, 2632/92, 1684/93, 1848/93, and 2509/93). From this point of view, inclusion of the clause "Give notice to Congress" as a section of the NUD would be sufficient. This clause was included in most of the NUDs but not in all of them. On the other hand, Congress evidently did not need

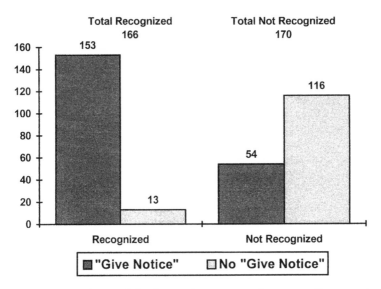

Figure 2.3 Inclusion of the clause "Give notice to Congress . . ." as a section of NUDs (Source: *All data collected by the authors*)

formal notification to take action repealing or ratifying NUDs. Data regarding notification from the executive is included because it shows in part the attitude of the president in relation to the legislative branch. Figure 2.3 sums up this information.

Figure 2.3 shows some curiosities. First, of 166 NUDs the executive recognized as such, 13 did not include the clause "Give notice to Congress." On the other hand, of 170 nonrecognized NUDs, 54 did include the clause. In some cases this was because NUDs ordered the executive to notify the Congress about all the political initiatives taken in a given area (NUD 1930/90). But that is not the case of all of these 54 NUDs. According to some government officials we consulted about this apparent discrepancy, the clause "Give notice to Congress" was a kind of implicit recognition of the nature of the decree.

How many NUDs were effectively communicated to Congress? Not all of the NUDs that included the clause "Give notice to Congress" were communicated. Take 1991 as an example. Of the 85 NUDs issued, only 21 (25 percent) were communicated to Congress, although the "Give notice to Congress" clause appeared in 66 of the NUDs. Of the 59 decrees the executive recognized as NUDs, Congress was notified of only 16 (27 percent); the other 5 that were communicated to Congress were nonrecognized NUDs. In short there has been no clear pattern between the executive's recognition (versus nonrecognition) of NUDs, on the one hand, and its willingness to submit new policies implemented by decree for congressional consideration, on the other.

How did Congress respond to the NUDs? Of the 336 NUDs issued by President Menem in the period under consideration, Congress completely ratified 26, 1 was partially ratified, and another was ratified with some modifications. In total, 28 NUDs (8 percent) were ratified during this period – 16 of them in December 1993 by Act 24,307 alone. During the same period Congress repealed 3 NUDs entirely and 1 NUD partially. Thus, Congress took no action at all in response to more than 90 percent of the NUDs issued by President Menem between 1989 and 1993, as shown in Figure 2.4. Moreover, in the few cases where Congress did act – particularly when it resisted executive initiatives – its incapacity relative to the executive was exposed. The executive upheld the congressional repeal on only one of these three occasions – the repeal of NUD 752/92 by Act 24,138. In the other two cases, the president used partial vetoes to eliminate from congressional acts the sections repealing NUDs. Act 23,982 provides an instructive example of Menem's attitude toward congressional challenges to decree authority.

Act 23,982 (Consolidation of Public Debt Act) repealed two chapters of NUD 1757/90, although it reiterated that the repeal did not pertain to the rest of the NUD. Menem partially vetoed the bill, eliminating the sections repealing the chapters of NUD 1757. Subsequently, when the president issued some regulatory decrees to implement Act 23,982, he repealed the same two chapters of NUD 1757/90 originally rejected by Congress. The substantive compliance with Congress' mandate, however, should not be interpreted as deference to congressional will. Menem made a procedural point of promulgating Act 23,982 initially, without the clause repealing NUD 1757/90. The message was: "The executive is the only one who can decide on the policy implemented by an NUD" (Spisso 1992:90). On four other occasions the president wholly vetoed laws enacted by Congress, because they contradicted policies established by NUDs.[20] The same reason justified partial vetoes of nine other laws.

Although the reaction has rarely gone beyond individual action – especially from the UCR and minor parties – many legislators have strenuously objected to the increase in the executive's law-making activity.[21] General objections to the practice of legislating by NUDs, however, were never passed in either chamber of Congress. This is not surprising, considering the support that the government party had in Congress and the fact that even non-JP legislators have not been united in opposition to the *decretazo*. Indeed, some have even requested that the executive issue NUDs.

Why did Congress react in this way? The opposition parties may have preferred to challenge presidential initiatives, but they did not have the votes to force debate on the ratification or rejection of NUDs. Across the aisle, Peronist legislators, both in the Senate and the Chambers of Deputies, did not want to foster debate on NUDs for three main reasons. First, President Menem specifically asked the leaders of the Peronist Party in Congress to support executive initiatives. As long as Menem remained the unchallenged leader of his party, he could count on congressional support. Second, in case of a floor debate on NUD ratification, the JP was not always certain to have the necessary votes. The JP held a majority

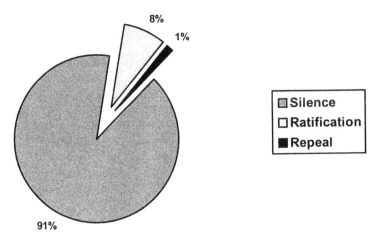

Figure 2.4 Congressional action regarding NUDs (Source: All data collected by the authors)

of Senate seats throughout this period. In the Chamber of Deputies, however, the JP held partisan pluralities but not majorities. Because congressional ratification was not necessary for NUDs to take force, the JP had good reason to accede to NUDs rather than to take direct action on them. Third, in some cases, NUDs simply anticipated legislators' preferences and, just as important, allowed for the adoption of controversial policies favored by Congress without public debate. According to constitutional scholar and UCR Deputy Jorge Vanossi, "The worst thing is that the majority of NUDs are things Congress would have passed because the executive had enough parliamentary support. Why, then, did the president use decree? Because of the fear of public debate, it was more convenient to do them secretly" (Florit 1996).

THE SUPREME COURT: THE ABSENCE OF CHECKS AND BALANCES

What has been the judicial reaction to the *decretazo?* The Plan Bonex NUD and cinema tax NUD were the two NUDs that prompted the greatest number of judicial challenges. The Supreme Court had to rule in several cases related to NUDs, and the decisions were not similar in all cases. Moreover, like the reaction of other political actors, the Supreme Court's reaction to NUDs has varied according to whether the decrees directly affect the economic interests of the justices.

The Peralta Decision. The most relevant Supreme Court decision on the constitutionality of NUDs is the Peralta decision upholding NUD 36/90, which established the forced public loan for term deposits (Bianchi 1991; Bidart Campos

1991; CSJN 1990). In the Peralta decision, the Supreme Court established the following principles on which to justify legal validity of NUDs. The decision (CSJN 1990) said,

1. Separation of powers is a "historic category: it was an instrument of the political fight against absolutism." This principle cannot be interpreted as inviolable when to respect it would risk the survival of the state. Consequently, if the president "enacts laws" by NUDs like 36/90, this does not automatically mean that these NUDs are unconstitutional.
2. The validity of NUDs depends on two conditions:
   a. "that Congress does not pass laws different from NUDs regarding the involved issues of economic policy"; and
   b. NUDs have to be the political reaction to "a situation of serious social danger that requires an immediate response . . . the effectiveness of which is not possible by other means."

The Supreme Court based its ruling on the existence of an *implicit congressional consent through silence*. Because Congress passed no law repealing NUD 36/90, congressional consent should be presumed. The Court's thesis of presumed consent did not address the fact that the legislation to ratify NUD 36/90 was only passed by the Senate. The Court ruled that NUDs did not usurp congressional sovereignty over legislation because Congress technically could repeal or modify NUDs. Our review of Congress' success in such attempts demonstrates that this is a dubious assertion.

The second condition for constitutionality relates to the existence of a state of emergency and to the effectiveness of the response. The Supreme Court described an emergency as "an extraordinary situation that affects the economic and social order, with its effect of accumulated uneasiness, through scarcity, poverty and indigence, creating a state of necessity that requires solution." Again, the cases of various NUDs reviewed earlier demonstrate that many of them bore no relation whatsoever to any reasonable definition of such an emergency.

The compensation of justices. Nine months after the Peralta decision, the executive suspended the Supreme Court's authority to determine justices' compensation. NUD 2071/91 suspended for one year a section of the Judiciary Autarky Act (23;853), which endowed the Court with the authority to determine compensations for members and employees of the judiciary. The executive justified NUD 2071 on the grounds that the Supreme Court had not taken into account the economic emergency when determining compensations. The Supreme Court issued an *acordada* (Acordada 42/91, October 8, 1991) – an internal administrative resolution – declaring NUD 2071/91 null and void.[22] The Court's rationale was that NUD 2071/91 interfered with the implementation of some Court resolutions, which were issued on the basis of legally delegated authority, and that the Court had to declare NUD 2071/91 null and void "in order to safeguard separation of powers." It is self-evident that here the Court changed its interpretation of the relation between NUDs and the separation of powers relative to its decision in the Peralta case. The conflict ended a month later when the executive issued another NUD to restore the Supreme Court's authority to determine compensations (NUD 2356/91). The Court, in turn, immediately determined compensations according to the criteria established by the Ministry of Economy.

NUDs, DELEGATED DECREE AUTHORITY, AND THE CONSTITUTIONAL REFORM OF 1994

In November 1993 Menem and Alfonsin, as presidents of the Peronist (JP) and Radical (UCR) parties, respectively, negotiated and signed the *Pacto de Olivos*, stating the initial agreements on the reform of the Argentine Constitution. One of the stated objectives of the reform was the consolidation of the democratic system and of the equilibrium of power among the three branches of government. To achieve this goal, the reform would include – among other provisions – the constitutional regulation of NUDs. Alfonsin believed that the constitutional recognition and regulation of NUDs would curtail the powers of the president and would prevent the misuse of decree authority in the future (Alfonsin 1994:43; *La Nación* 6/21/94; *Página 12* 6/28/94). On the other hand those politicians who were against the *Pacto de Olivos* thought that the constitutional regulation of NUDs would codify the expansion of presidential power and would seriously damage checks and balances (Zaffaroni 1994). In December 1993, Congress passed Act 24,309, declaring the need for the constitutional reform on the terms established by the *Pacto*. Act 24,309 distinguished between the "core of basic agreement," which were those reforms included in the *Pacto* and other potential issues of reform. The core was to be considered as a unit, meaning that it had to be accepted or rejected in its entirety. The members of the Constitutional Assembly could neither amend nor accept only selected parts of the reforms negotiated by Menem and Alfonsin. The articles allowing the reelection of the president as well as those regarding NUDs and decree delegated authority were included in the core. By August 1994 the constitutional delegates adopted a broad slate of reforms, including the recognition and regulation of NUDs. Article 99.3 of the Constitution now reads, in part:

> The Executive Power shall never issue lawmaking decisions. These kinds of measures will be considered null and void.
> Only when exceptional circumstances make it impossible to follow the ordinary lawmaking process established by this Constitution, the Executive can issue NUDs insofar as they do not regulate penal, fiscal, electoral or political [party] matters. NUDs must be decided by the Cabinet assembled and must be countersigned by the Cabinet Chief and the other Ministers.
> Within ten days the Cabinet Chief will personally submit the NUD

to a Permanent Bicameral Committee which will be composed proportionally according to the political representation of the House and the Senate. The Committee will send its opinion to the floor within ten days. The House and the Senate must immediately consider the opinion. A special act, passed by the positive vote of the majority of the members of the House and the Senate, will determine the proceedings and effects of Congress' intervention in this matter.

The inclusion of NUDs in the Constitution has generated diverse reactions. Some authors think this new article is merely the recognition of existing constitutional custom (Garcia Lema 1993:205). Others believe that the constitutional regulation of NUDs will strengthen the president's power and will reinforce concentration of power in the executive (Ferreira Rubio and Goretti 1994b; *La Nación* 6/20/94). From a legal point of view, the introduction of NUDs removes any doubt as to their constitutional validity. At the same time, the provision for procedures to regulate NUDs may limit the president's discretion in their use. Article 99.3 states that NUDs will be null and void if they are related to penal, fiscal, electoral, or political party matters. Many of the procedural details of how Congress will exercise its regulatory authority remain to be determined by normal legislation. And Article 99.3 raises several questions that will certainly prompt diverse interpretations. For instance, who will determine the existence of "exceptional circumstances"? Can this decision be challenged judicially? Does the "impossibility" of following the ordinary law-making process include "political impossibility" (for instance, that the president's party does not have the necessary votes to pass a bill)? Whether Congress exercises control over the use of NUDs under the new Constitution any more effectively than it did before the reform remains to be seen. At the very least, the requirement of the countersignature of the Chief of the Cabinet and of all the other ministers is regarded as a limit to presidential authority.

The constitutional reform of 1994 also explicitly regulates delegated authority for the first time (in Article 76):

> Legislative delegation to the Executive is forbidden except in the case of determined matters of administration and public emergency, with a limited term for its effectiveness and within the standards for the delegation of authority established by Congress.
>
> The expiration of the term mentioned above will not cause the revision of the legal relations born under the rules issued as a consequence of the legislative delegation.

This article, which was also part of the *Pacto de Olivos*, ratified the limits and conditions that the Argentine Supreme Court had established in 1927 regarding the constitutional status of decree delegated authority. According to Article 100(12), legislative or delegated decrees shall be controlled by the same Permanent Bicameral Committee mentioned by Article 99.3.

POSTSCRIPT AND CONCLUSION

In expanding and institutionalizing the use of decree in Argentina, President Menem has brought about significant changes in the process of government decision making. To understand these changes, one has to bear in mind the degree and intensity of the emergency that Argentina had undergone for years. Once democratic institutions were recovered, the economic agenda replaced the political agenda. Society began to demand a solution to the economic crisis that the Alfonsin administration seemed unable to solve. Although increasing citizens' demands concentrated on the presidency as the only institution that could manage the economic crisis, Menem had to confront the gap between democratic decision-making procedures and those tools needed to handle the crisis successfully (Torre 1993). He decided to rule by decree. Through early 1995, as a result of Menem's management of the economic crisis, his party's electoral fortunes continued to improve, even beyond the JP's emergence in 1989 as the country's most powerful political force. As part of the constitutional reforms of 1994, Menem even secured an amendment striking down the longstanding prohibition on presidential reelection, and in May 1995 he was elected to a new four-year term.

Emergency government in Argentina has given birth to a new institutional balance of power. The presidency has accumulated authorities that previously had been distributed among the other branches. Moreover, Menem has exhibited a new style of decision making – discretionary, informal, sometimes arbitrary, and with a low commitment to the sanctity of formal political institutions – one resembling the style of old local leaders, or *caudillos*. Concurrently, Congress has lost legitimacy and political capacity, reducing its ability to act in reaction to presidential initiatives. All these developments were responses to public opinion and public demands for quick and effective policy making. The presidency was better prepared, both structurally and in terms of leadership capacity, to satisfy those demands than Congress, which facees formidable collective action problems. As a consequence, reactions against presidential decree authority have been isolated and uncoordinated – they have primarily been responses to presidential measures that directly hurt specific political and economic interests.

The constitutional reform of 1994 may bring about some changes in the practice of government by decree, although it is too early to reach judgment. Article 99.3 formally recognizes the constitutionality of decree, but it also attempts to restore to NUDs the status of exceptional political devices, as they were until 1989, and it mandates a procedure by which all decrees must be reviewed and then ratified or rejected by Congress. Just as the intent of Article 99.3 is ambiguous, so too have been its effects. Creation of the Permanent Bicameral Committee required by Article 99.3 requires a new law; but more than two years after the constitutional reform, Congress had not passed such a law, so the commission does not exist. Meanwhile, NUDs remain central to the administration's governing strategy. As Menem stated in November 1996,

"Within this constitutional framework, in instances where I am able to take action by decree, I am going to do it" (Florit 1996). The rate at which the administration issues NUDs, however, has declined by more than 50 percent relative to the period before the reform. In the first twenty-seven months under the new 1994 Constitution, the administration issued sixty-two NUDs – less than its yearly average over the 1989–94 period. President Menem's reference to the constitutional framework, then, only highlights the ambiguity of the current status of decree in Argentina. Decree is now constitutional, and Menem has established the precedent of its centrality to the law-making process. On the other hand, its very institutionalization corresponds to a decline in use. If Congress acts to establish the oversight mechanisms called for under the new constitution, then the executive's discretion to make law by decree may be further limited. Congress has been slow to act, however, and whether the institution is willing or able to do so remains unclear.

NOTES

1 NUDs are not the same as "decree-laws," which are, in Argentina, those laws enacted by de facto governments.
2 This third kind is called *decretos delegados* in Argentina.
3 The JP is sometimes known as the Peronists, after the party's founder and two-time Argentine president, Juan Peron.
4 Among other cases, this occurred on legislation dealing with the following issues: pensions (*La Nación* 6/03/92, *Página 12* 6/20/92 and 6/26/92); regulation of the right to strike (*La Nación* 7/26/90); consolidation of public debt (*Página 12* 8/16/91); the national budget (*La Nación* 8/17/91); privatization of the national oil company, YPF (*Clarín* 9/18/92). See also President Menem's declarations after three years in office (*La Nación* 7/8/92).
5 Act 23, 928 declares that one peso has the same value as one U.S. dollar and that the Argentine Central Bank will always retain sufficient holdings and gold reserves to cover all money in circulation.
6 See the complete version of the "Acordada 44" in *La Nación* (9/23/89). The Court stated, ". . . the Court is important for democracy. . . . such an institution cannot live with authoritarian administrations."
7 See President Roosevelt's "Message to the U.S. Congress" (2/5/37) and the letter from Chief Justice Hughes to Senator Wheeler (3/21/37) in Stephens and Rathjen (1980:47).
8 This decision was the immediate antecedent for one of President Alfonsín's NUDs: 2196/86.
9 Under Argentine law, intervention is an anomalous way of removing the legal authorities of an institution, one that replaces them with *interventores* who act as delegates of the authority who declared the intervention. For instance, the Argentine Constitution grants the Congress the authority to declare federal intervention in a province (Art. 75:31). The executive has the authority to order federal intervention when the Congress is not in session (Art. 99:20).

10 For example, the Salta Constitution (Section 142), the Río Negro Constitution (Section 181.6), and the San Juan Constitution (Section 157).

11 We are distinguishing constitutional governments from military or de facto governments, both of which ruled Argentina for much of this time.

12 Some of the NUDs issued in this period were the following:

- In 1880 a NUD declared Belgrano as Capital District in the context of an armed revolt that was led by the Buenos Aires governor against national authorities.
- In 1891 a new NUD authorized Treasury Bills.
- In 1915 a new NUD dissolved Buenos Aires' local legislature.
- NUDs 31.864 and 31.865, both issued in 1933, authorized the government to regulate corn market prices.
- NUD 2639/60 established a national security plan ("Plan Conintes").
- During the Peron-Peron administration (1973/1976) several NUDs were issued regulating the right to go abroad in case of *estado de sitio* emergencies.

Other examples can be found in Lugones, Garay, Dugo, and Corcuera (1992).

13 Our database only includes indisputable NUDs. Whenever there was the possibility of contradictory interpretations, we chose not to include the decree. For instance, among those excluded was decree 2184/90, which related to strike rights. The government presented it as a rule-making decree related to three acts: Act 14.786 (1958), Act 16.936 (1966), and Act 20.638 (1974). In our opinion the executive overstepped its authority, and the decree involved modifications of these laws – limiting strike rights, for example, to preserve essential services. Because this was a matter of legal dispute, we excluded this decree from our database.

14 These data were first presented by Ferreira Rubio and Goretti (1994a). In this paper 1992 showed a total of 67 NUDs because we included only those NUDs published in the Official Bulletin until December 31, 1992. The increment of one NUD for 1990 is due to the fact that it had been published only partially, and we did not include NUDs until we could verify the complete text. The data for 1993 were first presented in Ferreira Rubio and Goretti (1995). In this paper 1993 showed a total of 61 NUDs because we included only those NUDs published in the Official Bulletin through January 11, 1994.

15 Law 24,241 had created a privately funded and administered pension system, and it established rules governing the choices that employees were allowed over whether to participate in the existing public pension system or the newly created private one. Menem issued five NUDs directly contradicting, modifying, or replacing some sections of Law 24,241, as well as more than 100 rule-making and delegated legislative decrees related to the implementation of the law.

16 The policy implemented by NUD 36/90 was known as Plan Bonex because of the name of the Treasury Bills involved.

17 NUDs 99/90, 100/90, 296/90, 340/90 (which stated that nonprofit organizations would be exempted from the forced loan), 591/90 (which established an exception for persons older than 75), 853/90, and 2670/91 (issued almost two years later). All these exceptions were general, but the executive also issued NUD 581/90, which created an individual exception. This interesting NUD created a special privilege for a private publicity agency – Thompson Argentina Inc. The preamble

of that NUD justified this privilege by stating that Thompson was working for UNICEF and that the term deposit corresponded to what UNICEF had paid for Thompson's private professional services; it also stated that because UNICEF was a nonprofit organization, Thompson's term deposits should be excluded from the forced loan.

18 We included in our database of 336 NUDs those NUDs that created exceptions to NUD 435/90 only when they had been recognized by the executive, in spite of the fact that the president had stated that in order to modify NUDs, it was necessary to issue new NUDs (see, e.g., the preambles of NUD 1854/91).

19 See the paid advertisement titled "Justicia, verdades y video." The argument is that NUDs are good when they deregulate or suspend benefits and privileges (others' benefits and privileges, of course) but not when they impose taxes (*La Nación* 4/23/93). Other cases of objections to NUDs driven by particularistic economic interests abound. For instance, there were the lawyers' reaction to NUD 34/91 (*Página 12* 4/3/91), to NUD 2071/91 (*La Nación* 10/5/91 and 10/11/91), and NUD 2077/93 (*Página 12* 10/22/93); the architects' reaction to NUD 34/90 (*La Nación* 5/3/91); the accountants' reaction (*Página 12* 6/27/91); the U.S. Embassy's demands for legal guarantees for U.S. corporations (*Página 12* 8/12/93; *La Nación* 8/12/93 and 9/27/93).

20 For example, Act 23, 889, which was passed by Congress in September 1990, created a series of exceptions to the policies implemented by NUDs 435/90 and 612/90. The president vetoed that bill because he thought "it was inconvenient to make exceptions to the policies established in NUD 435/90."

21 Among others, the following statements and reports by individual legislators and legislative committees can be mentioned: Senator Britos (Justicialist Party), Expte S–1451–90, DAE 4/29/91; Senator De la Rúa (*Unión Cívica Radical*), 12/93; Senator Rodríguez Saa (Justicialist Party), Expte S–1174, DAE 03/8/91; Senator Romero Feris (Pacto Autonomista Liberal – Corrientes), asking for the impeachment of the president (09/17/92), Expte 320, Sec. P; Deputy Baglini (UCR), Expte 4437–D–91, TP 12/27/91; Deputy Baylac (UCR), Expte 383–D–91, TP 5/10/91; Deputy Hernández (UCR), Expte 4343–D–91, TP 12/19/91; Deputy Vanossi (UCR), Expte 3564–D–91, TP 10/4/91.

22 In order to reach an agreement on the resolution, the Court suspended its decision on specific compensations for sixty days.

3

PRESIDENTIAL DECREE AUTHORITY IN RUSSIA, 1991–95

Scott Parrish

INTRODUCTION

Since the introduction of an independently elected president in Russia in May 1991, presidential decrees have played a central role in the political development of the country. Under both constitutions in effect since the collapse of the Soviet Union, the president has been granted significant Constitutional Decree Authority (CDA), and in the First Russian Republic (1991–93), the assembly delegated sweeping powers to President Boris Yeltsin. The nature and extent of presidential decree authority and the political and institutional context in which it was exercised, however, varied considerably between the two post–Soviet Russian republics. Russia thus provides valuable opportunities for examining the origins and the exercise of both constitutional and delegated presidential decree authority.

The role of presidential decrees in the development of Russian democracy has been highly controversial. President Yeltsin's use of decrees has often been termed "autocratic" (Wishnevsky 1992, 1993b), although some Western analysts have seen Russia as a paradigmatic case of "delegative democracy," in which the president rules by decree and thus usurps or at least marginalizes the powers and function of the assembly[1] (Kubicek 1994; Linz 1994; O'Donnell 1994; Roeder 1994). Such a democracy, these critics hold, is less representative of the popular will than one in which an assembly plays a major role, and it is also more prone to breakdown. Russia, they argue, because of its staggering geographic, economic, cultural, and religious diversity, is particularly ill-suited for this form of rule, which may undermine Russia's nascent democratic institutions. These judgments about the role of presidential decrees and the extent of presidential dominance over the policy agenda in Russia since 1991 deserve closer scrutiny. They capture a large amount of the truth, particularly about the 1991–93 period, but they are still somewhat exaggerated and may not accurately describe the development of the Second Russian Republic (1994–present), particularly in the post–Yeltsin era.

In the First Russian Republic (1991–93), the president's Constitutional Decree Authority (CDA) was limited. This case is thus consistent with the predictions of Carey and Shugart (this volume, chapter 1) because the Constitution was effectively written by the assembly, the Congress of People's Deputies. Economic and political crises, however, led the politically fragmented assembly to grant sweeping Delegated Decree Authority (DDA) to President Yeltsin in November 1991. Consistent with Carey and Shugart's hypotheses, urgency played a major role in this delegation decision. Yeltsin subsequently exercised this decree authority to influence almost every aspect of Russian society, although his decrees were sometimes overturned by a Constitutional Court that was independent of the executive. As Russia fell deeper into economic crisis in 1992 and 1993, an intense political struggle emerged between the assembly and Yeltsin over the extent of his DDA. This conflict culminated violently in October 1993, when Yeltsin issued a series of paraconstitutional decrees abrogating the existing constitution, dissolving the assembly, and suspending the Constitutional Court. Although his opponents did not immediately capitulate, Yeltsin ultimately gained the upper hand in a subsequent power struggle that spilled out into the streets of Moscow for several days.

What followed was a process of constitution drafting completely dominated by the executive. Yeltsin took a constitution largely drafted by officials of his administration and submitted it to a national referendum in December 1993, completely bypassing the elected assembly in the ratification process. The resulting constitution of the Second Russian Republic, not surprisingly, strongly supports Carey and Shugart's hypotheses linking the process of constitution drafting with the extent of presidential decree authority. Rather than checking or limiting presidential decree powers, the constitution's authors, all presidential appointees, bolstered them in a number of ways. Consequently, the Russian president wields decree authority that exceeds that of any other democratically elected chief executive.

Article 90 of Yeltsin's custom-designed 1993 Constitution grants the president authority to issue decrees on any subject, as long as they do not contradict existing law or the Constitution itself. Because the slow pace of legal reform in Russia has left many gaps in legislation relevant to an emerging democracy and market economy, Yeltsin has had considerable room for initiative. And in contrast to the situation in the First Russian Republic, the 1993 Constitution gives the president an effective veto, which Yeltsin has used on several occasions to block the politically divided bicameral Federal Assembly from overruling his decrees. In addition the constitutional amendment process is quite difficult, so that the Russian president cannot easily be stripped of his decree powers. All of these features of the new Constitution create an institutional framework in which the Russian president has both proactive and reactive instruments that allow him or her substantial control over the policy agenda.

Nevertheless, although Yeltsin may enjoy strong decree authority, future Russian presidents will probably find themselves more constrained. Much of Yeltsin's room for maneuver is not entirely the result of the institutional framework created by the Constitution, but rather it is an artifact of current conditions in Russia that are less likely to be shared by his successors. For example, the new Constitution revives the independent Constitutional Court, which has the power to review presidential decrees. Yeltsin was able to pack the Court with his supporters, and it has been deferential to him so far. But the Court's judges have twelve-year terms, so that Yeltsin's successors, particularly if they have political views that differ from his, may find the Court a constraint on their actions. And although there are many gaps in the Russian legal code now as a result of the turmoil of the transition, future presidents will undoubtedly face a more fully developed system of laws, constraining their ability to invoke Article 90.

The remainder of this chapter is divided into two sections; each one examines the origins and nature of presidential decree power in the two Russian Republics, using detailed case studies to test the hypotheses put forward in the introduction to this volume. The discussion of the Second Russian Republic also presents some basic data on the frequency and types of decrees that Yeltsin has issued since January 1994. Each section also analyzes the role of the Russian Constitutional Court in adjudicating the legality and constitutionality of presidential decrees.

PRESIDENTIAL DECREE AUTHORITY IN THE FIRST RUSSIAN REPUBLIC (1991–93)

An independently elected Russian presidency emerged in 1991 from the struggle between the increasingly conservative Soviet central government of President Mikhail Gorbachev and the reform-minded Supreme Soviet of the Russian Federative Soviet Socialist Republic (RSFSR), which was led by Boris Yeltsin. In January 1991 reformist deputies in the legislature of the Russian Republic proposed creating a presidency to oppose the central Soviet authorities over issues like control of the economy and republican sovereignty. They felt that the current governmental structure of the Russian Republic did not give the head of the government, the Chairman of the Russian Supreme Soviet, sufficient authority to successfully counteract the conservative central authorities (Rahr 1991:27).

The lengthy process that led to the creation of the Russian presidency reflected the byzantine structure of the Soviet-era political institutions under which Russia was then governed. According to the 1978 Russian Republic Constitution, Russia was a "socialist all-people's state," whose political will was to be expressed through the Supreme Soviet, which was designated the "supreme organ of state power" (*Konstitutsiya* 1992:1,104). In 1990, as part of Gorbachev's program of democratization, a series of amendments to the 1978 Constitution changed the process by which the assembly was formed and created an unusual bifurcated legislature.

At the base of this system was the 1,068-member Congress of People's Deputies, whose members were all elected from single-member districts on the basis of a majority run-off formula. The Constitution granted the Congress the totality of state power, meaning that there was no separation of powers in this model of government. The Congress itself met only periodically, but it alone could amend the Constitution (by a two-thirds supermajority) and elect the powerful Chairman of the Supreme Soviet. It also selected from among its members a smaller standing legislature, one consisting of two houses, which retained the traditional name of Supreme Soviet. The Supreme Soviet could adopt laws and other acts, subject to review by the Congress[2] (Remington, Smith, Kiewiet, & Haspel 1994: 160–3).

Continuing Soviet practice, the Constitution also gave considerable powers to an inner chamber of the Supreme Soviet, called the Presidium. Its powers included oversight of the legislative process, responsibility for the operations and agenda of the Supreme Soviet, and also the right to issue certain kinds of decrees. The Chairman of the Presidium, who was elected by a simple majority vote of the Congress for a five-year term, was in effect the head of state of the Russian Republic. The Chairman also played a role in the selection of the Chairman of the Council of Ministers of the RSFSR, who was the head of government. According to the Constitution, the Chairman of the Council of Ministers was accountable to the Supreme Soviet, and so the Chairman of the Supreme Soviet in principle had strong levers of control over the government.

The First Congress of People's Deputies elected Boris Yeltsin as Chairman of the Supreme Soviet in a very close vote at its first June 1990 meeting. By early 1991, however, with the Soviet Union – and Russia along with it – increasingly gripped by political and economic crisis, the executive authority of the Chairman seemed insufficient. In April 1991, for example, Yeltsin told the Congress that the weakness of the Russian executive could trigger "a veritable paralysis of power." He then suggested "redistributing the responsibilities of the supreme bodies of power," supporting the idea of an independent presidency (FBIS-SOV, 4 April 1991:70).

Despite opposition from communist deputies, the Supreme Soviet passed a law creating a Russian presidency on April 22, 1991. This law was then endorsed by the Fourth Congress of People's Deputies (May 1991), which amended the Constitution to take into account the new office. A competitive election for the post was held on June 12, 1991. From a field of six candidates, Yeltsin was elected, with 57.3 percent of the popular vote (*Pravda*, 25 June 1991). Thus, the Russian presidency was grafted onto a Soviet-era constitution for the express purpose of bringing Russia out of the deep economic and political crisis into which it had been plunged by the shortcomings of Mikhail Gorbachev's perestroika.

CONSTITUTIONAL DECREE AUTHORITY

The 1991 constitutional amendments appear to indicate that the Russian president had only limited Constitutional Decree Authority (CDA). Under Article 121:8 of the amended Russian Constitution, the president could issue decrees on subjects "within his competence," as long as they did not contradict existing law or the Constitution. Article 121:5 gave the president some maneuvering room, insofar as it charged him with protecting "state and social security," and almost any decree which did not contradict existing law could be rationalized as a defense of "social security." However, the Constitution specified that existing law or the Constitution would trump any presidential decree in the case of conflict (Article 121:8).

As originally written, therefore, the Constitution was supposed to limit the president's decree powers. The primary intent was to give the executive the power to implement decisions of the Congress and Supreme Soviet rather than to endow the president with the power to launch new policies independently. Sergei Shakrai, Chairman of the Supreme Soviet Committee on Legislation and one of the authors of the amendments creating the presidency, assured deputies at the Fourth Congress (May 1991) that the president would have the power only to issue decrees that were "subordinate to the law" and would not be able to usurp the functions of the Supreme Soviet and Congress of People's Deputies through the use of decree authority (FBIS-SOV, 22 May 1991).

Furthermore, the amended Constitution provided the Supreme Soviet and Congress with several checks against presidential abuse of decree authority. As Carey and Shugart hypothesize, the legislature, in drafting constitutional amendments, did not give the president an effective veto. The president could return bills to the assembly for reconsideration, but his or her objections could be overridden by a simple majority vote (Article 121:5). The Supreme Soviet could thus supersede presidential decrees with new legislation relatively easily. As a last resort, the president could be impeached for violations of the Constitution or the laws of the Russian Federation by a vote of two-thirds of the members of the Congress of People's Deputies (Article 121:3).

Finally, because of the procedure that was established for constitutional amendment, the president did not have a truly independent source of political authority. The Congress, after all, was the "supreme organ of state power" and could amend the Constitution with the approval of a two-thirds supermajority (Article 185). It would have been just as easy for the Congress, then, to vote the president out of existence as to impeach any particular president. Although this requirement did not make the president dependent on shifting day-to-day majorities in the Congress for his political survival, it did create a rather dependent presidency, one which was subject to significant interference by the Congress. With a constitution relatively easy to amend, the Congress did not need to fear extreme agency loss to the president by the extension of the limited decree powers granted to the president under Article 121:8.

This brief examination of the extent of the CDA granted to the Russian president under the 1991 constitutional amendments lends support to Carey and Shugart's hypothesis H1. The amendments were drafted by an assembly, and because the executive in effect did not yet exist, its influence was minimal. Consequently, the 1991 amendments granted the president only limited decree power, while guarding against agency loss by depriving the president of an effective veto and by retaining for the assembly the possibility of amending the Constitution relatively easily.

THE CONSTITUTIONAL COURT

To create a third pillar in a Western-inspired system of checks and balances, a Russian Constitutional Court was also created in 1991. As the preamble of the law creating the Court stated; "[I]n accordance with the principles of the separation of powers, constitutional oversight is to be entrusted to the judicial power as the most dispassionate and independent" (Sharlet 1993a:3). Its mandate empowered the Court to rule on the constitutionality of presidential decrees and also allowed it to resolve disputes between the other branches of the federal government. It would prove instrumental in this role for more than a year, sometimes even overturning presidential decrees, before President Yeltsin took paraconstitutional action to circumvent it in October 1993.

The constitutional amendments creating the Court were passed by the Fourth Congress of People's Deputies in May 1991, but because of political disputes, the judges were not actually selected until the Fifth Congress in October, and they were finally sworn in on October 31 (*RFE/RL Daily Report*, 31 October 1991). The Court consisted of fifteen judges elected by the Congress of People's Deputies from a list of nominees submitted by the president. Yeltsin presented twenty-three nominees, from whom the Congress elected only thirteen judges. Political maneuvering was evident during the voting, as members of the Congress clearly anticipated the possible political impact of the Court's future decisions.

Some deputies complained about the cursory nature of the screening process, because the Congress was able to question each candidate for only five minutes prior to the vote, thus suggesting that political affiliations were more important than professional qualifications. A critical article in the newspaper *Moskovskie novosti* commented that very few of the new judges had judicial experience, and it questioned the impartiality of several of the new appointees, including the Chief Judge, Valerii Zorkin, who had earlier held positions in Yeltsin's government (Thorson 1991b:13). As the Court began work, its members became so politicized that when Yeltsin suspended its activity nearly two years later, the final two vacancies on the bench remained unfilled (Sharlet 1993a:11).

Judges were appointed for limited-life tenure, meaning that once appointed, they could remain on the bench until age sixty-five, which gave the Court some independence from the other two branches of government. The relative ease with which the Constitution could be amended, however, meant that the Congress could potentially abolish the Constitutional Court if two-thirds of its members chose to do so. Without resorting to paraconstitutional means, however, the president had far fewer levers of influence over the Court. While he or she could nominate candidates for vacancies on the Court, the requirement that they be approved by the Congress restricted presidential influence over the composition and political views of the court.

PRESIDENTIAL DECREE AUTHORITY IN PRACTICE, 1991–93

Although it is often contended that Yeltsin had a tendency to ignore the assembly and rule the country by executive fiat during the First Russian Republic, this is not an accurate picture of the entire period. In fact Yeltsin met frequent resistance from the other branches of power, and in those areas where he had the greatest impact, he was often operating within the scope of a very sweeping blanket delegation of decree authority granted him by the Congress of People's Deputies. In short, Yeltsin did not always control the policy agenda, and when he did, it was often with the blessing of the other branches of the Russian government. Ultimately, however, Yeltsin did choose to rule by fiat. Unsatisfied with the restraints placed on him by the Constitution, the Congress, and the Constitutional Court, he increasingly flouted them and finally resorted to paraconstitutional action to sweep those institutions aside and engineer a wholesale change in Russian politics.

Attempting to Ban Political Opponents by Decree. Almost as soon as he became president, Yeltsin began to issue decrees testing the limits of his CDA. On July 20, 1991, Yeltsin issued a decree with the lengthy title, "On terminating the activity of the organizational structure of political parties and mass public movements in state agencies, institutions, and organizations of the RSFSR." The decree banned "political activity" by mass organizations or political parties within state institutions during working hours. It also stated that while working, government employees were "bound by the demands of RSFSR legislation" and not subject to "the decisions of political parties and mass public movements" (*Sovetskaya Rossiya*, 23 July 1991).

Although it did not say so openly, the decree targeted the Communist Party of the Soviet Union (CPSU) and its Russian branch, the Russian Communist Party (RCP). The communist parties had so-called primary organizations or cells in state institutions across the country, including factories and government ministries. This network served as a vital part of the system of "party control" over state institutions in the Soviet Union. It in effect created a parallel chain of command throughout the state bureaucracy, which, despite modest reform, continued to control most of the Russian economy. These cells could threaten Yeltsin's control over the RSFSR state apparatus (Teague and Wishnevsky 1991:2). Having such a network also gave the RCP, which opposed Yeltsin's call for radical economic reform and political sovereignty for Russia, an advantage over all other Russian political parties, none of which could claim anything approaching its organizational depth. Yeltsin used this disparity to justify his decree, terming it necessary to ensure "equal rights of political parties" as guaranteed in the Russian Constitution (*Sovetskaya Rossiya*, 23 July, 1991:2).

Although Yeltsin was undoubtedly correct about the Communist Party's organizational advantages, he was stretching the limits of his constitutional decree authority under Article 121:8. It was far from clear that the decree could be justified as an action taken to "implement" the Constitution's guarantee of equal political rights. Because the RCP represented a significant political threat to Yeltsin, his action looked transparently self-serving. Not surprisingly, pro-Yeltsin politicians from the reformist side of the Russian political spectrum hailed the decree. Critics, on the other hand, those who were mainly from the RCP itself, quickly attacked Yeltsin for exceeding his authority. The Politburo of the RCP, for example, accused Yeltsin of violating the constitutional rights of Communist Party members. It also contended that Article 121:8 empowered the president only to issue decrees "in fulfillment of the RSFSR Constitution and laws passed by the RSFSR Supreme Soviet," and it argued that neither provided any grounds for restricting the activity of any political party. The RCP also pointed out that attempts to push legislation restricting the RCP through the Supreme Soviet had failed on several earlier occasions. Hence Yeltsin's decree had "no legal basis" and was "illegal" (*Pravda*, 24 July 1991:2). As the RSFSR Constitutional Court had not yet been formed, it could not adjudicate this dispute.

The furor over Yeltsin's decree, however, was soon overtaken by events. The failed August 1991 coup in Moscow and the subsequent disintegration of the U.S.S.R. emboldened Yeltsin to take even harsher action. On August 23 and 25, Yeltsin issued two additional decrees; pending a judicial investigation into the role both parties played in the August coup (Thorson 1991a:5), he suspended the activity of the RCP and confiscated its property and that of the CPSU. Finally, on November 6, two months after the coup attempt, Yeltsin issued another decree banning both the RCP and the CPSU altogether (Wishnevsky 1993a:6).

By the time Yeltsin issued the November decree banning the communist parties, the Russian Constitutional Court had been created, and its judges had been selected. The RCP quickly petitioned it to review Yeltsin's August and November decrees on the RCP and CPSU. The Court, despite a prohibition in its enabling statute against reviewing "political questions," accepted the petition, a decision which guaranteed its entanglement in one of the hottest political controversies in Russia during 1992. In fact the expectation that the so-called CPSU Case would come before the Court had been one reason for both the delay and political maneuvering surrounding the selection of the Court's members (Sharlet 1993a:17).

The Court waited until May 1992 to hold its first hearings, but the case then dragged on through most of the year. The arguments against the decrees were rather strong on constitutional, if not on political, grounds (Thorson 1992:2–3).

In an implicit admission of the weak legal basis for the decrees, a group of pro-Yeltsin politicians submitted their own counterpetition just a few days before the Court began hearings. The counterpetition asked the Court to verify the constitutionality of the CPSU and RCP. According to an amendment to the Russian Constitution, which had been passed only in April 1992, political organizations that advocated the violent overthrow of the current constitutional order were banned, and the Constitutional Court was given authority to enforce this provision. In a politically charged and legally questionable procedural move, the Court decided to hear both the original petition and the counterpetition as one case. This decision gave the Court more latitude than it otherwise might have had, given that the original decrees were on shaky constitutional ground.

The political biases of some of the judges on the Court obviously motivated this procedural maneuver. Chief Judge Zorkin, for example, told an interviewer in February 1992 that in the event conservative pro-communist forces gained the upper hand in Russia, then "dreams about any changes for the better will be ruined at the root" (Thorson 1992). The maneuver did, however, let the Court extricate itself from a difficult political dilemma. Absent the counterpetition, the Court would have faced a stark choice between either clearly flouting the law and the Constitution by validating Yeltsin's decrees or politically backing the CPSU and the RCP by overturning those decrees. With the counterpetition under consideration, the Court had a "fudge factor," which allowed it to reach a compromise decision.

When that decision was announced, even its timing was politically motivated, coming as it did on December 1, 1992, only a day before the opening session of the Seventh Congress of People's Deputies, which promised to be a political slugfest between Yeltsin and his parliamentary opponents. The decision tried to split the difference between the Yeltsin administration and the communists. Although the decrees were ruled constitutional, the Court only partially upheld Yeltsin's ban on the RCP and CPSU, allowing him to close the central executive apparatus of the CPSU and the RCP, but permitting local organizations of the RCP to continue functioning. As to the confiscation of the property of the CPSU and the RCP, the decision referred most of the vexing issues to courts of arbitration for final decision (Wishnevsky 1993a:5–7). Yeltsin thus avoided a politically embarrassing decision overturning his decrees, while the RCP was given an opportunity to continue its political life.

The final vote on the Court's decision was 11–2. One of the dissenting judges, however, wrote an angry dissenting opinion. Judge Luchin argued that Yeltsin had exceeded his competence in issuing the decrees and that the Court had erred in merging the two petitions into a single case. The final decision, he contended, was based more on political expediency than on the law, and it showed that the members of the Court themselves were more politicians than jurists. This view contrasted sharply with Zorkin's appraisal that the decision had been "guided only by law and conscience" (Sharlet 1993a:30).

The decision did not, however, validate the principle that the president could ban political parties by decree. On October 28, 1992, Yeltsin issued a decree banning another political movement, the extreme rightist National Salvation Front (NSF) (*Rossiiskaya gazeta*, 30 October 1992). Like the communists, the NSF petitioned the Constitutional Court to rule on the constitutionality of the decree. The NSF, in contrast to the CPSU and RCP, had just begun to organize when Yeltsin banned it. Even some liberal supporters of Yeltsin felt the decree went too far (Wishnevsky 1993a:7). Although Yeltsin weakened the decree in January 1993, the Court nonetheless struck it down in February. It judged the decree unconstitutional because it usurped the functions of the legislative and judicial branches (ITAR-TASS, 12 February 1993). On balance, then, Yeltsin's attempts to use his decree authority to eliminate his political opponents in the 1991–93 period met with only limited success, and the Constitutional Court provided a loose institutional counterweight to the president in this regard before its suspension in October 1993.

DELEGATION BY THE CONGRESS OF PEOPLE'S DEPUTIES

Yeltsin's most sweeping decree authority during the First Russian Republic, however, derived not from the Constitution but from delegated authority. After the failed August 1991 coup, Russia's economic difficulties intensified. Yeltsin began to call for an augmentation of his powers in order to deal with this crisis. On the eve of the Fifth Congress of People's Deputies in late October 1991, where Yeltsin planned to request a delegation of decree authority, the Russian economy was in headlong decline. Experts were forecasting a GNP decline of about 15–20 percent for the year. The government budget deficit was soaring – it was approaching 20 percent of GNP – whereas inflation, virtually unknown in the Soviet era, was expected to reach 200 percent for 1991 (Bush 1991:1). This decline continued despite the introduction of six "reform programs" by the central Soviet government during the previous two years.

Yeltsin thus urged the Congress to grant him powers that were "adequate for today's emergency situation" (*Izvestiya*, 30 October 1991:2) and sufficient to implement a radical economic reform program. He submitted a bill allowing him to issue decrees with the force of law, even if they contradicted existing legislation. He also requested authority to form a government without approval by the Supreme Soviet or the Congress, as normally required by the Constitution. He further proposed that any economic legislation submitted to the Congress or the Supreme Soviet be previously cleared with the president. To cement his authority to oversee implementation of his reforms, Yeltsin asked for the power to directly appoint regional heads of administration (governors), and he requested the power to overrule actions of regional and local officials (ibid.).

Although some critics complained that these powers would make the president a virtual dictator, Yeltsin was able to convince the Congress to approve most of what he requested. On November 1, 1991, the Congress approved Yeltsin's proposed economic reform program, and then it voted 876–16 to give Yeltsin the powers he had requested to carry it out for a period of one year. Although the delegation itself was explicit, its terms were not. The president was empowered to issue decrees on questions of "banking, the stock market, currency and financial [affairs], foreign economic [activity], investment, customs activity, the budget, price formation, taxation, property, land reform, and employment" (*Rossiiskaya gazeta*, 5 November 1991). Such decrees could be overruled by the Supreme Soviet, but if it did not act within seven days, the decree would enter into force (ibid.).

This decision represented a very sweeping delegation of power to the Russian president, because the wide range of topics it covered allowed the president, with a little creative argumentation, to issue decrees on almost any subject. What factors motivated this decision? First, although it is difficult to define, urgency clearly played a role in the decision. The economic situation in the country was worsening, and immediate action seemed imperative. One media account of the Congress suggested that many deputies felt "the country stands on the edge of an abyss, and radical reforms are indispensable, otherwise there will be total chaos and collapse" (*Izvestiya,* 4 November 1991:4).

Bargaining problems also played a role in motivating the Congress' decision. The Congress, with its 1,068 members, was hardly an efficient forum for reaching decisions. Nor was the smaller standing legislature, with its two chambers, necessarily much better, given that its most important decisions would require ratification by the larger Congress. The cumbersome two-level legislative institutions bequeathed to independent Russia by the Soviet Union exacerbated the already severe bargaining problems involved in embarking on a difficult transition to a market economy. Hence, delegation to a unitary and decisive executive appealed to many deputies. Since the delegation statute contained a clause that allowed the Supreme Soviet and the Congress to review any decrees that the president issued, agency loss on particular issues could be minimized. In addition, the existence of the independent Constitutional Court meant that a "third force" could check any extreme abuses of delegated decree authority.

The makeup of partisan political forces in the Congress may also have operated to encourage the Congress to delegate extensive powers to Yeltsin. There was, at the time, almost no party structure in the Congress. When it had been elected in 1990, political parties had played no significant role in the selection and financing of candidates. An exception to this statement, of course, must be made for the CPSU, which did play a significant role in the nomination and election of some of the candidates. However, although 86 percent of the deputies elected to the Congress were members of the Communist Party, the party itself had begun to fragment by this time. Thus, these communist deputies came from across the political spectrum and did not represent a coherent bloc of votes even on individual issues (Remington et al. 1994:162). As a result, it is safe to say that party discipline, as such, was extremely low in the Congress, which on the face of it would increase the salience of bargaining problems and perhaps influence deputies to support the delegation of powers to the president in order to avoid economically costly political deadlock in the legislature.

Partisan support for Yeltsin, on the other hand, does not seem to have been a major factor. The support for the delegation to Yeltsin was overwhelming, but an analysis of other votes in the Fifth Congress as well as in the four preceding Congresses shows that the deputies were polarized into two roughly equal blocs along a left–right ideological dimension. One group represented defenders of the old order, whereas the other could be roughly characterized as "reformist" (Remington et al. 1994:164; Sobyanin 1994:182–3). Thus, although Yeltsin won the vote on the powers he asked for, his victory did not reflect a strong partisan majority supporting Yeltsin; no such majority existed. This was the same Congress, after all, that had only very narrowly selected Yeltsin as its Chairman in 1990 at its first meeting.

At the Fifth Congress itself, there was a vivid illustration of the bargaining problems connected with this distribution of partisan interests. A proposal was put forward to revoke the current ten-year ban on the sale or transfer of privatized land. After a lengthy discussion the Congress could not muster the votes to repeal the ban, and the issue remained deadlocked. One observer said that this fruitless debate showed that "the Congress is running true to form" and remained unable to address the crucial issues facing the country (*Izvestiya*, 1 November 1991).

The situation was so bad that some of the deputies who opposed Yeltsin's conception of market-oriented reform on principle obviously preferred delegation to the president over sticking with the status quo, which, given the cumbersome apparatus of the Congress and Supreme Soviet, precluded the rapid implementation of decisive measures to cure the ills of the economy. Others, although opposing Yeltsin, voted to delegate responsibility over the management of the economy to him in order to transfer the political cost of economic reform to the president. Whether one believed that the "shock therapy" that Yeltsin told the Congress he was prepared to implement would work or not, it was bound to prove economically painful in the short run. And as one journalist observed, some Yeltsin opponents were counting on this sort of logic; they declared themselves "ready to give Yeltsin full power – let him fail and then be swept away" (*Izvestiya*, 2 November 1991).

Economic Reform by Decree. The powers which had been delegated to Yeltsin would be used over the next two years to dramatically alter many aspects of the country's political and economic life. Almost immediately after the delegation went into effect, Yeltsin launched an attempt to implement a program of Polish-style shock therapy in Russia. He quickly used the authority delegated to him by the Congress to appoint himself prime minister and Yegor Gaidar, a reform-minded economist, as deputy prime minister with responsibility for the economy (*RFE/RL Daily Report*, 6 November 1991; 7 November 1991). He then proceeded to issue a package of ten decrees on November 15, 1991, which aimed at the rapid transformation of the Russian economy. The decrees covered a wide

range of issues, transferring control of most elements of the economy to Russia
from the collapsing Soviet Union government, liberalizing foreign trade, decon-
trolling many transactions in foreign convertible currencies, and establishing a
minimum wage (*Izvestiya*, 18 November 1991:1). Subsequently, many of the
most important economic reform initiatives would be issued in the form of presidential decrees rather than be passed as laws by the Supreme Soviet or the
Congress of People's Deputies.

A brief look at two of the most important areas of the overall economic reform
program – industrial privatization and agrarian reform – will quickly demonstrate the key role played by presidential decrees issued under the blanket delegation from the Congress. In the area of industrial reform, presidential decrees
laid out both the basic framework of the privatization program and the specific
mechanisms for its implementation. The result was a policy conceived and executed largely within the executive branch, one with enormous distributional
consequences. Yeltsin first outlined the industrial privatization program in a
decree on "Privatization of State and Municipal Enterprises" on December 29,
1991, which laid out general guidelines for which types of enterprises would be
privatized. Overall, the decree called for the privatization of one-fifth of state-
owned industry by the end of 1992 (*Rossiiskaya gazeta*, 15 January 1992; Bush
1992:43). The following June the Supreme Soviet passed a law on privatization
that corresponded on most points with the decree, one that set a deadline of
October 1 for state-owned firms to begin selling shares; this law also exempted
twenty-five different categories of industry from privatization, such as military
equipment and raw materials producers (Sakwa 1993:231).

However, in a dramatic nationally televised speech on August 19, 1992, President Yeltsin announced that the privatization program would be carried out on
the basis of voucher auctions, with each citizen of Russia receiving a voucher
worth 10,000 rubles that could be used to bid for shares in privatized industries.
The goal of the program, he said, was to ensure that the privatization process
would create "millions of owners, not a small group of millionaires" (ITAR-
TASS, 19 August 1992; Djelic 1992:40). The parliament had not called for such
a voucher program in its earlier law, and conservative opponents of economic
reform argued for the passage of a law that would supersede Yeltsin's decree
creating this program. The opponents failed to muster enough votes to force the
issue onto the parliament's agenda in September, thus leaving Yeltsin's initiative
intact (Sakwa 1993:232). The result was that the voucher program – an executive
initiative – dominated the process of industrial privatization in the 1992–93
period (Djelic and Tsukanova 1993). Although these decrees played a major role
in the transformation of the Russian economy, they largely fell within the bounds
of the powers delegated to Yeltsin by the Congress of People's Deputies.

Presidential decrees played an equally weighty role in the area of agrarian
reform. Although agrarian reform had gotten underway in 1990 in a decree issued
in December 1991, Yeltsin greatly accelerated the process by ordering that by
the end of 1992 all state and collective farms, which controlled the bulk of the

land in Russia, should be restructured. Under the terms of the decree, "chronically unprofitable" firms would have to adopt a new form of labor organization. One of the objectives of the decree was to promote the formation of private farms by allowing individual peasants to withdraw from the collective and state farms with a share of land. By the middle of 1993, more than 90 percent of all collective and state farms had been reorganized, with an increasing number of private farms – numbering 58,000 by July 1993 – being created by peasants who had struck out on their own using the provisions of the decree (Wegren 1993:44–45).

Although the Sixth (April 1992) and Seventh (December 1992) Congresses of People's Deputies placed restrictions on the use of land by the new private farmers and prevented the development of a private market in land, Yeltsin's decree nonetheless opened the door to gradual change in the Russian agricultural sector. The slow pace of change has been in large measure attributable to local bureaucratic resistance and the difficult conditions for private farming in Russia. This situation demonstrates, however, that in the current chaotic environment of Russia, a presidential decree may not always be rigorously implemented outside the capital. The issuance by Yeltsin of a decree "On the Regulation of Land Regulations and Agrarian Reform in Russia" in October 1993 suggested that local resistance had hindered the implementation of earlier decrees on the subject, because it simply repeated many provisions of the 1991 decree and called for local officials to be fined if they failed to carry out its provisions (Sigel 1995:16).

Attempting to Merge the Security and Interior Ministries. Yeltsin also used his DDA from 1991 to 1993 for purposes other than economic reform, although he did not always do so with such dramatic effect. Because the Congress had delegated to him the power to form the government without its consent, Yeltsin assumed that this gave him the right to organize the government however he wished. Accordingly, he decreed on December 19, 1991, that the Russian Ministries of Interior and Security be merged, along with the domestic elements of the former Soviet KGB, to form a single Russian Ministry of Security and Internal Affairs. The new ministry would be more efficient and centralized than its fragmented predecessors, said presidential spokesmen (*RFE/RL Daily Report,* 20 December 1991).

This action quickly provoked a public outcry. Journalists noted that on three previous occasions in recent Soviet history, these ministries had been merged into one institution – in 1934, 1941, and 1953. Each time, the move had signaled the opening of a campaign of Stalinist repression (Wishnevsky 1993a:2). Critics in the Supreme Soviet pushed through a resolution calling for suspension of the decree and asked the Constitutional Court to rule on the decree (*RFE/RL Daily Report,* 27 December 1991). The Court, in one of its first cases, issued a resounding rebuke to Yeltsin by overturning his decree in a decision handed down in January 1992. The Court held that the president did not have the authority to create new ministries; only the Supreme Soviet or the Congress could do so. Reportedly, Yeltsin was shocked by the verdict, but he agreed to abide by it nevertheless, and he ordered the re-separation of the Interior and Security Ministries (Sharlet 1993a:7,14). In the future Yeltsin used his powers to create institutions that lay outside the ministerial structure, like the Security Council, but he did not attempt again to alter the structure of the government itself (Sakwa 1993:51–2). Again, Yeltsin's decree power had been checked by another branch of the government.

Increasing Conflict with the Supreme Soviet and Decree 1400. As Yeltsin's economic team moved into high gear in early 1992, its policies quickly met with opposition from the Supreme Soviet, which did not agree with many of the prescriptions of shock therapy. Increasingly, as 1992 and 1993 progressed, the Supreme Soviet and the Sixth (April 1992), Seventh (December 1992), Eighth (March 1993), and Ninth (March 1993) Congresses of People's Deputies attempted to counteract the very decree powers that they had earlier delegated to Yeltsin, and they even threatened to revoke them entirely. At the seventh Congress, for example, Yeltsin was forced to sacrifice Yegor Gaidar, the architect of shock therapy, but the Congress backed down from its threat to revoke Yeltsin's delegated decree authority. Nevertheless, as conflict over such issues as monetary policy, privatization, and others increased between the Supreme Soviet and Yeltsin, each began to try to use its powers to circumvent the other. As one commentator put it in August 1993, "The President issues decrees as if there were no Supreme Soviet, and the Supreme Soviet suspends decrees as if there were no President" (*Izvestiya*, 13 August 1993).

The conflict over privatization, mentioned earlier, provided a good example of this form of legislative–executive combat. In May 1993, for example, Yeltsin issued a decree intended to accelerate the process of voucher privatization that he had initiated in August 1992. Critics in the Supreme Soviet did not like the provisions of the decree, feeling both that too much power was being concentrated in the hands of the State Property Committee, which was subordinate to the president, and that forcing the pace of privatization was leading to socially inequitable results. The Supreme Soviet thus voted to suspend the decree and asked the Constitutional Court for a ruling on its legality. Yeltsin didn't hesitate – he responded with a second decree of his own, which reiterated the provisions of the first one – and even further accelerated the timetables for privatization. The Supreme Soviet countered with another suspension; Yeltsin quickly followed up with a third decree on the same issue (Gualtieri 1993:12–13). In another month Yeltsin's paraconstitutional dissolution of parliament would render the issue moot, but already at this point, in the summer of 1993, a checkmated Yeltsin was increasingly exceeding even the generous delegation of decree authority granted him in 1991, and he was sliding into the zone of paraconstitutional action.

The conflict between the Supreme Soviet and the president came to a head in the fall of 1993. The Supreme Soviet prepared a series of amendments to the Constitution for consideration at the Tenth Congress of People's Deputies, which was scheduled to take place in November. The amendments would have stripped Yeltsin of most of his powers and effectively would have transformed the presidency into a ceremonial head of state. The leader of the Supreme Soviet also intended to revoke Yeltsin's delegated decree powers; at the same time planned additions to the criminal code would have made it a crime for government ministers to disregard parliamentary instructions and would have added enforcement powers for rulings of the Constitutional Court (Sharlet 1993b:326).

Rather than endure another bruising confrontation with the Congress and the Supreme Soviet, which were hindering the implementation of his policy programs at every turn, Yeltsin chose to take paraconstitutional actions to break the political deadlock between the branches of government. He preempted the plans of his parliamentary opponents, and on September 21, 1993, he issued Decree 1400, entitled, "On gradual constitutional reform in the Russian Federation." The decree dissolved the Congress and the Supreme Soviet, and it suspended the existing Constitution, pending elections of a new parliament.

Yeltsin justified his action in a manner that would have been familiar to many chief executives in other countries. On two grounds Yeltsin claimed to be more accurately representative of popular sentiment than the assembly. First, he claimed that he was elected by "all the people," whereas the two assemblies were not. Second, he accused the Congress and the Supreme Soviet of ignoring the results of an April 1993 referendum, one in which a majority of voters had expressed "confidence" in the president. The Supreme Soviet and the Congress, then, should be disbanded because they failed to adequately represent the popular will, which was best expressed in the policies of the president. In addition Yeltsin also based his action on Article 121:5 of the Constitution itself, which charged the president with protection of "social security" (ITAR-TASS, 21 September 1995).

Many members of the Supreme Soviet did not recognize the authority of the president to dissolve it, and a tense standoff ensued. The crisis came to a violent conclusion when some supporters of the assembly attacked riot police who had cordoned off the building on Yeltsin's orders. A short-lived insurrection followed, but within twenty-four hours, the Russian army had cast its forces into the balance on the side of Yeltsin, and the Supreme Soviet was shelled into submission. Yeltsin's paraconstitutional initiative had succeeded. The First Russian Republic had ended, and the decree authority of the Russian president was now for all intents and purposes unlimited.

PRESIDENTIAL DECREE AUTHORITY IN THE SECOND RUSSIAN REPUBLIC (1993–PRESENT)

THE INSTITUTIONAL CONTEXT

After dissolving the Supreme Soviet in October 1993 and imprisoning its leaders, Yeltsin scripted a new constitution which would alter the rules of the game in

Russian politics to fit his political requirements. Initially, Yeltsin seems to have planned for a newly elected assembly to adopt a constitution. This idea was quickly jettisoned, however, because it could have allowed regional political elites the opportunity to strengthen themselves at the expense of the federal government (Slater 1994). Instead, Yeltsin administration officials took a draft constitution written the previous summer by the consultative Constitutional Assembly and made some additional modifications to it. Yeltsin then issued a decree on October 15, 1993, announcing that a new constitution would be adopted by plebiscite, and he subsequently delivered a nationally televised speech on November 9, outlining the provisions of the constitution and announcing that the referendum would be held on December 12 (*Rossiiskie vesti*, 15 October 1993; ITAR-TASS, 9 November 1993).

The executive branch thus totally dominated the process of constitution-drafting (Slater 1994; Urban 1994). The only constraint on Yeltsin was that the draft constitution had to secure the support of the electorate in the upcoming referendum. But under the rules laid out in Yeltsin's decree, even this constraint remained modest. In order to pass, the draft constitution would need only the support of a simple majority of those voting, although for the election to be valid, at least 50 percent of registered voters had to participate. Hence, with the support of only 25 percent of the Russian electorate, Yeltsin could enshrine his custom-designed constitution as the fundamental law of the land.

In the referendum the Constitution appeared to have squeaked through, in the wake of a vigorous government campaign to ensure its adoption. The official results claimed that 54.8 percent of the electorate participated in the referendum, with 56.6 percent of that total voting for adoption of the Constitution. Serious discrepancies in the reporting of the results, however, led critics to claim that the Central Electoral Commission and local officials had padded turnout to ensure that the Constitution passed (Slater 1994). These allegations of fraud were subsequently verified on a local level by a number of regional courts and procurators, leading President Yeltsin to appoint a special commission to study the issue. In May 1994, after months of work, the commission concluded that only 46 percent, or 49 million of Russia's 106.2 million registered voters, had participated in the referendum, making it invalid. Thus, the new Constitution was not really ratified, even by the rules that Yeltsin himself had laid out (*Izvestiya*, 4 May 1994; Tolz and Wishnevsky 1994). However, a presidential spokesman subsequently announced that despite the commission's conclusions, the Constitution would remain in force. Opposition politicians, although sometimes critical of the new Constitution, have not seriously called for its suspension (*RFE/RL Daily Report*, 6 May 1994). Subsequently, the Central Electoral Commission destroyed the original ballot papers, making it impossible to ascertain with certainty whether the fraud charges were true.

Article 90 of this custom-designed constitution, in language similar to Article 121:8 of the previous Russian Constitution, gives the president the authority to issue decrees. These decrees have the force of law, come into force immediately upon publication, and are obligatory for implementation by all levels of government. Although they do not require any confirmation by the assembly and are not subject to any time restrictions, they cannot contradict existing law or the Constitution itself (*Konstitutsiya* 1993). Although the previous Constitution limited such decrees to addressing subjects "within the competence" of the president, the 1993 Constitution does not contain any such limitation. The president thus has sweeping CDA which allows him or her to make new policy in virtually any area not covered by existing statutes. In a December 1995 interview with the author, one judge of the Russian Constitutional Court even asserted that if a presidential decree contradicted legislation adopted under the previous Constitution, the decree would have precedence. Given the state of Russian legal development, then, the president has considerable room to legislate by decree.

Other features of the 1993 Constitution reinforce the president's CDA. First, the new Constitution created a bicameral assembly, called the Federal Assembly, which consists of a lower house, the State Duma, and an upper house, the Federation Council. Yeltsin even considered making the upper house appointive rather than elected, but he discarded that idea rather quickly. Nonetheless, although the upper house remained elective, the unitary executive now faces a divided legislature, meaning that other things remaining equal, it is more difficult to overturn presidential decrees than it would have been under a unicameral system. Even more importantly, the 1993 Constitution, unlike its predecessor, gives the president an effective veto over legislation. If the president vetoes a bill which has come to him or her for signature, a two-thirds supermajority in both houses is required to override.[3] Hence the president needs only the support of one-third of one house of the Federal Assembly to avoid having his decrees superseded by new legislation, which is the only way for the Assembly to block such presidential initiatives.

This combination of veto and decree authority has proven crucial to Yeltsin's ability to legislate by decree. While his custom-designed constitution "passed" in the referendum of December 12, 1993, the simultaneous elections of the new bicameral Federal Assembly delivered less satisfactory results from Yeltsin's point of view. The main pro-presidential party, Russia's Choice, did far worse than was expected, whereas the opposition, including the Communist Party of the Russian Federation, the Agrarian Party, and especially Vladimir Zhirinovsky's Liberal Democratic Party, did far better. Of the eleven parties and factions which later formed in the Duma, the lower house, Russia's Choice gained the largest number of seats, but it could only claim 76 seats out of 450, whereas three of the next four largest parties, all opposed to Yeltsin, had over 160 seats. The result was a politically fragmented assembly in which neither of the two houses could be reliably counted upon to support the president, although the upper house, dominated by regional political elites, has generally been more sympathetic to the executive than has the Duma.

The Duma elections of December 1995 did not substantially change this picture. Yeltsin's opposition, especially the Communists, did even better than in

1993, coming just short of gaining a working majority. The Communist Party of the Russian Federation won 149 seats, and two factions allied with it took another 72 seats, giving them 221 total. The pro-government Our Home Is Russia party, by contrast, won only 55 seats. But the remaining seats are divided among parties across the political spectrum, so that mustering the supermajority needed to override presidential vetoes remains extremely difficult. Changes introduced in 1995 to the procedure for forming the Federation Council made it an indirectly, rather than directly, elected body. Originally the upper house had consisted of two directly elected senators from each of the eighty-nine constituent members of the Russian Federation. Now the governor and the chairman of the regional assembly will automatically be their region's senators. For the time being, because many governors are Yeltsin appointees, this body remains largely sympathetic to the president on many issues.

The Constitution's authors also locked in these presidential powers by making the 1993 Constitution difficult to amend. Whereas the old Constitution could be amended by a two-thirds majority of the Congress of People's Deputies, Article 136 of the new Constitution sets higher barriers. Proposed amendments must pass the lower house of the Federal Assembly by a two-thirds majority, then it must receive the support of a three-fourths majority of the upper house. Then the amendment must be approved by the legislatures of two-thirds of the eighty-nine republics and regions that make up the Russian Federation. These conditions are quite stringent, and few amendments are likely to survive the complex multi-stage process.[4] Only one set of constitutional amendments has so far completed even part of this process. On June 21, 1995, the Duma passed three proposed amendments that would have expanded the control of the assembly over the executive branch. The amendments failed to gain approval in the Federation Council, however, garnering only 75 votes out of the necessary 134 (Russian Television, 8 July 1995). Many future amendments seem likely to suffer a similar fate.

The 1993 Constitution also makes it nearly impossible for impeachment to be used against the president as a means of restricting his or her decree authority. The authors of the Constitution clearly had in mind Yeltsin's situation during the 1991–93 period, when the old Congress of People's Deputies threatened impeachment on many occasions, a threat that had some substance to it because it required only a two-thirds vote of the Congress and a finding by the Constitutional Court that the vote had been carried out properly. The new Constitution, by contrast, establishes a very cumbersome process for impeachment.

According to Article 93, the impeachment process begins if one-third of the Duma accuses the president of "treason or other high crimes." This accusation must then be supported by a two-thirds majority of the Duma and confirmed by findings of both the Russian Supreme Court and the Constitutional Court. Only then can the president be convicted and removed from office, but only if a two-thirds majority of the Federation Council agrees that the president is guilty. Only the most criminally culpable president is likely to be removed from office under these procedures. Despite the political furor that often surrounds Yeltsin, for example, none of the frequent impeachment attempts by opposition deputies has made it past the second stage of the impeachment process.

All of these considerations suggest that the dominance of the executive over the constitutional drafting process in 1993 resulted in a constitution that grants the president sweeping constitutional decree authority and provides few levers with which an assembly majority might attempt to counteract a president determined to implement a policy program by decree. However, like its predecessor, the new Constitution creates a third force in the shape of the Constitutional Court, which may operate to limit and restrain the decree authority of the president. Under Article 125 of the Constitution, the Court is empowered to adjudicate the constitutionality of presidential decrees. Like its predecessor, the new Court will be able to overrule presidential decrees that it decides are not in accordance with the Constitution. Other duties of the Court might also indirectly affect the constitutional decree authority of the president, including the resolution of conflicts between branches of the federal government and the interpretation of the Constitution.

Yeltsin had suspended the old Constitutional Court shortly after it ruled that his September 1993 decree dissolving the Supreme Soviet and the Congress of People's Deputies was unconstitutional. But he did not disband it. The old judges were allowed to retain their positions under the transitional provisions of the 1993 Constitution. However, since the old Court had not been sufficiently pliant to Yeltsin's will, the 1993 Constitution provided that the Constitutional Court would consist of nineteen judges. Under the previous Constitution the Court had consisted of only fifteen judges, and political divisions in the Congress of People's Deputies had meant that only thirteen seats were filled when the Court was suspended in October 1993. Because the new Constitution provides for judges to be appointed by the Federation Council from a list presented by the president, Yeltsin gained the opportunity to stack the Court with six additional politically sympathetic judges. Partly for this reason, the Court has not constrained Yeltsin much yet. However, since new judges are appointed for twelve-year terms and can be removed only by impeachment once appointed, the Court will be much less subject to influence by future presidents, who may well find it a significant constraint on their constitutional decree authority.

NUMBER AND TYPES OF DECREES, 1993–96

The assertion that Yeltsin has been ruling Russia by decree is quite common in both Russian and Western commentary. Given the constitutional powers outlined in previous sections, it would be strange indeed if Yeltsin did not have a major impact on the Russian policy agenda. However, in determining just how fully Yeltsin dominates the legislative arena and to what extent his decree powers enable him to usurp the law-making authority of the Federal Assembly, one should first seek to establish the frequency and content of Yeltsin's decrees and

Table 3.1 *Number and types of decrees issued by President Yeltsin, 1994–96*

Year	Normative decrees	Nonnormative decrees	"Secret" decree	Total decrees	Federal laws
1994	256	1,477	526	2,259	78
1995	290	507	548	1,345	229
1996 (Jan.–Oct.)	407	591	470	1,468	118
Totals	953	2,575	1,544	5,072	425

Source: Data collected by the author from *Sobranie aktov Prezidenta i Pravitelstva Rossiiskoi Federatsii*, issues 1–17 (January–April 1994); *Sobranie zakonodatelstva Rossiiskoi Federatsii*, issues 1–35 (May–December 1994), issues 1–52 (January–December 1995); issues 1–43 (January–October 1996).

also to compare them to the output of the Federal Assembly. What follows here is a preliminary attempt to do just that.

The first point worth noting is that the word *ukaz* in Russian, which translates to *decree*, covers a broad range of executive actions, ranging from sending in the tanks to closing down the Supreme Soviet to appointing ambassadors. So simply observing that Yeltsin issues hundreds of *ukazy* each year does not demonstrate that he is setting new policy in many areas and usurping the assembly. Fortunately, the official Russian collection of laws and executive acts divides presidential decrees into two categories: normative and nonnormative. Normative acts are defined in Russian legal usage as those that establish a new precedent of some sort, whereas nonnormative acts merely implement existing policy, law, or administrative practice. At most, then, only Yeltsin's normative decrees should be counted as executive initiatives aimed at setting new policy. Even this probably overstates the number of times Yeltsin makes new policy, because some normative decrees may be setting new norms under existing legislation, but it is a reasonable first cut at how many policy-making decrees Yeltsin issues.[5]

Table 3.1 shows the results of counting all the officially published decrees that Yeltsin issued under the new Constitution from January 1994 to October 1996. In those thirty-four months, Yeltsin issued 953 normative decrees, in comparison to 2,575 nonnormative decrees. The majority of his output of decrees, then, consists of nonnormative acts, such as pinning medals on veterans, filling executive branch positions, and so on. During this same period the Federal Assembly passed – and Yeltsin signed – 425 federal laws. It is clear, then, that Yeltsin is outstripping the Assembly in terms of raw output, but he is not doing so nearly as much as one might think if one used the total number of decrees Yeltsin issued rather than looked at just the normative ones.

Interestingly, although Yeltsin has outstripped the assembly overall, in 1995, the one year in which the system established by the Constitution operated somewhat normally, Yeltsin issued 290 normative decrees, whereas the Assembly passed 229 laws, a ratio which indicates a much lesser extent of executive dominance. In 1994 the Assembly spent the first half of the year just getting on its feet, thus limiting its ability to pass legislation. The first half of 1996 was dominated by the presidential election, which led Yeltsin to issue a plethora of decrees aimed at securing reelection, whereas the opposition leaders in the assembly were occupied with campaigning, not legislating. The pattern of 1995, then, may be more indicative of the future of normal Russian politics than either 1994 or the first half of 1996. Even if this turns out not to be the case, the overall pattern in Table 3.1 shows that without a careful examination of Yeltsin's decree output, one could easily leap to the conclusion that he totally overshadows the assembly in terms of producing new policy initiatives.

To this argument must be added the caveat, however, that Yeltsin appears to issue a large number of unpublished, secret decrees each year. Each decree published in the official government register is given a number, starting with decree number 1 in January and continuing on in numerical order through the end of December. Some numbers, however, never appear in the register. For example, in 1994, the last decree Yeltsin signed on December 31 was numbered 2,259, but adding up all the published decrees that year produces a total of only 1,733. Simple subtraction leads to the conclusion that 526 unpublished – or "secret" – decrees were issued that year.

This conclusion is supported by an examination of the regulations of Yeltsin's administration, the 1993 Constitution, and recent practice. In 1992 Yeltsin issued a decree on issuing decrees, which stated that all decrees were to be published, except those containing state secrets (*Sobranie aktov Prezidenta i Pravitelstva Rossiiskoi Federatsii #1*, 6 July 1992:3–4), clearly implying that some decrees should remain secret. The 1993 Constitution specifies (Art. 15) that all federal laws must be published in order to take effect, but it is less categorical about "normative acts," a term which includes decrees. It says they require publication if they touch on the "rights, freedoms, and obligations of citizens." This apparently allows the president's administration not to publish decrees that it feels do not touch on those rights, freedoms, and obligations – in other words, it again establishes a legal basis for secret decrees. Finally, in the Chechnya case, discussed in a later section, it emerged that Yeltsin had issued a secret decree ordering that "illegal armed formations" in Chechnya be neutralized, thus showing that secret decrees are issued.

What is surprising is not the existence of secret decrees – all executives engage in some classified activities – but their scale. If my rough calculations are correct (see Table 3.1), Yeltsin has issued 1,544 secret decrees since 1994 – more than the 953 normative decrees he issued. Although many of these secret decrees may have touched on classified military and intelligence matters, their sheer number, as well as the example of Chechnya, suggests that they may also impact on other areas of policy. This shows that the principle of accountability still has only weak roots in Russia, because it is difficult for the press, deputies in the Assembly, or ultimately the voters to bring in a verdict on secret presidential action. It also makes it hard to say much about the overall mix of the decrees that Yeltsin issues, since some of these secret decrees, as in Chechnya, could touch on major issues of policy and thus change the balance between normative and nonnormative decrees outlined earlier. Unfortunately, then, the existence of these secret decrees means that the picture outlined here must be taken with a grain of salt. The next section will examine several cases of Yeltsin's use of presidential decrees to initiate new policy since the new Constitution came into operation. Although not a comprehensive review of the use of decrees since the new Constitution came into effect, these cases do illustrate both the possibilities and limitations of presidential decree authority under the 1993 Constitution.

The Anticrime Decree: Making New Policy. A June 1994 decree intended to combat organized crime presents one of the most obvious examples of Yeltsin's effort to make new policy by decree despite opposition from the Federal Assembly. Criminal activity has reached epidemic proportions in Russia since the collapse of the U.S.S.R. Russian legislation has failed to keep pace with the emergence of new forms of crime that had been unknown to the Soviet planned economy but that have arisen during Russia's transition to a market economy. Organized crime has also grown much faster than has the capacity of the weak Russian state to cope with it. In July 1995, for example, Interior Ministry officials complained that Russian law still had no definition of "organized criminal group"; nor was membership in such a group considered a crime. Draft legislation on the subject still had not been passed by the Federal Assembly eighteen months after it had begun operation (*OMRI Daily Digest*, 19 July 1995).

Following a series of particularly brutal gangland slayings in Moscow during the spring of 1994, President Yeltsin issued a decree on June 14 entitled, "On urgent measures to protect the population from banditry and other forms of organized crime." The decree was justified by reference to the need to protect the lives and property of Russian citizens "until the passage of legislation by the Federal Assembly," thus implicitly invoking Article 90. It also clearly aimed to steal the political credit for taking action against crime away from opposition deputies in the Federal Assembly.

Among other provisions, the decree gave Russian police authorities sweeping search powers, allowing them to search the premises of individuals suspected of belonging to organized criminal groups, as well as the residences of their relatives and anyone they had lived with in the past five years. Evidence obtained in such a search could be used as "proof of guilt" in any subsequent criminal trial. The police were also empowered to trawl through business and financial records of such suspects. None of these searches required any preliminary court approval under the terms of the decree. In addition these suspects could be detained for up to thirty days without being formally charged, and the decree explicitly stated that bail and other legal means of temporarily leaving police custody – including appeal to the courts – would not apply to such individuals (*Izvestiya*, 15 June 1994).

Although these harsh measures were designed to appeal to crime-weary public opinion, they immediately provoked howls of protest from the Federal Assembly. Deputy Viktor Pokhmelkin told a press conference on June 16 that the decree effectively amended the Russian Criminal Code, which only the legislative branch was permitted to do under the 1993 Constitution. He complained that the decree allowed police to carry out searches before a criminal case was even opened and then to use the evidence obtained as proof that a crime had been committed, thus reversing the procedural order specified in the Criminal Code. Preventive detention of suspects for up to thirty days without bail also contradicted the existing criminal code, Pokhmelkin added (*Nezavisimaya gazeta*, 15 June 1994).

Others pointed out that many provisions of the decree violated the Constitution itself. It is not possible to list all the possible contradictions, but among the most obvious was the provision for imposing up to thirty days' preventive detention without court approval. This provision clearly contradicts Article 22 of the Constitution, which declares that no one may be detained longer than forty-eight hours without a court order. Because it creates a class of individuals who can more easily be searched than others, the provision for searches, without court approval, of those suspected of organized crime and their families was judged by many observers to be a violation of Article 19 of the Constitution, which states that "all are equal before the law." Critics also charged that the provisions for searches of bank and financial records without a court order violated Article 23, which holds that all personal correspondence shall be considered confidential and that this right can only be infringed upon on the basis of a court order (*Nezavisimaya gazeta*, 16 June 1994).

Beyond accusing Yeltsin of exceeding his constitutional decree authority, critics of the decree argued that these draconian provisions would undermine legal business in Russia and provide the legal basis for the resurrection of a Soviet-style police state. On the floor of the Duma, deputies debated about how to respond to Yeltsin's initiative. Viktor Ilyukhin, a member of the opposition Communist Party of the Russian Federation and a vocal critic of the president, said, "[I]f the president today suspends the operation of the criminal code, what guarantee is there that he will not suspend the operation of all courts tomorrow?" (*Nezavisimaya gazeta*, 23 June 1994). He protested that Yeltsin had promised to submit draft laws on the fight against organized crime to the Duma but that he had not done so – and instead had issued this decree. A minority of deputies supported the president, arguing that the harsh measures were necessary to combat rising crime. But on June 22, the Duma adopted a resolution by a vote of 246–6 entitled, "Onto protection of constitutional rights and freedoms of citizens during the fight against crime," which called on Yeltsin to suspend the decree (ibid.).

The following day, Yeltsin announced that he would reject the Duma's advice and implement the decree despite its objections. The Duma resolution was not a law, after all, and thus Yeltsin was not obliged to follow its recommendations. He did make a small concession to the critics by charging his Human Rights

Ombudsman, Sergei Kovalev, with the responsibility of monitoring the implementation of the decree and reporting directly to him if its implementation led
to regular violations of constitutional rights (ITAR-TASS, 23 June 1994). But
this was a symbolic move, because the decree remained in force and Kovalev's
role was purely advisory.

When the Duma failed to pass a law of its own on the subject before its summer
recess at the end of July, Yeltsin's decree remained in force. It was much easier
for the politically fragmented Duma to denounce Yeltsin's decree than to cobble
together a majority in support of a positive program of its own. Because the new
Constitutional Court had not resumed operation – its enabling statute had been
passed only at the end of July, and six of its seats remained unfilled – there was
nowhere for aggrieved Duma deputies to go to appeal the decree. In September
1994 a presidential advisory body even expressed concern that the decree's provisions were leading to widespread violations of civil rights, but Yeltsin spokesmen reiterated that the president would not suspend its operation (*RFE/RL Daily
Report*, 27 September 1994).

About one year after the decree went into effect, a conference of Russian police
officials concluded that despite its draconian provisions, enforcement was lagging
and crime continued to increase (*Rossiiskaya gazeta*, 2 June 1995). Apparently,
however, the decree will lapse only when a revised version of the Russian Criminal
Code goes into effect. A new code was finally passed by the Federal Assembly
and signed by Yeltsin in June 1996, and it went into effect, as scheduled, on
January 1, 1997. For 2 ½ years, then, this controversial decree remained in force,
despite its paraconstitutional character and the opposition of an overwhelming
majority in the lower house of the legislature. In this case Yeltsin succeeded in
imposing his preferred policies on the country by decree despite substantial opposition. Although the decree has not suppressed criminal activity, it certainly
represented a victory for Yeltsin over the new Assembly. It should not be taken
as proving the total dominance of the president over the Assembly, however,
because the decree did not prevail against a competing law that the Assembly
had passed, but rather it filled a legislative vacuum created by the Assembly's
own failure to muster a coherent majority behind new anticrime legislation.

That Yeltsin viewed the experience of the decree as a victory is underlined by
his decision to issue another similar anticrime decree about two years later: on
July 10, 1996. Coming only a few days after Yeltsin's reelection in the July 3
presidential runoff election, the new decree was apparently intended to show that
Yeltsin was serious about his campaign promises to fight crime and corruption.
It may also have been a concession to Aleksandr Lebed, Yeltsin's newly appointed
Security Council secretary, who had finished third in the first round of presiden-
tial balloting and whose support had helped Yeltsin defeat his communist chal-
lenger, Gennadii Zyuganov, in the runoff. Fighting crime and corruption had
been cornerstone pledges of Lebed's campaign. The decree, which was entitled
"On Urgent Measures to Reinforce Law and Order and Strengthen the Fight
Against Crime in Moscow and Moscow Oblast," contained provisions calling for

dramatic increases in police personnel in Moscow and a crackdown on vagrants in the capital, and it allowed the police to confiscate "unclaimed property," including rubles and foreign currency. Finally, it also permitted the "temporary suspension" of government officials who were suspected of "involvement in organized criminal activity" by any law-enforcement agency (*Rossiiskaya gazeta*, 16 July 1996).

As before, observers quickly commented that many provisions of the decree violated aspects of the existing Criminal Code, Criminal Procedures Code, and the Constitution itself. The human rights monitoring group Express-Khronika, for example, pointed out that provisions of the decree allowing the Moscow procurator to order the detention for thirty days of homeless vagrants violates three different articles of the Constitution: Article 22, which prohibits detention for longer than forty-eight hours without a court order; Article 27, which grants Russian citizens freedom of movement and allows them to choose their own place of residence; and Article 129, which states that the procurator's office is regulated by federal law, not by presidential decrees. The group also criticized the provisions both for the confiscation of "unclaimed property" and for the temporary suspension of government employees, because they contradicted the current Russian Civil Code and because they were so vague as to encourage abuse by police authorities. Mainstream newspapers like *Izvestiya* and *Trud* also criticized various provisions of the decree as inconsistent with existing legislation (*Izvestiya*, 16 July 1996; *Trud-7*, 26 July 1996).

Nevertheless, as with the earlier decree, Yeltsin showed no sign of rescinding it, and when a series of bomb blasts on Moscow trolley buses took place only a few days after its issuance, a police crackdown followed, one in which several thousand people were arrested on charges of violating residence permit regulations (ITAR-TASS, 15 July 1996). Even though Yeltsin later decided to fire Lebed, other figures in his administration will likely push for similar extraordinary measures to combat crime. Since the Duma also chose not to protest over this more recent anticrime decree, having learned from previous experience not to challenge the president on this politically charged subject, the way seems open for future paraconstitutional decrees along these lines.

Privatizing the Airwaves by Decree. Another case in which Yeltsin has been able to carry out his preferred policies by decree is in the area of privatization of state-owned television. In November 1994 Yeltsin issued a decree reorganizing the main state-owned television broadcasting corporation, Ostankino. Ostankino controls Channel One, the most-watched television channel and the one with the widest distribution network in Russia. It is the only channel that reaches most parts of the former Soviet Union, and it has a potential audience of nearly 200 million people. As one Russian newspaper put it, "[W]hoever controls Ostankino, controls Russia" (*Kommersant-Daily*, 17 March 1995). Ostankino was generally pro-government in its orientation, and Yeltsin relied upon it to attempt to shape public opinion at various times, such as during the December 1993 elections. In response to the dramatic failure of pro-government candidates – led by Yegor Gaidar's Russia's Choice – in the elections, which many observers attributed in part to the opposition's superior use of TV advertising, Yeltsin had already begun to overhaul the management of Ostankino early in 1994. At that time he appointed Aleksandr Yakovlev, a former close associate of Gorbachev, to direct Ostankino (Belin 1995:2; Orttung 1995a: 11).

Together, Yakovlev and Yeltsin developed a strategy to reorganize Ostankino and make it more responsive to Yeltsin's political needs, while removing it farther from the influence of his parliamentary opponents. The November decree was an integral part of this strategy. It called for the reorganization of Ostankino into a new company, called Russian Public Television (ORT), which would continue to control Channel One. The state would keep 51 percent of the new company, which would be managed by the State Property Committee, whose members were presidential appointees. The other 49 percent would be auctioned off into private hands (*Rossiiskaya gazeta*, 2 December 1994). This partial privatization would give the new company a greater degree of financial independence, thus reducing the ability of Yeltsin's opponents in the Duma to use the power of the purse to influence the content of television programming. The private shares in ORT were subsequently sold to a variety of banks and firms with close ties to Yeltsin and his political supporters.[6] In December Yakovlev was elected chairman of the board of ORT. Despite Yakovlev's claim that the creation of the new channel was a step forward for democracy, critics termed the new station "the president's channel" (Orttung 1995a:12). According to the original decree, ORT was to take over broadcasting on Channel One by February 1, 1995, but its debut was delayed until April 1 to give it additional time to prepare.

Yeltsin's opponents in the Federal Assembly did not simply sit by and watch as the ownership and control of the most influential media outlet in the country was transformed in a manner calculated to injure their political interests. They responded to Yeltsin's decree by introducing legislation in the Duma to regulate the privatization of state-owned television. If such legislation passed and if a supermajority could be mustered in both houses to override the inevitable presidential veto, then Yeltsin's decree could be overturned. A bill sponsored by the Liberal Democratic Party of Vladimir Zhirinovsky, which called for the renationalization of ORT and its subordination to Assembly control, garnered the support of only 199 deputies on March 10, but this total was less than the 226 needed to pass and far fewer than the 300 required to overcome a presidential veto. However, a milder bill, one which would have suspended the transformation of Ostankino into ORT until the assembly passed special legislation on the privatization of television, passed in the Duma on April 5 by the vote of 275–2[7] (*Ekho Moskvy*, 5 April 1995).

The Federation Council subsequently passed this bill by the vote of 98–8 on May 23. According to press reports a major factor in the votes was the feeling among many deputies in both houses that the new pro-presidential ORT would be an obstacle to a fair parliamentary election campaign in December 1995 and that the shift from Ostankino to ORT would make their own reelection campaigns more difficult. However, the margin in each house was far short of the two-thirds majority required to override a presidential veto, even if one assumed that many of the deputies absent on the first ballot would support an override (*Kommersant-Daily*, 24 May 1995). Yeltsin did not surprise anyone when he vetoed the law on June 6, thus thwarting the Assembly and leaving his decree intact (*Ekho Moskvy*, 6 June 1995). And the Assembly has never managed to override that veto, meaning that ORT continues to operate.

On June 7, in another response to Yeltsin's veto, the Duma formally requested that the Constitutional Court review the constitutionality of the decree (*Segodnya*, 8 June 1995). But after considering the petition over the summer, the Court decided not to hear the case, ruling that "the president's right to issue decrees of this nature follows from the constitution" (*OMRI Daily Digest*, 6 November 1995). The failure of the Court challenge and the inability to muster the supermajority needed to override Yeltsin's veto have left the assembly majority with no way to hamper Yeltsin's control of ORT. As opposition deputies surely foresaw, ORT played an important role in helping Yeltsin dominate the media during the 1996 presidential campaign, airing what outside observers have agreed was very biased coverage.

The Duma continues to harangue Yeltsin on the issue, however, publicizing in May 1996 the results of an audit of the network, which concluded that it had misused budgetary funds (*OMRI Daily Digest*, 16 May 1996). After the presidential elections, the Duma on July 17 passed a nonbinding resolution again appealing to Yeltsin to renationalize the network (*OMRI Daily Digest*, 18 July 1996). But although the Duma can fulminate publicly, Yeltsin has clearly won a major victory over his opponents on this issue.

A similar instance of a presidential decree remaining in force against the inability of a divided assembly to override it emerged in 1996 with respect to a new land code. Since 1991, Yeltsin has issued a series of decrees on land reform, which have allowed collective and state farmworkers to leave their collectives and take possession of a portion of the land when they do so. But in the absence of new comprehensive legislation on the topic, clearly defined property rights in land have not yet emerged, even though the 1993 Constitution guarantees the right of citizens to own land. Yeltsin's most recent decrees on the subject, which were issued in October 1993 and March 1996, have somewhat expanded the rights of those who have received landholdings under previous reforms, and they have begun to lay the basis for the development of a market in land, which is bitterly opposed by his Communist and Agrarian Party opponents. Agrarian Party leader Nikolai Kharitonov attacked the March 1996 decree, for example, and promised to appeal it to the Constitutional Court (*OMRI Daily Digest*, 8 and 12 March 1996).

The opposition majority in the Duma, however, has been unable to block Yeltsin's moves toward land reform. An Agrarian-backed land code, which would ban the sale of farmland and allow it to be leased only to those with agricultural training, passed the Duma overwhelmingly by a 288–18 vote in May, but it was rejected by the Federation Council the next month after Yeltsin threatened that he would veto it if it passed (*OMRI Daily Digest*, 23 May and 27 June 1996). A subsequent attempt by the Duma to override the Federation Council failed by a 269–53 vote, falling 31 short of the 300 votes needed. As long as the assembly is unable to come up with a compromise land code, Yeltsin's decrees will continue to operate here, as they do in the area of state television.

Raising the Minimum Pension: President Forces Compromise. On another issue – the level of the minimum state pension – Yeltsin has also shaped policy by the use of his decree authority. Here, however, Yeltsin ultimately accepted a compromise with the assembly majority, and currently policy in this area is made through the normal legislative process rather than by presidential decree. In early 1995, with inflation in Russia continuing to increase, many members of the Duma – especially deputies from the Communist Party of the Russian Federation and the Agrarian Party, who were elected with the support of older, more conservative voters – argued that the minimum state pension should be increased again in order to prevent the further impoverishment of many pensioners. The Yeltsin administration, on the other hand, hoping to maintain the endorsement of the International Monetary Fund (IMF) and the $6 billion standby credit that would accompany it, opposed a major pension increase, claiming it would drastically increase the budget deficit and torpedo government plans to use "tight" monetary policy to bring inflation under control.

Populist deputies in the Duma cared less about the endorsement of the IMF than about the welfare of voters who could return them to their seats in the next election. On January 18 the Duma accordingly passed a bill by a 246–5 vote that increased the minimum state pension from 19,600 rubles per month to 54,100 rubles per month (*Dnevnik zasedanii Gosudarstvennoi Dumy*, January–February 1993; Russian Radio, 18 January 1995). The Federation Council shared the Duma's enthusiasm for a pension increase and quickly endorsed the same bill on January 20 (ITAR-TASS, 20 January 1995). President Yeltsin responded by vetoing the proposed increase. He justified his veto by claiming that the pension increase, which he estimated would cost 23 trillion rubles in 1995, would bankrupt the state pension fund (ITAR-TASS, 30 January 1995).

Not to be outdone in populist political theater by the Federal Assembly, Yeltsin simultaneously issued a decree that raised the minimum pension to 39,360 rubles per month. That doubled the former rate, but it was considerably less than that established by the vetoed law (*Sobranie zakonodatelsva Rossiiskoi Federatsii*, 6 February 1995:474). Once again, by vetoing the law and issuing a decree on the same subject, Yeltsin had used his constitutional decree authority to force through his own political preference (financial austerity) over the preference of the Assembly majority (maximizing social benefits for its members' constituents). Two attempts by the Duma to override Yeltsin's veto failed (*Interfax*, 24 February and 10 March 1995).

Realizing that it could not muster the necessary votes to overcome Yeltsin, the Duma voted on March 24 to form a joint "conciliatory commission" with the government to discuss pension increases (ITAR-TASS, 24 March 1995). The work of this commission produced a new law on pensions which Yeltsin signed on June 29, 1995. It raised the minimum pension to 52,486 rubles per month and increased all other pensions by 20 percent (Russian Radio, 29 June 1995). Subsequent legislation, worked out jointly by the assembly and the government and signed by the president, raised the minimum pension to 55,000 rubles per month, effective August 1, 1995 (ITAR-TASS, 27 July 1995). Although in nominal terms this figure appears to indicate a victory for the assembly, with inflation running at an average monthly rate of 10.1 percent during the first six months of 1995, 55,000 rubles in July was worth considerably less in real terms than 54,000 rubles would have been in January, when the two houses passed their original bills. By using his decree power, Yeltsin compelled the assembly majority to compromise and accept a lower increase in minimum pensions than it would have enacted otherwise. However, pressure from the assembly also influenced the president, who might otherwise have increased pensions less. The bottom line is that although Yeltsin's constitutional decree authority did not allow him to completely dictate the level of the minimum pension, it did give him more leverage than he would have had without it – or armed only with his veto powers.

The Anti-Fascism Decree: More Smoke than Fire. Although it is true that Yeltsin has used his decree powers to force through his policy preferences in the face of assembly resistance, some decrees at first glance appear to make new policy but in fact do not do so. These decrees really amount to little more than administrative orders, and even though they may on occasion provoke significant political criticism, they cannot be seen as evidence that Yeltsin is dominating the policy agenda by decree. A case in point is the so-called Anti-Fascism decree that was signed by Yeltsin on March 23, 1995 (*Sobranie zakonodatelstva Rossiiskoi Federatsii*, 27 March 1995:1127). The decree provoked a small furor among members of the opposition in the Duma, especially in the Communist Party of the Russian Federation and in Vladimir Zhirinovsky's Liberal Democratic Party, whose members feared its terms might be used to suppress their activities in the upcoming parliamentary election campaign.

While Yeltsin undoubtedly had political motives in issuing the decree, a close examination of the text shows that it does not actually lay down any new standards for or issue any new prohibitions on particular activities or groups. The opening of the decree sounds like a policy pronouncement, with its declaration that the emergence of extremist and fascist groups in Russia presents "an extremely serious threat to the foundations of constitutional order." One might have expected a list of new policies, with no basis in existing legislation, to have followed, as in the anticrime decree. Instead, this anti-fascist decree basically orders Yeltsin's subordinates in the executive branch to intensify enforcement of existing laws prohibiting extremist activity, such as fomenting interethnic hatred through the publication of racist materials (Orttung 1995a:4).

In fact presidential advisors who commented on the decree after its publication told journalists that it specifically avoided the imposition of any new prohibitions or sanctions, in part because of fears that the Constitutional Court might overturn it if it did. An early draft of the decree had apparently called for confiscating the property of those who engaged in extremist activities, but the expectation that this provision would be judged unconstitutional led to its removal from the final version (Orttung 1995b:4). So in essence, the decree is nothing more than an administrative order, one telling local officials to perform their duties efficiently.

The political motivation of the decree was transparent. Concern with the activities of extremist groups has been growing in Russia, as reflected in a letter to Yeltsin written by several leading cultural figures in October 1994, a letter which questioned if he "was sufficiently informed about the growth of Russian fascism and the large number of publications seeking to convince the public to support ethnic cleansing" (Orttung 1995b:5). The scandal that followed extremist Alexei Vedenkin's public promise on national television in February 1995 to kill two leading human rights advocates also underlined this concern. With the decree Yeltsin could portray himself as a fighter for democratic liberties against extremist forces seeking to overthrow the Constitution. In this way Yeltsin might succeed in attracting back to himself some of the support of liberal politicians and voters in Russia who had distanced themselves from him after the brutal December 1994 military intervention in Chechnya (ibid.).

But although the decree may have been a new step in Yeltsin's public relations campaign, it did not really initiate new policy or new law on the subject of fascism. Like many of Yeltsin's decrees, this one, despite its political content, was strictly administrative in character, and it hardly supports the notion of a president issuing decrees to usurp the legislative authority of the Federal Assembly. Although the official government register lists the decree as "normative," then, it actually does not set new policy. This suggests that using the number of normative decrees discussed earlier to gauge how often Yeltsin makes new policy by decree gives one a rough estimate at best – and one that likely overstates how often Yeltsin has used his decree powers in this fashion. After all, in July 1995 both houses of the Federal Assembly passed – and Yeltsin signed – a series of amendments to the Russian Criminal Code, updating its provisions with respect to extremist political activity.

THE NEW CONSTITUTIONAL COURT AND DECREE AUTHORITY

As of late 1997, the impact of the Constitutional Court on the CDA of the Russian president remains uncertain. The new Court took much longer to resume operations than the Federal Assembly. This delay resulted from political maneuvering over two aspects of the new Court: its enabling statute and the selection of new judges to fill the six vacancies created by the new Constitution. The 1993 Constitution states that a "federal constitutional law" should be passed to regulate the "powers, formation, and activity" of the Constitutional Court. Such "constitutional laws" must be supported by a two-thirds majority in the Duma and three-fourths majority in the Federation Council to pass, but in contrast to constitutional amendments, they do not need to be ratified by the constituent regions of the Russian Federation.

Although the newly-elected assembly began to discuss the constitutional law on the new Court very rapidly, its content was hotly debated, and it was only seven months later, in July 1994, that Yeltsin signed the law. The main point of contention was, unsurprisingly, political. Critics of the old Court had felt that access to it was too easy, prompting politicians unable to achieve their political preferences by other means to flood the Court with petitions that dragged the Court into day-to-day politics, thus hopelessly clogging its docket. Some opposition members of the new Duma, anticipating that Yeltsin would use his decree authority liberally, wanted to maintain easy access to the Court in order to oppose his policies there. Supporters of the president – and others who wanted a more orderly legal system – wanted more limited access. Ultimately, the new law on the Court had more restrictive access provisions than its predecessor, a compromise that emerged after months of debate in part because continued delay in passing the law meant that Yeltsin was utterly unconstrained by any judicial authority (Sharlet 1995:5).

Once the law passed, political maneuvering intensified as Yeltsin began submitting nominees for the six vacancies on the Court to the Federation Council for confirmation. Although some observers had anticipated that Yeltsin would easily manage to pack the Court with supporters, the Federation Council proved less compliant than expected. It took another six months to fill the vacancies; in a series of sessions throughout this period, Yeltsin nominated a total of fourteen candidates for the six vacancies, eight of whom were rejected (Ostankino Television, 15 February 1995). It was not until February 7, 1995, more than a year after the new Constitution went into effect, that the final vacancy was filled, and only on March 23 did the new Court issue its first ruling (*Segodnya*, 8 February 1995; ITAR-TASS, 23 March 1995).

The potential of the Court to overrule presidential decrees obviously influenced the selection of judges to the Court. Several of Yeltsin's nominees were transparent attempts to pack the Court with supporters, such as the then-Justice Minister, Yurii Kalmykov, as well as a member of the presidential staff, Robert Tsivilev. Both were rejected by the Federation Council. As the lengthy process of filling the seats continued, one Russian newspaper commented that the process followed a pattern. It suggested that the less that was publicly known about a particular candidate for the Court, the more likely he or she was to be confirmed by the Federation Council (Nikitinskii 1994).

Although that may have been an exaggeration, nominees with close ties to the president often were rejected by the Council in favor of those with less obvious political preferences. When filling the last vacancy, for example, the deputies had a choice between two nominees: Marat Baglai, an academic, and Anatolii Vengerov, the chairman of a council for resolving disputes involving the mass media under the president. Baglai was chosen for the position. Both candidates had been endorsed by the Council's Committee on Constitutional Legislation as "highly qualified." The difference between them, quipped one deputy, was the phrase "under the president." Another deputy said that the upper house had felt "a sort of political sympathy" for Baglai (*Segodnya*, 8 February 1995). In any event the Council took its responsibilities seriously and collectively worked to prevent Yeltsin from obviously stacking the Court in his favor, although the results of this effort remain unclear.

It is worth pointing out here, however, that the Russian president has a significant advantage in shaping the political views of the Court because he or she has the initiative in the appointment process. The powers of the Federation Council in the selection process are strictly negative. It can turn down presidential nominees, but it cannot force the president to nominate candidates who are more to its liking. If the president has a good idea of the median preferences of the Federation Council, then, he or she should usually be able to secure approval of a candidate closer to his or her ideal preferences than to those of the Council. This is so because the initiative of proposing candidates lets the president make a "take it or leave it" offer to the Council. And since the Council cannot dismiss judges after they are appointed, it has no incentive not to approve the first minimally acceptable candidate that the president nominates (Shugart and Carey 1992:106–10). Yeltsin appears to have learned to use this advantage during the nomination process, insofar as his more obvious attempts to pack the Court came in his first few nominations, whereas his later nominees tended to be less clearly connected to the president and his policies (although as will be shown shortly, Yeltsin still cemented a deferential majority on the Court, reflecting the advantages just discussed).

The rebirth of the Constitutional Court could have a significant impact on the extent of the Russian president's constitutional decree authority, because the Court has the power under the 1993 Constitution to adjudicate the constitutionality of presidential decrees. In each of the cases already described, the Court, not being in operation, could not act as a counterweight to the president. In the future this will not be the case, and Yeltsin may find himself more tightly constrained. However, to what extent this will be the case remains uncertain. Despite the efforts of the Federation Council, the Court still has a number of Yeltsin supporters among its members, and the election by the judges from among their number of Vladimir Tumanov as the Court's Chief Judge was taken by some observers to indicate the "total victory of the presidential line in the Constitutional Court." Tumanov was one of the first new judges confirmed by the Federation Council in November 1994. Reportedly among the authors of the 1993 Constitution, he has been described as "fairly close to the president" in political orientation (*Nezavisimaya gazeta*, 17 February 1995). However, Tumanov turned seventy in October 1996, an age which forced his retirement. Given the potential of regional elections to shift the balance of power in the Federation Council, the president may have a more difficult time getting supportive justices in the future.

In its first ruling touching on presidential decree authority, the Court, by omission, appeared to support a fairly broad definition of Article 90. A group of deputies – it requires ninety signatures for a petition to be valid – in the Duma had asked the Court to review a presidential decree regarding the state-owned nuclear industry in the city of Zheleznogorsk. In the Court hearing on the decree, Deputy Valerii Gorbachev claimed that it should be struck down because it provides for the import and processing of foreign radioactive waste at a Zheleznogorsk facility, whereas existing legislation forbids the importation of radioactive materials. Arguing the presidential side of the case, Valerii Savitskii said that the decree, which issued instructions only to one government body and had only a limited time-frame, was not a "normative" act (*Kommersant-Daily*, 8 June 1995). Such "nonnormative" decrees fall outside the jurisdiction of the Court, so it cannot overrule them. The Court accepted the arguments of the president and closed the case, allowing Yeltsin's decree to stand. Observers predicted that the case might set a precedent for future Constitutional Court rulings on presidential decrees (*Kommersant-Daily*, 10 June 1995).

These predictions were validated when the Court issued a similar verdict in the Chechnya case on July 31, 1995. In November and December of 1994, President Yeltsin had issued a series of decrees which ordered the Defense and Interior Ministries to dispatch troops to the breakaway North Caucasus republic of Chechnya and to "restore constitutional order." One of these decrees was "secret," and hence it was not published. The outcry against Yeltsin's action was immediate, and it intensified as the military campaign against the forces of separatist Chechen President Dzhokhar Dudaev degenerated into a bloody stalemate in which indiscriminate shelling and bombing by federal troops killed thousands of civilians; at the same time tough Chechen resistance led to heavy Russian casualties.

Deputies in the Federation Council, which represents the eighty-nine constituent members of the Russian Federation, were particularly incensed that the president had issued a decree authorizing the use of military force inside the country without consulting them and without declaring a state of emergency. According to Article 88 of the Constitution, the president can declare a state of emergency but must inform both houses of the Federal Assembly "immediately." Article 102 gives the Federation Council the authority to "confirm decrees of the Russian President invoking a state of emergency," implying that the president cannot introduce a state of emergency without its approval. However, Article 88 adds that a federal constitutional law will regulate states of emergency. No such law has been passed, so the legal basis on which a state of emergency could be introduced remains uncertain. A 1991 law on states of emergency remains on the books, but it outlines a process in the framework of the old Constitution, and hence it is now of dubious legitimacy.

Nevertheless, petitions from both houses of the Federal Assembly reached the Constitutional Court in early April 1995, requesting that it review three presidential decrees on Chechnya and one government directive issued in accordance with those decrees. The petitions challenged the constitutionality of the decrees on several grounds. First, the deputies argued that Decree 1,833 of November 2, 1994, which elaborated on the fundamental principles of Russian military doctrine, was unconstitutional because it provided for the use of regular army troops inside the country. Decree 2,137-s of November 30, on disarming "illegal armed formations" in Chechnya, was unconstitutional, said the deputies' petition, because it was secret and hence unpublished, whereas Article 15:3 of the Constitution says that unpublished laws and decrees have no force. And finally, they said, Decree 2,166 of December 9, on restoring constitutional order in Chechnya, should be overturned because it sanctioned the use of military force inside Russia without the declaration of a state of emergency (*Segodnya*, 8 and 14 April 1995).

The Court accepted the petitions but carried out a leisurely preliminary investigation. Officially, the Court attributed the delay to procedural irregularities in the petitions from the Duma and the Federation Council. But observers speculated that the Court wanted to let the situation in Chechnya come to some sort of political or military resolution before holding formal hearings (*Rossiiskie vesti*, 7 July 1994). The Budennovsk events of mid-June 1995, however, created a situation in which it seemed likely that the conflict might soon be resolved through political talks, thus potentially reducing the significance of the case.[8]

As the renewed negotiations in Chechnya made creeping progress, the Court began hearings on July 10. The parliamentary representatives reiterated the arguments made in their petitions, especially stressing that the president could not use military forces within the country without declaring a state of emergency and securing the approval of the Federation Council. They added that all the decrees contradicted the Constitution because their implementation had led to the widespread violation of human rights in Chechnya. The presidential delegation, led by Yeltsin's Chief of Staff Sergei Filatov and Deputy Prime Minister Sergei Shakrai, countered by citing Article 80 of the 1993 Constitution, which charges the president with maintaining the territorial integrity of the Russian Federation. The administration had tried for three years to negotiate a political settlement with the separatist Dudaev government, argued Shakrai, but ultimately had no choice but to use force to maintain the integrity of Russia. As Shakrai put it, under these conditions, the decrees authorizing the use of military forces in Chechnya were fully justified, and the government and the president "not only had the right, but were obliged to take these actions" (*Kommersant-Daily*, 11 July 1995).

After hearing several days of expert testimony, the Court retired to deliberate on July 17 and issued a verdict on July 31. It then ruled, as it had in the earlier case on nuclear energy, that two of the three decrees were outside its jurisdiction. Decree 1,833, on military doctrine, said the Court, was not a normative act, because it only laid out general principles and did not issue any specific instructions or make new law in any way. It remained in force. The secret decree (Decree 2,137-s) on disarming illegal armed formations in Chechnya was out of the Court's jurisdiction, the decision ruled, because Yeltsin had annulled it a few days after its issuance, and hence it no longer required a ruling from the Court.

Decree 2,166, on restoring constitutional order in Chechnya, was upheld by the Court as fully constitutional; so too was the subsequent government directive that implemented it, with the exception of two relatively minor provisions, which the court struck down (*Rossiiskie vesti*, 1 August 1995; *OMRI Daily Digest*, 1 August 1995). The Court decision also criticized the parliamentarians who had initiated the suit against the president in a clause which lamented the lack of relevant legislation regulating the introduction of a state of emergency. In the absence of such legislation, the Court said, the executive was justified in taking direct action to meet its constitutional obligations (*Segodnya*, 1 August 1995). The implicit message was that the deputies should spend more time on their legislative functions and less time challenging presidential acts in court. Not surprisingly, Filatov told journalists he was "fully satisfied" with the decision after its announcement. The deputies who had come to hear the judgment, on the other hand, left the Court building without even commenting to the press (Russian Television, 31 July 1995).

The Court decision, however, should not be taken to mean that the Court will refuse to overturn any other decrees that Yeltsin issues. It is hard to imagine an issue in Russian politics more charged than Chechnya, and the majority on the Court clearly wanted to avoid a head-on confrontation with the president over the conflict. The Chechnya decrees were also more emergency decrees than anything else, and hence the decision upholding them may not set a long-term precedent for decrees in more normal spheres of politics. Finally, the verdict was not unanimous. Four of the Court's nineteen members told journalists later that they fundamentally disagreed with the verdict; Valerii Zorkin, the former chairman, and Nikolai Vitruk were the most vocal of these critics. Vitruk especially attacked the notion that the president could enforce general provisions of the Constitution even if there was no legal basis for doing so. This aspect of the decision could lead to a dramatic expansion of presidential power, especially decree authority, Vitruk warned (*Izvestiya*, 8 August 1995). Another three or four judges also filed special opinions outlining their differences with the majority opinion.

So far, however, the Court has not demonstrated much proclivity for overruling presidential decrees. In the other major decree-related case during 1995, the Court refused to hear the Duma's appeal of Yeltsin's decree privatizing the state-run television network, as noted earlier. Overall, then, the Court has been very deferential to Yeltsin on this issue. Reviewing the work of the Court since it resumed work, its chairman, Vladimir Tumanov, in a July 1996 interview, felt compelled to explain that although the Court had rejected more petitions from the Duma and Federation Council than from the president, that did not mean the Court was biased in favor of Yeltsin. Rather, he said, deputies often appealed

Yeltsin decrees that were intended only to remain in force until the passage of appropriate legislation. If the Court struck down such decrees, said Tumanov, it would open gaping holes in the Russian legal system. Instead of appealing such decrees to the Court, he added, the deputies should concentrate on passing necessary legislation, which would then supersede the Yeltsin decrees to which they objected (*Nezavismaya gazeta*, 25 July 1996). Given Yeltsin's veto powers and the fragmentation of the assembly, however, Tumanov's arguments are disingenuous at best, because the assembly cannot pass new laws to overcome Yeltsin's decrees unless it bows to his wishes or musters a supermajority to overcome his veto. Thus, even if Yeltsin claims his decrees are temporary, he can maneuver in the current Russian political environment to make them nearly permanent.

Ironically, it was a lower court that recently issued the most direct legal challenge to a Yeltsin decree, but it did so on strictly procedural – not constitutional – grounds. In December 1994, at the urging of Yevgenii Nazdratenko, the governor of Primorsk Krai, Yeltsin had issued a decree removing from office the elected mayor of Vladivostok, Viktor Cherepkov, a fierce political opponent of Nazdratenko. The decree simply cited Nazdratenko's request and Cherepkov's "failure to carry out his duties" as justification for removing him from office. On the face of it, the decree was patently illegal, because the federal president has no constitutional authority to remove local elected officials – even if they have violated the law (Cherepkov was charged with corruption). However, the regional police obeyed both Nazdratenko and Yeltsin and forcibly ousted Cherepkov from his office. He was replaced by a Nazdratenko appointee.

Subsequently, after the corruption charges against him had been dismissed for lack of evidence, Cherepkov challenged the legality of his ouster in a Moscow court, insofar as Yeltsin had issued his decree in Moscow; and as a nonnormative act, which affected only one individual, Cherepkov claimed it did not fall under the jurisdiction of the Constitutional Court. After an eighteen-month trial, the Khamovnicheskii municipal court handed down a verdict voiding Yeltsin's decree as illegal, an act which *Izvestiya* termed "unprecedented" in Russian legal practice (ITAR-TASS, 14 August 1996; *Izvestiya*, 16 August 1996). Yeltsin and Nazdratenko subsequently acquiesced in the decision, and Cherepkov resumed the post of mayor. Since the decree in question was nonnormative and affected only a single individual, it will not set a precedent with regard to normative decrees that set new policy. But the case at least demonstrates that not all courts in Russia are willing to accept executive explanations of questionable presidential decrees.

CONCLUSIONS: THE PROSPECTS FOR PRESIDENTIAL DECREE AUTHORITY

What are the prospects for the future development of presidential decree authority under the 1993 Constitution? As of late 1996, the constitutional decree powers of the Russian president seem quite sweeping. In many cases Yeltsin has been able to use his decree powers to dominate the policy agenda and force the assembly to accept his policy preferences. Nor does the Constitutional Court seem to be an effective counterweight, one that could prevent the sweeping use of decrees by the president; furthermore, the possibility that local courts may overturn some of Yeltsin's individual nonnormative decisions will not prevent him from dominating the larger national policy agenda. It is tempting to conclude that this situation will become permanent and that Russia is indeed likely to become a "delegative democracy," as described by O'Donnell, one based on the premise that "whoever wins election to the presidency is thereby entitled to govern as he or she sees fit, constrained only by the hard facts of existing power relationships and by a constitutionally limited term of office" (O'Donnell 1994:59).

A number of factors underlined in this chapter support such a conclusion. First, Article 90 of the new Constitution itself gives the president a very sweeping mandate to rule by decree, whereas the difficulty of enacting constitutional amendments seems to give this power some permanence. Legislative opposition to presidential *policy making-by-decree* seems unlikely to prove successful in the current Russian political environment. The Federal Assembly is highly fragmented and cannot present a determined president with a united front, and this situation thus opens the gate to legislation by decree. Fragmentation of the Duma has decreased since the 1995 elections, but not sufficiently to allow any party or coalition to consistently muster majorities, much less the supermajorities needed to overcome presidential vetoes. In the Duma elected in 1995, for example, there are seven registered parties and factions, as opposed to eleven in the previous one. It is true that the largest faction, the Communist Party of the Russian Federation, has 149 seats (33 percent of the total), whereas the largest faction in the previous Duma had only 76 seats (or 17 percent of the total). But the other six factions in the current Duma, which are spread across the political spectrum and are not especially well-disciplined, have only 35–55 members. It is the rare issue, then, that can provoke a majority to form in opposition to a presidential decree, much less the supermajority needed to override a veto. The new Duma is little different from the old one in this respect.

Nor does the Constitutional Court seem like an effective counterweight to the president. The current Court, despite the efforts of the Federation Council, seems to have a comfortable pro-presidential majority, one that is disinclined to overturn Yeltsin's decrees. After Yeltsin's reelection in July 1996, a reorganization of his presidential administration consolidated power over the drafting of decrees in the hands of his talented and ambitious chief of staff, Anatolii Chubais. Before he was removed, former Security Council Secretary Aleksandr Lebed claimed that Chubais was not just controlling what draft decrees Yeltsin signed but that he was using a facsimile stamp to issue decrees under Yeltsin's signature which the president, then seriously ill with a heart condition, had not actually signed. These developments point to both a concentration of effectively-legislative power in the president, but they also reflect the dangers for democracy of making policy by presidential decree, when an unelected official like Chubais may be issuing significant policy decisions with only minimal legislative involvement and public scrutiny. Overall, when looking at the three branches from the perspective of the fall of 1996, then, it is hard to avoid the conclusion that the presidency, in no small measure because of its sweeping decree powers, is the dominant branch.

On the other hand, there are some reasons to believe that Yeltsin's decree authority – and especially that of his successors – will decrease and that we may already have seen the peak of presidential influence over policy making in Russia. Barring a democratic breakdown, a number of factors point to the diminution of the Russian president's constitutional decree authority in the future. Much of the president's apparent power stems less from the institutional arrangements specified in the Constitution itself than from the current political situation in Russia. The role of the Federal Assembly is a case in point. It is currently highly fragmented; this is especially true of the lower house. Over time, however, this fragmentation is likely to decrease. Although the incentives created by the Russian electoral system and the Constitution itself are not strong enough to dramatically reduce the number of political parties from its current level, one would still expect a moderate reduction over the next few election cycles, and the figures cited earlier demonstrate that the last election did indeed produce such a trend. A more consolidated lower house will probably emerge over time.

The upper house, or Federation Council, has often proven useful to Yeltsin in blocking Duma initiatives and allowing his decrees to stand. The Council, however, is about to undergo a transformation that may change its political complexion and make it less inclined to support the president than it has been in the past. Originally, the 178-member Council was directly elected, and it consisted of two deputies from each of the eighty-nine constituent regions of the Russian Federation. Under a 1995 law, however, the Council is now formed ex officio; the two seats for each region are now held by its governor and the head of the regional legislature. Over the long run, an upper house that represents the interests of local political elites may frequently disagree with the president, although coalitions of local interests which are large enough to override presidential vetoes may still be rare. Nonetheless, future Russian presidents will face a more independent upper house than Yeltsin has.

Even more importantly, the assembly itself, especially the lower house, is gradually finding its place in Russian politics and organizing internally, and the parties in it are becoming better at overcoming collective action problems and reaching compromise decisions. These developments suggest that future presidents will face a more coherent assembly, one better equipped to oppose presidents who attempt to rule by decree. In the same vein, as the figures in Table 3.1 show, if one discounts the presidential election year of 1996, the Duma is accelerating its production of new legislation, and hence it is filling in the gaping holes in the Russian legal system. Over time, as more and more laws are passed, the maneuvering room for future presidents will be reduced, because it will become increasingly difficult to issue decrees on important policy issues that do not contradict existing law.

The role of the Constitutional Court may also change over time. In part the currently deferential attitude of the Court toward presidential decrees reflects transient circumstances. The Court's current stance reflects the fact that Yeltsin was able to appoint six new judges. Despite the efforts of the Federation Council to prevent him from packing the Court, he has a majority of supporters on the current bench. The close links between Yeltsin and the current Court were the source of some criticism after the Chechnya decision. For example, the pro-communist opposition newspaper *Pravda* complained that the verdict showed the president had the Court in his pocket (*Pravda*, 31 July 1995). Other critics pointed out that after the verdict was announced, its chairman, Tumanov, retired to his private office in the company of presidential Chief of Staff Filatov, taking this as evidence that the Court and the president have very close ties (*Moskovskii komsomolets*, 2 August 1995).

Although the current makeup of the Court may help Yeltsin retain the initiative now, it could easily hinder his successors in the future, especially if they do not share Yeltsin's political orientation. According to the law on the Court, judges are appointed for twelve-year terms (up to age seventy), and because of grandfather provisions covering those appointed before 1993, some of the current judges will be on the bench until 2018. Even if Yeltsin survives his full term and a new president is not elected until 2000, that president will face a similar pro-Yeltsin majority on the Court, which could act as a serious constraint on presidential decree authority, depending on the political preferences of Yeltsin's successor.

Furthermore, the current Court, so soon after the bracing experience of its October 1993 suspension by Yeltsin, is obviously reluctant to provoke controversy by overturning presidential decrees on politically charged issues. In an interview with the author in December 1995, one of the Court's judges admitted as much. In this light the Chechnya case may prove a poor predictor of the future rulings of the Court on presidential decrees in general, insofar as the Court seemed determined to limit its verdict to the narrowest ground possible in order to avoid too much political furor (*Segodnya*, 1 August 1995). As the Court continues to operate, it may become less cautious in this regard, insofar as, like the Duma, it begins to find its place in the Russian political order. That some of the judges who dissented from the Chechnya ruling would have taken a more aggressive stance toward the president's decrees suggests that the base of a more activist coalition is already on the Court. So even a future president who broadly shares Yeltsin's political preferences, like Viktor Chernomyrdin, could well find him- or herself more constrained than Yeltsin does now. Although it has not yet ruled on the issue, the Court will also have considerable discretion in defining what Article 90 means when it says decrees cannot contradict existing law. A narrow interpretation of this clause could drastically restrict future presidential action, whereas a broad one could leave the president much room for maneuver even if the gaps in the Russian legal system are filled.

Finally, the development of federalism in Russia, with local and regional officials striving to gain autonomy from the central government, as well as the continued inefficiency of the Russian bureaucracy, have combined to reduce the actual impact of Yeltsin's decrees, even in those cases when he wins his political battles with opponents in Moscow. It is not a coincidence that Yeltsin often issues the same decree more than once, the second time warning that officials who fail to implement his instructions will be punished. Successive decrees on land reform, as noted earlier, were sabotaged at the local level. The problem is endemic and intractable, as suggested by Yeltsin's issuance of two decrees in 1996 that ordered the more efficient implementation of his decrees by the bureaucracy and introduced "personal accountability" for failure to follow his orders (*OMRI Daily Digest*, 11 November 1996). So the dominance of the executive in Moscow may not be as complete as it seems at the first glance of often–Moscow-centered foreign observers. As Russian federalism is consolidated, this trend may accelerate.

All these factors taken together suggest that while Yeltsin has very broad constitutional decree authority now, his successors will quite likely face far more severe political and institutional constraints than he does. And this conclusion gives one modest hope that the transition to institutionalized representative democracy may yet prove more successful in Russia than some would have us believe.

NOTES

1 O'Donnell's *delegative democracy* should not be confused with the term *delegated decree authority* (DDA), which is also used in this volume. O'Donnell's concept is much broader, and it is intended to characterize the political system as a whole, not just the delegation of decree powers to the executive by the assembly.

2 There was only one Congress of People's Deputies (CPD) elected during the First Russian Republic (1990–93). The numerical designations of the Congresses in this paper (First, Second, Third, etc.) refer to different sessions of that same Congress, which met only once every few months. References to these sessions will include dates for clarity.

3 Bills not falling into specified categories do not require the approval of the upper house, the Federation Council, but they can be sent directly to the president for signature if the Federation Council does not explicitly reject them within fourteen days (Arts. 105 and 106). If the president vetoes such a bill, however, it still requires a two-thirds supermajority in both houses to override.

4 The procedures resemble those in the American Constitution, which has been amended relatively few times in the more than 200 years of its operation.

5 Time limitations made it impractical for the author to read and carefully classify all 953 of the normative decrees Yeltsin issued through October 1996. Future

work might focus on the content of these decrees to ascertain exactly how many of them really initiate new policy. On the basis of the case studies reported in the text, there is reason to believe that not all of them could be considered as executive attempts to make new policy.

6 For example, one of the shareholders is the gas monopoly, Gazprom, which has very close ties to its former director, Yeltsin's current prime minister, Viktor Chernomyrdin. Another is entrepreneur Boris Berezovskii, who is reputed to have helped bankroll Yeltsin's 1996 presidential campaign as well as the campaign of Aleksandr Lebed, the third-place finisher who later backed Yeltsin in the runoff.

7 Absenteeism is a chronic problem in both houses of the new Federal Assembly. It is routine for 100 or more of the 450 members of the Duma to be absent at any given session, whereas the Federation Council has repeatedly canceled sessions because of difficulty in mustering a quorum. Under the rules of the Duma, deputies may choose not to vote on any given measure, and they are then recorded as "not voting," a category distinct from abstentions that must be registered. Hence on this vote, a large number of deputies were not present, whereas some in the hall chose not to vote.

8 In mid-June 1993, a group of separatist Chechen fighters attacked the southern Russian city of Budennovsk and took over 1,000 of its inhabitants hostage. After a bloody botched rescue attempt by federal special forces, the Russian government agreed to begin political negotiations on the terms of ending its military intervention in Chechnya in return for the release of the hostages. The Budennovsk events thus changed the nature of the struggle in Chechnya and raised the prospect that a negotiated settlement would emerge, although as of August 1995 the talks had only produced a cease-fire, not an overall settlement (Parrish 1995).

4

PRESIDENTIAL USURPATION OR CONGRESSIONAL PREFERENCE?

THE EVOLUTION OF EXECUTIVE DECREE AUTHORITY IN PERU

Gregory Schmidt

The only element of democracy in Peru today is the electoral process, which gives Peruvians the privilege of choosing a dictator every five years. Rule making is subsequently carried out in a vacuum, with the executive branch enacting new rules and regulations at a clip of 134,000 every five years (an average of 106 each working day) without any feedback from the population.
HERNANDO DE SOTO, THE INTERNATIONALLY RENOWNED
ADVOCATE FOR PERU'S VAST INFORMAL SECTOR,
AND DEBORAH ORSINI (DE SOTO AND ORSINI 1991:106)

Peru appears to be very inhospitable terrain for exploring the ideas ventured in the introductory chapter of this volume.[1] Guillermo O'Donnell categorizes the country as one of the purest cases of "delegative democracy," in which elected presidents govern with few, if any, institutional constraints (1994). Lending credence to such a characterization is a variety of recent works by prominent experts on Peru.[2] During the 1980s the administrations of Fernando Belaunde and Alan García faced few obstacles in using various kinds of decree to routinely promulgate major policies and supersede legislation passed by Congress. In the 1990s Peru's current president, Alberto Fujimori, has epitomized the sort of messianic, anti-institutional leader typically found in O'Donnell's delegative democracy. If periodic elections to choose a "dictator" for the next presidential term are indeed the only important characteristic of Peruvian democracy, then it makes little sense to distinguish among different types of decree authority, to analyze legislative or other institutional checks on decree, or to consider congressional preferences. Instead, decrees of all sorts can be indiscriminately lumped together and regarded as prima facie evidence of executive dominance (see De Soto 1989:192, 196–7).

In contrast to the caricature sketched by De Soto and O'Donnell, which reflects the prevailing "presidential usurpation" view of decree in the literature, this chapter paints a much more variegated picture of executive decree authority under democratic regimes in Peru. It shows that members of successive constitutional assemblies have placed significant constraints on presidential powers, although these constraints have seldom been enforced by pro-government majorities in Congress. In other words, if democratic governance in Peru frequently resembles delegative democracy, this is primarily because legislators from the president's party have usually given him broad latitude to use decree and not because of the assembly's institutional weakness. Presidents lacking partisan majorities have faced much greater scrutiny from a powerful Congress. Nevertheless, even chief executives in the latter category have made extensive use of decree when they could muster the support – or could count on the acquiescence – of most legislators. Thus, the sorts of variables emphasized in the introductory chapter – the distribution of powers between the executive and legislative branches, the standing of the president's party in Congress, the preferences of legislators, and the institutional source of decree – are all important for understanding decree authority in Peru.

Although most decrees promulgated by democratic governments have been supported – or at least not opposed – by legislative majorities, controversy over the bounds of executive decree authority has been frequent, sometimes with severe repercussions. Indeed, the most important source of decree authority in Peru evolved from successive presidents' controversial use of an ambiguous clause in the 1979 Constitution regarding economic and financial regulation. Moreover, decrees promulgated by the executive branch or policies implemented by such decrees were among the major issues of consequence in the constitutional breakdowns of 1948, 1968, and 1992. In the most recent of these three years, in a clear act of usurpation, Fujimori "called out the tanks" to seize absolute power in the *autogolpe* (presidential or self-coup), and he did so following congressional attempts to assert control over various types of executive decree authority. Nevertheless, as democracy was restored under international pressure, significant new restrictions on different kinds of decree were incorporated into the 1993 Constitution.

The first section of this chapter highlights the strong constitutional powers of Congress and the "volcanic" character of executive–legislative relations since 1933, with an emphasis on events leading up to the 1992 constitutional breakdown. Employing the conceptual framework developed in Chapter 1, the second section in the chapter examines the general parameters of executive decree authority under Peru's three most recent constitutions (1933, 1979, and 1993). Subsequent sections focus on specific types of decree authority – rule making, DDA, emergency CDA, and standard CDA – and assess the role of Peru's hybrid judiciary in mediating disputes over decree.

Drawing on evidence from the complex Peruvian case, the concluding section addresses the theoretical issues posed by John Carey and Matthew Shugart in the first chapter. Some of the editors' arguments and hypotheses are supported, often strongly. In other instances there are inconsistencies between their expectations and the Peruvian experience with decree, but these anomalies nevertheless raise important issues for future research. Thus, this chapter demonstrates that the approach developed by the editors is very useful even in Peru, a country in which many knowledgeable observers might well expect the conventional "presidential usurpation" interpretation to prevail.

"VOLCANIC" EXECUTIVE–LEGISLATIVE RELATIONS SINCE 1933

Although Peru has had thirteen constitutions, there has been remarkable continuity in the powers of its legislative and executive branches of government since the mid-nineteenth century. Compared with other Latin American countries, Peruvian constitutional tradition has tilted the balance of power between the president and Congress toward the latter during periods of (relative) democracy. Particularly noteworthy is Peru's president–parliamentary regime, under which the prime minister and cabinet members are appointed by the president but subject to congressional confidence.[3] Peruvian presidents traditionally have exercised only a weak veto, and until recently Congress could amend the Constitution with relative ease.[4] According to modern Peruvian charters special congressional majorities have not been required either to declare the presidency vacant as a consequence of "moral or physical incapacity" or to impeach a sitting president or former chief executive. These removal powers are reinforced by historical precedents, beginning with the dismissal of Peru's first president, José de la Riva-Agüero, in 1823.

During the course of modern Peruvian political history, executive–legislative relations have resembled volcanic activity: Long periods of relative tranquillity have been interrupted by short spurts of furious activity. Although Congress has seldom been quiescent, it has usually deferred to the president when in session during periods of extraconstitutional government or limited democracy (1933–36, 1939–45, 1950–56), as well as when it was controlled by a majority coalition supportive of the chief executive (1956–62, 1980–90, 1992–95, 1995–present). However, conflicts between the two branches erupted during the 1945–48, 1963–68, and 1990–92 periods when the president's supporters were minorities in Congress. All three eruptions contributed to breakdowns of democracy, although this outcome was by no means inevitable.

PRESIDENTIAL WEAKNESS AND EPHEMERAL DEMOCRACY

Following the twelve-year dictatorship of Augusto Leguía Salcedo (1919–1930), Peru held elections for a new president and Constituent Congress to serve a concurrent five-year term beginning in December 1931. Lacking his own political organization, Luis Sánchez Cerro, the military hero who had overthrown Leguía, won the presidential contest under the banner of the Revolutionary Union (UR), a party founded by a small group of right-wing nationalists. However, supporters of the other major candidate, Víctor Raúl Haya de la Torre of the populist American Popular Revolutionary Alliance (APRA), refused to accept the results of the presidential election, charging instead that it had been stolen through fraud.

The UR ran lists of candidates for the Constituent Congress selected by its leadership (Stein 1980:120–1). Thanks to Sánchez Cerro's popularity, the UR slates won a strong plurality of seats and achieved a working majority through alliances with several smaller parties. Fresh memories of Leguía's dictatorship prompted the Constituent Congress to increase the relative power of the legislative branch (Basadre 1983, X:270–4). Most notably, the 1933 Constitution eliminated the presidential prerogative to reject legislation, although a weak veto with a simple majority override was later exercised paraconstitutionally (Bernales 1971). The delegates also emphatically reinforced the longstanding prohibition of immediate presidential reelection. Article 142 of the new Charter stipulated that this proscription could not be altered by constitutional amendment and that sponsors of any proposed modification would automatically be disqualified from holding public office. Thus, UR delegates and other supporters of Sánchez Cerro were not dependent upon the president for their reelection.

The 1933 Constitution, however, was affected by the severe political conflict between the followers of Sánchez Cerro and APRA, a conflict which escalated into virtual civil war while the Charter was being drafted. In January 1932 the pro–Sánchez Cerro majority passed a repressive emergency law requested by the government, one which the latter used to exile APRA delegates the following month (Basadre 1983, X:201–3, 207–10). In an abrupt shift from its immediate predecessors, the 1933 Constitution granted the executive emergency CDA to suspend certain civil liberties.

Shortly after he promulgated the new charter, Sánchez Cerro was assassinated by an *aprista* (member of APRA). The Constituent Congress elected General Oscar Benavides to serve out the remainder of Sánchez Cerro's term and later extended his mandate for another three years, during which time he ruled by decree without a legislature. As his extended term wound down in 1939, Benavides convoked an extralegal plebiscite to approve ten constitutional amendments designed to strengthen the executive vis-à-vis Congress, including provisions for a strong veto and broad DDA during congressional recesses. These reforms benefited Benavides' immediate successor, Manuel Prado (1939–45), who won a restricted election, but they were quickly annulled by Congress after the relatively open 1945 election.

José Bustamante i Rivero, who won the presidency by a landslide in 1945, was elected with APRA's support, and the congressional lists of his National Democratic Front (FDN) included many *apristas*. The very disciplined APRA congressional delegation held a majority in the Senate and, thanks to the support of other FDN members, a working majority on most issues in the Chamber of Deputies. In a highly charged political atmosphere, APRA employed this congressional power to methodically enact its legislative program, both to the chagrin of the moderate president and the alarm of the conservative opposition. Congress forced two key members of Bustamante i Rivero's first cabinet to resign after fewer than three months in office, and four different cabinets were formed during the first two years of his term.

In a context of increasing polarization and political violence, conservative and moderate senators used a boycott to prevent Congress from convening in July 1947, leaving the president to rule controversially by decree. Bustamante i Rivero attempted to resolve the congressional standoff and restore the veto and other executive powers, but the president's economic policies along with his reluctance to crack down on APRA alienated the conservative elite. After an attempted coup by young *aprista* militants failed in early October 1948, a conservative faction of the military led by General Manuel Odría overthrew Bustamante i Rivero at the end of the same month.

Executive–legislative relations were much less contentious under Odría's authoritarian government (1948–56) and Prado's second, constitutional administration (1956–62), both of which could count on pro-government congressional majorities. However, conflict between the two branches once again erupted in 1963 when Fernando Belaunde, a reformist whose Popular Action (AP) party was strongest among newer middle sectors that had emerged after World War II, was elected president without a congressional majority. An opposition coalition of APRA as well as supporters of General Odría sabotaged even Belaunde's watered-down reform program, using interpellation to harass the cabinet and forcing ten ministers to resign through censure or the threat of censure (Hilliker 1971: 133–5). Belaunde went through seven cabinets and made sixty-one appointments to fill the nine civilian ministries that existed at that time, including four finance ministers during his last year in office (V. García Belaunde 1988:3–5; Kuczynski 1977:76).

The congressional opposition competed with the government to deliver benefits through rapidly expanding public expenditures, but it blocked new taxes until the last year of Belaunde's term. Although the economy was growing at a brisk pace, a mushrooming fiscal deficit fueled inflation and contributed to a politically charged devaluation in September 1967. Executive–legislative conflict epitomized the failure of Peruvian democracy to address the country's major social and economic problems – a failure that was the core motivation for the 1968 coup and the military's so-called Peruvian Revolution.

A STRONGER EXECUTIVE WITH SUPPORTIVE MAJORITIES

As Peru returned to democracy a decade later, members of the 1978–79 Constituent Assembly sought to avoid a repetition of the first Belaunde administration by strengthening the power of the executive vis-à-vis Congress.[5] Nevertheless, the delegates were not inclined to change the fundamental model of executive–legislative relations that had emerged in previous constitutions. All of the major political parties could expect to win seats in Congress, which was elected by proportional representation, mostly in medium and high magnitude districts; but none had a clear edge at the presidential level. Moreover, 74 of the 100 delegates to the Constituent Assembly ran for Congress in the 1980 election.[6] These aspiring legislators had a personal stake in maintaining the institutional integrity of their prospective branch of government.

APRA, whose highly disciplined congressional delegations had frequently used legislative prerogatives to great advantage, held a plurality of thirty-seven seats in the Assembly. The Popular Christian Party (PPC), whose ranks include some of Peru's most prestigious legislators, had twenty-five representatives, the second largest delegation. An APRA-PPC alliance drafted most of the 1979 Constitution, which a large but fragmented leftist bloc refused to sign. Belaunde's AP had boycotted the Constituent Assembly election and was not represented.

Although the 1979 Charter established an explicit veto, it could be overridden by only absolute majorities in each legislative chamber. Similarly, requirements for interpellation and censure were tightened, but ministers still could be forced to resign by an absolute majority of the Chamber of Deputies, except in the last year of the five-year term concurrently served by the executive and legislative branches. In contrast to the terms of the 1933 Constitution, the new Constitution allowed the president to dissolve the lower chamber and hold new elections once per term, but only if three cabinets had been censured or denied confidence, and not while emergency CDA was invoked or during the last year of a term. Only the president could introduce expenditure bills; however, Congress usually altered executive proposals during the appropriations process.

The 1979 Constitution incorporated explicit provisions for DDA, an addition that was strongly influenced by a positive experience with ad hoc delegation at the very end of Belaunde's first administration. The Constituent Assembly delineated two regimes of exception for emergency CDA – the state of emergency and the state of siege – but it rejected explicit provisions for standard CDA. Nevertheless, a little-noticed passage in Article 211(20) evolved into a very potent source of standard CDA.

During the 1980s Congress was not inclined to flex its constitutional muscles

Table 4.1 *Presidential vetos under the 1979 Peruvian Constitution, 1980–92*

Type of Initiative	Fernando Belaunde 1980–85	Alan García 1985–90	Alberto Fujimori 1990–92	Total
Number of bills passed by Congress	724	665	67	1,456
Number (%) of bills vetoed	38 (5.2)[a]	60 (9.0)	35 (52.2)	133 (9.1)
Number (%) of vetoed that were:				
Overridden	0 (0)	3 (5)	8 (23)	11 (8)
Sustained	4 (11)	5 (8)	4 (11)	13 (10)
Not contested, no action	33 (87)	48 (80)	23 (66)	104 (78)
Not contested, formally withdrawn	0 (0)	3 (5)	0 (0)	3 (2)
Not contested, another bill submitted	1 (3)	1 (2)	0 (0)	2 (2)

[a]Percentages are in parentheses.
Source: Adapted from Delgado-Guembes (1992:43, 226).

because pro-government majorities controlled both chambers during the second presidency of Fernando Belaunde (1980–85) and during Alan García's administration (1985–90).[7] Although the opposition parties had sufficient votes to interpellate one of Belaunde's and three of García's cabinets, as well as individual cabinet members, neither president lost a minister through censure.[8] As illustrated in Table 4.1, these presidents returned relatively few bills to Congress, and only three vetoes were overridden during the decade.

FRAGMENTATION AND DEMOCRATIC BREAKDOWN

Although the Belaunde and García administrations both enjoyed strong support in Congress, neither was able to reverse Peru's long economic decline or effectively deal with the Shining Path insurgency and the Túpac Amaru Revolutionary Movement (MRTA), whose ability to inflict violence greatly increased during the 1980s. By the end of the decade, Peruvians' faith in their political and governmental institutions, especially parties, had plummeted to all-time lows. During the final six weeks of the 1990 general election campaign, support for Alberto Fujimori, a political outsider, surged from less than 1 percent in public opinion polls to 29 percent of the valid vote, placing him a close second to neoliberal candidate Mario Vargas Llosa, the overwhelming favorite. With support from

APRA and the two major leftist fronts, Fujimori went on to defeat Vargas Llosa in the June presidential runoff by a landslide (Schmidt 1996).

The new Congress was extremely fragmented, with 6.06 effective parties in the 180-seat Chamber of Deputies and 6.12 in the 62-seat Senate.[9] After losing the presidential runoff, Vargas Llosa's Democratic Front (FREDEMO), which had won a plurality of seats in both houses, splintered into its component parties – AP, the PPC, and the Liberty Movement. APRA held more seats than any single party in each chamber, with Fujimori's Change 90 (C90) second. Two leftist fronts, each composed of distinct political parties, had delegations in both houses. Minor parties filled thirteen seats in the lower chamber and one in the Senate.

Despite this fragmentation Fujimori could have formed a majority center–right coalition with the former FREDEMO parties or a majority center-left coalition with APRA and the leftist fronts. Instead, the president chose to maintain his independence from the traditional parties – the key quality that had made him attractive to voters. Continuing a popular theme from his campaign, Fujimori aggressively ridiculed Congress, the parties, and other institutions. Behind the scenes, he increasingly relied on a small inner circle of advisers and began to build a power base in the intelligence service and the military.

Lines of support for and opposition to the government were ambiguous and fluid. After Fujimori broke his major campaign promise by implementing "shock" economic policies, a block of C90 legislators frequently voted against him; some were later expelled from the party. Only one member of C90 served in the cabinet, which was primarily comprised of political independents. Although the president made a series of tactical alliances with APRA, the ex-FREDEMO parties generally supported his market-oriented economic policies. Prominent leftist politicians initially held several cabinet portfolios, but the key posts of prime minister and economics minister were invariably filled by individuals sympathetic to the right.

The extreme partisan fragmentation in Congress precluded the sort of legislative dominance that had marked most of the first Belaunde administration. Although Fujimori exercised his relatively weak veto much more frequently than either of his predecessors in the 1980s, he was overridden less than a quarter of the time (see Table 4.1). There were only four ministerial interpellations and only one minister was forced to resign after being censured.[10] Nevertheless, in marked contrast to the 1980–90 period, legislators began to challenge executive actions that were not clearly within the bounds of the 1979 Constitution, such as Fujimori's partial veto of the 1991 budget law.

In May 1991 Congress overwhelmingly approved Law 25,327, which provided the executive with DDA for 150 days on three key issues: national pacification (counterinsurgency), job creation, and the promotion of private investment. APRA backed Law 25,327 in exchange for Fujimori's continued support of former President García, who faced impeachment and prosecution on charges of corruption. However, to the chagrin of APRA and the left, Fujimori and Economics Minister Carlos Boloña used the delegated authority to implement sweeping market-oriented reforms. Most of the 117 decrees issued under Law 25,327 reached Congress in early November, when APRA was no longer beholden to the president after the congressional votes against García the previous month. APRA and some of the leftist parties prepared some 200 bills to repeal the neoliberal decrees, but most of them were defeated by the ex-FREDEMO parties and C90.[11] Legislators from APRA and the left then filed fifteen petitions of unconstitutionality before the Tribunal of Constitutional Guarantees.

Although Fujimori found congressional support for most of his economic decrees, legislators of all political stripes united to oppose draconian provisions in the counterinsurgency decrees that threatened civil liberties and democratic governance.[12] Before the end of its regular session on December 15, Congress passed bills repealing or modifying some of the more controversial decrees dealing with both economic and counterinsurgency matters. After presidential vetoes of these bills and other key legislation, two-thirds of the members of each chamber signed petitions to convoke themselves in special session. During January and early February 1992, Congress overrode the president to pass all of the vetoed legislation into law, and it also approved new bills overturning or revising decrees. All told, Congress repealed 16 of the 117 decrees issued under Law 25,327, modified 14 others, and delayed final action on 9 until its next regular session in April.[13] Among the legislation passed over Fujimori's veto was the Law of Parliamentary Control Over the Normative Acts of the President of the Republic (Law 25,397, hereafter the Law of Parliamentary Control), which had the backing of all parties except the pro-Fujimori faction of C90. This law, which is discussed further in subsequent sections of this chapter, defined procedures for DDA and, more significantly, asserted congressional authority to review various kinds of decree issued under CDA.

As legislators became more assertive, Fujimori accelerated his rhetorical attacks on Congress. For example, in December 1991 the president insinuated that legislative opposition to one of the counterinsurgency decrees was motivated by a desire to protect the launderers of drug money. The very same day, the Senate unanimously passed a resolution that was widely interpreted as a threat to declare the presidency vacant by virtue of "moral incapacity." After Congress overrode his veto of the 1992 budget law in special session, Fujimori charged that legislators were the beneficiaries of extravagant spending on congressional salaries and pensions.

Yet while Fujimori was taunting Congress in public, his third prime minister, Alfonso de los Heros, quietly negotiated with the ex-FREDEMO parties during the congressional recess. By late March 1992 the two sides had ironed out common language on the key counterinsurgency decrees still at issue. They also agreed to end *aprista* control of the judiciary by rescheduling the ratification of Supreme Court justices and setting a new mandatory retirement age of seventy for magistrates of the Tribunal of Constitutional Guarantees. These latter agreements were motivated by recent judicial decisions: a December 1991 ruling by the Supreme Court throwing out the corruption charges against Alan García and resolutions by the Tribunal in March 1992 that had overturned three of the neoliberal decrees issued under Law 25,327.[14]

Legislation to implement these agreements was scheduled to be introduced in Congress on April 7. However, on April 2 the Senate formed a special committee to investigate allegations by First Lady Susana Higuchi de Fujimori that her husband's family was selling donated clothing from Japan – a process that would have focused on the president's secretive inner circle. In this context, Fujimori decided to activate longstanding plans for an *autogolpe*. In a late-evening televised address on April 5, the president attacked the "handcuffing" of his constitutional prerogatives by the Law of Parliamentary Control, among other denunciations. He then announced the dismissal of Congress and the reorganization of the judiciary.[15]

THE 1993 CONSTITUTION: PLUS ÇA CHANGE. . . . ?

In his address to the nation, Fujimori promised to appoint a commission to draft changes in the 1979 Constitution, which then would be put to a vote in a national plebiscite. International reaction to the *autogolpe*, however, was "swift and universally unfavorable" (Ferrero Costa 1993:34). At a May meeting of the foreign ministers of the Organization of American States in the Bahamas, the president announced elections for a Democratic Constituent Congress that would serve until the end of his term in July 1995, functioning both as a legislature and a constituent assembly. Following the dramatic capture of Abimael Guzmán, the evasive leader of the Shining Path, in November 1992, Fujimori's New Majority-Change 90 (NM-C90) alliance won 44 of the 80 seats in the unicameral Constituent Congress.

Most political observers expected a strongly presidentialist charter to emerge from the Constituent Congress, given Fujimori's majority, his marked authoritarian streak, and the fragmentation of the opposition. Indeed, the new Constitution, narrowly approved in an October 1993 referendum, allows the president to serve two consecutive terms and gives the chief executive authority over high-level military promotions and ambassadorial appointments. The 1993 Constitution also stipulates that Congress can be dissolved and new elections held if only two, instead of three, cabinets are censured or denied confidence.[16] More importantly, whereas the president previously could dissolve only the lower chamber, unicameralism and explicit provisions on votes of confidence make dissolution a more viable political option. In a major departure from previous charters, constitutional amendments must be approved by (1) two-thirds of the members of Congress in consecutive regular sessions; or (2) an absolute majority of Congress and a favorable vote in a national referendum.

Nevertheless, the pro-Fujimori majority, which followed the wishes of the president, backed away from a comprehensive overhaul of executive–legislative relations. Although some of Fujimori's advisers had circulated a hyperpresidentialist draft in December 1992,[17] the Constitution Committee used the 1979 Charter and some specific proposals from the majority as the points of departure for debate.[18] The new constitution could not be seen as perpetuating the president's authoritarian rule. An opposition boycott of the Constituent Congress or of the referendum to approve the new Charter could have tarnished Fujimori in the eyes of the United States and other key international actors, who had reserved final judgment on the process of redemocratization.

The 1993 Constitution maintains previous voting margins for veto overrides, interpellations, and censures, while continuing to allow congressional rules to define margins for votes of confidence, declarations of vacancy, and impeachment. Moreover, unicameralism further undermines the already weak presidential veto. Peru's latest Charter also abolishes the previously required two-thirds majority for censure during the last year of the five-year term; it places significant new restrictions on DDA, emergency CDA, and standard CDA; and it eliminates the executive's role in judicial appointments.

Fujimori won a landslide victory in the 1995 presidential election, receiving 64 percent of the valid vote in a field of fourteen candidates. Moreover, his NM-C90 alliance, whose list of candidates was selected by a small committee of presidential confidants and presumably approved by Fujimori himself, claimed 67 of 120 seats in the new unicameral Congress. Of the 44 NM-C90 delegates to the Constituent Congress, 42 reportedly wanted to run for Congress in 1995,[19] 28 were included on the NM-C90 list, and 24 won election.[20]

In August 1996 Congress tried to make Fujimori eligible for a second reelection in 2000 by passing Law 26,657, which stipulates that any presidential term initiated before the 1993 Constitution took effect is not to be counted toward the limit of two consecutive periods of service. This statute soon came under legal challenge, and the president's eligibility for reelection remains in doubt, as discussed in the penultimate section of this chapter.

EXECUTIVE DECREE AUTHORITY

Myriad decrees emanating from the Palace of Pizarro in Lima are poorly understood. As elsewhere, understanding has been hampered by the failure to distinguish among different kinds of decree authority and inconsistencies in terminology. This section provides an overview of the sources, instruments, and frequency of decree. It then analyzes the roles of the cabinet and Congress vis-à-vis executive decree authority.

INSTITUTIONAL SOURCES OF DECREE

Employing the typology developed in Chapter 1, Table 4.2 lists the various sorts of executive decree authority under Peru's three modern charters, their consti-

Table 4.2 *Typology of executive decree authority in Peru*

Type of decree authority	Relevant articles in respective constitutions		
	1933	1979	1993
Delegated Authority			
Rule making	154(8)	211(11)	118(8)
	DS, RS	DS, RS	DS, RS
Legislative (DDA)	40, 49, 123(23)	188, 211(10)	104
	DS*	DLeg	DLeg
Constitutional Decree Authority (CDA)			
Emergency powers	70	132, 211(18), 231	118(15), 137
	DS	DS	DS
Standard decree authority	154(8)	211(11)	118(8)
Residual	DS, RS	DS, RS	DS, RS
Economics and finance			
(general purpose in		211(20)	118(19)
practice)		DS, DSE	DU
Tariffs		211(22)	118(20)
		DS, RS	DS
International agreements		104	57
or treaties		DS, RS	DS, RS
Budget and executed			
budget (if Congress			
fails to act by		198, 200	80, 81
deadline)		DLeg	DLeg

Codes for Legal Instruments: DS – *Decreto Supremo*; RS – *Resolución Supremo*; DS* – *Decreto Supremo with Force of Law*; DLeg – *Decreto Legislativo*; DSE – *Decreto Supremo Extraordinario*; DU – *Decreto de Urgencia*

tutional basis, and the most common legal instruments used in their implementation. The discussion here follows the scheme in the table.

Provisions for rule-making authority have been included in all of the country's major constitutions. In contrast the 1933 Charter foresaw DDA only for the specific purposes of limiting property rights and lowering the price of basic goods, as outlined in Articles 40 and 49. However, Article 123(23), which allowed Congress "[t]o exercise the remaining essential attributes of legislative power," was sometimes interpreted as a license for broad legislative delegation. A procedure for DDA is explicitly outlined in Articles 188 and 211(10) of the 1979 Constitution and in Article 104 of the 1993 Charter. These articles allow Congress to delegate legislative authority on (a) matter(s) and for a time period specified in the authorizing law. Subsequent congressional approval of presidential decrees issued under DDA is not constitutionally mandated.

All three modern constitutions have given the president emergency powers to suspend civil liberties in times of unrest, as outlined in Articles 70, 231, and 137 of the 1933, 1979, and 1993 Charters respectively. Article 211(18) of the 1979 Constitution and Article 118(15) of the 1993 Charter provide the chief executive with extensive wartime powers, but they have never been invoked. Article 132 of the 1979 Constitution, which gave the state extraordinary economic authority in emergency situations, was cited in the 1987 decree issued by President García to seize control of private banks and insurance companies.

There are several types of standard CDA in Peru. All three modern constitutions have allowed a sort of residual CDA that permits the president to issue decrees as long as he or she does not contravene existing laws. Thus, chief executives have been able to promulgate decrees that are not based on any specific law. Recent charters also have given presidents the authority to grant pardons, although this is a subject beyond the scope of this chapter.

The most important and controversial type of standard CDA originated in an obscure passage in Article 211(20) of the 1979 Constitution. The last part of this article allowed the president "to dictate extraordinary measures on economic and financial matters, when so required by the national interest and with the duty to give notice (*dar cuenta*) to the Congress." Beginning in the second Belaunde administration, the executive maintained that decrees issued under 211(20) had the force of law, and, indeed, these extraordinary measures sometimes superseded legislation passed by Congress. Because "economic and financial matters" could be stretched to cover almost any subject, Article 211(20) became a form of general purpose CDA in practice.

Because Article 211(20) was so controversial, it could plausibly be classified as a paraconstitutional source of decree authority. However, as decrees based on Article 211(20) became routine during the 1980s under the Belaunde and García administrations, constitutional interpretation evolved to support this article as a legitimate basis for CDA. By the beginning of Fujimori's first term, even most critics of 211(20) accepted this article as a bona fide source of executive decree, but they debated how to best place limits on its use. A more explicit version of Article 211(20) appears in the 1993 Constitution as Article 118(19).

Additional, specific sources of standard CDA are also present in the 1979 and 1993 charters. Article 211(22) of the former and Article 118(20) of the latter have given the president authority to set tariffs. Although both the 1933 and 1979 Constitutions required congressional approval of treaties, under Article 104 of the latter Charter, the president could contract, ratify, or adhere to international agreements "in matters of his (her) exclusive competence" without the prior approval of Congress. For example, in May 1991 President Fujimori infuriated legislators by signing an antinarcotics agreement with the United States without consultation. Congress subsequently specified certain topical restrictions on international executive agreements in the Law of Parliamentary Control. Articles 56 and 57 of the 1993 Constitution eliminate the distinction between treaties and international agreements, while using the same sort of criteria outlined by the Law of Parliamentary Control to define a residual sphere of executive authority.[21]

Finally, Articles 198 and 200 of the 1979 Charter and Articles 80 and 81 of the 1993 Constitution have allowed the president to promulgate his (her) budget proposal or to approve the Controller General's audit of the executed budget (called the *Cuenta General*) if Congress fails to meet certain deadlines. The 1985, 1987, and 1989 budget laws were decreed in this manner, although in each case the executive had adopted the proposal of the Bicameral Budget Committee. However, in an interesting legal twist, the 1985 and 1989 budget laws delegated authority to the executive, using this limited form of CDA as a source of DDA.[22]

LEGAL INSTRUMENTS

As is glaringly obvious in Table 4.2, there is not a one-to-one correspondence in the three constitutions between the various types of decree authority and the legal instruments employed to issue executive decrees. Several legal instruments have been used to implement more than one kind of decree authority, and most sorts of decree have been carried out through more than one legal instrument. Thus, one often must read individual decrees in order to classify them by type of decree authority.

Prior to the 1979 Constitution, all major kinds of executive decree authority were exercised through *Decretos Supremos* (DSs), which are issued by the president. In the case of DDA, chief executives promulgated DSs "with the force of law." *Resoluciónes Supremas* (RSs), which are issued by ministers with the president's initials, were also used for rule making and residual CDA. Under the 1979 and 1993 Charters, emergency CDA has continued to be exerted through DSs, whereas DSs and RSs have remained the legal instruments for rule making, residual CDA, and international agreements or treaties. Article 74 of the 1993 Constitution stipulates that tariffs are to be regulated by DSs, whereas either DSs or RSs could be used under the 1979 Charter.

The 1979 Constitution created the *Decreto Legislativo* (DLeg) for exercising DDA. DLegs also could be employed to promulgate the budget and *Cuenta General* if Congress failed to act, serving in this capacity as an instrument of CDA. Under the 1993 Charter, DLegs continue to be utilized for both purposes.

Several legal instruments have been used to exercise the controversial CDA that originated in Article 211(20) of the 1979 Constitution. Decrees promulgated under 211(20) were initially issued as DSs. They were later called *Decretos Supremos Extraordinarios* (DSEs) under the Law of Parliamentary Control. Article 118(19) of the 1993 Charter, which replaced Article 211(20), created a new decree mechanism, the *Decreto de Urgencia* (DU), for this type of CDA.

FREQUENCY UNDER THE 1979 CONSTITUTION

Table 4.3 contains data on the most important kinds of decrees issued under the 1979 Constitution from July 28, 1980, to April 5, 1992. During this period Presidents Belaunde, García, and Fujimori promulgated 768 DLegs. Only three

Table 4.3 *Number of executive decrees issued by each administration under the 1979 Peruvian Constitution**

Type	Number per presidential term (Number per month during term)			
Legal instrument	Fernando Belaunde 1980–85	Alan García 1985–90	Alberto Fujimori 1990–92	Total
Delegated decree authority (DDA)				
DLeg	348 (6)	262 (4)	158 (8)	768 (5)
Constitutional decree authority (CDA) DS under				
Art.211 (20)	667 (11)	1,338 (22)	575[a] (29)	2,580 (18)
Residual CDA; also rule-making authority within bounds of existing legislation.				
Other DS	5,990 (100)	4,860 (81)	1,339 (67)	12,189 (87)

*Rate of decrees (number per month) in parentheses
[a]Of these, 32 were issued as *Decretos Supremos Extraordinarios* after passage of the Law of Parliamentary Control (Law 25,397) in February 1992.
Sources: Abad Yupanqui and Garcés Peralta (1993:103), Delgado-Guembes (1992: 226–7), and unpublished data supplied by César Landa Arroyo.

of these decrees concerned the budget; the rest were used to exercise DDA. Article 211(20) CDA was the basis of 2,580 DSs, whereas 12,189 DSs were published under other auspices, primarily residual CDA and rule-making authority. These three presidents also initialed tens of thousands of RSs, again primarily for residual CDA and rule making.

Although DLegs were more versatile and had greater legitimacy than 211(20) DSs, many measures could be implemented through the latter once it gained general acceptance. Moreover, whereas these executives had to anticipate congressional expectations when requesting DDA, they could use 211(20) CDA to create a fait accompli that was harder for Congress to alter (cf. Timothy Power's chapter in this volume on the use of decrees in Brazil). The ratio of 211(20) DS to DLegs was 1.9:1 under Belaunde. It soared to 5.1:1 under García, who preferred to totally bypass Congress; and then it declined somewhat to 3.6:1 under Fujimori.

Nevertheless, the frequency and relative importance of major executive decrees increased overall under Fujimori, who promulgated measures under both DDA and 211(20) CDA – about 8 and 29 per month respectively – at a rate higher than either of his predecessors (see Table 4.3). Even disregarding the 30 DLegs issued under Law 25,327 that were repealed or modified by Congress, more *Decretos Legislativos* ultimately became law per month under Fujimori than under either Belaunde or García. Most striking is the fact that the ratio of major executive decrees (DLegs and 211[20] DSs) to laws enacted through the conventional legislative process increased from 1.4 under Belaunde to 2.4 under García, and then to 10.9 (!) under Fujimori.[23]

THE CABINET CONNECTION

All official acts of Peruvian presidents, including decrees, must be countersigned by one or more ministers. In addition the full cabinet must approve all DLegs and DUs, as well as DSs and RSs specified by law (1993 Const. Art. 125[2]). Peruvian ministers, however, do not exercise independent political authority, because the chief executive can dismiss the cabinet or any of its members. When a minister refuses to ratify a decree, presidents usually ask another member of the cabinet to countersign, or they arrange for the vice-minister to do so when the minister is out of the country.[24]

Nevertheless, the requirement of ministerial approval appears to exert a moderating influence on executive decree authority and may even work against agency loss by Congress. Ministers are politically accountable to the legislature, as well as to the president, and are also legally responsible for the acts that they sign or countersign. In addition the cabinet as a whole is responsible for any violations of the Constitution or the law by the chief executive; a minister is absolved of this responsibility only if (s)he resigns. Ministers or former ministers can be impeached and prosecuted for using decree authority in an illegal or unconstitutional way – or for allowing a president to do so!

Members of Congress have frequently held key cabinet posts. Indeed, all but one prime minister during the 1980–90 period were members of the legislature (Chirinos Soto 1991:89). Although Fujimori has seldom appointed members of Congress to his cabinets, Dante Córdova, the first prime minister to serve in his second term, is an exception. Because the tenure of a cabinet member is almost always shorter than a legislative term, ministers holding seats in Congress are usually motivated to maintain good relations with their congressional colleagues. During the 1980s two long-serving prime ministers, Manuel Ulloa and Luis Alva Castro, were elected president of their respective chambers after returning full-time to Congress.

The cabinet is a deliberative institution, one which is chaired by the prime minister in the president's absence. Some decrees proposed by Fujimori, who attended fewer than half of all the cabinet meetings held before the *autogolpe*, were modified during the course of cabinet debate.[25] Moreover, after strong opposition in Congress and by his own cabinet, in early 1991 the president backed away from decrees of dubious constitutionality, such as those that would have established a regional development authority in Peru's principal coca-growing region and set up a sort of parallel cabinet in charge of increasing direct citizen participation in decision making.[26]

CONGRESSIONAL CONTROL OVER
DELEGATED AUTHORITY

Ultimate congressional control over delegated authority (rule making and DDA), as well as residual CDA, is well established. Since at least the 1860s, Peruvian congresses have not hesitated to repeal executive decrees (Basadre 1983, V.9:41, 43–4). By virtue of a long tradition and explicit articles in the 1979 and 1993 Constitutions, laws supersede acts of an inferior category, such as DSs and RSs used for rule making and residual CDA.[27] If a decree of either kind should transgress or pervert existing legislation, Congress can repeal it by passing a new law. Indeed, many Peruvian statutes include a generic clause that revokes any conflicting law or decree already on the books. Similarly, DLegs used to exercise DDA can be modified or repealed through legislation, as already illustrated.

In addition to ex post legislation, Congress has frequently exerted ex ante control over DDA through provisions of dubious constitutionality, and it has done so in enabling statutes that establish intermediary commissions primarily or exclusively composed of legislators. Although the names and composition of these intermediary commissions have varied, all have been empowered to (1) review or revise the draft decree proposed by the executive, or (2) elaborate a draft decree for the president to promulgate. The executive sometimes has been represented on commissions performing the first function and is usually represented on those that undertook the second.

The first mode of ex ante control has been used frequently for tax legislation. Although intermediary commissions were largely window dressing during the 1980s, a period when pro-government majorities controlled Congress, they became more assertive during the 1990–92 period.[28] In 1991, for example, an APRA-dominated Special Bicameral Economic Commission rejected a proposed decree establishing a "solidarity tax" on Peruvians with relatively high incomes, one that was drafted by Economics Minister Boloña, although it did approve an extraordinary one-time levy on assets (DLeg 643).

The second sort of ex ante control – under which enabling statutes establish intermediate commissions to draft legislation for the president to promulgate – has been employed less frequently.[29] However, the distinction between the two modes blurs when an intermediary commission has the authority to revise decrees drafted by the executive. In the case of legal codes, which are usually enacted through DDA, the commissions have often significantly altered the executive's proposal, in effect crafting much of the legislation themselves. Presidents cannot modify draft codes adopted by intermediary commissions in this manner, but they can decline to use their DDA to promulgate them.[30]

CONGRESS AND CDA

In marked contrast to delegated authority and residual CDA, the power of Congress to annul, suspend, or repeal both decrees issued under emergency and most types of standard CDA was never firmly established while the 1979 Constitution was in effect. This lack of authority was largely academic as long as the legislature was controlled by pro-government majorities during the 1980s, but it became increasingly untenable after Fujimori took office.

Almost all CDA was exercised through DSs or RSs, which were subordinate to laws under Article 87 of the 1979 Charter. Moreover, as discussed later in this chapter, Congress' authority to overturn 211(20) DSs had been explicitly recognized during the 1980s by one of Belaunde's economics ministers and in 1990 by Fujimori's first labor minister. However, Article 87 also established the supremacy of the Constitution – and thus, arguably, decrees used to carry out CDA – over laws. Following the latter line of reasoning, Fujimori ignored an article in the 1991 budget law that prohibited its modification by 211(20) decrees, and then he used this source of CDA to repeatedly countermand budgetary legislation passed by Congress.

Congress was extremely reluctant to directly challenge 211(20) decrees, although they were sometimes superseded by subsequent legislation.[31] It did not annul a decree based on 211(20) until early 1992 – at the peak of the confrontation with Fujimori.[32] Law 25,401 of February 7, 1992, overturned two such decrees that had established sanctions against striking teachers. While Congress was in its summer recess, the president vetoed another bill that would have annulled a 211(20) decree modifying the income tax system (*Resumen Semanal*, Nos. 651, 654, 657). Legislators never got a chance to override this veto, due to the *autogolpe*. Had they done so, the president could have simply reissued the decree on the basis of his competing claim to constitutional authority.

The Law of Parliamentary Control was a more systematic congressional attempt to check emergency and standard CDA by invoking a superior source of constitutional authority. This statute cites Article 186(2) of the 1979 Charter, which specifies the following power as an attribute of Congress: "To oversee adherence to the Constitution and to the laws, and to take appropriate steps to hold violators accountable." Prominent legal scholars and legislators also argued that Congress could regulate CDA and DDA on the basis of "to give notice" (*dar cuenta*) clauses in the respective articles of the Charter, which they interpreted to mean a rendering of accounts for congressional review and potential action.[33]

Some specific provisions of the Law of Parliamentary Control are treated in subsequent sections of this chapter. Here it is important to note that this law established a sort of constitutional review by Congress for four types of CDA under the 1979 Charter: emergency powers (Art. 231), emergency economic powers (Art. 132), economic and financial matters (Art. 211[20]), and international agreements (Art. 104). The law empowered Congress, meeting in joint session, to suspend any decree deemed to be at odds with the respective constitutional criteria, as fleshed out in the law itself. This statute did not establish a right to legislate on these matters or to overturn an executive decree on the basis of substantive policy disagreements, although the latter possibility could have occurred under the guise of constitutional interpretation.

In vetoing the Law of Parliamentary Control, Fujimori argued that Congress' interpretation of Article 186(2) was erroneous and violated the principle of separation of powers. This article, he maintained, could not be used to restrict the executive's constitutional authority, nor did "to give notice" (*dar cuenta*) mean anything more than informing Congress. According to the president, only the Tribunal of Constitutional Guarantees and the courts could rule on the constitutionality or legality of executive decrees.[34] Indeed, Fujimori and his supporters later maintained that Peru's constitutional order was disrupted by the Law of Parliamentary Control rather than by the *autogolpe*.[35] Nevertheless, the president ultimately accepted significant constraints on emergency and standard CDA in the 1993 Charter.

RULE MAKING

Executive rule-making authority is exercised through DSs and RSs. The former, which are intended for more general matters, must be signed by the president and countersigned by one or more ministers. A specific kind of DS is the *reglamento*, a set of comprehensive administrative regulations that fleshes out and interprets a major law or DLeg. RSs, which are supposed to treat more specific matters, are signed by the relevant minister and only initialed by the president (Furnish 1971:113–15; DLeg 217, Art. 3).

DSs and RSs are part of a hierarchy of decrees that has largely evolved through custom and usage (Furnish 1971:92, 112). DSs take precedence over RSs, which in turn have more legal weight than administrative decrees issued solely by ministers and lower ranking officials. Reality, however, is considerably messier. Whether a decree should be a DS or RS is often a matter of judgment. Presidents have been known to camouflage policies on sensitive issues through RSs or even administrative decrees of lesser rank. Conversely, regulations on relatively narrow matters are sometimes issued by DSs in order to elevate their importance and legal standing.[36]

Because legislation in Peru, as elsewhere, is often vague, significant agency loss can occur in the often numbing details of *reglamentos* and other rules. Presidents sometimes have attempted to use rule-making authority to implement policies that are not consistent with congressional preferences. On other occasions they have delayed the promulgation of *reglamentos*, without which most major legislation cannot be implemented.

THE EVOLUTION OF DDA

The 1933 Constitution did not establish a procedure or legal instrument for DDA. Nevertheless, the 1931–36 Constituent Congress delegated authority to the chief executive on several occasions and gave President Benavides broad legislative powers during the three-year extension of his term. Using Articles 40, 49, or 123(23), which were discussed earlier, or simply using the rationale that delegation was not constitutionally prohibited, subsequent congresses passed at least ten different enabling statutes for DDA before 1968.[37]

DDA was first used prolifically in 1968.[38] As Belaunde's first term drew to a close, APRA, which smelled victory in the 1969 election, realized that continued obstruction of tax legislation would, at best, lead to its inheritance of fiscal chaos, and, at worst, provoke a military coup. Thus, APRA and most of Belaunde's AP cooperated to resolve the impasse. On June 19 Congress passed Law 17,044, which provided Belaunde with DDA for sixty days to "dictate measures of extraordinary character to solve the structural disequilibrium in public finances, to strengthen the country's international balance of payments and to encourage the integrated development of our economy." Although members of a new cabinet friendly to APRA had to approve the decrees, *aprista* leaders avoided congressional review, because they did not want to be held responsible for new taxes.

In a torrent of over 300 DSs issued under Law 17,044, Belaunde and Finance Minister Manuel Ulloa overhauled the Peruvian fiscal and financial systems. Severely stretching the authority of the enabling legislation, the government also negotiated the settlement of a longstanding and highly sensitive dispute with the International Petroleum Company (IPC), a subsidiary of Exxon. The fiscal reforms implemented under Law 17,044 were remarkably successful in restoring economic confidence, but their positive impact was soon eclipsed by controversy over the IPC settlement, which ironically became the immediate precipitant of the October 3, 1968, coup.

Under Article 188 of the 1979 Constitution, "[T]he Congress may delegate to the Executive Branch the power to legislate, by means of *decretos legislativos*, on the matters and until the deadline that the authorizing law specifies." Article 188 did not place any restrictions on subjects that could be delegated, but some prominent scholars and legislators maintained that other provisions in the Charter precluded the use of DDA for constitutional functions, such as approving international treaties or amendments; tax and budgetary legislation; statutes mandated by the Constitution; and organic laws, which have a higher rank in Peru's legal hierarchy.[39] Although Congress has jealously guarded its constitutional prerogatives, during the 1980s pro-government majorities ignored the other potential proscriptions on the use of DDA and instead delegated authority for most constitutionally mandated statutes, fifty-two organic laws, key tax legislation, and modifications of the budget.[40]

During the 1980s DLegs usually dealt with more substantive issues – such as governmental organization, legal codes, public finance, banking, and development – than did laws passed by Congress. The Belaunde and García administrations, their supporters in Congress, and sometimes even members of the opposition maintained that extensive delegation on these matters was justified by their complexity, technical character, or urgency. However, perhaps the primary motive for delegating authority was avoidance of extensive congressional debate on sensitive topics, especially taxation and austerity measures (Eguiguren 1990b:181–3). Although there were various proposals during the decade to eliminate or restrict DDA through constitutional amendment or statute, none was brought to a vote. Only one DLeg was repealed during the 1980s.

Frustrated by the extensive use of DDA and the short-circuiting of congressional debate, opposition parties frequently charged that pro-government majorities had abdicated their legislative responsibilities by passing vague or excessively broad authorizing laws and by failing to review DLegs promulgated by the president – or that the executive had exceeded the scope of delegation. These allegations were often little more than political rhetoric, but some had merit. For example, Law 23,230 of December 1980 gave the executive 180 days to modify or repeal much of the legislation enacted by military governments during the 1968–80 period. Yet under its auspices, the Belaunde administration altered legal norms that antedated the previous regime, revised laws passed by the military that were not covered by the enabling statute, and even issued DLegs that did not address any specific legislation passed during the aforementioned period.[41]

During the 1990–92 period extreme partisan fragmentation in both chambers of the legislature greatly complicated collective action on critical issues. Congress was unable to pass any legislation during the first 2 ½ months of its first session, and the first five laws that it approved were enabling statutes for DDA. As discussed previously, Law 25,327, by far the most important authorizing statute during this period, provided Fujimori with DDA for pacification, job creation, and the promotion of private investment. There was broad consensus in Congress that major changes in policy were desirable on each of these issues, but it was difficult to reach agreement on specific legislation.[42] Thus, legislators delegated authority to the president despite his strident attacks on their institution.

Enabling statutes were passed at a higher rate under Fujimori before the *autogolpe* (15 in 20 months) than under Belaunde (26 in 60 months), but they were passed at a slower pace than under García (51 in 60 months).[43] Moreover, as previously noted, Fujimori actually employed DDA more often than his two predecessors, who both had congressional majorities. This higher rate of DDA under Fujimori is all the more remarkable because he also used 211–20 CDA more frequently than either Belaunde or García (see Table 4.3).

Although the Law of Parliamentary Control was passed in the aftermath of the November 1991 deluge of DLegs, this statute mostly dealt with CDA. The law's provisions regarding DDA were essentially a commitment not to abdicate authority in the future: they required more specific criteria in enabling statutes and outlined a procedure for reviewing DLegs. Congress' right to repeal DLegs was taken for granted. After the *autogolpe* the 1992–95 Constituent Congress approved authorizing legislation far less frequently than in previous periods – only five enabling statutes in thirty-one months. Less than one DLeg was promulgated per month – a much slower pace than under previous administrations.

The 1993 Constitution, rather surprisingly, places greater restrictions on DDA than the 1979 Charter and potentially narrows its scope by calling for a "specific matter" to be delineated in the enabling statute. No longer may Congress delegate authority to pass organic laws (now defined as those dealing with institutions and matters specified in the Charter) or the budget, initiate constitutional amendments, or approve treaties (1993 Const. Arts. 101[4], 104, 106). However, Article 74 explicitly allows DDA to be used for tax legislation, thus putting an end to a major controversy since 1979. The other major change is that Congress can now delegate legislative authority to its Permanent Committee, although the same proscriptions apply. Supporters of this provision argued that it will reduce the use of DDA (Torres y Torres Lara 1994:66–68,74).

Although Fujimori has a congressional majority in his current term (1995–2000), during his first sixteen months in office, enabling statutes (5) and DLegs (about 6 per month) were less frequent than in the 1990–92 period.[44] This low incidence of DDA is not explained by the new role of the Permanent Committee, which had not passed any legislation at the time of this writing (in late 1997). Among the laws enacted by DDA during this most recent period are the establishment of the Ministry of Women and Human Development (DLeg 866) and the very controversial privatization of health care services provided by the social security system (DLeg 887).

Over the years several significant procedural issues have arisen with regard to DDA. More than a score of DLegs on security matters have never been published, in apparent violation of the 1979 and 1993 Constitutions. An additional irritant, particularly under Fujimori, has been substantive alteration of DLegs through "corrections" subsequently published in the official gazette.[45] Moreover, during the November 1991 deluge of decrees, First Vice-President Máximo San Román signed three DLegs while Fujimori was abroad, although he did not have clear constitutional authority to do so.

EMERGENCY CDA

Article 70 of the 1933 Constitution allowed the executive to suspend certain civil liberties (protection against arbitrary detentions, searches of domiciles without warrants, and exile; freedom of assembly and travel) "[w]hen the security of the State may require it." Article 231 of the 1979 Charter outlined two regimes of exception: the state of emergency and the state of siege. The former could be enacted in the event of internal disorder, catastrophe, or grave circumstances; could last for sixty days, with no limit on renewal; and had effects similar to the suspension of guarantees under the 1933 Constitution, although exile was proscribed. The more serious state of siege could be decreed in the case of invasion, foreign war, civil war, or the imminent threat of any of these three. All personal guarantees, except arguably those protected by the Inter-American Human Rights Convention, could potentially be suspended for periods of up to forty-five days (Eguiguren 1989:265, 278). Congress only had to be given notice (the *dar cuenta* clause) of states of emergency, but it was required to immediately convene upon the promulgation of a state of siege and to approve any extension of such a state of siege.

No state of siege was declared while the 1979 Constitution was in effect, but a majority of Peruvians eventually lived under constantly renewed states of emergency promulgated in response to the Shining Path and the MRTA. Opposition political parties, especially those on the left, frequently attacked the counterinsurgency policies of the Belaunde and García administrations, and they condemned often flagrant abuses of human rights by government security forces. Nevertheless, the executive's use of emergency CDA per se was not challenged by Congress in the 1980s (see Power Manchego-Muñoz 1989:177–8).

Much more controversial was the establishment of Political-Military Commands (CPMs), through which a military officer coordinated the operations of the entire public sector in some regions on the basis of a sentence in Article 231 that allowed the president to put the military in charge of internal order (see García Sayán 1987:286). However, in June 1985, shortly before the end of Belaunde's second term, Congress incorporated the CPMs into law. Taking advantage of an ambiguity in Article 231, the Belaunde administration also passed legislation that was interpreted by most courts as suppressing the use of habeas corpus and *amparo* (the protection of fundamental rights other than personal liberty) in the areas under emergency rule.[46]

After Fujimori became president, Congress took a more restrictive view of the executive's emergency CDA powers without directly challenging the periodic renewal of states of emergency. In February 1991 legislators overturned a decree of dubious constitutionality that had placed all actions of military personnel in emergency zones under the jurisdiction of military courts (*Resumen Semanal*, Nos: 601, 607). Overriding a veto in February 1992, Congress passed Law 25,398, which prohibited the suspension of habeas corpus and *amparo* during states of emergency or siege (Fernández Segado 1994:59). Through the Law of Parliamentary Control, legislators claimed authority to void regimes of exception that they deemed to violate Article 231.

Article 137 of the 1993 Constitution basically reiterates the regimes of exception established by the 1979 Charter, although some changes in its language point to more restrained use. However, Article 200 stipulates that the processes of habeas corpus and *amparo* cannot be suspended during either states of emergency or siege, and it allows judicial review of measures taken under both regimes of exception.[47] More than two years into Fujimori's second term, neither the Shining Path nor the MRTA had been totally defeated, and emergency CDA was still being used routinely.

STANDARD CDA BY "CONSTITUTIONAL MUTATION"

The 1978–79 Constituent Assembly, which was wary of a powerful executive after twelve years of military government, rejected explicit provisions for CDA approved by its Principal Committee, the body charged with reconciling drafts approved by other committees. Nevertheless it approved the previously quoted passage in Article 211(20), with little debate. Most delegates apparently did not realize that this article could become a constitutional source of executive decree, because the debate over CDA had centered on other proposals. Moreover, the wording of Article 211(20) (i.e., "extraordinary measures") reassuringly resembled Law 17,044, the statute passed at the end of Belaunde's first term that had authorized the most important use of DDA prior to 1979 (Eguiguren 1990a: 29–33).

The Belaunde and García administrations employed Article 211(20) to modify laws and to enact policies without any delegation of authority from Congress. This article was frequently used for tax legislation and to approve credit agreements, even though Articles 139 and 140 of the 1979 Constitution stipulated that laws were required for governmental action on these matters. Among other important and controversial uses of 211(20) were frequent changes in annual budget statutes, the establishment of foreign exchange controls, and the 1987 takeover of banks and insurance companies. (The latter was also based on Article 132.) Other 211(20) DSs dealt with more mundane matters, including the approval of regulations for bingo games (Eguiguren 1990b:233–5).

The frequent use of Article 211(20) to promulgate important and not-so-important policies prompted a debate over executive decree authority. Responding to an inquiry by the Senate Constitution Committee after he had used 211(20) to make major changes in the 1983 budget statute, Economics Minister Carlos Rodríguez Pastor argued that DSs issued under this article were tantamount to laws. He did, however, recognize Congress' authority to overturn these decrees through legislation.[48] Although the Constitution Committee concluded that the executive's use of Article 211(20) was unconstitutional (Rubio and Bernales 1988:402), during the 1980s various proposals to assert congressional authority through legislation or constitutional amendment failed to gain adequate political support (Fernández-Maldonado Castro and Melo-Vega Castro 1989:405–7). Moreover, under both Belaunde and García, pro-government majorities did not attempt to annul 211(20) DSs or to challenge ministers who had countersigned them (Eguiguren 1990b:225).

Although some respected scholars argued that 211(20) decrees could not have the force of law,[49] the dominant current of constitutional interpretation evolved to provide qualified support for Rodríguez Pastor's position.[50] Writing in 1990, Francisco Eguiguren, a leading expert on the 1979 Charter, maintained that congressional acquiescence to the executive's frequent use of Article 211(20) during the 1980s had created "a sort of constitutional mutation." Yet, Eguiguren and most others who viewed 211(20) as a source of CDA also believed that this article had been abused by the executive and called for limits on its use (Eguiguren 1990b:215–16).

The political spotlight once again focused on Article 211(20) when Fujimori used this form of CDA to implement shock economic policies in August 1990. Barely a month after the new president had assumed office, Labor Minister Carlos Torres y Torres Lara, who had countersigned two key austerity decrees, resurrected Rodríguez Pastor's arguments, bluntly asserting that measures issued under 211(20) could modify laws. His remarks sparked a firestorm of protest in Congress and the press. However, most leading constitutional scholars and the Lima Bar Association essentially supported Torres y Torres Lara's position. After the minister had recognized congressional authority to overturn 211(20) decrees, C90 and the ex-FREDEMO parties defeated a motion of censure by APRA and the left (see Torres y Torres Lara 1991).

Before the *autogolpe* Fujimori issued 211(20) decrees at a pace a third faster than García and at more than 2 ½ times the rate of Belaunde (see Table 4.3). Following the examples of his predecessors, he employed Article 211(20) to modify the budget, the annual finance law, and tax legislation. Fujimori also broke new ground by using 211(20) DSs to make basic changes in labor legislation, to enact numerous austerity measures, and to strengthen property rights in agriculture.[51]

Although Congress and most constitutional scholars acknowledged Fujimori's right to invoke Article 211(20), an emerging consensus also favored limits on its use. The Law of Parliamentary Control stipulated that executive decree authority based on this article, as well as on Article 132, was to be exercised through a new legal instrument, the DSE, which could remain in effect for no longer than six months and had to be approved by the cabinet and initialed by the prime minister. DSEs could "suspend the effects of law" in order to "restructure" the budget, "temporarily modify or suspend taxes," complete emergency credit operations, and intervene in the economy in accordance with Article 132 (law 25,397, Art. 4). The law also stipulated that the Constitution Committees of each chamber were to review DSEs within fifteen days to verify that each decree fulfilled constitutional and procedural criteria. In the case of a negative finding, Congress or its Permanent Committee could choose to suspend the DSE.

Between the publication of the Law of Parliamentary Control in early February 1992 and the April 5 *autogolpe*, the Fujimori administration complied with the statute, submitting thirty-two DSEs to Congress. Most of these decrees modified tax legislation, including major changes that could not be enacted through DDA because Congress had refused to delegate the necessary authority after the November 1991 deluge of DLegs.[52] Nevertheless, hoping to pass some of the tax reforms into law after an accommodation with the president, the ex-FREDEMO parties defeated an effort by APRA and the left to have the Permanent Committee suspend or overturn these DSEs before Congress reconvened.[53] After the *autogolpe*, in another ironic twist, the Constituent Congress employed the Law of Parliamentary Control to review DSEs used to enact financial commitments in order to assure creditors of their legal validity.[54]

The hyperpresidentialist draft of a new Constitution circulated by some of Fujimori's advisers contained provisions for sweeping executive decree powers, including absolute authority over government organization, counterinsurgency, and national defense. Nevertheless, the Constitution Committee of the Constituent Congress rapidly reached consensus on adjustments to the basic paradigm of standard CDA that had evolved during the 1980–92 period.[55] Following the lead of the Law of Parliamentary Control, Article 118(19) of the 1993 Charter states that DUs – as the decrees used to exercise CDA for economic and financial matters are now called – have "the force of law." However, in contrast to the Law of Parliamentary Control's rather oblique model of congressional oversight through constitutional interpretation and review, this article straightforwardly establishes Congress' authority to modify or annul DUs for whatever reason it may choose. The executive, moreover, will not be able to veto legislative resolutions overturning or altering DUs.

Unlike DSEs issued under the Law of Parliamentary Control, there is no time limit for DUs, but the latter cannot be employed for tax legislation, which had been the single most important use of 211(20) decrees (1993 Const. Art. 74). This proscription and the executive's apparent willingness to accept congressional oversight may reflect a realization that unfettered CDA had contributed to an uncertain business climate, especially from the perspective of international investors.[56] More generally, Fujimori's neoliberal policies, now enshrined in the new Charter, can be expected to decrease government intervention in the economy – and thus the frequency of economic and financial CDA. Indeed, whereas about eighteen DSs based on Article 211(20) were issued each month during the 1980–92 period, with a sharp upward trend during this period (see Table 4.3), DUs averaged only nine per month during the first three years of the 1993 Constitution.[57]

Despite its less frequent use, this form of standard CDA continues to spark controversy. Many recent DUs have been used to exempt public agencies from competitive bidding procedures, such as when a presidential airplane was purchased in 1995.[58] In November 1996 this instrument was employed to procure a dozen MIG-29 fighters from Belarus, escalating the arms race with neighboring Ecuador.

In the unlikely event that the president dissolves Congress under the 1993 Charter, (s)he may govern through DUs until a new Congress is elected (Art. 135). Although DUs cannot be used for tax legislation during this interlude, it is not clear that they are restricted to economic and financial matters. Thus, if this situation were to arise, yet another strain of standard CDA might emerge from a new "constitutional mutation."

JUDICIAL REVIEW

Prior to the 1979 Constitution, judicial relief from unconstitutional or illegal norms was possible only on a case-by-case basis (Furnish 1971:99–110, 118). The principle of constitutional supremacy was explicitly established in Articles 87 and 236 of the 1979 Charter, which created a hybrid judicial system combining a European-style constitutional tribunal with a U.S.-style, litigation-based review in the regular courts. By 1992 this hybrid system had begun to play an important role in mediating disputes involving executive decrees, although the reputation of the judiciary was badly soiled by widespread allegations of corruption, politicization, incompetence, and intimidation. The 1993 Constitution lessens the judiciary's susceptibility to direct pressure from the executive branch and provides for clear jurisdiction over standard CDA. However, at Fujimori's behest, NM-C90 congressional majorities subsequently passed measures that have made a mockery of judicial independence.

THE 1979 CONSTITUTION

Under the 1979 Charter the Tribunal of Constitutional Guarantees was composed of nine magistrates, with the executive branch, Congress, and Supreme Court each choosing three members. The magistrates served staggered, six-year terms and could be reappointed. Judges of the Supreme Court and superior courts were named by the president from nominees submitted by the National Council of the Magistracy,[59] the former were also ratified by the Senate. Similarly, lower-level judges were nominated by circuit-level magistracy councils and were chosen by the chief executive. Judges normally served until at least the age of seventy.

The Tribunal reviewed the constitutionality of laws and DLegs but maintained that it lacked jurisdiction over 211(20) DSs (see 1979 Const. Art. 298–1; see also Torres y Torres Lara 1991:227–58). Petitions of unconstitutionality could be filed by the president, Supreme Court, chief state's attorney, one-third of the members of either legislative chamber, or 50,000 citizens. DSs, RSs, and other executive decrees that are nominally subordinate to laws came within the Tribunal's purview only if related to habeas corpus and *amparo* cases, and even then its role was limited to ensuring adherence to proper procedure in the regular courts (1979 Const. Art. 298[2]).

The Tribunal frequently could not reach decisions because its organic law was interpreted as requiring six votes (two-thirds of the Court's full membership) for *the same opinion* on constitutional issues.[60] Thus, not only was a supermajority required to find a law or DLeg unconstitutional, but the magistrates had to support the same legal reasoning in order to do so. Nevertheless, in a politically explosive March 1992 ruling, the Tribunal partially overturned DLeg 650, which had established a less generous system of severance pay, because it violated the state's obligation to protect workers' rights under Article 42 of the 1979 Constitution (Rodríguez Brignardello 1993). Two other neoliberal decrees were also declared unconstitutional the same month.[61]

During the course of litigation, the regular courts could invalidate laws or decrees that were unconstitutional or illegal (1979 Const. Art. 236). However, on more than one occasion the Supreme Court ruled that 211(20) DSs had the effect of law.[62] Decrees also could be challenged before the regular courts through the process of *amparo*. For example, in 1986 a Lima civil court suspended a 211(20) DS that had changed summer working hours (Pareja Pflücker 1987:82). After President García seized the banks and insurance companies in 1987, their principal shareholders and employees obtained numerous injunctions against the takeovers (Abad Yupanqui 1990:391–400).

THE 1993 CONSTITUTION

Acting as dictator following the *autogolpe*, Fujimori oversaw the restaffing of the regular courts, but he never replaced the magistrates of the Tribunal of Constitutional Guarantees. Under the 1993 Charter, the seven magistrates of the new Constitutional Tribunal are elected by a two-thirds majority of the members of Congress, serve concurrent five-year terms, and cannot stand for immediate reelection. The new Constitution stipulates that judges of the regular courts and state's attorneys are elected by a two-thirds vote of the National Council of the Magistracy, whose broader-based membership no longer includes appointees from the executive branch.[63] The Council also must ratify judges and state's attorneys every seven years after an evaluation of their performance, and it may dismiss them at any time for misconduct.

The jurisdiction of the new Tribunal was expanded to encompass DUs (formerly 211[20] DSs and DSEs) that were issued under standard CDA, treaties, and congressional rules, as well as the norms that could be reviewed by its predecessor (1993 Const. Arts. 200[4] and 202[1]). Petitions of unconstitutionality can be filed by the president and chief state's attorney, as before, although no longer by the Supreme Court. It now takes only one-fourth (rather than one-third) of the members of Congress to impugn legal norms, and the threshold for citizen challenges was lowered dramatically, from 50,000 to 5,000. In addition the newly created Defender of the People (ombudsman) may file petitions of unconstitutionality.

As under the 1979 Constitution, the regular courts can rule that laws and executive decrees are unconstitutional or illegal during the course of litigation (1993 Const. Art. 138). Moreover, the procedures for challenging decrees that are subordinate to law, *acción popular* and *las acciones contencioso-administrativas*, remain under their exclusive jurisdiction.[64] In addition the regular courts have initial jurisdiction over habeas corpus and *amparo* cases, as before, and over two new processes – *cumplimiento* and habeas data – designed to protect individual rights.[65] When hearing habeas corpus or *amparo* cases, the courts may overturn government actions taken under emergency CDA that are deemed to be unreasonable or disproportionate (1993 Const. Art. 200). On the other hand citizens accused of terrorism or treason are now tried in military court – a constitutional provision that has been severely criticized by jurists in Peru and abroad.

Although the 1993 Charter generally strengthened the judiciary vis-à-vis the executive branch, after it took effect pro-Fujimori congressional majorities adopted legislation that has severely compromised judicial autonomy and review powers. The Organic Law of the Constitutional Tribunal, passed by the 1992–95 Constituent Congress, requires a six-sevenths majority to declare a legal norm unconstitutional (Law 26, 435, Art. 4). Installed in August 1996, the new Constitutional Tribunal included some distinguished independent jurists among its magistrates, but the will of the majority was soon frustrated by the six-sevenths rule and two solidly pro-Fujimori colleagues. Nevertheless, in late December 1996, four of the seven magistrates voted to reject a petition of unconstitutionality against the six-sevenths rule filed by opposition members of Congress, thus upholding this provision of the Organic Law (*Resumen Semanal*, No. 901).

Beginning in November 1995, the new unicameral Congress passed a series of laws that gave various special commissions, which were headed by Fujimori appointees, effective control over the budgets and personnel policies of the regular courts, as well as the appointments of new state's attorneys. In August 1996 legislators considered a bill that would have stripped the regular courts of their authority to declare laws and decrees unconstitutional during the course of litigation. Although the bill was withdrawn after protests from the opposition, this sort of legislation could be quickly passed if a court threatened to overturn a legal norm of critical importance to the government. Indeed, pro-Fujimori majorities had previously enacted laws that thwarted politically sensitive judicial processes, most notably in the case of the Cantuta massacre.

In January 1997 the Constitutional Tribunal circumvented the six-sevenths rule to render a politically explosive decision on Law 26,657, which allows Fujimori to run for reelection again in 2000. Four members of the Tribunal, including its president, Ricardo Nugent, abstained from voting on this matter because they had publicly expressed an opinion. The other three magistrates, who asserted that the Tribunal could also exercise litigation-based review like the regular courts, found Law 26,657 to be "inapplicable" to Fujimori's case. Nugent validated this decision on the basis of Article 4 of the Tribunal's Organic Law, which stipulates that nonconstitutional matters are settled by a majority of those voting (*Resumen Semanal*, Nos. 904–6).

In May 1997 a furious NM-C90 majority impeached and removed the three magistrates who had voted for the inapplicability of Law 26,657, citing alleged procedural violations. Nugent, who also faced charges, soon resigned in solidarity with his deposed colleagues. Public opinion, which had consistently supported Fujimori's attacks on pre-1993 institutions, decisively favored the deposed magistrates, and it did so despite a surge in the president's popularity following the daring raid on the Japanese ambassador's residence that had freed MRTA-held hostages in late April. Ironically, Congress' dismissal of the magistrates did not overturn their decision, leaving the chief executive's eligibility for reelection in doubt. As this chapter went through final revisions, pro- and anti-Fujimori forces were maneuvering to influence the composition of the National Board of Elections (JNE), which also has jurisdiction over the reelection matter. The Peruvian people might well have the final say in a referendum.

CONCLUSIONS

The conceptual framework developed by Carey and Shugart in Chapter 1 is essential for understanding executive decree authority in the often tumultuous context of Peruvian politics. The framework helps us to distinguish the sources of decrees from the legal instruments employed to implement them, to relate different kinds of decree authority to other features of constitutional design, and to quickly grasp the implications of various constitutional combinations for executive–legislative relations.

In contrast to the presidential usurpation interpretation of decree, congressional powers and legislative preferences have clearly mattered in Peru. However, most legislators usually have supported – or at least accepted – executive decrees. During their respective first terms, neither Belaunde nor Fujimori could impose their wills on Congresses in which their partisans were minorities, but each of these presidents made extensive use of DDA when he could muster adequate legislative support. The fragmented 1990–92 Congress displayed a remarkable degree of solidarity vis-à-vis Fujimori in repealing the more controversial decrees issued under Law 25,327, but nevertheless it opposed neither most DLegs promulgated by DDA nor the executive's continuous use of emergency CDA. Moreover, even though this Congress asserted its authority over various types of CDA by passing the Law of Parliamentary Control, a majority of legislators refused to censure Torres y Torres Lara for his use of 211 (20) CDA or to overturn tax legislation implemented by DSEs. During other periods pro-government majorities have been broadly supportive of executive decrees of all sorts.

In addition the Peruvian case corroborates some of the principal hypotheses in Chapter 1. Executive preferences were reflected by provisions for extremely strong CDA in the draft of a new charter circulated by Fujimori's advisers (cf. Hypothesis 1), although international pressure precluded their adoption. As predicted by Hypothesis 4, DDA has been used more frequently for policy issues that were generally considered to be urgent, regardless of party alignments or the overall state of executive–legislative relations. The very frequent use of DDA under the 1979 Constitution, with its relatively weak veto, supports Hypothesis 6. Since 1992, unicameral assemblies have passed enabling legislation for DDA much less frequently (.21 delegations per month) than the bicameral legislatures of the 1980–92 period (.66 delegations per month), a pattern that is consistent with Hypothesis 3.[66]

This case study also illustrates the premise of Hypothesis 7 – namely, that a malleable constitution provides legislators with their best check against CDA (assuming, of course, the continuity of a democratic regime). If Fujimori had ignored the Law of Parliamentary Control or if he had successfully challenged the law before the Tribunal of Constitutional Guarantees,[67] in less than two years absolute majorities of each chamber of Congress could have amended the 1979 Constitution to limit or even abolish various types of CDA (see Note 4, cited earlier). There was not, however, a direct link between these features of constitutional design in the drafting of the 1979 Charter, because the members of the Constituent Assembly did not consciously approve CDA. Although the 1993 Constitution combines strong CDA with more onerous amendment procedures, this combination was primarily due to presidential influence and, thus, does not contravene the hypothesis. Moreover, the combination of unicameralism and strong CDA in the 1993 Charter is not at odds with Hypothesis 3 for the same reason.[68]

Other evidence from the complex Peruvian case is less consistent with the editors' expectations. Some reflection on these anomalies points to five ways in which the arguments and hypotheses developed in Chapter 1 might be refined or supplemented during the course of future research.

First, Carey and Shugart assume that members of constituent assemblies who aspire to become legislators will defend the institutional integrity of Congress. This assumption proves to be correct in the case of the 1931–36 Constituent Congress and the 1978–79 Constituent Assembly. Members of the first body increased congressional powers, even though most were supporters of the incumbent president. Delegates to the second body strengthened the presidency but nevertheless maintained the basic parameters of executive–legislative relations. Although the 1993 Charter largely followed these parameters as well, this fundamental continuity with Peruvian constitutional tradition reflected Fujimori's desire to regain international legitimacy for his regime, not the role of the majority in the 1992–95 Constituent Congress. Indeed, this author could find no evidence that the NM-C90 delegation defended the institutional prerogatives of Congress. In contrast to the supporters of Sánchez Cerro in the 1931–36 Constituent Congress, members of the pro-Fujimori majority stood little chance of being included on the NM-C90 list in the 1995 election if they did not faithfully follow directions from the presidential palace.[69] Thus, the Peruvian case suggests that constituent assemblies or congresses may not protect the role of regular legislatures if a majority of their members are dependent on an incumbent president who is likely to stand for reelection.

Second, recent Peruvian experience demonstrates that the logics for controlling DDA and CDA can be quite different. Whereas decrees issued under the former could always be repealed by legislation, the latter could be definitively checked only by a claim to superior constitutional authority under the Law of Parliamentary Control or an explicit constitutional provision, which eventually was added in 1993. Moreover, executive vetoes cannot be used against Congress' constitutionally enshrined powers (such as the right to annul DUs under the 1993 Charter) when they are wielded through legislative resolutions rather than through laws. Thus, although a relatively weak veto in Peru has contributed to the frequent use of DDA, as noted earlier, it has been largely irrelevant to the exercise of CDA (see Hypothesis 6). The peculiar constitutional traditions of each country appear to be more relevant for controlling the latter than the former.

Third, the experiences of the 1963–68 and 1990–92 periods suggest that different sorts of collective action considerations can contribute to significant DDA even when the executive does not have majority support in the legislature (Hypothesis 5). In 1968 *aprista* legislators believed that unpopular economic measures, especially tax increases, would reduce the risk of a military coup and improve their chances of successfully governing after an anticipated victory in the 1969 election. By delegating authority to implement these policies to the outgoing Belaunde administration, APRA tried to become a "free rider," reaping the anticipated future benefits of the adjustment policies without incurring the current costs. It would appear that such a deliberate free-rider strategy, as opposed to a mere shirking of responsibility, is more likely when Congress is controlled by a cohesive opposition party or coalition.

In contrast, during the 1990–92 period, the increased difficulty of collective action in a very fragmented assembly provided a strong incentive for DDA. Indeed, the fragmented 1990–92 Congress delegated authority more frequently than the pro-government majorities of 1980–85, 1992–95, and 1995–96. However, frequent delegations to Fujimori during the 1990–92 period tended to be more circumscribed by ex ante controls and more cautious than those to presidents of the majority party in the other periods. Thus, it appears that an assembly lacking a stable majority has a greater incentive to delegate but also a greater motivation to limit the scope of DDA or make it contingent on some sort of ex ante control.

Fourth, a corollary of the previous point is that chief executives who lack majority support in Congress have an incentive to squeeze maximum advantage from any enabling statute that might be passed, especially if the opposition is fragmented and thus unlikely to successfully challenge decrees. When Congress finally delegated authority to the first Belaunde administration in 1968, the president took advantage of an ambiguous phrase in the enabling law to settle the highly sensitive IPC dispute. Similarly, DDA was used more frequently to issue decrees during the 1990–92 period (when Fujimori did not have a congressional majority) than when presidents enjoyed majority support during the 1980s, under the 1992–95 Constituent Congress, and in the first sixteen months of the 1995–2000 term. According to former Prime Minister Alfonso de los Heros, in 1991 the Fujimori administration tried to use Law 25,327 "to the last drop, to the last centimeter, to the legal and constitutional limit."[70]

Fifth, with respect to Hypothesis 8, under the 1993 Constitution Peruvian courts may have little real power to overturn decrees within their formal jurisdictions, even though the president no longer has a hand in selecting judges. As

Larkins (1996) points out, impartiality is a necessary but not a sufficient condition for judicial independence. Although several members of the Constitutional Tribunal were widely respected for their integrity, Congress's power to impose procedures and remove magistrates has frustrated judicial review. It should be noted that these restrictions on judicial independence could be reversed by future legislatures, each of which will appoint a new Tribunal. The coordinated attack on the courts in the mid-1990s has been led by a congressional majority in support of a co-partisan president. Strategic interaction among the Court, Congress, and executive may play out quite differently under different partisan configurations – for example, when a president faces an opposition majority or when no partisan majority exists. In the long run, the Tribunal may function as an agent of Congress rather than as an impartial arbiter of disputes, with the judiciary's will and ability to challenge executive decree authority largely dependent on congressional support.

A few predictions are appropriate at the conclusion of this chapter. Both external and internal factors make it likely that the strong congressional prerogatives embedded in Peru's constitutional tradition will outlast Fujimori, just as they have survived numerous *caudillos* since the mid-nineteenth century. The president's authoritarian proclivity will almost certainly be checked by powerful international actors that are committed to democracy. Within the democratic rules-of-the-game, Fujimori will find it extremely difficult to alter the longstanding model of executive–legislative relations due to the more onerous procedures for amending the 1993 Constitution and the widespread reluctance of Peruvians to give any leader too much power. Furthermore, most future presidents (including Fujimori if he runs and wins again in 2000) will probably not enjoy congressional majorities, given the system of electing Congress by proportional representation in a single national district.[71] Thus, even if Peru resembles a delegative democracy for the rest of Fujimori's current term, the approach developed by the editors of this volume is likely to be useful for understanding executive decree authority in the future, as well as in the past.

NOTES

1 The author gratefully acknowledges support for fieldwork in Peru from the Center for Latino and Latin American Studies of Northern Illinois University. He wishes to thank César Delgado-Guembes, an expert on the Peruvian Congress at the Catholic University in Lima, and Wilo Rodríguez, director of Peru's congressional archive, for their invaluable assistance, suggestions, and friendship. John Carey and Matthew Shugart made stimulating comments and suggestions. John Reese Alexander and Verónica Gonzales Casanova graciously shared critical sources.
2 For example, see Conaghan and Malloy (1994: esp. 145–8, 203–28), Cotler (1995: esp. 337–53), McClintock (1996), Palmer (1996), Roberts (1995), Rudolph (1992: esp. 78–9), and Wise (1994).

3 For a definition and analysis of president–parliamentary regimes, see Shugart and Carey (1992: esp. Chapters 2, 4, 6, and 8).

4 Peru's longest-lived constitution, the 1860 Constitution, allowed amendment by simple majorities in each legislative chamber in two consecutive annual regular sessions. This threshold was raised only slightly to an absolute majority by the 1933 and 1979 Charters.

5 See the exposition of motives by APRA's Carlos Enrique Melgar, who was head of the committee on executive–legislative relations, in Comisión Principal de la Asamblea Constituyente 1978–1979, *Anexos y ponencias*, Tomo II (Lima, n.d.), pp. 115–31.

6 Calculated by comparing the membership of the Constituent Assembly, reported in Tuesta Soldevilla (1994: 74–5), with party lists in the 1980 election, recorded in Jurado Nacional de Elecciones (JNE) (1982: 91–188).

7 Belaunde's AP had a majority in the Chamber of Deputies, and an alliance with the PPC provided him with a majority in the Senate until March 1984. García's APRA enjoyed majorities in both chambers.

8 Bernales (1989:148) and interview with César Delgado-Guembes (12 August 1994). All interviews cited in this chapter took place in Lima.

9 The effective number of legislative parties refers to the standard party system fragmentation index elaborated by Laakso and Taagepera (1979). The figures for Peru were calculated from the distribution of seats reported in Tuesta Soldevilla (1994: 65–8).

10 Delgado-Guembes (1992:276) and *Resumen Semanal*, nos. 648–9.

11 Interview with Lourdes Flores Nano, a prominent deputy during the 1990–92 period (15 August 1994).

12 For example, *Decreto Legislativo* (DLeg) 733 made all citizens eligible for conscription, required them to supply any information requested to fight terrorism or narcotic trafficking, and gave the government sweeping powers of requisition. Anyone resisting "mobilization" could be charged with treason. DLeg 743 created a sort of war cabinet controlled by the president and the military, but it was not accountable to Congress. DLeg 762 mandated prison sentences for publishing or broadcasting any information pertinent to national defense deemed secret by the government.

13 Cámara de Diputados, Dirección Técnica General Parlamentaria, "Estado situacional de los Decretos Legislativos promulgados al amparo de la Ley 25327" (Lima; 31 March 1992).

14 This account of the behind-the-scenes negotiations between the executive and legislative branches is based on interviews with Alfonso de los Heros (17 August 1995) and with two prominent congressional participants in the negotiations, AP Senator Javier Alva Orlandini (19 August 1995) and PPC Deputy Lourdes Flores Nano (28 August 1995).

15 "Manifesto a la Nación del 5 de Abril de 1992," reproduced in Ferrero Costa (1992:129–35).

16 Although the once-per-term limit on dissolution was dropped, the previous proscription during the last year was maintained. Congress can be dissolved during a state of emergency, but not a state of siege.

17 "Constitución Política del Perú" [draft proposal] (2 December 1992).

18 Interviews with Carlos Ferrero Costa (NM), August 21, 1995, and Lourdes Flores

Nano (PPC), August 28, 1995. Both served on the Constituent Congress' Constitution Committee.

19 José Reyes Apesteguía, "Comenzó el sacamanteca electoral," *Oiga* (16 January 1995), pp. 17–20. Ironically, the statute decreed by Fujimori to convene elections for the 1992–95 Constituent Congress had specified that the delegates elected would not be eligible to run for Congress in 1995. However, this provision was subsequently ignored by most members of the Constituent Congress, who claimed autonomy, and by Fujimori himself.

20 Overall, 57 of the 80 delegates to the Constituent Congress ran for Congress in 1995. Of these, 38 won seats, including all members of the key Constitution Committee. These figures were derived from comparisons of the membership of the Constituent Congress, reported in Tuesta Soldevilla (1994:64–5), with party lists posted on the World Wide Web by the National Board of Elections (JNE) and with the winning candidates listed in JNE (1995:18–20).

21 Congress must approve all treaties (or revocations thereof) dealing with human rights, sovereignty, national defense, and financial obligations, as well as those that involve taxes, require changes in existing law, or need new legislation for implementation. The president has the authority to approve (and revoke) all other treaties that do not alter constitutional provisions, and (s)he can do so without any congressional action, although Congress apparently may choose to act.

22 Barrientos Silva (1990), D. García Belaunde (1991:45), and Pareja Pflücker (1987:67).

23 Calculated from data in Table 4.3 and Delgado-Guembes (1992:226).

24 Interview with de los Heros.

25 Ibid.

26 Alfonso de los Heros, who was the Minister of Labor at the time, confirmed press accounts of cabinet opposition to these decrees, whose primary advocate was, ironically, Hernando de Soto.

27 See Furnish (1971:92,112), 1979 Const. Arts. 87 and 236, and 1993 Const. Arts. 51 and 138.

28 Interview with Armando Zolezzi of the Catholic University, a leading tax expert who participated in many negotiations between the government and intermediate commissions during the 1980s and 1990s (23 August 1995).

29 This mode was used several times during the last year of Belaunde's second term as president, for medical legislation under García, and in a couple of delegations to Fujimori before the *autogolpe*. See Laws 23,974, 23,978, 24,038, 24,057, 24,131, 25,186, 25,296, and 25,297.

30 Previously cited interview with Javier Alva Orlandini (19 August 1995), a member of five commissions that revised legal codes during the 1980s and 1990s.

31 Interviews with Armando Zolezzi, César Landa Arroyo, and Ana Velazco of the Catholic University (23 August 1995).

32 The author is very grateful to Wilo Rodríguez and his associates in the congressional archive, who searched through all bills introduced to annul or repeal decrees while the 1979 Constitution was in effect.

33 See Bernales (1990:150–5), Eguiguren (1990b:218, 237, 241–2), and the comments of Deputy Lourdes Flores Nano, chair of the Constitution Committee in the Chamber of Deputies, at the beginning of the floor debate in the lower house

(4 December 1991, afternoon session, *turno* 15 of the unpublished congressional record).

34 These arguments were developed in Fujimori's letter of veto to the president of the Permanent Committee of Congress, sent as Oficio No. 005-92-PR on January 7, 1992.

35 For example, see Enrique Chirinos Soto, "La pugna entre los poderes del Estado," *El Comercio* (8 June 1992), p. A-2.

36 Interview with Delgado-Guembes (op. cit.).

37 See Basadre (1983, X:275), Eguiguren (1990b:176–7), and Furnish (1971:95–6). Examples of DDA before 1933 are discussed in Basadre (1983, X:275) and Planas (1992:272–3).

38 This discussion of DDA under the first Belaunde administration draws on Kuczynski (1977:esp. 222, 226, 230–43, 260–76).

39 See Bernales (1981:69–70, 75–6), Eguiguren (1990b:185–97), and D. García Belaunde (1989:24–8). Before 1993 constitutionally mandated statutes and organic laws were overlapping categories.

40 See Bernales (1989:163) and Eguiguren (1990b:180–3). In the case of organic laws, a convention evolved whereby the authorizing legislation was passed by absolute majorities, the same margin required for their approval through the regular legislative process.

41 Bernales (1981:74) and Bustamante Belaunde (1981:49). The opposition parties could not challenge any of the 201 DLegs issued under Law 23,230 before the Tribunal of Constitutional Guarantees, which was not operational until 1982.

42 For example, see Pedro Planas, "Congreso revisará convenio [Interview with Senator Luis Bustamante]," *Oiga* (20 May 1991), pp. 32–7. Ironically, congressional support for DDA was greatest on the issue of pacification. Legislators did not anticipate the sort of draconian counterinsurgency decrees that would be drafted by the Fujimori administration.

43 The figures for Belaunde and García are based on Barrientos Silva (1990:117–226), supplemented by additional research undertaken by the author. The number of enabling laws under Fujimori is provided by Abad Yupanqui and Garcés Peralta (1993:104), who used the same methodology.

44 This paragraph draws on information provided by César Delgado-Guembes.

45 See Bustamante Belaunde (1981:48) and "El cartel de las erratas," *Oiga* (4 November 1991), pp. 23–5.

46 Eguiguren (1989:265–6, 279–83). The day after the massacre of captured Shining Path insurgents in 1986, President García issued a DS declaring the affected prisons to be in a "restricted military zone" outside of the jurisdiction of civilian justice, but this decree had no basis in Article 231 and was patently unconstitutional (Eguiguren 1989:274). García's role in the prison massacre was the focus of an unsuccessful attempt to impeach him in 1990 – that is, after he had left office.

47 Peruvian human rights organizations had vigorously lobbied the Constituent Congress to include these important changes. Interview with Francisco Eguiguren (17 August 1994).

48 Oficio No. 275-84-EFC/60 of March 19, 1984, reproduced in Bernales (1984: 126–31).

49 See Pareja Pflücker (1987:79–81) and Rubio and Bernales (1988:402–3).
50 Interview with Domingo García Belaunde (20 August 1993). Also see Eguiguren (1990b:221–4).
51 See especially *Resumen Semanal*, nos. 613 and 642.
52 Oficina de Iniciativas Parlamentarias, "Relación de Decretos Supremos Extraordinarios de conformidad con el inciso b) del Artículo 4 de la Ley N° 25397"; Boloña Behr (1993:98); and Planas (1992:285–8).
53 Interview with Flores Nano (28 August 1995). Congress had previously converted some 211 (20) decrees into law.
54 Interview with Landa Arroyo (23 August 1995).
55 The author interviewed four members of the Constitution Committee – Carlos Ferrero Costa (NM) and Lourdes Flores Nano (PPC), as cited above; Enrique Chirinos Soto (Renewal Party: 16 August 1995); and Henry Pease García (Democratic Movement of the Left: 24 August 1995).
56 See *Apoyo al Congreso* Año 2, no. 3. On the other hand, Eguiguren (1994:190) points out that one of the first DUs issued under the 1993 Constitution apparently affects taxes.
57 Information provided by César Delgado-Guembes.
58 "¿Cuál es el Cau Cau?," *Caretas* (7 November 1996), p. 23.
59 Under the 1979 Constitution, the National Council of the Magistracy was headed by the chief state's attorney, a presidential appointee. The Supreme Court, the legal profession, and university law faculties each elected two representatives.
60 Interviews with former Congressman Valentín Paniagua, who argued a key case on the 1985 electoral law before the Tribunal (16 August 1994); and César Landa Arroyo, a leading expert on the constitutional court (29 August 1995).
61 Information supplied by César Landa Arroyo.
62 Interview with Domingo García Belaunde in *Apoyo al Congreso* Año 2, no. 3, p. 8; and Torres y Torres Lara (1991:93–5).
63 Making up the new Council are two representatives from nonlegal professional associations and single members designated by the Supreme Court, the national bar associations, the presidents of public universities, the presidents of private universities, and state's attorneys. The Council also may elect two additional members from nominees submitted by entrepreneurial and labor organizations.
64 Although both of these procedures were included in the 1979 Constitution, the enabling law for *acción popular* was delayed until 1988, and the implementing legislation for *las acciones contencioso-administrativas* did not take effect before the *autogolpe*.
65 The Constitutional Tribunal now serves as the court of last appeal, rather than as a court of review for these procedures (1993 Const. Art. 202[2]). *Cumplimiento* is a process under which authorities can be compelled to implement laws and decrees. Habeas data is designed for freedom of information, right of privacy, and libel cases.
66 However, it is by no means clear that DDA is actually *used* more by presidents facing a bicameral Congress. DDA was employed to issue approximately 5.5 DLegs each month under the bicameral Congresses of the 1980–1992 period, in contrast to 6 DLegs per month during the first sixteen months of the 1995–96 unicameral Congress. DLegs were used very sparingly (.6 per month) during the tenure of the 1992–95 unicameral Constituent Congress, but this low frequency

was probably a historical aberration, because it followed a deluge of important legislation promulgated during Fujimori's brief dictatorship.

67 An unlikely outcome, given domination of the Tribunal by APRA at that time.

68 Interviews with Ferrero Costa; and interview with Flores Nano (28 August 1995).

69 The leaders of most other parties in Peru also control congressional nominations, even though the country has employed a form of open-list proportional representation since 1985. Thus, using these conflicting indicators to measure party discipline, we find that the independent variable in Hypothesis 2 is problematic in the Peruvian case.

70 Previously cited interview. Among the decrees issued under this law was DLeg 695, which authorized the reorganization of the national sports system on the theory that Peruvians would be less inclined to support terrorism if their teams had greater success in international competition!

71 The new electoral law for 2000, which was passed in late September 1997, maintains the single national district, a system favored by Lima-based congressmen and one that facilitates Fujimori's tight grip on NM–C90. However, the improbability of any single party winning a majority would not be reduced significantly if the single national district were to be replaced in future elections by the principal alternative: regional districts of medium and high magnitude.

PRESIDENTIAL DECREE
AUTHORITY IN
VENEZUELA[1]

Brian F. Crisp

EXECUTIVE–LEGISLATIVE RELATIONS

Democratic rule has now lasted nearly forty years in Venezuela, although the system has recently been shaken by a mismanaged neoliberal, austerity package; public riots and military overreaction; two attempted coups; and presidential impeachment proceedings. It is the oldest extant democracy in South America, and as such, it has the longest historical record of currently existing regimes. Brewer-Carías' description of the Venezuelan system, through its own ambiguity, may best capture its mixed nature: *el sistema presidencial con sujeción parlamentaria*, or "a presidential system subject to the parliament" (1985b: 153–190; 1985a: 131). The ambiguity of this phrase accurately reflects the complexity surrounding the president's use of the office's constitutionally allocated powers. In comparative terms the formal powers of Venezuelan presidents are quite minimal, yet it is widely perceived that the president dominates the political arena. An empirical analysis of presidential decree authority helps sort out this apparent contradiction.

In Venezuela the president's formal powers are comparatively few, but a number of factors, in a sense, can magnify their importance. Venezuelan presidents use their nonlegislative decree powers to great effect. They draw attention to and study particular issues, draft legislation, appoint government functionaries, regulate the economy – and they determine the limits of constitutional guarantees. However, they never receive binding legislative powers unless the Congress delegates it to them. So, presidents are always operating within bounds set for them by the legislative branch. Therefore, to understand presidential decree authority, we will have to account for electoral regulations, internal party rules, and the partisan composition of both branches. To get a sense of how important presidential decree authority is to executive–legislative relations, we will leave decree authority aside for a moment and examine the other powers of the three branches.

Without this decree authority, the conclusion that the executive dominates will seem untenable. Then, once we account for presidential decree authority, both legislative and nonlegislative, it will become clear how presidents are able to compete with Congress for power.

Most basic to the relationship between executive and legislature is the fact that the president has the independent popular electoral base and fixed term inherent in a presidential system. Because the executive is directly elected, the administration does not depend on congressional confidence to continue governing. In terms of appointments executives have the right to name cabinet ministers without congressional approval (Art. 190:2) and, until recently, state governors (Article 190:17, but they are now directly elected). The president and his ministers have the right to propose legislation (Art. 165), and ministers have the right to address Congress at any time (Art. 199) and to participate in the discussion of legislation (Art. 170). However, the president has only a suspensive veto over legislation.[2] There are less tangible signs of power too, including the relative attention given presidential races and the amount spent on presidential – in contrast to congressional – campaigns. It is certainly the case that the president receives the most media attention and as a result has the ability to put issues on the nation's political agenda.

However, no president can govern comfortably without the support of Congress. Congress is the source of all laws and, as noted earlier, can override a presidential veto with a simple majority (Art. 173). It has the right to question ministers (Art. 199), who must submit to Congress an annual account of their expenditures (Art. 190). Likewise, the president must give an annual message accounting for the actions and plans of his government (Art. 191). In terms of appointments, the Senate must confirm some presidential appointees, including the procurator general and the heads of diplomatic missions (Art. 150:7). The power of Congress to name functionaries in the executive branch has been increasing through specific pieces of legislation, such as the Administrative Career Law of 1970 and the Prices, Costs, and Salaries Law of 1983 (Brewer-Carías 1985a:134–5). In addition the Chamber of Deputies, with a two-thirds majority, can censure, censure and remove, and/or order the trial of a minister. Some administrative functions, including the signing of contracts "of national interest" (Art. 126) and the disposition of national territory (Art. 150:2), require congressional approval. Finally, the Senate must give the president permission to leave the country (Art. 150:6).

The judicial branch is relatively weak in Venezuela, as it is in much of Latin America. What passed for legal theory in predemocratic Venezuela was often nothing more than an effort to justify the actions of the current dictator, and the reliance on knowable, impartial rules has been slow to develop in the democratic era as a result of this lack of historical experience (Kelley 1986:43–4). The independence of the judiciary is established by Article 205 of the 1961 Constitution, but that Constitution left many important characteristics of the judiciary to be determined by future laws (see Arts. 207–10, 212, and 217). This vacuum resulted in politicization – or a decrease in the potential independence – of the judicial branch. For example, judges are named for relatively short terms, and their reappointment is dependent upon the political balance in the other two branches. Supreme Court justices are elected to nine-year terms by a joint session of Congress, and one-third of the Court is renewed every three years. Judges in lower courts were originally appointed jointly by the president and an administrative arm of the Supreme Court (Coppedge 1994:33). However, during the first administration of President Rafael Caldera, the unified opposition in Congress moved the authority to appoint 2,500 to 2,800 judges to the Judicial Council (*Consejo de la Judicatura*). The Judicial Council is made up of representatives of all three branches, but the Congress is guaranteed the majority (Velásquez 1976:307). When Caldera exercised his suspensive veto on the law containing this change, he was overridden. In response to the override, he challenged the constitutionality of the law before the Supreme Court, and he proceeded to use the old method of nominating judges. The administrative arm of the Supreme Court, which was controlled by Acción Democrática (AD) and Unión Republicana Democrática (URD) and which had to approve his nominees, refused to act. The Supreme Court later upheld the reform and the creation of the Judicial Council by a vote of eight to seven (Velásquez 1976:308). The judicial system has, thus, been grounds for conflict between the other two branches, and it remains a site for battle among the parties in Congress.

Recall, though, that this examination of constitutional powers does not account for presidential decree authority. At the agenda-setting stage the president can create high-profile commissions which bring executive branch authorities and the representatives of interest groups together to study issues of the president's choice. At the stage of policy formation, similar commissions are often charged with drafting the actual legislation that the president will then submit to Congress for adoption. Given the extreme party discipline enforced in the Venezuelan Congress, there are greater incentives to lobby the highest party elites who determine the parties' positions in Congress and to lobby the executive branch than to lobby individual legislators. Presidents often have the ability to act on this consultation through the decree authority they have when constitutional rights are suspended or restricted or when the legislature delegates decree authority to them. However, the Congress has the right to effectively revoke the suspension or restriction of constitutional guarantees, and it is never obligated to decree authority (these forms of decree authority are discussed in detail later). The executive branch also drafts and proposes a great deal of legislation, but the process of approving executive-initiated policy in the legislature is usually nothing more than an opportunity to modify that policy's specific content. The participatory commissions created in the executive branch give groups their first and best opportunity to influence draft legislation, but the opposition parties and/or coalition members (if the president does not have majority support in Congress) take the legislative debate as an opportunity to press for further changes – sometimes quite successfully. The president's discretionary powers involved in overseeing the enormous bureaucracy give the executive branch one last opportunity to influence policy outcomes.

Presidential decree authority plays a key role in the policy-making process, but even this brief account shows that the use of decree authority is no simple case of usurpation. In the next section I will describe the various types of decree authority defined in the Venezuelan Constitution and illustrate how they have been used throughout the democratic era. I will show how patterns in their use are related to the partisan composition of government and to party behavior more broadly. In the Conclusion I will turn to the theme of what the particular inter-branch relations that characterize Venezuela mean for democratic rule more generally.

TYPES OF PRESIDENTIAL DECREE AUTHORITY

The range and use of decree authority in Venezuela are defined in the Constitution which was enacted on January 23, 1961 – three years to the day after the fall of the dictator Pérez Jiménez.[3] It was drafted and adopted in a period of highly consensual politics. Between January 23, 1958, and December 7, 1958, the country was ruled by the *Junta de Gobierno*, which was originally composed exclusively of military figures but evolved over the course of the year into a body made up primarily of civilians. Elections on December 7 brought Acción Democrática candidate Rómulo Betancourt to the presidency and gave his party a majority in Congress.[4] The new Congress took office on January 28, 1959, and appointed the Bicameral Commission for Constitutional Reform in less than a week. The Commission was composed of twenty-two members of Congress, who were appointed in proportion to the recent electoral performance of their parties – eight representatives of AD, which had become a more centrist multiclass party since its first try at governing between 1945 and 1948; four of COPEI (the Christian Democratic Party); four of the Unión Republicana Democrática (URD) that represented the noncommunist left; three of the Venezuelan Communist Party (PCV); and three independents. The deliberations of the Commission were relatively shielded from public view, and the process of drafting and adopting the new Constitution was completed in a very nonpoliticized manner (Kornblith 1991: 71–2). Carey and Shugart hypothesize that where the executive or those who expect to hold executive office have influence over constitutional design, the likelihood of constitutional decree authority (CDA) is greatest. The Venezuelan case supports this hypothesis – the legislature dominated the drafting of the Constitution and did not provide for CDA. I will describe the types of decree authority that are available under the 1961 Venezuelan Constitution, give an overview of the actual use of each one across administrations, and provide specific examples of their content.

DELEGATED AUTHORITY

Rule making. In Venezuela presidential rule-making decrees are provided for by Article 190:10 of the 1961 Constitution, and their use is commonplace. Though this capacity is provided for directly in the Constitution and does not require explicit congressional delegation or consent, Congress must pass a law before the president can issue a decree regulating the law's administration.

Rule making involves the issuing of seemingly minor regulations that are necessary to implement a piece of legislation, and they are constitutionally prohibited from changing the spirit, purpose, or motivation of the legislation (Bacalao Octavio 1973:11). The legislative initiative granted the Venezuelan executive has led to the use of rule-making decrees for obtaining advice, for consulting on policy choices, and for the process of drafting legislation as described earlier.

Delegated legislative authority. Article 190:11 of the Venezuelan Constitution of 1961 allows presidents, when Congress is not in session, to create public services or modify existing ones as long as they have the prior approval of the Delegated Commission of Congress, which remains in session when the full Congress is in recess. No presidential decree has been justified by this constitutional provision.

More importantly, Article 190:8 allows the president in a meeting of his Council of Ministers "to dictate extraordinary measures in economic and financial matters when the public interest requires it and he has been authorized to do so by a special law." These special laws are referred to as *leyes habilitantes*, or enabling laws. Delegated legislative authority has been granted rather infrequently and in exceptional circumstances. However, the vagueness of Article 190:8 does not theoretically prohibit more frequent use of this option in Venezuela. Decree authority in economic and financial matters has been delegated to the president five times since 1961. In the first three instances authority was delegated for one full year. The circumstances surrounding the delegation and the nature of the decree authority allowed have varied widely.

On June 29, 1961, the Law of Urgent Economic Measures was passed by an AD-controlled Congress, one that delegated decree authority on economic and financial matters to President Betancourt, also of AD (*Gaceta Oficial* 26,590, 6/29/61). The enabling law gave the president broad authority by specifying a wide array of issues to be faced and by only loosely defining exactly how they should be addressed. It authorized the president to reorganize the decentralized public administration, to reorganize public services, to defer collective contracts, to fix prices of goods of primary necessity, to modify the Property Tax Law, to modify inheritance and other national taxes; and to establish an insurance system for deposit and savings accounts. These powers are quite wide-ranging and are only loosely defined, thus leaving a great deal of discretion to the president.

Given this leeway, Betancourt's use of the authority seems quite moderate.

Over the course of the next year, he used this authority to issue fifteen decree laws. In the area of collective contracts, he lowered public employee salaries, suspended these employees' current contract, and postponed their ongoing contract negotiations until 1962. On taxes he revised several tax laws, some of them more than once. He made a number of moves to make credit for building urban housing more available, including the establishment of a particular credit fund for this purpose, the release of funds to banks, and the provision of incentives for private lenders. In terms of public administration and services, he intervened in the management of the Social Security Institute, created the School of Public Administration, and reorganized the telecommunications services (Brewer-Carias 1980:108–11).

While all these measures are important, they are also limited in number and clearly within the bounds of the enabling legislation. Betancourt may have been circumspect in his actions because he was pledged to follow a "common minimum government program" (Crisp 1997b) which had been approved by the major parties prior to the election and because he had created a grand coalition government with cabinet representation for other parties. These characteristics point to the Venezuelan tendency to protect the democratic system first and pursue partisan goals second (ibid.).

Decree authority in economic and financial matters was next delegated to Carlos Andrés Pérez of Acción Democrática; again AD had a majority in both houses of the legislature. In April 1974, a month after taking office, Pérez asked Congress for the power to dictate measures to transform the economic structure of the country in light of the tremendous increase in income from petroleum exports, and the next month Congress obliged with enabling legislation on May 31, 1974 (*Gaceta Oficial* 30,412, 5/31/74). Congress did grant Pérez substantial powers, although these powers were less broadly defined than those for which he had asked. In particular the enabling law omitted the right to decree a tax reform. Pérez, at the urging of Finance Minister Hector Hurtado, wanted to reform the tax system in order to begin shifting "the burden of budget financing from the oil sector to the internal sector of the economy" (Abente 1990: 201–2). Despite omitting this authority, the enabling law did give Pérez one year to dictate measures to reform the national finance system and capital markets, to modify the Organic Law of the National Public Finance, to create the Venezuelan Investment Fund, to arrange and invest funds of the Treasury, to stimulate the transformation of sectors of production, to nationalize the iron ore industry, to pay off the debt of the Venezuelan Social Security Institute, to uphold the seniority and pension rights of workers, and to determine minimum salaries and salary and wage hikes. This is an incredibly diverse array of issues, and the particular instructions within each issue area were not very well defined.

Pérez took advantage of this loose leash and dictated fifty-three decree laws (he actually issued thousands of more decrees and decree laws, but on different constitutional grounds to be discussed later). Most of the decrees were designed to distribute the oil wealth to the economy through credit institutions, to develop plans for particular industries (including aeronautics and automobiles), or to subsidize types of producers (such as small and medium industry). The sheer number of decree laws and their wide scope indicate the degree to which the executive assumed legislative authority. The authority was delegated, not taken on the president's initiative (although he did propose the delegation law to Congress), but it was done in such a vague manner that these far-reaching decrees did not fall outside its limits.

To its credit, Perez's own party, the AD, through its majority in Congress attempted to prevent his complete autonomy and to avoid the opposition charge that the AD was bypassing the legislature altogether, and it did so by including in the enabling law a congressional vigilance committee. This committee was composed of thirteen members from eight parties and was to receive all decrees before they were promulgated; it was also supposed to get trimesterly reports from the Venezuelan Investment Fund, a financial institution that the enabling legislation required the president to create. In practice none of this happened. The Pérez administration ignored the commission. The congressman often received decrees after they were issued, if at all. In stages, the opposition parties resigned from the commission in protest over what they saw as Pérez's *decrotamania* and AD's blatant disregard for the separation of powers critical to democratic rule (Fernandez 1976:35–98; Karl 1982:220–1). AD as a party was either unwilling or unable to rein in Pérez, and it was unwilling to do so because much of the time Pérez was carrying out policies it found acceptable and because he and his supporters were significant factors in the party leadership bodies. In addition an intraparty split would jeopardize the party's future electoral winnings. The congressional delegation of AD was unable to further limit Pérez's activities because individual members of Congress were bound by party discipline and because, after creating the oversight committee, the party lacked any institutional mechanisms to enforce compliance, unless it rescinded the delegation completely or passed countervailing legislation.

President Jaime Lusinchi of Acción Democrática received decree authority next on June 20, 1984 (*Gaceta Oficial* 33,005, 6/22/84). By the mid-1980s the oil price hikes had ended, and servicing Venezuela's extensive foreign debt was putting a drain on government revenue. Due to the economic downturn, Congress delegated authority for an extensive array of activities. The list of items to be addressed totaled nearly twenty. Most of them focused on cutting government spending, on raising government revenue, and on refinancing public debt. What distinguishes them from previous delegated tasks is their specificity. For example, the president was given authority to decrease government spending by cutting public salaries – and, in fact, the percentage was defined for him (10 percent). Likewise, he was told he had authority to increase revenue by raising the tax on alcohol, but, again, the range (between 5 and 30 percent) was defined for him. He was given somewhat greater leeway in reorganizing the public sector for efficiency, including the right to dissolve public enterprises. The enabling law also required that the president report his activities to Congress.

Lusinchi issued a grand total of seventy-one decrees that were justified in this manner, but the sheer number is tempered by the significant repetition of particular acts. Although many of the decrees were used to carry out the array of objectives listed in the enabling legislation, more than half (thirty-six) of these decrees were used for the single purpose of selling government bonds to refinance the public debt – which was also explicitly called for in the enabling legislation. Unlike the Pérez case, it appears that the powers delegated were much more clearly expressed and carefully followed as a result of both the specificity of the instructions given Lusinchi and the oversight placed on his activities. This is true despite the fact that, like Pérez, Lusinchi's AD party had a majority in both houses. It may be the case that the legislators learned from their broad delegation of authority to Pérez, and as a result, they did not risk losing their efficacy in the case of Lusinchi. It is also likely that the differences in the motivating factors behind the delegation – an economic boom under Pérez and a bust under Lusinchi – and the leadership styles of the executives made a difference in how the decree power was exercised. The original draft of the enabling legislation was written by the executive branch itself, and it is likely that many of these moderating factors were reflected in the president's original request.

Power was next delegated to President Ramón J. Velásquez on August 23, 1993 (*Gaceta Oficial* 35,280, 8/23/93). Velásquez, an independent in Congress, was the interim president serving the remainder of Carlos Andrés Pérez's second term. Pérez's administration, after surviving public riots, the unpopularity of the military's action to quell those riots, and two attempted coups, had been forced from office as a result of corruption charges. Due to his interim status and the upcoming elections in December, Velásquez received delegated decree authority only until the end of the year – the end of his interim term. Article 1 of the enabling legislation granted the president decree authority in "the *specific* economic and financial areas" listed in the rest of the article (emphasis added). Article 1 takes up more than two pages of the *Gaceta Oficial* detailing ten areas in which Velásquez was instructed to act, including tax reform, banking regulation, provision of credit for low-cost housing, the sale of a government-owned airline, and the stimulation of the agricultural sector. The tax reform was intended to raise government revenue (by establishing both a wholesale sales tax of between 5 and 15 percent, depending on the particular good or service, and a tax on corporate assets) and to promote foreign investment in petroleum-related industries by covering such companies under the normal tax laws rather than under their previously exceptional status. The banking reform was designed to standardize oversight and regulation and to open the industry to increasing foreign participation. Stimulation of the agricultural sector included increased credit, refinancing of existing debt, promotion of exports, and protection against imports.

Other than the rather vague instructions to promote agricultural export, to protect domestic agricultural producers from foreign competition, and to establish in the decree itself (Art. 2) the sanctions for those disobeying the decree laws, these provisions were characterized by their specificity. What is more, the remaining three articles of the enabling legislation detailed the means of congressional oversight. Article 3 required that if a decree law modifies existing legislation, the original legislation and modifications must be published in full (which is commonplace in Venezuelan legislative activity). Presumably, this would have allowed legislators to examine the legislative impact of the decree in the context of specific preexisting laws rather than in a relative vacuum. Article 4 required that the executive give a detailed account of each decree law within ten days after it is approved by the Council of Ministers and before it is enacted. No specific provision was made for what Congress could do if it found a decree unacceptable, although it could clearly pass countervailing legislation. Article 5 required that the president appear before Congress within the first ten days of its 1994 session to account for his actions in fulfilling the tasks assigned in Article 1.

The importance of the power to establish sanctions for those disobeying the decree laws should not be overlooked. For the first time in Venezuelan history, the president was given the power to modify the penal code, an act previously reserved exclusively for the legislature. This provision was also included in the enabling legislation that delegated authority to Caldera in 1994. Although the crimes created by this power might be narrow in their impact, this again indicates an area where the separation of powers between branches has become blurred in the executive's favor.

As a result of Velásquez's interim status, the recent lack of confidence granted the executive branch, previous presidential zealousness in the use of delegated decree authority, and the coalition nature of the legislative majority that delegated the authority, the powers granted in 1993 were carefully defined and closely monitored. Velásquez issued only thirteen decrees as a result of the delegation. The limited number should not detract from the importance of the issues addressed, including value-added and income taxes, but Velásquez's autonomy, relatively speaking, was constrained. The parties that controlled Congress used this opportunity to find another actor to carry out tough reforms. They asked the president to carry out tasks for which they did not want to be held accountable by voters in the future. The value-added tax was particularly unpopular, but, by virtue of the way it was adopted, no one had to take responsibility for it. Instead, an interim president who was officially independent of all political parties (and, like all other presidents, unable to run for immediate reelection) was saddled with the job. Congress would later delegate authority to another president to overturn it.

On April 14, 1994, Congress delegated presidential decree authority in economic and financial matters to President Rafael Caldera, who was formerly of COPEI but who was supported in the 1993 elections by the *Convergencia* coalition, Movement Toward Socialism (MAS), and others (*Gaceta Oficial* 35,442, 4/18/94). It gave the president decree authority for only thirty days. Interestingly enough, the initiative behind this delegation of decree authority came from the opposition party (AD), which had a plurality of seats in Congress. Until this time, delegation of decree authority was always suggested by the president himself, and the executive branch even submitted a draft of the delegating legislation. In this case, however, Caldera had always opposed, in principle, the way in which delegated decree authority operated. Caldera had argued publicly that the force of presidential decrees issued in this manner should only endure as long as the delegated authority itself and that the decrees should be abrogated once the duration of the delegated authority was over (Caldera 1981:22–3). Thus, in the cases of Pérez and Lusinchi, for example, Caldera argued that the decrees they issued should have only been in force for the year that the authority to decree laws in economic and financial matters was delegated. This interpretation had never been accepted in Venezuelan practice, but, nonetheless, it would have been embarrassing for Caldera or his supporters in Congress to ask for a decree power that he had argued should not exist. Instead, AD instigated the delegation, and Caldera made no complaint about accepting it.

Article 1 of the enabling legislation authorized the president to establish a luxury tax, a wholesale sales tax, and a tax on savings accounts. It also gave him power to reform a number of existing tax regulations and to abolish the extremely controversial value-added or wholesale tax. Subsequent paragraphs detailed exceptions that could be made, ranges for tax rates, and the requirement of an expression of congressional support for particular tax rates established during the reform of existing tax regulations. It also authorized Caldera both to establish norms for contracting with private companies that were to provide public works and public services and to abolish parts of existing laws that restricted this possibility. It gave the president a great deal of discretion to enforce these changes and to establish punishments for people found to be disobeying them. In the thirty days allotted him, Caldera issued only four decrees justified by the enabling legislation. He partially reformed the budget regimen, he put a .75 percent tax on bank deposits, he declared a wholesale sales tax and a tax on luxury consumption, and he established mechanisms for contracting out public services to private companies. Congress did restrict his authority through a relatively limited list of tasks, some detailed instructions regarding their completion, the limitation of thirty days, and the requirement that he report his actions.

It appears then that delegated authority has grown substantively more specific and temporally shorter over time. One explanation for this trend is that Congress learned from its early agency loss, especially to Carlos Andrés Pérez in the 1970s. The severity of this lesson was compounded by the fact that Pérez has been one of the most activist of Venezuelan presidents and was governing by decree in a time of abundance, so his activities were not constrained by budgetary concerns.[5]

In support of Carey and Shugart's hypothesis that delegated decree authority (DDA) is more likely when the president's party controls Congress, the first three times that presidential decree authority in economic and financial matters was delegated, it was to presidents from AD by Congresses where AD had a simple majority in each chamber (Betancourt, Pérez in his first term, and Lusinchi). Of the eight regularly elected presidents since 1958, every president with a majority

Table 5.1 *Partisan support for Venezuelan presidents in Congress and party system fragmentation*

Administration	Seats in the Senate	Seats in the Chamber of Deputies	Index of fragmentation
Betancourt (AD)	AD = 63%	AD = 55%	.66
1959–64	COPEI = 22%	COPEI = 26%	
Leoni (AD)	AD = 47%	AD = 37%	.79
1964–69	COPEI = 17%	COPEI = 21%	
Caldera (COPEI)	AD = 37%	AD = 31%	.84
1969–74	COPEI = 31%	COPEI = 28%	
Pérez (AD)	AD = 60%	AD = 51%	.70
1974–79	COPEI = 28%	COPEI = 32%	
Herrera Campins			
(COPEI)	AD = 48%	AD = 44%	.68
1979–84	COPEI = 48%	COPEI = 42%	
Lusinchi (AD)	AD = 64%	AD = 56%	.66
1984–89	COPEI = 32%	COPEI = 30%	
Pérez (AD)	AD = 48%	AD = 48%	.70
1989–93	COPEI = 43%	COPEI = 33%	
Velásquez			
(Independent)[a]	AD = 48%	AD = 48%	.70
1993–94	COPEI = 43%	COPEI = 33%	
Caldera (*Convergencia/*			
MAS)	AD = 32%	AD = 27%	.82
1994–99	COPEI = 28%	COPEI = 26%	

[a]Velásquez was an interim president chosen by the Congress; he was not directly elected.
Source: Rey (1994a) and author's calculations based on Consejo Supremo Electoral figures.

in both houses has been delegated decree authority. AD's majority in the Senate ranged from approximately 60 to 64 percent in each case, and its majority in the Chamber of Deputies ranged from approximately 51 to over 56 percent (see Table 5.1). The bare majority of 51 percent was enough to delegate authority to Pérez despite the fierce opposition by COPEI, which had only 32 percent of the seats in the Chamber. Because of the populist policies guaranteed in the enabling legislation, the delegation also received the support of many smaller parties (Karl 1982:213–20). This pattern lends support to the idea that congressional majorities did not fear agency loss by delegating authority to a president from their own party.

Of the five times that decree authority was delegated, the first two, to Betancourt and Pérez, were substantively the broadest and of long duration (one year).

In each case the president had a majority in both houses of Congress. Legislative decree authority was also delegated to Jaime Lusinchi for a year in the mid-1980s by a majority Congress. In this case he was substantively more constrained than the previous two presidents. This may in part be due both to the "learning experience" that resulted from Pérez's prolific issuing of decrees and to the relative economic austerity of the times. These judgments are complicated by the fact that enabling legislation usually originates in the executive branch itself, so the responsibility for oversight provisions is difficult to discern.

The delegation of authority to Caldera (the *Convergencia*/MAS candidate) in 1994 does not contradict the importance of the partisan composition of the legislature for explaining delegation. In both chambers of the legislature, no party had more than 32 percent of the seats; in addition there were five parties in the Chamber of Deputies and four parties in the Senate with at least 10 percent of the seats. Using Rae's (1971:55–58) index of fragmentation, party system coherence reached its second lowest score (Fe = .82) in the democratic era (see Table 5.1).[6] Thus, it is a highly divided legislature that was willing to delegate authority – but only for a short time and in a carefully defined manner. What is more, in support of Carey and Shugart's hypothesis that delegating authority to a president with a weak veto does not threaten congressional interests, it should be recalled that Venezuelan presidents have only a suspensive veto, so their decrees could be relatively easily countermanded with subsequent legislation. In addition, again as Carey and Shugart hypothesize, the court that adjudicates executive–assembly disputes is highly politicized – mostly because of legislative rather than executive appointment of judges – so legislators might assume the president could be controlled through legal action.[7]

The only other instance of delegation was to Ramón J. Velásquez, who, after Pérez was forced from office in 1993 on corruption charges, was agreed upon by the legislative parties as an interim candidate because of his independent status. At this point AD had a majority in the Chamber of Deputies and a plurality of nearly 48 percent in the Senate. Velásquez as the consensus choice of AD and COPEI, the two largest parties in each house, was able to count on their support during his term.

Even most of the cases when decree authority was not delegated seem to support the importance of the partisan composition of Congress. In no case has a president faced an opposition majority. Leoni and Pérez (in his second term) from AD were not delegated authority by congresses in which their party had clear pluralities, but no majorities, in both houses. The two Copeyano presidents have faced opposition pluralities. Caldera as a member of COPEI until the 1990s did not receive decree authority during his first presidency from a Congress in which AD had a plurality in both houses, and Herrera Campins also from COPEI did not receive decree authority from a Chamber of Deputies in which AD had the plurality and a Senate in which AD and COPEI had an equal number of seats. The party system was particularly fragmented during the Caldera government (Fe = .84), but the opposition parties proved to be able to work together, especially in a spirit of opposition to COPEI and the president. For example, recall that it was during this period that the president's role in appointing lower court judges was eliminated; it was also when representatives of organized labor (where AD affiliated leaders were numerically superior) were put on the governing boards of public enterprises (Coppedge 1994:338–40).

When authority is delegated, the substantive leeway given the president and the duration of the delegation are related to the partisan composition of the legislature. Presidents ask for and receive decree authority when they have a majority in Congress that will give it to them, and they can be assured of its original acquiescence and continued support because of the strong role for party elites. Presidents play a key role in determining their party's stance, and they use the party discipline exercised in Congress to assure the consent of their congressional delegation to any decrees they might issue. Minority presidents are only given authority to carry out unpopular tasks or to address particularly difficult situations. Although we have no agreed upon measure of informational advantages, the Venezuela case offers some support for these hypotheses. The president has access to an array of consultative commissions and an enormous federal bureaucracy, whereas Congress is understaffed and lacks internal structure. Because of the president's informational advantage, his or her co-partisans give him long and wide-ranging decree authority when they have a majority. When the president's party does not have a majority, he gets carefully defined decree authority to carry out unpleasant tasks.

Carey and Shugart hypothesize that a legislative branch with intrabranch bargaining problems is more likely to delegate authority. Venezuela does have a bicameral legislature, thus complicating legislative branch unity, and decree authority has been delegated to five of eight presidential administrations. Contrary to their hypotheses, however, Venezuelan congressional delegations are highly disciplined. It may be that disciplined legislative delegations are better able to agree on whether or not decree authority should be delegated and with what provisions.

Does the provision for delegation of decree authority in Article 190:8 of the 1961 Venezuelan Constitution undermine the separation of powers and checks and balances and, as a result, lead to presidential dominance? The evidence from these case studies is mixed. In defense of the position that democratic institutional arrangements are not endangered, we can conclude that

1. the Constitution restricts delegated decree authority to economic and financial matters.
2. the authority has been delegated only five times.
3. the time for which such authority is granted is limited (increasingly so as of late).
4. the instructions provided the president by the Congress can be quite detailed.
5. the provisions for oversight can be fairly rigorous.

On the other hand, what constitutes economic and financial matters has been broadly defined at times, the flurry of presidential activity that can occur within a year is tremendous (witness Pérez in 1974 and 1975), the instructions provided can also be vague and unrestricting, and the provisions for oversight can be nonexistent or ignored. However, even if we conclude that the separation of powers is occasionally being blurred, we must keep in mind that the pattern is only explainable if we account for constitutionally allocated powers of both the executive and legislative branches and the partisan composition of each one. Zealous use of power by heads of government is not inherent in the presidential system as it is defined in the Constitution of 1961. When such zealousness occurs, it can only be explained by looking at the party system and the relative strengths of parties in government (Crisp 1997b).

DECREE AUTHORITY GRANTED THE PRESIDENT DIRECTLY BY THE CONSTITUTION

Restricted or suspended constitutional guarantees. Venezuelan presidents can assume decree authority through a number of provisions related to unusual circumstances that fall short of an official state of emergency (which will be discussed later). For example, Article 244 allows them to restrict the personal liberty of anyone threatening the public order.

More importantly, the president has the right to suspend and restrict constitutional guarantees and to issue decrees related to these rights, and such decrees have the force of law as long as the guarantees are suspended (Art. 190:6 and Art. 241). The president is prohibited from tampering with the right to life (Art. 58); neither can the president tamper with the prohibition against being held *incommunicado* or tortured (Art. 60:3), as well as the prohibition against being sentenced to cruel and unusual punishment (Art. 60:7). Otherwise, the president, by suspending any of the individual, social, economic, and political guarantees in the Constitution, can assume "powers that normally correspond to the Congress" (Brewer-Carias 1985b:521). The president must submit decrees related to the suspension or restriction of constitutional rights to Congress within ten days of their taking effect. The legislature does not have the right to disapprove of or modify individual decrees, but it can declare that the motivating factors for the suspension or restriction of rights have expired and thus render all decrees justified in this manner null.

In cases where rights are totally suspended, the president can issue decrees or take actions that would not be legal in ordinary times. When a constitutional guarantee is completely suspended, the executive branch is not required to issue further decrees regulating its exercise. Instead, the government is free to act in these areas without issuing any notification whatsoever. If the president only restricts the right, the successive decrees can only determine how the right will be exercised within previously established legal bounds during the period of restriction. However, this distinction between the suspension and restriction of constitutional guarantees has been all but ignored recently (Rey 1994a:2–3).

The presidential initiative to promulgate decrees justified by the suspension or restriction of constitutional guarantees has been used, literally, since the Constitution of 1961 was adopted (and, in fact, before it). Due to the continued threats of military coups and leftist insurrections in the early days of the democratic regime, Betancourt felt the need to suspend or restrict a number of constitutional guarantees. When he took office, the Constitution of 1953 was still in force, and it was through it that he first suspended rights on November 29, 1960. The day the new Constitution went into effect – on January 23, 1961– Betancourt set aside the same constitutional rights with Decree #455 (*Gaceta Oficial* 26,463, 1/23/61). He suspended the prohibition of arrest without a warrant and the guarantee of a full defense (Art. 60:1); the inviolability of the home (Art. 62); the inviolability of private communications (Art. 63); free transit (Art. 64); freedom of expression (Art. 66); the right to assembly (Art. 71); and the right to peaceful protest (Art. 115). He restricted the right to strike (Art. 92) and the right to economic liberty (Art. 96). Less than a year later – in early January 1962 – Betancourt was comfortable enough to reestablish some constitutional guarantees completely (Art. 60:1, 62, 63, 64, and 92) and others partially (Art. 66, 71, and 115); again he did so through a decree – Decree# 674 (*Gaceta Oficial* 26,746, 1/8/62). The right to economic liberty remained restricted in its original form, and I will discuss this right in much greater detail later.

When Acción Democrática split later that year, the opposition temporarily gained a legislative majority and used it to reestablish all the remaining suspended or restricted rights, except that of economic liberty as provided for in Article 96 (*Gaceta Oficial* 26,821, 4/7/62). However on May 5, 1962, a naval battalion in the port city of Carupano attempted a rebellion, and as part of the means to maintain order, Betancourt suspended some of the same rights again (Art. 60:1, 62, 63, 66, 71, and 115) (*Gaceta Oficial* 26,839, 5/4/62). Two political parties were associated with the rebellion – the Movement of the Revolutionary Left (MIR) and the Venezuelan Communist Party (PCV) – and Betancourt was able to suspend their operation as a result of the guarantees he set aside. The Minister of Interior Relations, future President Carlos Andrés Pérez, used the suspension of Article 96 to require that publishers receive government approval before reporting on disturbances (Resolution #8, *Gaceta Oficial* 26,890, 7/3/62). Betancourt reestablished the rights at the end of July (*Gaceta Oficial Extraordinario* 811, 7/31/62). On October 7, 1962, as a result of the increasing number of leftist attacks designed to overthrow the government, Betancourt again set aside these rights, as well as the right to release from detention by public order (Art. 60:6) and the minimal protections offered citizens who were considered to be "dangerous" but who had not committed a criminal act (Art. 60:10) (*Gaceta Oficial Extraordinario* 811, 10/7/62). Again Pérez, as Minister of Interior Relations, clamped down on the press (Resolution #9, *Gaceta Oficial* 26,971, 10/8/62). Shortly before leaving office, Betancourt completely reestablished all constitutional rights, except the right to economic liberty as provided for in Article 96 (*Gaceta Oficial* 27,030, 12/18/62 and *Gaceta Oficial* 27,040, 1/3/63).

With Decree #1,084 of March 28, 1968, President Raul Leoni suspended several constitutional guarantees in the state of Zulia due to disturbances by waste management workers in Maracaibo. He suspended the right to due process (Art. 60:1), the prohibition against imprisonment after an order of release (Art. 60:6), the inviolability of the home (Art. 62), free transit (Art. 64), freedom of expression (Art. 66), freedom of assembly (Art. 71), and political protest (Art. 115) (Leoni 1968).

Excluding the right to economic liberty, constitutional guarantees were not suspended or restricted again until the second administration of Carlos Andrés Pérez. The Pérez administration approved of a hike in bus fares, but most independent operators doubled their rates, going beyond the government-approved increases. The administration failed to communicate the policy and its motivation to the population at large, and as a result, workers only learned of it when they tried to take a bus to work Monday, February 27, 1989. Their outrage at the situation was exacerbated by its timing – the very end of the month, when most of them were desperately awaiting paychecks (Naim 1993:31–4). Spontaneous rioting and looting ensued, and when the government finally responded, it was with a very heavy hand. During the riots and following military crackdown, at least 300 people were killed (*El Nacional* 1990:127–9), but many estimates put the number in excess of 2,000. With Decree #49 on February 28 (*Gaceta Oficial* 34,168, 2/28/89), Pérez suspended the individual rights to liberty and security (Art. 60),[8] the inviolability of the home (Art. 62), free transit (Art. 64), freedom of expression (Art. 66), and the right to gather publicly and privately (Art. 71). He also suspended the political right to peaceful protest (Art. 115).[9] He partially reestablished the right to liberty and security (Art. 60:10), and he also completely reestablished freedom of expression (Art. 66) on March 8, 1989, through Decree #67 (*Gaceta Oficial* 34,175, 3/9/89) and the remaining rights through Decree #98 on March 22, 1989 (*Gaceta Oficial* 34,184, 3/22/89).

During this nearly month-long period, not one decree or resolution was issued that defined how these rights were to be exercised. Instead, the government was free to act in these areas without restrictions, and one could argue that Venezuelans lived in the complete absence of a state of law (Brewer-Carias 1989:21). This complete absence of qualifications to government authority also means that it is impossible to trace government activity through official documents. Instead, one is forced to rely on the mass media, and in this state of legal informality, the government also relied upon them. So, for example, the Minister of Education suspended educational activities and later reopened primary schools and then secondary schools through pronouncements reported by the press. Likewise, the Minister of Defense declared, modified, and lifted a curfew through government communications that were reported on television and by the papers without a single presidential decree or ministerial resolution. And a curfew can restrict other constitutional guarantees for many, including the right to work and the rights to assemble or protest (at certain hours), even though these rights were never formally modified (Brewer-Carias 1989:23).

After the attempted coup on February 4, 1992, Pérez suspended the same rights as in 1989, but this time, he also suspended the right to strike (Art. 92) with Decree #2,086 (*Gaceta Oficial Extraordinario* 4,380, 2/4/92).[10] He reestablished some of the rights (Art. 64, 66, and 92) in approximately two weeks (Decree #2,097, 2/13/92; *Gaceta Oficial* 34,905, 2/17/92). He did not reestablish the remaining rights until April (Decree #2,183, 4/9/92; *Gaceta Oficial* 39,941, 4/9/92). Again, the president issued no further decrees indicating the limitations to government activity on the basis of this suspension of constitutional guarantees.

After a second attempted coup on November 27, 1992, Pérez suspended the same rights as in 1989 (Decree #2,668, 11/27/92; *Gaceta Oficial* 35,101, 11/27/92). This time, a limited number of official government pronouncements did follow. The curfew that was constitutionally put in place from 6:00 P.M. to 6:00 A.M. was established by a resolution from the Ministry of Interior Relations (Resolution #517, 11/27/92; *Gaceta Oficial* 35,101, 11/27/92), and a second resolution shortened its duration from the hours of 10:00 P.M. to 5:00 A.M. (Resolution #518, 11/28/92; *Gaceta Oficial Extraordinario* 4,496, 11/28/92). More importantly, the president issued a subsequent decree which established a number of military courts and gave them jurisdiction over proceedings related to the coup for both civilians and members of the armed forces (Decree #2,669, 11/27/92; *Gaceta Oficial Extraordinario* 4,496, 11/28/92). This action was justified by reference to the decree which suspended the rights and particular articles of the Military Code of Justice but not by reference to particular constitutional guarantees. These military courts proceeded to detain and judge a number of people, but their activities were later declared unconstitutional by the Supreme Court for violating Article 69 of the Constitution, the article which declares that no one can be tried, except by their natural judges, or condemned on any basis except preexisting laws (Cova 1993:195–205). Unlike the undocumented acts taken during earlier suspensions, there was an official record of government activity which could be used to challenge the constitutionality of government behavior.

On November 28, Pérez modified Decree #2,668 with Decree #2,670 (*Gaceta Oficial Extraordinario* 4,496, 11/28/92), allowing the meetings of political parties that would be participating in the upcoming elections (by reestablishing Art. 64, 66, and 71). He reestablished some of the still suspended rights (Art. 64, 66, and 71) on December 1, 1992 (*Gaceta Oficial* 35,103, 12/1/92). Despite the fact that Pérez's party had a plurality of approximately 48 percent in each house, Congress issued an Accord on December 18 which reestablished Articles 60:6, 60:10, 62, and 115, but it expressly left due process (Art. 60:1) and the prohibition against unlawful of detention (Art. 60:2) suspended. The accord itself does not give the reasoning behind this move, but the Constitution (Art. 243) allows a joint session of the legislature to reestablish rights if it deems that the motivating circumstances no longer exist. Pérez reestablished the remaining rights

(Art. 60:1 and 60:2) on January 16, 1993 (*Gaceta Oficial Extraordinario* 4,519, 1/16/93).

Pérez felt compelled to suspend guarantees again, but this time only in the state of Sucre. The governor's term ended on January 12, 1993, but questions regarding the election results from December, 1992, had yet to be resolved. As a result, Pérez suspended the right to free transit (Art. 64), the right to assembly (Art. 71), and the right to peaceful protest (Art. 115) (Decree #2,765, 1/16/93; *Gaceta Oficial Extraordinario* 4,519, 1/16/93). Based on the peaceful behavior of the citizens and the prudent actions of government officials, as the justification for the decree declared, Pérez reestablished the rights on January 25 (Decree #2,780, *Gaceta Oficial* 35,138, 1/25/93). However, complications brought about by the lack of a governor led Prez to declare an official state of emergency in the states of Sucre and Barinas the very next day. This is the only state of emergency in the history of Venezuela, and it will be discussed in greater detail later.

President Rafael Caldera, who was elected to his second term by a coalition of small parties in December 1993, assumed decree authority as a result of what he called the "economic-financial emergency" in which the country found itself (Decree #241, *Gaceta Oficial* 35,490, 6/27/94). This should not be confused with the declaration of an official state of emergency or the delegation of decree authority in economic and financial matters. Caldera suspended the individual rights that prohibited arrest without a warrant (Art. 60:1), that established the inviolability of the home (Art. 62), and that guaranteed free transit (Art. 64). He also suspended the economic right to property (Art. 99 and 101) and the right to economic liberty (Art. 96).[11]

As one human rights organization put it, "the measure appeared to be interpreted individually by each minister and used for different ends" (*Suspensión de las Garantias Para Qué?* 1994:1). One goal was to seize the property of banking officials who were accused of gross mismanagement and to shake the confidence of speculators. However, the suspension of rights also appears to have been used to justify efforts to uncover evidence of plans for an uprising. Citizens in poor sections of Caracas were considered suspect, and social activists and leftist party leaders were detained.

This was the first time in the history of the 1961 Constitution that property rights were abridged (Rey 1994a:3). This raises an important question beyond the nontrivial issue of government by decree being used to intervene into a new and important facet of people's lives. Recall that decrees justified by the suspension or restriction of constitutional guarantees are only valid for as long as the right remains suspended. The suspension of Articles 99 and 101 have been used, for example, to seize the property of important officials in banks that went under due primarily to poor management. What happens when property rights are reestablished? What is the status of the seized property? Does it still belong to the government, or does it revert to its original owners (its state prior to the suspension)? The government sold this property as part of the bank bail-out, so it clearly assumes that there is no going back to the state of ownership prior to the decree. However, this is a new use for presidential decree authority, one that is justified by this means, and significant legal questions may be raised once the suspension of constitutional guarantees no longer shrouds the government's behavior from legal action.

On July 21, 1994, Congress, in which Caldera's coalitions of parties did not have a majority or even a plurality, decided that reasons for these suspensions did not exist, and it reinstituted all the constitutional guarantees – all of them except Article 96, the right to economic liberty (*Gaceta Oficial Extraordinario* 4,754, 7/22/94). The measure was supported by members of AD, COPEI, and Causa R,[12] but it was opposed by *Convergencia* and MAS. Within hours Caldera called a meeting of his Council of Ministers and resuspended all the same guarantees. The turn of events occurred so rapidly that the congressional agreement and the new presidential decree (#285) were published back-to-back in the same *Gaceta* (*Gaceta Oficial Extraordinario* 4,754, 7/22/94). Never in the history of presidential decree authority had a president so baldly overridden the desires of Congress (Rey 1994a:4). Caldera did not attempt to argue that new motivating factors required resuspension. He simply contradicted Congress by stating that the crises in the financial and exchange systems, as well as difficulties surrounding the supply of goods,[13] had not ceased and that the executive required sufficient powers to confront these issues. He also explicitly reconfirmed the suspension of Article 96, even though this issue was not in question, and he "ratified" several decrees issued between June 27 and July 22, even though some of them were not justified in terms of Decree #241, which originally suspended the rights. By "ratifying" rather than reissuing these decrees, Caldera was indicating that the rights had never been reestablished – even momentarily – between the congressional accord and Decree #285. The new decree itself made no mention of congressional action, but in a dialogue carried on with congressional leaders through the press, Caldera made it clear that he would not brook another challenge. He made it known that if he was challenged again, either through another accord or through a challenge in the courts, he would appeal directly to the people regarding his right to rule by decree. Fearing a Fujimori-like *autogolpe* (self-coup), Acción Democrática, with the largest legislative delegation, backed down and left the coalition trying to reinstate the constitutional guarantees. Regardless of the constitutionality of Caldera's actions, the rights remained suspended, and he only reinstated them with Decree #739 (see *Gaceta Oficial Etraordinaria* 4,931 7/6/95) on July 6, 1995, after Congress passed the last of three pieces of legislation (discussed later in greater detail under emergency powers) which enhanced the executive's ability to intervene in the economy.[14]

The situation surrounding the right to "dedicate oneself freely to the profitable activity of one's preference," as outlined in Article 96 of the 1961 Constitution, deserves special comment. The article also calls for the law to prevent usury, unduly high prices, and monopolies. This article was one of the ones restricted by Betancourt on January 23, 1961 (Decree #455; *Gaceta Oficial* 26,463, 1/23/61) when the Constitution took effect, and it remained restricted until July 4,

1991 (Decree #1724; *Gaceta Oficial* 34,752, 7/10/91). It was suspended completely, not restricted, on February 28, 1994 (Decree #51; *Gaceta Oficial* 35,410, 2/28/94), but it was reinstated on June 1, 1994 (Decree #208; *Gaceta Oficial* 35,473, 6/1/94). It was suspended again less than a month later on June 27, 1994 (Decree #241; *Gaceta Oficial* 35,490, 6/27/94), and was reestablished again on July 6, 1995 (Decree #739). Interestingly, when Congress and Caldera clashed over the suspension of guarantees in July 1994, neither branch tried to reinstitute the right to economic liberty.[15] This near permanent restriction has served as the justification for numerous presidential decrees related to a rather wide range of activities, and, as a result, it has been used to effect policy changes in a manner similar to constitutional decree authority (CDA). Between 1961 and 1994 this presidential initiative was used to issue at least 194 decrees (Presidential Commission for the Reform of the State 1985: 9–23; see also *Gaceta Oficial*). See Figure 5.1 for how these decrees have been spread over time.

Many of the decree laws issued in the early 1960s focused on the control of the exchange rate. During the late 1960s there were relatively few decrees, but their range of activity broadened considerably. They did everything from regulating private armed guard companies, to establishing the number of animals to be processed daily in slaughter houses, to eliminating a chain of state-owned gas distributors. In general Betancourt (AD) made occasional use of the initiative and Leoni (AD) hardly any. The pace of decrees began to increase slightly during the Caldera (COPEI) administration from 1969 through 1973, and their range of activity continued to be quite broad. Caldera addressed interest rates, urban housing, services for the hydrocarbon industry, and the importation of fireworks, among other things.

In the mid- to late-1970s under Pérez (AD), the promulgation of decrees due to the restriction of economic rights accelerated dramatically. These decrees fixed consumer prices, encouraged employment, set interest rates, and raised prices that wholesalers were to pay farmers, among many other activities (Brewer-Carias 1980: 107–144). Herrera Campins (COPEI) appears to have made relatively little use of this power until near the end of his term in 1983. Much of this flurry of activity was related to the differential exchange rates designed to help enterprises with a large foreign debt deal with the currency devaluation. It was this same area of activity on which Lusinchi (AD) focused from 1984 through 1988, and it was also this same area of activity that would lead to scandal over the determination of who would receive preferential rates. His interventions concerning exchange rates, debt classification, foreign exchange, and the convertibility of money allowed for a great deal of discretion, and this discretion was apparently misused as debtors with apparently identical characteristics were treated quite differently, thus leading to many allegations of kickbacks for preferential treatment. It should be noted that Pérez and Lusinchi, the two most prolific issuers of these types of decrees, had majorities in both houses of Congress. One could interpret this in two ways. Perhaps these presidents felt compelled to issue such decrees despite having relatively cooperative congresses. Or, conversely, their use

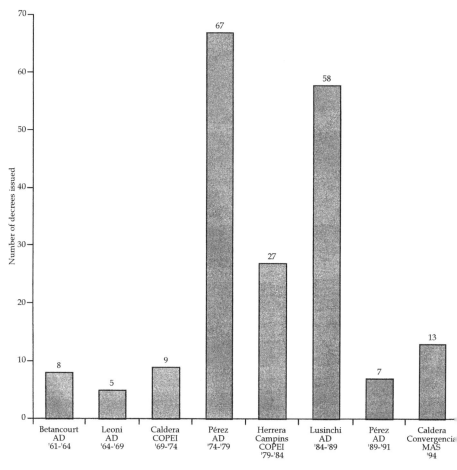

Figure 5.1 Number of decrees justified by the suspension of economic rights between January 23, 1961, and August 31, 1994 (Source: All data collected by the author from Comisión Presidencial para la Reforma del Estado {1985}, 13–23; and the Gaceta Oficial de la República de Venezuela)

of decree was tolerated because the products of their initiatives benefited the current congressional majorities and their supporters.

Pérez's second term stands in a marked contrast to his first one. He reinstated the right to economic liberty on July 4, 1991, which means he only had the power for a year and a half; this stands in contrast to his entire first, five-year term in the 1970s. The fact that he reinstated the right, as well as his relatively limited use of the power, indicates his newly adopted neoliberal strategy. Pérez surrounded himself with a number of market-oriented academics who supported the policies promoted by international lending agencies, which called for a decreased role for the state in Latin American economies. Perez's use of the right to restrict economic rights is a clear indicator of his changed position. In fact, of the seven decrees he issued, four were used to repeal previous presidential decrees justified by the restriction of economic rights, including the fixing of prices and the offering of preferential exchange rates.

In his second term, this time as the candidate of *Convergencia*, MAS, and others, Caldera suspended Article 96 twice. The distinction between restriction and suspension has not always been clear, but the case of Caldera's first suspension illustrates it well. The Constitution says that if a guarantee is restricted, the executive branch must issue decrees and resolutions indicating how it will be exercised.[16] Thus, the 181 decrees discussed thus far fulfilled this requirement. However, if the right is completely suspended, the executive branch does not have to formalize into decrees or resolutions its activities in any related area. As a result, there is no systematic means of monitoring executive branch behavior. For example, Caldera suspended Article 96 in February 1994, and when he reinstated it in June, he reasoned in the decree itself that the motivating circumstances had ceased, because the executive had been able to reform the tax system and because the exchange and financial markets had been stabilized. Yet between February and June, no decrees justified by the suspension of economic rights were issued. Caldera considered the suspension of the Constitution necessary in order to carry out significant policies, but he did not have to justify these policies in terms of or explicitly connect them with this suspension of the Constitution. After the resuspension of the right at the end of June, Caldera did justify several decrees on this basis. He used this authority to create two new government entities: the Financial Emergency Board (Decree #248, 6/29/94; *Gaceta Oficial* 35,492, 6/29/94) and the Exchange Administration Board (Decree #268, 7/9/94; *Gaceta Oficial Extraordinario* 4,744, 7/9/94). These entities were given wide-ranging economic and financial powers, including the right to punish violators of their policies. The new boards issued ministerial-like resolutions, the force of which was justified by the suspension of Article 96.

Other than the suspension of economic rights, Venezuelan presidents have rarely taken decree authority by suspending or restricting constitutional guarantees, and usually they do so only in dire circumstances, including the imminent threat of coups, insurrections, or mass disturbances. However, some of the actions they have taken to limit individual rights during these periods were subsequently declared unconstitutional. Human rights activists and legal scholars have decried the rather capricious behavior of several governments. Excluding economic rights, only Betancourt, Pérez (in his second term), and Caldera (in his second term) have taken this initiative. However, Caldera's suspension in 1994 seems less clearly supported by Article 241, and his failure to accept Congress' reestablishment of guarantees seems to violate the intent of the Constitution and marks a new and dangerous stage in executive–legislative relations.

Given the motivating factors in the case of Betancourt and Pérez, it is not surprising that these suspensions and restrictions are unrelated to the partisan

composition of the legislature and the resulting potential for interbranch stalemate or intralegislative bargaining problems.[17] Betancourt had a congressional
majority, Pérez had a congressional plurality, and Caldera had a congressional
minority in which no party had a simple majority. Caldera's suspension and his
consequent struggle with the legislature were very likely motivated by his lack
of support in Congress and by the potential difficulty he would face in pushing
through a program. If Caldera's precedent of overriding Congress holds up, then
there is no check on the president's ability to suspend the Constitution and issue
related decrees.

The near permanent restriction or suspension of economic liberty and the
number of decrees issued as a result do not show anywhere near as clear a relationship to the partisan compatibility of the branches as is the case with delegated
decree authority. First, no Congress, regardless of its partisan composition, ever
reinstated this constitutional guarantee, thereby eliminating the president's decree authority. The two presidents who did reinstate it did so when they did not
have majorities in Congress, so they could not have been assuming that they
could count on support for their initiatives in the legislature. As Figure 5.1
indicates, the relative use of this authority has varied widely over time. Pérez (in
his first term) and Lusinchi issued the most decrees, and they had congressional
majorities. This might indicate that presidents exercise this authority when Congress will not reinstate the right or issue countermanding legislation. However,
this does not explain Betancourt's relatively scant use of this authority when he
had a congressional majority, not unless he was constrained by the common
minimum government program and the grand coalition nature of his government. Herrera Campins and Caldera made relatively frequent use of decrees when
they had congressional minorities. It is possible that they anticipated the reaction
of Congress and issued decrees that would not provoke a reestablishment of the
guarantee by the legislature. Given the contradictory evidence, however, it is
difficult to conclude which branch's preference is being pursued through the
decrees justified by the suspension of the right to economic liberty.

Given the near permanent restriction or suspension of the right to economic
liberty (Art. 96), the use of this decree authority in Venezuela appears much like
constitutional decree authority (CDA) in other countries. There are two critical
differences however – in Venezuela, the legislature had the right to reestablish
Article 96 at any time, thus ending the president's ability to issue new decrees,
and it also had the right to render null and void all previous decrees justified in
this manner. Thus, this form of decree authority falls in a gray area between
constitutional and delegated authority. It resembles CDA to the extent that presidents can initiate it without prior congressional consent, and it has been used
by every president in Venezuelan democratic history (see Figure 5.1). On the
other hand, it resembles a retrospective form of DDA to the extent that Congress
does not delegate authority prior to its initiation, but it has the ability to revoke
it once it is taken.

Because decree authority obtained by suspending or restricting the Constitution is not an example of CDA, this authority's relationship to Carey and Shugart's hypotheses is difficult to sort out. They hypothesize that CDA is more likely in cases where the legislature is likely to face bargaining problems and where the legislature is least likely to suffer agency loss. Venezuela is mixed in each area. The legislature may suffer from bargaining problems because it is bicameral, but on the other hand, the electoral system has been designed to minimize the chances of a divided legislature. In addition legislative parties are disciplined. Likewise, the Constitution is difficult to amend, so the legislature would find it difficult to respond to agency loss, but the president's veto is weak, so regular legislation has had the potential to countermand him. The mixed nature of the independent variables fits perfectly with the mixed nature of decree authority from the suspension or restriction of constitutional guarantees. The bicameral legislature and the weak veto are consistent with the legislature's willingness to tolerate the president's initiation of this process, whereas the disciplined legislative delegations and the difficulty in amending the Constitution are consistent with the legislature's tendency to retain the right to end the process.

Emergency powers. Article 240 of the Constitution gives the president, in his Council of Ministers, the right to declare a state of emergency in situations of domestic or foreign conflict or when established facts indicate that one or the other situation will occur. The Constitution does not define any additional powers that accrue to the president in a state of emergency, except the right to suspend or restrict constitutional guarantees, which he or she can do directly without a state of emergency. There has only been one instance when a state of emergency was declared. The validity of the results of the 1992 gubernatorial elections in the states of Barinas and Sucre was challenged, and the challenges were not resolved by the time the previous governors' terms had expired. Carlos Andrés Pérez declared a state of emergency in these states (Decree #2,781, 1/26/93; *Gaceta Oficial* 35,139, 1/26.93), because only the governor has the right to make payments on behalf of the state and because the financial difficulties that could result from a paralyzed state government might lead to unrest.

Because the justifications for a state of emergency are more narrowly defined than the justifications for suspending or restricting rights directly (in states of emergency, in situations that could disturb the peace of the Republic, or in grave circumstances that affect economic and social life) and because no additional powers resulted from the state of emergency, presidents have had little reason to invoke this condition. However, Venezuelan legislation has been defining additional presidential powers for states of emergency, and these powers may lead to increased use of this provision. For example, the Organic Law of Security and Defense, which was adopted in 1976, named the president maximum authority in everything related to security and defense, and it defined these areas very broadly as "involving directly or indirectly all the activities of the state" (Rey 1989: 150–5). It declares that in a state of emergency, the president along with the National Council of Security and Defense, a body consisting of only presidential appointees and military officials as members that was created by the law, will have broad powers to mobilize the military and to sustain order.

Similarly, the Caldera government convinced Congress to increase the president's emergency powers by modifying of the consumer protection law, adopting the exchange control law, and adopting a law increasing the president's powers to intervene in banking activities. In addition to broadening the justifications for a state of emergency beyond those listed in the Constitution, these laws defined a series of presidential powers that would result immediately from a state of emergency rather than from the requirement that constitutional guarantees be suspended. The consumer protection law allows the president to take actions against ill-defined crimes such as hoarding, speculation, usury, and the propagation of rumors. The exchange control law allows the president to decree currency controls at will (*Economist* 1994: 45–6). The financial emergency law, which took the longest to pass, allows the president to intervene in banks, freezing accounts and seizing assets. Because ending a state of emergency (by presidential decree in the Council of Ministers along *with* the authorization of Congress in joint session) requires action by both branches of government, the president's powers would be even less subject to congressional control than they are through the suspension of constitutional guarantees. Recall that suspended guarantees can, theoretically, be reinstated by either branch (although Congress failed to accomplish this in 1994), but a state of emergency requires consensus between the branches. As a result, such powers open the real possibility that a state of exception could become government by decree in relatively normal times.

PARACONSTITUTIONAL USES OF PRESIDENTIAL DECREE AUTHORITY

Decree authority delegated by the Congress in a paraconstitutional manner. It may seem paradoxical that a legislature would willingly abdicate its lawmaking responsibility in the absence of constitutional grounds for doing so. There are no instances in Venezuela in which Congress has obviously disregarded the Constitution in order to grant decree authority to the president. However, the extremely broad delegation of decree authority in economic and financial matters under the justification of Article 190:8 has bordered on paraconstitutional delegation. What constitutes an "economic or financial matter" has included, for example, the authority to create a school of public administration. The earliest cases of delegation – to Betancourt on June 29, 1961, and to Pérez on May 31, 1974 – were the broadest and of the longest duration, and Pérez, in particular, took advantage of this opportunity. The delegations to Velásquez and Caldera also raise the constitutional issue of the right to define the penal code. This is significant not because of the number of people who would be guilty of violating presidential decrees but because it signifies a critical breakdown in the constitutional separation of powers. The precedent established by allowing the president to create crimes and punishments is an enormous danger. In addition the legislature's willingness to leave economic rights suspended by presidential decree, as outlined in Article 190:6 and Article 241, and its failure to pass legislation that would replace these decrees indicate a failure to fully implement the Constitution. In both cases where Congress acted to reestablish constitutional rights suspended by the president, it left Article 96 concerning economic liberty suspended.

Decree authority taken by the president in a paraconstitutional manner. Again, it is difficult to evaluate whether this situation has occurred in Venezuela. Opposition politicians in Congress argued that Pérez's *decretomania* of every theoretical type in the 1970s was an usurpation of the legislature's power – an usurpation at least tacitly supported by AD's majority in Congress. COPEI's congressional delegation, in particular, argued that Perez's claim that he needed special powers to implement his program and deal with the international economy was unjustified, especially given his party's majority in Congress (Fernandez 1976: 35–98). In the end he was given the authority with the support of both his own party and the opposition parties on the left – but much to the chagrin of COPEI. He used this delegated authority, his rule-making authority, and the suspension of economic rights to issue more than 3,000 decrees during his term. His access to tremendous petroleum-generated revenue only served to make his activities seem limitless.

The example that most closely approximates usurpation is Caldera's defiance of Congress in 1994. The Constitution gives only the executive branch the right to suspend and restrict constitutional guarantees, but it gives both the executive and legislative branches the right to declare at an end the extraordinary circumstances that justified the suspension. Caldera's brash resuspension of guarantees immediately on the heels of congressional reestablishment seems to usurp the power granted Congress (Art. 243) both to declare extraordinary circumstances and, therefore, to declare that presidential decree authority is no longer in existence.

PRESIDENTIAL DECREE AUTHORITY AND THE NATURE OF DEMOCRACY IN VENEZUELA

When one reads the Constitution of 1961, one finds that the formal powers given to the president are relatively limited and unequivocal. The mere use of decrees does not necessarily indicate that presidents are threatening the separation of powers and short-circuiting institutional checks and balances. The phenomenon is too complex to justify such a broad conclusion. Yet Venezuelan presidents have used their limited powers quite effectively. For example, the president in the past has used his rule-making and other forms of decree authority to institutionalize the opportunity to consult with and influence important interest groups (Crisp 1997a). Presidents have also used their initiative to suspend or restrict constitutional guarantees as a way to achieve nonlegislative decree authority. Particu-

larly in the case of the guarantee of economic liberty, presidents have been able
to act without legislative participation for extended periods. Since January 23,
1961, this constitutional right has only been guaranteed from July 7, 1991, to
February 26, 1994, and from June 1 to June 27, 1994. This suspension has led
to hundreds of decrees concerning a long list of economic issues – some of them
only tangentially related to Article 96 of the Constitution (Comisión Presidencial
para la Reforma del Estado 1985: 2–12). Finally, five presidents have been delegated decree authority in economic and financial matters for as long as a year,
and what constitutes "economic and financial matters" has often been interpreted
broadly.

   Most forms of decree authority, even those that theoretically have no substantive content, can result in cases where presidents governed with little daily participation by the legislature. The most notorious case in Venezuela is the first
term of Carlos Andrés Pérez, when he issued more than 3,000 decrees of one sort
or another. His party had a majority in both houses of the national Congress, in
all the state congresses, and in most of the municipal governments. He asked for
and got delegated authority, and he could issue decrees justified by the restriction
of the right to economic liberty – not to mention that he had all the resources
of the oil boom at his disposal. Although this case is extreme, it serves to highlight the degree of power that can be made available to a Venezuelan president.

   The ways that legislative and nonlegislative decree authority are used in Venezuela make the president a powerful player in the legislative process. However,
this power varies significantly as a result of the partisan composition of the legislature, and it can only be understood in the context of mechanisms of interest
group representation, electoral regulations, and the nature of parties (Crisp
1997b). Presidents have been fairly prolific in issuing decrees after restricting or
suspending the Constitution. However, after the *decretomania* of Pérez, the legislature has been careful when delegating decree authority in economic and financial matters – that is, when it has done so, it has issued relatively detailed
instructions. And in the case of Velásquez and Caldera, presidents without majority support in Congress have been delegated decree authority for only very
short periods. In these cases the legislature has used the executive branch, with
its greater speed and more extensive resources, to carry out the legislature's will.
Under Betancourt, Pérez, and Caldera (in his second term), Congress has been
willing to declare that the extraordinary circumstances which justified the suspension or restriction of rights (other than the right to economic liberty) were
no longer, if ever, valid. (However, in the case of Caldera, the president was able
to resuspend constitutional guarantees.) In each of these instances, the president's
party, at least temporarily, did not have a majority in Congress.

   Thus, all presidents appear to make substantively significant use of their limited decree powers, but minority presidents find their prerogatives curtailed relative to majority presidents. Minority presidents are equally free to consult with
interest groups, to draft legislation, to appoint important government officials,
and to use any discretionary authority provided by the large decentralized public

administration. However, they are unlikely to be delegated broad or lengthy decree authority, and their efforts to set aside constitutional guarantees are more likely to be contested. Therefore, the relative activism and strength of Venezuelan presidents can only be explained in the context of the party system and the partisan composition of government.

It is the composition of the legislature that determines the boundaries of presidential behavior, but in order to understand the role of Congress, we must account for the nature of Venezuelan parties. Because a large role for party elites is guaranteed by both the candidate selection process and the electoral system, parties are highly disciplined and able to act as coherent units in the legislature. The same constitutional allocation of powers with undisciplined parties would probably lead to more frequent interbranch immobilism. Majority presidents would not be able to count on consistent support from their own parties, minority presidents would find it difficult to bargain for issue-specific coalitions, and the internal workings of the legislature itself would be more chaotic.

It may seem paradoxical, but even though Congress determines the limits of presidential decree authority, the legislature itself is relatively inactive, approving only twenty-eight bills per year on average (Coppedge 1994:335–6).[18] This lack of action, combined with the large, interventionist nature of the Venezuelan state, indicates that many critical political decisions must be taking place elsewhere. "Elsewhere" means within the parties themselves and in the executive branch. The Constitution gives only limited powers to the president, yet Congress is prevented from being a locus for debate and decision making because of strong party discipline. The combination might be expected to lead to government paralysis and ineffectiveness, but, generally, it has not. Instead, majority presidents have been given a loose leash, and minority presidents have been able to strike deals with disciplined parties. The result is that the executive branch is active far beyond its constitutionally allocated powers, and it turns out that the legislature is more tangential to the day-to-day process of policy making than the Constitution would make it seem.

NOTES

1 For helping me sort out the details of the Venezuelan case, I am deeply indebted to Dr. Juan Carlos Rey of the Instituto Internacional de Estudios Avanzados. I would also like to thank John M. Carey and Matthew Soberg Shugart for their comments on earlier versions of this chapter.

2 If a joint session of Congress overrides the president's initial return for reconsideration, he or she may have the right to return it yet again. That is, if the majority overrides the first veto with a two-thirds majority, the president must execute the law within five days, but if it overrides it with a simple majority, the president has the option to return it a second time. Even so, the second suspensive veto can still be overridden with a mere majority (Art. 173).

3 The editors will offer comparative data regarding the impact of the constitutional
   amendment process on the provision for decree authority. In Venezuela the
   amendment process is relatively cumbersome, and there have only been two
   amendments to the Constitution since it was adopted. An amendment must be
   proposed by at least one-quarter of one house of the legislature during an ordinary
   legislative session or by one-quarter of the state assemblies. Once proposed, it
   must be approved by one-half of the legislature in joint session. It is then sent
   to the president, who submits it to all the state assemblies. One-half of the state
   assemblies must approve it before it can be adopted.

4 Betancourt ruled until January 23, 1961, under the previous Constitution, which
   had been adopted in 1953.

5 My other work on the creation of advisory commissions for consulting with sec-
   toral interests indicates that petroleum financed abundance does not appear to be
   the explanation, because Pérez was just as active in this area in his second term
   as in his first (Crisp 1994).

6 The fragmentation index is:

$$\text{Fe} = 1 - (\cdot T_i^2)$$
$$i = 1$$

   where n equals the number of parties participating in the election and T_i equals
   any party's decimal share of the vote. Thus a value of Fe $= 0$ would indicate a
   perfect one-party system; Fe $= .5$ would indicate a perfect two-party system; and
   Fe $= 1$ would indicate that each voter selected a different party (total fraction-
   alization). For 1993 I calculated the index using votes by party for the Senate (Fe
   $= .817$), votes by party for the Chamber of Deputies (Fe $= .821$), and votes by
   single-member district candidates for the Chamber of Deputies (Fe $= .823$). Prior
   to 1993 all legislators were elected through a single ballot.

7 Despite the independence of the judiciary from the executive branch, Caldera
   was able to avoid a related dispute (to be discussed later) in 1994.

8 Specifically, he suspended due process (Art. 60:1), the prohibition against detention for acts not previously defined as unlawful (Art. 60:2), the prohibition against
   imprisonment after an order of release (Art. 60:6), and the minimal protections
   offered citizens deemed "dangerous" without having committed a specific crime.
   (Art. 60:10).

9 Interestingly, Congress issued an Accord (*Acuerdo*) "authorizing" the suspension
   of guarantees even though the Constitution requires no such confirmation (*Acuerdo*
   3/10/89; *Gaceta Oficial* 34,183, 3/21/89).

10 Again, Congress issued an Accord (*Acuerdo*) "authorizing" the suspension of guarantees even though the Constitution requires no such confirmation (*Acuerdo* 2/4/
   92; *Gaceta Oficial* 34,897, 2/5/92).

11 On February 28, 1994, shortly after taking office, Caldera suspended Article 96
   of the Constitution, the right to economic liberty (Decree #51, *Gaceta Oficial*
   35,410, 2/28/94). He reestablished the right on June 1, 1994 (Decree #208,
   Gaceta Oficial 35,473, 6/1/94). He resuspended the right to economic liberty,
   along with others, less than a month later. The exceptional case of this right will
   be discussed in further detail later.

12 Causa R supported the reestablishment of all the rights, including the right to economic liberty (Article 96).

13 The supply of goods was not explicitly mentioned as a motivating factor in Decree #241 which originally suspended the other decrees.

14 Some guarantees remained suspended in limited areas along the Colombian border due to the armed conflict between Venezuelan forces and Colombian guerrillas.

15 The Causa R delegation in Congress was alone among the major parties in its support for reestablishing the right to economic liberty in July 1994.

16 Unfortunately, due to their sheer number, it was impossible to compile a list of all the ministerial resolutions justified by this and other forms of decree authority, although they would be another important indicator of executive branch activities.

17 Comparative data are used by the editors to evaluate the impact of bicameralism and party cohesiveness on collective action – and therefore the use of decree authority. Venezuela's Congress is bicameral, but there has only been one time when the party that had the most seats in the Chamber of Deputies did not also have the most seats in the Senate – and in that case it was tied for the number-one spot. Collective action problems as a result of a bicameral legislature have not been an issue in Venezuela because, until 1993, each voter only cast one congressional ballot for a party, not a candidate. Seats in both the Chamber of Deputies and the Senate were given out on the basis of a closed-list, proportional representation system by state, a system based on this single ballot. It was possible to split one's ticket between executive and legislature but not within the legislature. In the 1993 congressional elections, some seats were still determined in this fashion, but another group was made winner-take-all by district. As a result, the two houses could, in fact, be controlled by different parties in the future, and collective action difficulties as a result of bicameralism could become an issue. Interestingly enough, in 1993 the top five parties finished with very similar seat totals in each house, and AD and COPEI remained number one and number two respectively in both houses.

Venezuela's parties are extremely cohesive in Congress. They are so cohesive that procedures for counting vote totals are rarely enforced, because everyone knows the outcome before the vote is cast. Thus, if collective action is a problem, it is not normally due to internal party procedures. There are instances when there is insufficient intraparty agreement to impose a party line, but these cases have been relatively rare.

18 Although he defines majority and minority government somewhat differently from the way the terms are used here, Coppedge argues that the aggregate legislative output of majority vs. minority governments is roughly equal, with legislatures in majority governments being somewhat more productive. Thus, increased decrees justified by delegation or suspension of constitutional rights by majority presidents do not appear to replace regular legislation. Although Venezuela has experienced majority and nonmajority governments, there is no instance of an opposition-controlled Congress with which to compare these levels of output.

PART II

CONSTITUTIONAL DECREE AUTHORITY AND CONFLICT BETWEEN THE BRANCHES

6

DANCING WITHOUT
A LEAD
LEGISLATIVE DECREES IN ITALY

Vincent Della Sala and Amie Kreppel

Perhaps in no other advanced industrialized democracy has government use of decree legislation become so common in the legislative process as it has in Italy since the mid-1970s. There is a certain paradox in this development, because decrees often are seen as the expropriation of the legislature's decision-making powers by an executive intent on providing leadership and direction. Yet Italian governments, which have been so generous in their use of decrees, have been described as anything but strong and decisive; nor have they been able to provide policy and political leadership (Cassese 1980). This brings us to one of the questions raised by Carey and Shugart in the first chapter of this book – namely, do decrees necessarily imply the displacement of law-making and political powers from the legislature to the executive? If not, what factors may account for the use of decrees and what does this tell us not only about the legislative process, but of the balance of power between institutions and between political forces?

The Italian case suggests that some significant revisions in the conventional understanding of decree legislation may be in order.[1] First, Italy has a parliamentary and not a presidential system of government. As other chapters in this volume indicate, attempts by presidents to usurp law-making powers of legislatures are not uncommon in many presidential systems. However, the conventional view of parliamentary systems assumes that the legislature's ability to discipline the executive discourages the use of nondelegated decree authority in law making. As we will see shortly, this is hardly the case in Italy, where every government since the mid-1970s has relied heavily on initiating decrees to promote its legislative agenda. Second, Italy is an advanced industrialized democracy with an entrenched constitution and a consolidated democratic institutional order. Decrees are often used as necessary instruments by executives in regimes engaged in some form of transition: economic, social, and/or political. In the classic trade-off between representation and decision-making capacity, decrees are normally regarded as reflecting a tendency toward the latter – as devices used to impose coherence and timeliness to policy making (Dahl 1994: 23–24). The Italian case suggests that such an interpretation of decrees is potentially misleading. Regarding the trade-off between *garantismo* (representation) and *decisionismo* (decision-making efficacy), constitutional developments in postwar Italy have mostly favored the former, even as the use of decrees has exploded. Third, given that Italy is not a presidential system and that it is a consolidated democratic order, it is possible to examine decree authority in a context distinct from the transitional presidential regimes with which it is frequently associated. This allows us to explore both the extent to which decree is a specific product of such regimes and the extent to which other institutional factors, such as procedural rules and the nature of the party system, affect the use of decree across diverse political environments.

The aim of this chapter is to demonstrate that decrees in Italy are the product of the conjuncture of a weak legal position for the executive with a political context that has produced fragmented, incoherent governing coalitions. The result is a decision-making process that is characterized by the diffusion of political power, many access points, and bargaining among a broad range of forces. Decrees are an instrument that governments rely on to try to navigate this complex and sometimes protracted process. We argue that decrees, rather than being exceptional measures, have become a "normal" part of the legislative process in Italy. They are less frequently dramatic attempts to circumvent the will of elected representatives than strategic moves by players who do not have many tools at their disposal in the legislative game. In the Italian dance of legislation, decrees are an attempt by governments to lead – to promote their legislative agenda – but there is no guarantee that the legislature will decide to follow. This chapter will argue that decrees have remained an essential feature of decision making in Italy despite attempts throughout the 1980s to strengthen the position of the executive. We contend that this will continue to be the case until there is a significant change in the political landscape that will allow the development of strong, cohesive parliamentary majorities that are disciplined enough to follow the will of the executive. In short Italian governments have relied on constitutional decree authority because of a lack of dependable support in a highly fragmented and undisciplined parliament. Decrees in Italy are a sign of government weakness rather than strength.

LEGAL AND POLITICAL FRAMEWORK

It is difficult to understand the use and role of decree legislation in Italy without some knowledge of the legal framework and political environment that has governed their use. Legislative decrees are just one part of a constitutional and political order that has emphasized the diffusion of political power and consensus in decision making rather than timely, coherent policy direction.

LEGAL FRAMEWORK

There are two legal bases for the use of decrees in the Italian legislative process: the Constitution and ordinary legislation, which is enacted largely within the framework of the parliamentary rules of procedure. The framers of the 1948 Constitution were concerned primarily with avoiding a repeat of the fascist dictatorship, and they were not ready to put in place mechanisms that would make it easy for the executive to bypass Parliament (Hine 1988). Yet they also were sensitive to the dangers of completely disarming governments by not giving them recourse to some form of emergency power. The result was a compromise, which was enshrined in Article 77; this provision gives the government power to issue decrees when dictated by an emergency or by the need for urgent action. Decrees come into effect immediately, but they expire after sixty days if they are not approved or converted into law by Parliament. This struck an uneasy balance between the need to protect the law-making prerogatives of Parliament and the belief that governments needed to have access to some provision which would enable them to act swiftly and decisively in an emergency.

As with so many parts of the Constitution that sought to reconcile the needs of *decisionismo* and *garantismo*, Article 77 left many questions unanswered. For instance, could governments rule indefinitely by decree, issuing the same (or almost the same) *decreto* every sixty days even if Parliament rejected it or simply let it expire without voting on it? As we will see shortly, this problem has emerged as one of the central issues surrounding the use of decrees insofar as the vast majority of decrees presented in the 1990s are little more than recycled versions of earlier decrees that expired after sixty days. The framers of the Constitution assumed that both governments and Parliament would act responsibly. The former would introduce decrees only in the cases of emergency and would not use them as a "normal" legislative procedure, whereas the latter would act within sixty days. This assumption was reaffirmed by the Constitutional Court ruling no. 302 (1988 Corte Constituzionale), which lay blame on both the government and Parliament with respect to the persistent reiteration of decrees.[2]

The constitutional foundations of decree legislation are complemented by ordinary legislative procedures, primarily in the form of the parliamentary rules of procedure, which have been partly responsible for governments that have resorted to "emergency" measures instead of "normal" legislation.[3] The rules assumed an especially prominent role after their significant reform in 1971. The most important of these changes was to Article 23 of the new parliamentary rules, which stated that the parliamentary agenda would be determined by a unanimous vote in the *capigruppo*, the committee of representatives of all groups in Parliament. Moreover, the government could only send a single observer to this meeting, but this observer did not have a vote (Manzella 1991: 113–21). The result of this provision, along with the other changes in 1971, was to blur the divisions between the government and the opposition, as well as to introduce a form of "consociationalism" into the legislative process (Mammi 1987:71–3). The 1971 changes signaled to governments that they had lost control of the legislative timetable. Not only did government sponsored bills not have any priority on the agenda, but executives also were unable to control where and under which procedure their bills would be decided. They now had to enter into negotiations with all parliamentary forces if they wanted to place issues directly on to the agenda (Floridia and Sicardi 1991:230–236). Alternatively, they could resort to decrees. Article 23 of the rules of procedure, then, presented an obstacle to a planned legislative agenda for government as well as the emergence of clear, timely decision making.[4] This problem became apparent in the 1976–79 legislature, when groups such as the Radicals began to make use of the obstructionist tactics at their disposal. More importantly, the change in the legal rules meant that there was no formal center of power in the decision-making process (Cotta 1994:74).

There has been a gradual shift since the early 1980s. This shift has returned some control of the agenda to the government – or at least to the leadership offices in Parliament. The most important change was introduced in 1990. This change gave the President of the Chamber of Deputies the power to impose a legislative timetable for up to three months if unanimity were not attainable among the *capigruppi*.[5] The president is bound only to *consult* with all the groups in Parliament; thus unanimity is no longer required (Sterpa 1990:126). Moreover, the 1990 changes state quite clearly that in the absence of unanimity, the president's agenda must be based on suggestions brought by the government along with the views expressed by all the parties in the *capigruppo*. This change represents an important shift because the government position, which had no standing prior to 1990, is now given at least a weight equal to that of parliamentary groups. This improves the government's position because it is no longer hostage to the whims of even the smallest parties; however, Italian governments still do not possess the instruments, such as closure motions or constitutional priority for government legislation, available to most other west European executives (*Corriere della Sera*, 14 March 1990).

The desire to strengthen the legislative powers of the executive was responsible for two changes to the formal rules in 1988. First, the rules of procedure were amended to limit the use of secret ballots for votes in the Chamber. Prior to the change, the fate of legislation was left to votes by deputies, who were protected by the secrecy of the ballot box. Not only did governments have little control over the timetable for their legislation, but they also had few weapons to discipline their parliamentary majorities once legislation made it to Parliament (Casu 1986). The 1988 reform to the secret ballot was partly the result of the juncture of a number of political factors. First, the leader of the DC (Christian Democrats) for most of the decade, Ciriaco De Mita, had tried to break the grip of factions on the party (*La Repubblica*, 14 October 1988). Faction leaders and their deputies could use the secret ballot to undermine the party leadership, which for one of the few times in the postwar period, was also leading the government.[6] Second, De Mita and a large part of the DC were increasingly frustrated with their Socialist partner. It was clear that agreements laboriously crafted in the government were undermined once they came to a vote in the Chamber. Third, the Communist Party also recognized that it was not reaping the benefits of government defeats by the "snipers" in Parliament.[7] Moreover, the communist position in the wider debate on institutional reform was based on a demand for greater transparency and accountability in decision making; the party could hardly justify the use of the secret ballot without undermining its position. De Mita capitalized on the growing pressure to push through the reform that would at least give governments an indication of who had betrayed the government line.

The second major change in 1988 was the law that regulated the activities of the President of the Council of Ministers (as the prime minister is referred to in the Constitution). Article 95, which dealt with the prime minister, was the last part of the 1948 Constitution that required enabling legislation to be implemented. The 1988 law is important for our discussion not simply because it clarified the constitutional position of the prime minister and the organization of his or her office, thereby strengthening the executive, but also because parliamentary approval for the strengthening of the executive was secured by provisions in the law that governed the issuing of decrees (Hine and Finocchi 1991: 79–86). Governments would now have to include in the preamble of the decree a clear statement as to why the recourse to the emergency measure was necessary. In addition governments could not reissue decrees that had been rejected by Parliament or that had been ruled as unconstitutional by the Constitutional Court; however, the question of decrees that expired after sixty days was not resolved (Massai 1992:171–7). In practice the 1988 law had little direct effect on decree use. Article 77 of the Constitution remained silent on the question of reiteration of rejected decrees; but since constitutional practice dictated that bills that are rejected cannot be reintroduced in the same form, this change only formalized previous practice. The 1988 reform was the culmination of efforts throughout the 1980s to formalize the constitutional position of the prime minister, something which should have been done forty years earlier. It was concerned primarily with resolving issues internal to the government – and only less so with executive–legislative relations. This may explain why major issues, such as the question of decree legislation, were not addressed directly but only in a minor way, such as the provision that banned the re-introduction of decrees rejected by Parliament. By attempting to strengthen the executive, the reform sought to reduce the use of decrees in an indirect way – that is, a government that had clear policy direction and guidance would have less need to resort to emergency measures.

The parliamentary rules of procedure have provided governments with few legal instruments that would allow them to play a dominant role in law making in Parliament. The rules were complemented by the fact that the executive in general was in a weak legal position throughout the postwar period. Its legislation has no priority in Parliament; and the electoral system, which favored particularistic representation over efficacy, ensured fragmented coalitions. Additionally, the head of the government had few administrative or legal powers at his or her disposal. The late 1970s and the 1980s witnessed numerous attempts to reverse each of these limitations on executive strength. Periods have been set aside in the parliamentary timetable for consideration of the government's budget and for legislation dealing with Italy's policy commitments in the European Union (Hine 1993:Chapter 7). Changes were introduced in 1988 that strengthened the coordinating and policy-making powers of the prime minister's office. Finally, the electoral law was changed in 1993, leading to an additional-member, or mixed, system, with three-quarters of the seats allocated by plurality and the rest by proportional representation. These changes were expected to reduce the need for decrees insofar as governments were being given the tools needed to ensure that their legislation was considered in Parliament in a timely fashion (Cotta 1991:218–23). As we shall see, however, these attempts to reduce the number of decrees issued by the government have proven to be less than entirely successful.

POLITICAL FRAMEWORK

The weak legal and constitutional position of the Italian executive could have been tempered or countered by a political framework – primarily a party system – that provided the basis for political and decision-making leadership. However, this has not been the case and, as we will see shortly, recent attempts to change the legal framework have not been able to overcome the obstacles presented to executives with a weak political base. Italian postwar political history is too full to be given adequate coverage here. We will try to give a brief description of the main developments that affected the legislative process most directly and that may have led to the increased use of decrees.

In the period from 1948 to the beginning of the fourth legislature in 1963, the DC's hegemony was at its peak. The DC was by far the largest party in the country, the governing coalition encompassed a relatively narrow area of the ideological left–right spectrum, and, at least until the mid-1960s, this coalition involved a limited number of parties. Additionally, the main opposition party, the PCI, was struggling to achieve democratic legitimacy in the midst of the Cold War. The DC was able to combine these factors with favorable parliamentary rules of procedure to shape a relatively majoritarian system of government with the Christian Democrats, one that was located squarely in the center of the legislative process (Lijphart 1984).

The key to this position was the electoral strength of the centrist party (Di Palma 1977). The DC emerged from the first parliamentary elections of the new Republic (1948) as the largest party in Italy, and it was to retain that distinction until 1994. It was able to dictate the terms of government and to lead Parliament for over forty years, despite substantial internal divisions (Leonardi and Wertman 1989). Although the near absolute majority obtained in the first elections (48.4 percent) was not repeated in subsequent elections, the DC maintained a minimum lead of nearly 12 percentage points over the largest opposition party (PCI) and at least a lead of 25 percentage points over the other members of its own coalition through the 1968–72 legislature (this spread was well over 35 percent until the addition of the Socialists [PSI] to the governing coalition in 1963).

The governing coalitions for most of the period through 1963 included no more than three parties: the DC, the Liberals (PLI) or the Republicans (PRI), and the Social Democrats (PSDI). All three of the smaller parties together controlled only 9.1–14.5 percent of the votes (which translated into an even smaller percentage of the actual number of seats in the Parliament). As a result, the ideological spectrum included in the governing coalition was limited and, on the whole, dominated by the Christian Democrats. The cohesion of the governing coalition was somewhat reduced in 1963 with the "opening to the left" and the inclusion of the Socialists in the government.

The third factor that contributed to DC hegemony was the lack of a cohesive, organized, and legitimate opposition. In contrast to the Christian Democratic dominance of the center–right, the Communist Party was unable to control the internal schisms within the left. Repeated attempts by the Socialists to distinguish and distance themselves from the PCI were ultimately successful in dividing the left into three significant groups: the largely illegitimate Communist Party; the Social Democrats who, since 1948, were frequently members of the governing coalition; and the Socialists, who, until 1963, were unable to define their political role clearly. The inability of the left to form an appealing alternative to the entrenched governing formula centerd around the DC ensured the continued dominance of the DC in the legislative arena. The ultimate success of the Socialists to present themselves as potential partners in the governing coalition proved to be of great significance for the functioning of the legislative system as a whole, but it did not immediately aid in the creation of a viable alternative government of the left.

The combination of these three factors – coalitions across a narrow band of the ideological spectrum, DC dominance of relatively compact governments, and a lack of an effective alternative – left the Christian Democrats and their allies in an enviable position. There was broad public support for the new Republic, the opposition was mistrusted and internally divided, and the dominant position of the DC at the center of the political spectrum ensured its hegemonic position. Although there were internal divisions within the governing parties, these divisions had yet to reach the point where they affected parliamentary discipline.

Christian Democratic legislative hegemony was assaulted on many fronts in the second period of the postwar era, which began in 1963 and ended in the first part of the 1970s. Electorally, the DC fell from a high of over 48 percent of the popular vote in 1948 to only 38 percent in 1972; at the same time the Communist Party was able to increase its share of the vote from only 22.6 percent in 1953 to 27.1 percent in 1972 – and to over 34 percent in 1976. The difference in vote share between these two parties decreased from a high of 17.5 percentage points in 1953 to 11.6 percentage points in 1972 – and to only 4.3 percentage points in 1976. More importantly, DC hegemony of the political and decision-making processes was being eroded. A number of constitutional provisions that remained unimplemented since 1948, such as regional governments and the use of referendums, were finally realized more than twenty years later in the face of social unrest and pressure by the Socialists (PSI) within the government. The Socialists were intent as being seen as the voice of moderate reform, setting them apart form the Communists and the DC (Di Scala 1988). Trying to fill the space between the two large parties often meant that the PSI was not willing to be the pliant partner; it thus stood in contrast to many of the DC's traditional allies. The PSI was able to push for institutional reforms that opened up the political process to a wider range of political and social forces. The DC continued to be the dominant party at the center of a political system that rewarded centrist parties. However, the price for maintaining that position included increasingly fragmented coalitions, ideological divisions within and between governing parties, and institutional changes, such as the 1971 reform of the parliamentary rules, that diffused political and decision-making powers.

The mid-1970s was a period of great turmoil in Italian politics: The unrest of the late 1960s had generated a range of new demands and actors; the long run of economic growth seemed to have come to an abrupt halt; the terrorism of the left and the right presented serious challenges to the democratic order; and the party system seemed to be in a state of flux as the center–left governing coalition ended with no clear alternative coalition formula in sight. As mentioned earlier, the gap between the DC and the Communist Party narrowed significantly during this period, and there was speculation prior to the 1976 election that the PCI could emerge as the largest party. Moreover, the Communists made a serious attempt to be seen as a legitimate party, one that was committed to parliamentary democracy. This effort included the strategy known as the "Historic Compromise" in 1973, which posited a DC–PCI coalition to protect the democratic republic. Although the Compromise was never formally accepted by the DC and its allies, it did signal that the PCI was willing to play by the rules of the parliamentary game (Barbagli and Corbetta 1981).

The Historic Compromise did assume an embryonic form in the seventh legislature (1976–79), described as the period of national unity. Social unrest, the economic aftereffects of the decade's "oil shocks," and the growing public fear of terrorism (on both the right and the left) forced dramatic and concerted efforts from the political elite. For the first time since 1947, the Communists were allowed to actively and positively participate in government decision making. The DC governed alone but only with the parliamentary support of the Communist Party. Although the PCI never entered the government, it did hold the balance of power. The result was that Parliament became a central site for negotiation and decision making, and the lines between the government and opposition, already blurred by the 1971 reform of the parliamentary rules, became almost indistinguishable (Cotta 1994:75). The national unity governments collapsed in 1979, and the PCI never again came as close to entering into the government. Eventually, the DC was able to construct a five-party coalition (known as the *pentapartito*) that included the Liberals, Social Democrats, Republicans, and Socialists and that governed throughout the 1980s. However, the consensual decision-making style and the central role of Parliament that emerged in the 1976–79 period continued long after the political conditions that brought it about had disappeared (Della Sala 1993: 171).

The Christian Democrats continued in their downward slide at the polls during the 1980s, dropping from 38.3 percent in 1979 to 32.9 percent in 1983 – and finally to 29.7 percent in the 1992 elections. Moreover, the gap that separated the DC from the next largest party in the governing coalition dropped from a ratio of four-to-one in 1972 to two-to-one in 1992. At the same time the width of the ideological spectrum covered by the governing coalition increased still further, ranging from the Liberal Party on the right to the Socialists on the left. Christian Democratic hegemony within the *pentapartito* also faltered significantly as internal divisions became more pronounced and conflictive. These divisions were aggravated by the Socialist Party, which proved to be a difficult and demanding, but necessary, coalition partner.[8] The increasing fragmentation of the party system combined with the 1971 reforms, as well as with the changes in legislative behavior resulting from the national unity experience, to limit the ability of the government to pursue its legislative agenda successfully. As we will see shortly, one response to these limitations was increased recourse to the legislative decree after 1979.

The *pentapartito* coalition provided governments with volatile parliamentary majorities when it came to government legislation, but no other credible formula could be constructed. All of this was to change in the 1990s as the Italian party system underwent radical changes that produced uncertain results. The repercussions of the collapse of communism were felt in Italy as in no other western European party system. The main opposition party began its transformation before the fall of the Berlin Wall, and by 1991 it was known as the Democratic Party of the Left (PDS). Moreover, the end of communism in Europe meant that the linchpin of DC rule – that is, that it was the bulwark against communism – was undermined. The consequences of these challenges to the Italian party system are wide-ranging, and their long-term impact remains unpredictable. However, one of the most immediate changes was the near annihilation of the political parties of the postwar era. No major party (either governing or opposition) presented candidates under the same party label in both 1987 and 1994. A series of corruption scandals led to criminal investigations of or criminal charges against one-third of the deputies in the eleventh legislature (1992–94). An entire political class and the parties they served were discredited (Salvadori 1994).

The result was that the old parties transformed themselves to challenge new parties and new political forces. The bulk of the DC became the Italian Popular Party (PPI), with groups breaking away to form Catholic parties of the left and right. The Socialists, who had undergone a revival in the 1980s, were decimated by scandal, and their leader (Bettino Craxi) chose a self-imposed exile in Tunisia rather than face charges of corruption. The neofascist Italian Social Movement also tried to shed its historical baggage by attempting to transform itself into a traditional party of the right and calling itself the National Alliance. The Northern League emerged as one of the most significant political forces in northern Italy in the early 1990s, and it contributed to the decline of the DC in its traditional stronghold in the "white regions" of the northeast (Mannheimer 1991). Perhaps the most startling change was the rise of Forza Italia, a loose aggregation of political clubs that galvanized under the media magnate and political neophyte, Silvio Berlusconi. In a period that lasted less than six months, Berlusconi was able to launch his movement and sweep to power in the March 1994 elections. His center–right coalition with the Northern League, Forza Italia, and the National Alliance brought to an end nearly fifty years of DC-led governments (Diamanti and Mannheimer 1994).

The 1994 election signaled more than just the end of the DC era. It was fought under new electoral laws that introduced a mixed system: Three-quarters of the seats were assigned through plurality, and the remaining seats were assigned according to proportional representation. The new electoral laws were the product of popular pressure that effectively abolished the old electoral system in a referendum on April 18, 1993. The Italian electorate wanted a change in its political class and a new set of electoral rules that would produce greater clarity in the formation of government coalitions. The new electoral system was seen as a first step toward providing a sense of cohesion and focus to the executive; and it was partly responsible for the first parliamentary majority with an electoral mandate since 1948 (Diamanti and Mannheimer 1994). Prior to this time, governing coalitions following elections were formed after consultations between party leaders.

DECREES AND LEGISLATIVE OUTPUT

Italian governments have endured a period of political fragmentation in a legal framework that, despite recent changes, has not favored their legislative agendas and programs. Legislative decrees have become one of the few responses that governments may resort to in an attempt to buttress their fragile legal and political bases in the legislative process. This becomes readily apparent when looking at the fate of government legislation in the postwar period.

The data in Table 6.1 and Figure 6.1 reveal that the first twenty-five years of the Republic are distinguished from the period that followed. The success rate of legislation presented to the Chamber of Deputies demonstrates that governments were increasingly unsuccessful in their attempts to get their legislation approved. Governments have continued to present a relatively high number of bills to Parliament, but only a little more than half of them emerged successfully after the seventh legislature. There is a slight recovery in the 1987–92 period, perhaps reflecting some of the attempts to give the executive greater control of

Table 6.1 *Average yearly government-sponsored legislation, 1948–92*

Legislature	Average number of government bills introduced	Average number of government bills enacted	Average success rate for government bills
I (1948–53)	457	411	0.90
II (1953–58)	333	283	0.85
III (1958–63)	313	260	0.83
IV (1963–68)	313	248	0.79
V (1968–72)	241	173	0.72
VI (1972–76)	309	212	0.69
VII (1976–79)	333	189	0.57
VIII (1979–83)	332	189	0.57
IX (1983–87)	332	157	0.47
X (1987–92)	294	148	0.50

Source: Cotta (1994:61–2). Printed by permission of the University of Michigan Press. © The University of Michigan Press.

the parliamentary agenda and to limit the use of the secret ballot; but the figure hardly indicates an upward shift in the government's decision-making capacity.

The increasing difficulties faced by governments in getting their legislation approved corresponds to the period since the mid-1970s when the reformed rules of procedure combined with fragmenting governing majorities. It is important to note that there was a gradual decrease in the government's legislative record in the first twenty years of the Republic; perhaps this decrease reflected the growing importance of factions within the DC and the widening of the governing coalition with the center–left. However, there is a dramatic drop between the fifth and seventh legislatures – and again between the seventh and ninth legislatures. It seems that the reform of the parliamentary rules of procedure in 1971 did not have an immediate effect in the 1972–76 legislature. Rather, significant changes in legislative output became apparent during the national unity parliaments of the seventh legislature. The fact that the governments in this period could only survive with PCI support (or abstention) in Parliament meant that the legislature became the site for negotiation and compromise. It became apparent that the 1971 rules provided an ideal framework for this to take place. The 1971 rules *combined* with the political conditions of the national unity period to increase legislative assertiveness and resistance to government leadership in policy making.

The 1983–87 period is an interesting one because it saw relative stability in the government: The first Craxi government established a record for longevity in the postwar period (August 1983–August 1986), and the addition of the second Craxi government means that the Socialist leader led the executive for almost the

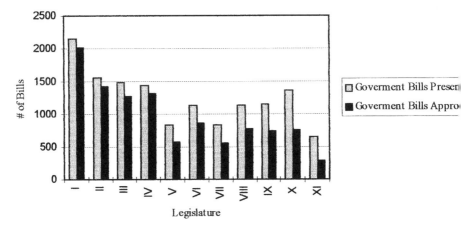

Figure 6.1 The fate of government bills, 1945–95 (Source: Cotta {1994}, pp. 61–2. Printed by permission of the University of Michigan Press. © The University of Michigan Press)

entire legislature. Moreover, Craxi placed a great deal of emphasis on making the executive the center of political and policy decision making; and his political strategy was based on his commitment to *decisionismo* (Hine 1986). Yet despite these factors that point to increasing government assertiveness, during the time of the ninth legislature, the trend of government failure to get its legislation approved continued. The changes in legislative behavior that emerged in the 1976–79 period continued long after the political conditions of the national unity period had disappeared and after changes to the formal rules in the 1980s tried to establish executive leadership in decision making.

There is evidence to suggest that governments began to use all the tools afforded to them by formal rules and parliamentary practice as more and more of their legislation failed to make it through Parliament. This was the beginning of the process which led to the extensive use of decrees. The figures in Table 6.2 start to reveal the extent to which governments have resorted to decrees as a "normal" legislative procedure to counter their difficult time in Parliament. Only 29 decrees were presented by governments during the first legislature.[9] There followed a gradual increase in the number of decrees through the first twenty-five years, going from 29 in the first legislature to 69 in the 1968–72 period. However, the gradual increase is overshadowed by the huge increase between the fifth (1968–72) and sixth (1972–76) legislatures. Subsequent legislatures would register similar large increases in the number of decrees presented to Parliament. The average number of decrees presented during the first five legislatures was 58, but this contrasts with the average of 305 for the period from the sixth to the eleventh legislature (1972–92). Although the period since the 1970s has been tumultuous, it is hard to see how substantive policy issues alone warranted nearly

Table 6.2 *Italian executive decrees, 1948–95*

Legislature	Decrees presented	Decrees converted	Decrees rejected	Decrees expired	Decrees reiterated	Reiterations as % of total
I (1948–53)	29	28	0	1	0	0
II (1953–58)	60	60	0	0	0	0
III (1958–63)	30	28	2	0	0	0
IV (1963–68)	94	89	2	3	1	1
V (1968–72)	69	66	0	3	4[a]	6
VI (1972–76)	124	108	0	16	5	4
VII (1976–79)	167	136	16	15	8	5
VIII (1979–83)	274	171	8	93	69	25
IX (1983–87)	302	136	30	99	92	30
X (1987–92)	459	187	15	249	207	44
XI (1992–94)	493	123	12	303	328	67
XII (1994–95)	322[b]	72	6	261	N.A.	83

[a]The total of the second through fourth columns may not be equal to the number of decrees presented because they do not take into account the fate of decrees that are carried over from one legislature to the next.
[b]May 1995
Sources: All data collected by the authors from Camera dei Deputati (1985, 1994a, 1995).

five times more recourse to "emergency" measures than in the past. Rather, we rely on institutional and political factors to explain this phenomenon.

The remarkable increase in the number of decrees issued in the period after the national unity government in the seventh legislature is complemented by another important trend – that is, a dramatic decrease in the rate of decree conversion by the legislature. Whereas Parliament converted an average of 95 percent of government decrees during the first through sixth legislatures (see Figure 6.2), it approved an average of less than 43 percent during the eighth through the eleventh legislatures. The preliminary figures for the twelfth legislature, one that was supposed to inaugurate a new era of executive leadership in policy making, seem to indicate that government frustration in getting decrees approved has not ended.

It should be noted that very few of the decrees that are not converted into law are actually rejected by a parliamentary vote. As the fifth column in Table 6.2 indicates, the largest group of unsuccessful decrees consisted of those that expired after the sixty-day period. For instance, only 15 of the 459 decrees presented during the tenth legislature (1987–92) were defeated in a vote in the Chamber, whereas only 187 were converted into law. This suggests that if governments have tried to bypass Parliament's control of the parliamentary calendar by putting issues directly onto the agenda with decrees, they have not entirely avoided

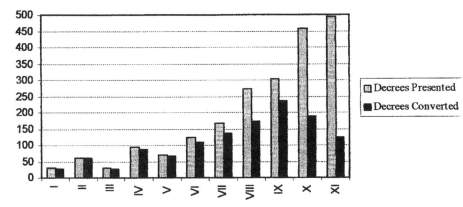

Figure 6.2 The fate of decrees, 1945–94 (Source: *All data collected by the authors from Camera dei Deputati {1985, 1994a, 1995})*

parliamentary inertia. Given that decrees must pass the gauntlet of parliamentary rules that are not designed for timeliness and alacrity in two chambers, it is hardly surprising to find that deputies can choose to simply do nothing rather reject a decree outright in a vote. As in the case of other types of legislation, governments cannot force a vote on decrees. Decrees also share another feature with other "normal" legislation – that is, they are part of an ongoing negotiation over policy choices between the executive and the legislature. Governments and parliamentary forces know that letting decrees expire does not mean an end to the bargaining process over policy. An indication that the issuing of decrees is just the first move in this game is the fact that beginning with the 1976–79 legislature, over two-thirds of the total number of decrees converted to law were amended in Parliament.[10]

The increasing number of decrees that expire in the second half of the post-war period, as shown in Figure 6.3, may be responsible for a closely related trend – that is, the frequent recourse of governments to repeated iteration of previous decrees. The figures in Tables 6.2 and 6.3 reveal that governments prior to 1979 rarely presented the same decree to Parliament for conversion into law after it had been rejected or had expired. Whereas the number of decrees being issued by the executive has been steadily increasing, the ability to get decrees converted into law has declined. As a result, governments are now forced not only to issue decrees in an attempt to affect the legislative output of the Parliament but also to continuously reiterate decrees in the attempt either to get them converted or to have a policy remain in effect. Governments seem to have responded to the frustration which has resulted from their relative inability to control the parliamentary timetable – thus leading them to have to sit idly while decrees expire – by presenting the same initiative every two months. The decree has the imme-

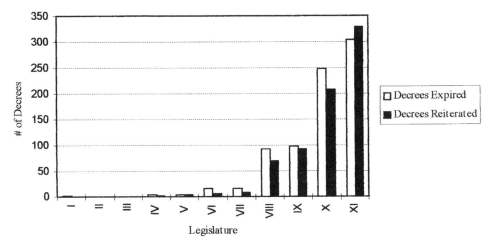

Figure 6.3 Decrees expired and reiterated, 1945–94 (Source: All data collected by the authors from Camera dei Deputati {1985, 1994a, 1995})

diate force of law, so governments can make policy indefinitely by reiterating the same proposal – or at least until Parliament decides to take a final vote on it.

The continuous reintroduction of previous decrees may be interpreted in one of two ways. The first, and perhaps more conventional, understanding of decree reiteration is that the executive is simply reissuing decrees with little or no substantive changes in order to rule by decree for extended periods of time. By repeatedly presenting the same decree, the executive can legislate *in spite of* Parliament for months and even years (some decrees have been issued more than ten times). This interpretation supports the conventional view that decrees are little more than the usurpation of legislative power by the executive.

A more complex interpretation of the growth of reiteration of decrees in Italy, however, requires a closer examination of the substantive content of reiterated decrees as well as their eventual fate. It is possible (and even probable) that the reiteration of legislative decrees serves effectively as a bargaining process between the executive and Parliament. A decree that has been left to expire by Parliament might be modified and reintroduced by the executive in the hopes of getting it converted. This process may be repeated any number of times. By approaching the legislative process in this way, the executive is able at least to ensure that its proposal is temporarily enacted and that Parliament is very much aware of it. (In fact, if the legislature continues to refuse to act, the government can credibly threaten to continue to reiterate the decree indefinitely.) In effect, according to this interpretation, the increase in reiteration of decrees in later legislatures ac-tually reflects an attempt by the executive to encourage Parliament to bargain over the government's legislative agenda rather than the outright imposition of

Table 6.3 *Decrees and government legislation, 1948–95*

Legislature	Total decrees presented	Success rate for decrees	Government bills approved	Converted decrees as % of government bills approved
I (1948–53)	29	97%	2,015	1.4
II (1953–58)	60	100%	1,427	4.2
III (1958–63)	38	95%	1,279	2.2
IV (1963–68)	94	95%	1,316	6.8
V (1968–72)	69	96%	572	11.5
VI (1972–76)	124	87%	866	12.5
VII (1976–79)	167	81%	565	24.0
VIII (1979–83)	275	61%	769	22.0
IX (1983–87)	307	44%	750	18.0
X (1987–92)	466	40%	740	25.3
XI (1992–94)	490	24%	292	42.0
XII (1994–95)	322[a]	—[b]	NA	NA

[a] April 1994 to May 1995.
[b] As there were still many bills before Parliament when this research was conducted, it would be difficult to assess the success rate or the percentage of government bills approved that are converted decrees.
Source: As in Table 6.2; also Servizio Informazione e Relazione Esterne della Camera dei Deputati (1994a).

executive leadership in decision making. The increase in reiteration demonstrates both the lack of other institutional options available to the executive – especially since 1971 – to force parliamentary consideration of its policy priorities and its inability to force Parliament to adopt (convert) its legislation.

Two examples serve to illustrate the point that reiteration of decrees is not necessarily evidence of government domination in policy making. The decrees on housing regulation that have been presented to Parliament almost continuously since 1985 are a vivid illustration (Guttenberg 1987). The fundamental points of controversy are no closer to being resolved after ten years of decrees (*La Repubblica*, 7 October 1994). But neither have government policy initiatives made by decree remained stable throughout the prolonged bargaining with Parliament on the issue. This raises interesting questions about compliance. For instance, some of the proposals presented over the years have included provisions for fines for those who have constructed housing without the proper permits, but there is little incentive for someone to pay the fines, because later decrees may have more lenient provisions, as has sometimes been the case (*La Repubblica*, 4 April 1991). Moreover, uncertainty about the stability of building regulation policy, due to its basis in frequently changing decrees and the lack of parliamentary ratification, has deterred local authorities from acting aggressively to sanction those who built without the proper permits.

A second example concerns a decree that regulated television exposure for political parties during the campaign leading up to regional and local elections in April 1995. In March the Lamberto Dini government decided the matter was urgent, given that no legislative action was imminent; and Silvio Berlusconi, leader of Forza Italia and one of the main contenders in the electoral contest, owned three national television networks. The government was so concerned about the issue that it is alleged that a special military aircraft was commissioned to fly to Ankara, where the President of the Republic was on a state visit to Turkey, so that he could sign the text of the decree that would allocate television time more evenly.[11] Despite the widespread political concern about the possible conflict of interest between electoral campaigning and media ownership, at least one of Berlusconi's networks apparently chose to ignore the decree in the expectation that it would expire and would be replaced by another. The Retequattro network allocated 256 minutes to Forza Italia and only about 6 minutes to the leading opposition parties (La Repubblica, 22 April 1995).

The reiteration of decrees, then, is inexorably linked to their expiration. Both features indicate that the increased use of decrees is a much more complex phenomenon than simply governments displacing the legislature. Rather, the issuing of most decrees is only the beginning of what may be a long decision-making process between Parliament and the government. The sixty-day limit does not seem to spur the legislature into action, and it is apparent that recent parliaments have been ready to accept the same decree over and over again. But does this mean that governments have been able to rule by decree? Observing Italian political behavior suggests that this would be too strong a conclusion, because although decrees may technically have the immediate force of law, they are difficult to enforce unless they are converted into law. Because decrees do not establish stable expectations about the shape of future policy among political actors, they frequently fail to elicit compliance, even in the short run.

Decrees, if combined with enhanced powers for an executive with a solid parliamentary majority, do have the potential to be powerful instruments that enhance the decision-making powers of that executive. On the other hand, if governments did have these institutional and political resources, there would be less need to resort to decrees. The changes introduced throughout the 1980s and 1990s that aimed to strengthen the powers of the executive – such as the 1990 reform of the parliamentary rules that give the government greater consideration in setting the legislative calendar – could lead to the assumption that governments no longer need to resort to decrees to guide policy making. However, if we look at the period since 1987, the use of decrees has continued to rise; and, in a related trend, there has been an increased number of expired and reiterated decrees during this same period.

The emphasis on giving governments a more central role in decision making was also expressed in the formation of governments and in who was chosen to

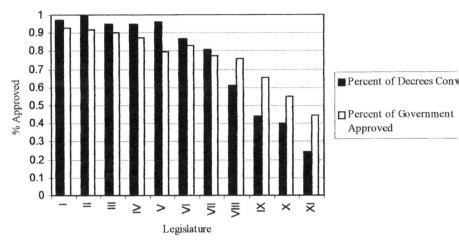

Figure 6.4 Success rates for decrees and government bills, 1945–94 (Source: All data collected by the authors from Camera dei Deputati {1985, 1994a, 1994b, 1995})

lead them. One would expect that if political forces were willing to entrust leadership of the government to a former governor of the Bank of Italy (such as Ciampi) or a constitutional expert (such as Giuliano Amato), then they would be more likely to support their legislative program too and allow governments to exert leadership in decision making. If this were the case, then executives might not feel the need to resort to decrees as other governments had. However, as illustrated by Figure 6.4, neither the Amato nor the Ciampi governments had a particularly easy time in Parliament. For instance, the Amato government in 1992–93 presented 149 decrees to Parliament: Of that total 47 were converted into law, whereas 97 expired and 89 were reissued. Ciampi had an even more difficult time in the 1993–94 period, when 295 decrees were presented; only 70 were converted into law and 225 expired (Camera dei Deputati 1994a: 99). It would seem that although there may be a willingness to create governments of technocrats who will give primacy to governing rather than to representation, parliamentary forces refuse to give them free rein in decision making.

Matters did not improve in the twelfth legislature, even after electoral reform was supposed to improve the cohesion of parliamentary majorities and executive leadership in policy making. The figures in Table 6.2 reveal that both the Berlusconi and Dini governments made ample use of decrees in the first year of the legislature (April 1994–May 1995). No decree issued by the Berlusconi government caused as much controversy as the one issued on July 13, 1994, that would change the rules governing protective custody of suspected criminals. The procedure was seen as one of the major instruments that helped investigating judges uncover political corruption at all levels and fight organized crime. However, it also raised serious civil liberties questions, because individuals could be arrested without being charged. The Berlusconi government issued a decree that freed over 2,000 individuals who were under "cautionary arrest." Public and political outrage ensued almost immediately, because Italians saw many leading political figures – those who had come to symbolize political corruption – walk freely from jail. Moreover, many accused Berlusconi and his government of acting to protect his friends and, perhaps, his own financial interests. The decree led to a serious split among some of the partners in his governing coalition, with ministers accusing each other of dishonesty. It was one of the few cases in which a decree was rejected in Parliament – many of the parties in the governing coalitions voted against it in response to public pressure (Camera dei Deputati 1994b: 1942–84; *La Repubblica*, 14 July 1994). This example reveals that even a government with an electoral majority, one which was committed to decision-making efficacy, was limited in how it could use decrees.

An examination of the substance of some of the decrees issued by the Berlusconi government reveals the extent to which they may not be so much "emergency" measures that usurp the power of the legislature as products of the fact that governments do not have the power to close debate and force a vote in Parliament in a timely fashion. For instance, *decreto-legge 30 giugno* (June 1994, n.424) issued provisions that closed certain fish industries for the remainder of the year. Perhaps there was a fishing "crisis" that required immediate action, but decrees were used because the government had no other way to get legislation approved in a rapid, timely fashion. It could not, as could governments in Britain, France, or Canada, go to Parliament and impose closure on debate and get legislation approved in a few days. There are no formal rules that prevent the legislature from acting with alacrity; however, the rules give many groups in the legislature an opportunity to slow down the process. There is no epicenter in the political and policy-making processes that will secure for a government a rapid response to an issue such as fisheries. Decrees, then, are one instrument that can come into play, but it is far from the most powerful and the final act.

CONCLUSION

The discussion reveals that the trends that characterized the 1980s – increased number of decrees issued, not converted, expired and reiterated – have become more pronounced in the 1990s. This trend has occurred both despite reforms to parliamentary rules that sought to strengthen the executive's capacity to provide legislative leadership and despite changes to the electoral law designed to produce majoritarian outcomes. This seems to suggest that although reform of formal rules aimed at providing cohesion and guidance to the legislative process are important, they must be accompanied by changes to the political framework and legislative behavior that point in the same direction. The governments of technocrats and the Berlusconi governments found a fate that was similar to that of their predecessors in Parliament, because they lacked strong, coherent parliamentary majorities that operated in a legal framework that favored the executive.

An examination of both the causes and the effectiveness of increased recourse to decree usage in Italy aptly demonstrates that the issuance of decrees alone does not signify the expropriation of legislative powers by the executive branch. In fact, the Italian case demonstrates the relative weakness of the executive in the legislative process and the relative futility of increased decree usage as a means to equalizing the legislative power between the executive and the legislature. The weakness of the executive, its continued reliance on the legislative decree (despite the fact that historically it has not proven to be a particularly effective tool), and the limited success in changing executive–legislature relations (such as the 1988 law formalizing the role of the prime minister and the 1990 procedural changes) suggest that it is difficult to shift the balance of power in an established constitutional democracy without complementary changes in the political arena. In the Italian case a continued reliance on legislative decrees by the government is a sign of its weakness and legislative impotence, not of its strength or dominance over Parliament. However, executive weakness does not necessarily mean Parliament provides legislative leadership. The fact that Parliament does not reject the vast majority of decrees but simply allows them to expire and to be presented anew indicates that it is not willing to assert some guidance over decision making.

The Italian case reveals that two of Carey and Shugart's factors that may shape executive–legislature relations through the use of decrees – the severity of bargaining problems among legislators and the severity of agency loss – have been important in determining decree usage in Italy. Low levels of party discipline and the lack of other constitutional authority over legislation by the executive led to great uncertainty about the fate of government legislation in Parliament. The political forces in the legislature looked to decrees as a mechanism to bypass, at least temporarily, the bargaining problems that the legislators faced. This was facilitated by the knowledge that decrees did not entail a dramatic expropriation of legislative authority by the executive, because the constitutional and political constraints that led to their use also ensured that decrees could only become law after sixty days with the consent of political forces within the legislature. Decrees, which were meant to be emergency measures, have become a normal legislative mechanism that reflects the combination of a weak executive with a lack of concern among political forces about guidance in the legislative process.

NOTES

1 As Power indicates in his chapter, the Italian experience has had a great deal of influence on the legal framework for decrees in Brazil.
2 The Court ruling was on a case brought forward by the Tuscany regional gov-

ernment, which claimed a government decree infringed on its powers in the areas of urban planning. Part of its argument was that the decree on abusive housing, of which more will be said shortly, should be ruled unconstitutional because it was reiterated for the tenth time (Corte Costituzionale 1988: 202–23).

3 The written rules of procedure are not, strictly speaking, ordinary law. They stem from Article 64 of the Constitution, which grants each chamber of Parliament full autonomy in its organization and functioning. Article 16 of the rules of the Chamber of Deputies states that those rules may be changed only with an absolute majority of all the members in the Chamber; this is different from the procedure for ordinary law, which states that only a majority of those voting are needed. Moreover, constitutional practice has established that a consensus (or as close to it as possible) is needed for any major changes in the written rules. A notable exception to this practice was the change in the voting procedures in 1988 that brought an end to the use of secret ballots for most pieces of legislation. The De Mita government put the motion as a question of confidence in the government, thereby establishing that only a majority of those voting was necessary for the change. However, this was an exceptional case, and has yet to establish a precedent (Longi 1994; Manzella 1991).

4 The 1971 changes must be seen within the wider context of the institutional reform of the late 1960s and early 1970s. Student and labor unrest, coupled with a center–left coalition in which the Socialist Party sought greater institutional channels for the PCI (Italian-Communist Party), produced a series of changes that diffused political power within and between institutions. The reform of the parliamentary rules, the creation of regional governments and neighborhood councils, and the introduction of the referendum mechanism may be seen as part of an attempt to create institutional channels for social conflict and demands. This trend reflected the "anomaly" of Italian democracy – that is, the two largest parties were "condemned" to their respective roles of government and opposition. This meant that close to one-third of Italians voted for a party that could never achieve executive power. The unrest of the late 1960s led to a widespread consensus in favor of diffusing power in order to create institutional outlets for social demands that may have been "permanently" excluded from power (Hine 1993).

5 It should be noted that the President of the Chamber of Deputies was a member of the opposition party (the PCI, later the PDS, the Democratic Party of the Left) from 1976–1994. After the 1994 elections, a member of the governing coalition was chosen – Irene Pivetti from the Northern league – thus breaking with parliamentary practice. However, the Northern League pulled out of the coalition in early 1995 even though Pivetti remained as the president.

6 With the possible exceptions of Alcide De Gasperi in the first legislature, Fanfani in the second, and De Mita in the 1980s, DC leaders normally did not assume the office of prime minister.

7 Deputies suspected of not holding to the party line and of voting against their government under the cover of the secret ballot are referred to as *franchi tiratori*, or snipers.

8 Throughout the 1980s, the Socialists maintained veto power in the *pentapartito*, insofar as their participation was necessary to achieve a numerical majority (Pasquino 1986).

9 A literal reading of Article 77 would suggest the dubious conclusion that the

demands of postwar reconstruction, tensions in the fledgling democracy, and the onset of the Cold War presented less than one-tenth the number of "emergencies" than were faced by the ninth legislature, which featured an economic boom, the longest surviving government in the postwar period, and the continuing decline of the PCI. Our argument is that the institutional determinants of decree explain this puzzle much better than the substantive policy determinants.

10 The figures for the percentage of converted decrees that were amended from the first to the ninth legislature are: I (1948–53) – 42.8 percent; II (1953–58) – 58.3 percent; III (1958–63) – 56.2 percent; IV (1963–68) – 56.2 percent; V (1968–72) – 66.7 percent; VI (1972–76) – 63.0 percent; VII (1976–79) – 72.8 percent; VIII (1979–83) – 76.3 percent; IX (1983–87) – 79.4 percent. Data are not available for subsequent legislatures, but evidence suggests that the trend has not been reversed (Camera dei Deputati 1985: 135–8; Camera dei Deputati 1987).

11 A silent player in the decree process is the President of the Republic, who must sign all decrees before they come into effect. *Silent* is the operative word, because this is almost without exception a mere formality. The president also must sign all legislation, including converted decrees, that is approved by Parliament. There are many cases where the president has sent bills back to Parliament. However, this has had less to do with the decree process itself than with the substance of the bill; more specifically, they contravened Article 81 of the Constitution that stipulates that all legislation incurring public expenditures must indicate the source of revenue (*Financial Times*, 22 March 1995; *La Repubblica*, 30 June 1995).

7

THE PEN IS MIGHTIER THAN THE CONGRESS

PRESIDENTIAL DECREE POWER IN BRAZIL[1]

Timothy J. Power

INTRODUCTION

For a brief moment in 1992, the forced resignation of a Brazilian president led journalistic observers to pursue a novel angle. In Latin America's largest country, where executives have traditionally sent assemblies packing, the reverse had finally come to pass. In the aftermath of the startling "Collorgate" affair, pundits wondered aloud about a new era of legislative ascendance. Would it henceforth be Congress rather than the president that would occupy the upper ground, employing its newfound assertiveness to reshape the national agenda?

In short, no. As subsequent events have made clear, the episode of Collorgate was an aberration and, as such, an unwelcome distraction from the real problems that underlie executive–legislative relations in Brazil.[2] Since the promulgation of a democratic constitution in 1988, both the president and Congress have struggled to define the acceptable bounds of behavior in the making of public policy. The intensity of this struggle is a testament to the deficiencies of the 1988 Charter, which has been at the center of political debate almost since its adoption. In the specific case of executive–legislative relations, the most controversial provision of the 1988 Constitution is its Article 62, which allows the president to decree "provisional measures with the force of law."

This chapter explores the effects of post-1988 decree power on executive–legislative relations in Brazil. Its purpose is explicitly empirical. Along with other case studies in this volume, it will allow us to explore a central topic in Latin American politics – a topic which has become more relevant than ever before in recent years but which still seems to produce time-honored generalizations rather than empirically based studies.

The chapter proceeds in seven sections. I begin by discussing the historical antecedents of contemporary CDA in Brazil. I then turn to an analysis of how it came into its most recent incarnation in the National Constituent Assembly of 1987–88. The next two sections examine the use and abuse of decree power by the first two postauthoritarian presidents; José Sarney (1988–90) and Fernando Collor de Mello (1990–92). These two executives established all of the major paraconstitutional precedents and defined most of the key controversies relating to CDA, and little has changed under their two successors, Itamar Franco (1992–94) and Fernando Henrique Cardoso (1995–present). The fifth section compares quantitative data on the 307 decrees signed by Sarney and Collor. In the sixth section I compare executive and legislative perceptions of decree power by drawing on survey data and personal interviews. Finally, I conclude by placing my findings on Brazil in theoretical perspective.

HISTORICAL ANTECEDENTS OF DECREE POWER IN BRAZIL

Presidential decree power in Brazil is nothing new. It has been used and abused by unelected as well as elected governments – some form of decree power has existed in at least three of Brazil's constitutions under different names and different guises. A brief review of some antecedents of the *medida provisória* (provisional measure) will illuminate the historical context which confronted the framers of the 1988 Constitution.

The history of republican Brazil is punctuated by numerous succession crises and/or regime transitions, often giving rise to provisional governments. Traditionally, these provisional governments have claimed the right to rule by decree. This was the case between the proclamation of the Republic in 1889 and the promulgation of the first republican Constitution in 1891.[3] A second provisional government was constituted by Getúlio Vargas in the aftermath of the coup of 1937. With the consequent dissolution of the legislature, the administration of Estado Novo was conducted entirely through decree-laws, which totaled more than 8,000 between 1937 and 1945.[4] In this period the power of the Brazilian presidency reached its zenith. Not only did Vargas grant himself executive, legislative, and judicial powers, but he also ran roughshod over federalist principles, centralizing power and intervening directly in the states.

With the overthrow of Vargas in 1945, yet another provisional government took power while elections were held for the presidency and a Constituent Assembly. This caretaker government also ruled by decree while the Assembly prepared the 1946 Constitution, thus inaugurating Brazil's first truly democratic regime. The framers of the 1946 document, much like their counterparts in 1987–88, reacted strongly against the excesses of an outgoing authoritarian regime. Both constitutional (presidential) decree authority (CDA) and delegated decree authority (DDA) were conspicuously absent from the text. In fact the 1946

Constitution explicitly prohibited any one of the three branches of government (executive, legislative, judicial) from delegating powers or attributes to another branch. This proscription on interbranch delegation was observed throughout the democratic regime of 1946–64, with the notable exception of the sixteen-month parliamentary interlude in the 1961–63 period.[5]

The military coup of April 1964 brought Brazil back full circle to an authoritarian regime, one that was based once again on arbitrary rule. The authors of the coup did not at first suspend the democratic Constitution of 1946, nor did they close down Congress; but by issuing a series of "Institutional Acts" (a euphemism for decrees originating in the military hierarchy, which were de facto constitutional amendments), they made it plain that the new regime was to be one of "executive absolutism" (Soares 1979). The Second Institutional Act (AI – 2), which was issued in October 1965, gave the president the power to issue decree-laws on matters of national security as well as the authority to recess all legislative bodies at will and to legislate in their place while they remained closed. The Fourth Institutional Act of December 1966 expanded the jurisdiction of decree-laws to include all financial and administrative legislation. In the following year the military finally abolished the 1946 Constitution and commissioned a new charter incorporating the decree-law (*decreto-lei*) as a permanent feature of presidential power. Article 58 of the 1967 Constitution permitted the president, "in cases of urgency or relevant public interest," to issue decree-laws on matters of national security and public finances. This was later amended to include a third area, one covering the creation of public employment and the setting of wages.

In contrast to Vargas thirty years earlier, the post-1964 military elites allowed the National Congress to function, albeit in an emasculated state. The assembly's role in examining decree-laws is illustrative of its general impotence under the 1967 Constitution. According to Article 58 decree-laws would take effect immediately upon their publication, and Congress would have sixty days to approve or reject them. No amendments were permitted. Even more striking was the provision that if Congress did not take action within the specified period of sixty days, the decree was "approved" automatically. This curious institution, known as the *decurso de prazo* – a kind of "pocket approval" by a rubber-stamp legislature – was used to great effect by the military governments, because the obstructionist tactics of pro-military legislators insured that Congress would never even consider many decree-laws. Finally, even if Congress explicitly rejected a decree-law (which rarely occurred),[6] this rejection would not undo the effects the decree had during its existence – that is, the legislature was permitted only *ex nunc* nullification of the decree-law.[7]

Throughout the authoritarian regime, the decree-law and the accompanying provision of the *decurso de prazo* provided the foundation for the military's administration of national affairs. As Table 7.1 shows, the five military presidents issued an average of about nine decree-laws per month, or about one every three days. In fact, while the 1967 Constitution was in force, these presidents and their postauthoritarian successor, José Sarney, legislated nearly as much as the National

Table 7.1 *The use of presidential decree power in modern Brazil*

Government	Number of decree-laws or MPs	Legislature in session?	Average number of decrees per month
Vargas era			
Estado Novo, 1937–45	8,154	No	85
Provisional Government	810	No	270
Military Republic			
Castello Branco, 1964–67	318	Yes	9
Costa Silva, 1967–69	486	Partially[a]	17
Military Junta, 1969	265	No[a]	133
Médici, 1969–74	253	Yes[a]	4
Geisel, 1974–79	357	Yes	6
Figueiredo, 1979–85	593	Yes	8
New Republic			
Sarney, 1985–88	209	Yes	5
(Constitution of 1967, DL)			
Sarney, 1988–90	147	Yes	9
(Constitution of 1988, MP)[b]			
Collor, 1990–92[c]	160	Yes	6
Franco, 1992–94[d]	505	Yes	19
Cardoso, 1995–96[e]	702	Yes	36

[a]Legislature suspended by Fifth Institutional Act (AI–5) from December 13, 1968, to October 22, 1969.
[b]Nine of Sarney's decrees are counted twice; in the protocol governing the transition between two constitutions, the last nine decree-laws were transformed into the first nine MPs under the Constitution of 1988.
[c]Removed from office September 29, 1992, during impeachment proceedings.
[d]Data from September 29, 1992, through December 31, 1994.
[e]Data from January 1, 1995, through August 15, 1996.
Sources: All data collected by author from *Diário da Assembléia Nacional Constituinte* (March 19, 1988), p. 8654; PRODASEN; and *Folha de São Paulo*, various issues.

Congress itself: 2,481 decree-laws versus 2,981 bills passed by the legislature (Câmara dos Deputados 1993). Congress was literally inundated by presidential decrees, which may explain why a constitutional amendment passed in 1982 that required the legislature to initiate "urgent" consideration of decrees immediately upon receipt (Santos 1991:198). The authoritarian and arbitrary nature of the *decreto-lei* and the *decurso de prazo* – as well as the fact that their use actually *increased* during the political liberalization of the late 1970s and early 1980s[8] – made these institutions prime targets of the democratic reformers of the new Republic.

CONTEMPORARY CDA: ITS ORIGINS IN THE NATIONAL CONSTITUENT ASSEMBLY, 1987-88

The opposition to the authoritarian regime of 1964–85 had as one of its main demands the convocation of a National Constituent Assembly (*Assembléia Nacional Constituinte*, or ANC) which would write a new constitution, thereby providing the basis for a new democratic regime. After some debate in 1985, it was decided that the National Congress elected in 1986 would sit simultaneously with the ANC. The ANC was sworn in on February 1, 1987, beginning deliberations which eventually concluded in September 1988.

Throughout the constitution-making process, former oppositionists were intent on dismantling the antidemocratic institutions imposed by the outgoing regime (nicknamed the "authoritarian debris" by then-Senator Fernando Henrique Cardoso), of which the *decreto-lei* was only one example. Despite these antiauthoritarian, reformist biases that were similar to those which had prevailed in the 1946 constitutional convention, a number of the *constituintes* of the 1987–88 period resisted the impulse to abolish presidential decree power entirely, and they were eventually successful in preserving it in a new form. The reasons for this unexpected outcome lie in the tumultuous history of the ANC itself and in the uneven crystallization of the draft document which eventually became the 1988 Constitution.

During the 1987–88 period Brazil came surprisingly close to abandoning its century-long experience with presidential rule. The first draft of the new Constitution, which was completed in July 1987, called for a "premier-presidential" system of government (Shugart and Carey 1992), one featuring a directly elected president but also a prime minister and cabinet subject to parliamentary confidence. It was not until March 1988 that then-president José Sarney, through an amendment that he supported, succeeded in rewriting the articles concerning the executive branch and restored the status quo system (pure presidentialism) to the constitutional text.[9] Therefore, for no less than fourteen of the twenty months of the ANC, the framers were working with a partially parliamentary draft, and in the final six months of the convention they did not entirely adjust the text to reflect the belated choice of pure-presidential government. As the discussion shortly will illustrate, this fact is fundamental to understanding why a form of CDA was retained in the constitutional text.

Not a single person or faction in the ANC defended the retention of the hated *decreto-lei* or *decurso de prazo*.[10] But a number of legislators were concerned that it would be unwise to deprive a Brazilian head of government of any and all extraordinary powers. According to then-Deputy Nelson Jobim of the Brazilian Democratic Movement Party (PMDB-Rio Grande do Sul), who was a supporter of premier-presidentialism, this viewpoint developed from a syndrome of three conditions which were abundantly clear to the legislators in

1987. First was the concern with the normal sluggishness of the Brazilian Congress in passing legislation. A second factor was the high degree of party fragmentation and the possibility that minority presidentialism would become a permanent feature of the new democracy. The third condition was the perceived need for the executive to intervene in crises – which in Brazil seem endemic – and to find a way to surmount them, especially in light of the two foregoing factors (Jobim 1993).

As one of the few congressmen trained in comparative constitutional law, Jobim himself (along with attorney Miguel Reale Júnior, legal adviser to the president of the Assembly) became a leading advocate of importing from the parliamentary constitutions of southern Europe a form of decree power which could equip the head of government with the desired agility. The institution which Jobim and Reale proposed was copied nearly verbatim from Article 77 of the Italian Constitution of 1947, which permits the prime minister to decree *provvedimenti provvisori con forza di legge* (provisional measures with force of law; see the contribution to this volume by Vincent Della Salla and Amie Kreppel). This phrase was rendered into Portuguese as *medidas provisórias com força de lei*. The term *medida provisória* (MP for short) can be translated literally as "temporary (or provisional) measures," although this is a euphemism for what we know as decree power.

The central drafting committee (*Comissão de Sistematização*) of the constitutional convention, which was dominated by partisans of premier-presidentialism, incorporated the idea of the MP into the initial draft of the constitution in mid-1987. According to this draft the president of the Republic was authorized to decree MPs only on the request of the prime minister. Later, pure-presidentialist forces carried the day and removed premier-presidentialism from the text, but the article creating the MP was simply revised to reflect the absence of a prime minister. The popularly elected president, now defined as the sole executive, was henceforth given the power to decree MPs.

In each of the two drafts, the institution of the MP was modeled closely on contemporary Italian CDA. The head of the government, in cases of "urgency and relevance," would be permitted to sign decrees which would have the force of law. They were to be submitted immediately to the National Congress, which, if in recess, would be convoked within five days to review the decree. If the legislature did not convert the MP into law within thirty days (compared to sixty in Italy), the decree would automatically become null and void. If an MP were invalidated in this way, Congress would rule retroactively on the effects of the decree while it was in force.

Although this new conception of CDA differed significantly from the *decreto-lei* of the authoritarian regime (for example, in essentially reversing the *decurso de prazo* and in allowing Congress to rule *ex tunc* on the decree's effects), important sectors of the constitutional convention were adamantly opposed to preserving *any* form of presidential decree power under democracy. These forces eventually challenged the PMDB leadership with an amendment which would have eliminated the MP altogether. When the amendment came to a vote on March 18, 1988, the debate was heated. Ironically, the leader of the effort to kill the MP was a member of the formerly pro-military PDS party, Deputy Adylsson Motta of Rio Grande do Sul, who claimed that the MP was nothing more than a continuation of the hated *decreto-lei* under a new name. For his efforts he won the support of two small leftist parties, along with that of a number of sympathizers from his own party and even a few dissidents from the majority PMDB, whose leadership endorsed the MP. The debate prior to the vote revealed that the defenders of MP, including Nelson Jobim and the chairman of the drafting committee, Bernardo Cabral, were convinced that the MP was fundamentally different from the *decreto-lei* of the 1967 Constitution and that the National Congress would have the ability to deter any abuses by the executive. Jobim emphasized that the MP reversed the normal direction of legislation: The executive could "pass a bill," as it were (issue a decree), but the legislature could easily "veto" it. Cabral stressed that any decree not ratified by Congress within thirty days would automatically expire and that the legislature would be equipped with retroactive, corrective powers over any undesired effects of the decree. In the end, Deputy Motta's amendment to kill the MP received only 78 votes out of 360 cast (*Diário da Assembléia Nacional Constituinte*, March 19, 1988).

In their account of these debates, two Brazilian scholars (Figueiredo and Limongi 1994) note that the legislators who defended the creation of the MP – and who claimed it was *not* simply the abhorrent *decreto-lei* under a new name – framed their arguments against the backdrop of premier-presidentialism, which was the backbone of the constitutional draft at that time. Defenders of decree power argued that the dependence of the future prime minister on assembly confidence would deter abuses. But these debates were conducted and the MP was approved *before* the ANC voted on the system of government (Figueiredo and Limongi 1994: 42). After premier-presidentialism went down to a crushing defeat, the ANC did not revisit the issue of decree power, which in subsequent drafts was assigned to the directly elected president.

Why the ANC did not reexamine the decree article after the victory of pure presidentialism remains an open question. A likely explanation is that allies of President José Sarney, who was the prime force behind the change to presidentialism, wished to let sleeping dogs lie, believing that their patron would be well served by the preservation of CDA (which he was already accustomed to under the existing 1967 Constitution). Another hypothesis is that the three factors cited earlier by Nelson Jobim as justifications for decree power – especially the critical issue of minority presidentialism – remained sufficiently convincing to discourage further debate on the decree issue. In any case the issue was now closed, and the MP was incorporated into the text as Article 62 of the constitution promulgated on October 5, 1988.

THE EXPERIENCE WITH DECREE POWER
SINCE 1988: SARNEY

President José Sarney (1985–90) governed for approximately two-thirds of his term under the authoritarian Constitution of 1967, with the remaining third under the democratically written 1988 document. As a living bridge between two regimes and as the "test driver" of the 1988 Constitution, Sarney set important precedents for his successors in his handling of CDA.

Sarney had begun his presidential term in 1985 still equipped with the authoritarian decree power designed by the generals. In the spirit of the transition to democracy (and following on a pledge made by the deceased architect of the transition, Tancredo Neves), Sarney promised publicly not to use this power (*O Globo*, April 11, 1985, p. 7). Quietly, though, in his first year in office, Sarney resorted to the *decreto-lei* on ten different occasions without provoking an uproar (*Jornal do Brasil*, March 7, 1986, p. 11). A major turning point came on February 28, 1986, when Sarney issued DL 2283, better known as the *Plano Cruzado*, which applied a heterodox shock to the inflation-ridden economy. With the initial success of the Cruzado Plan, Sarney became phenomenally popular, and for a period of several months he had the latitude to act as he wished. But the gradual disintegration of the plan and its replacement by the Cruzado II in November 1986 reversed Sarney's fortunes entirely. For the remainder of his term, he became a weak and reclusive president, rarely appearing in public and relying increasingly on the military and on the selective use of patronage to get his way. Decree power also became a favorite tool of Sarney. The Cruzado Plan seems to have broken the taboo on the use of decree power, because nearly 200 more *decretos-leis* (DLS) were penned by Sarney while the 1967 Constitution was still in force. On twenty-one occasions, the National Congress challenged Sarney and overturned his DLs, something which happened only rarely to the military presidents.

Sarney's political isolation is essential to an understanding of the initial experience with the *medida provisória* when it replaced the *decreto-lei* in October 1988. By that time, as a weak, minority president in a chaotic multiparty system, Sarney had already developed a severe dependence on CDA as an instrument of governance. By virtue of his past[11] Sarney was a product of the post-1964 presidential culture of *decretismo*; by virtue of his actions Sarney helped to perpetuate this culture into the 1990s.

Overall, the adoption of the democratic Constitution and the new MP had little, if any, impact on Sarney's presidential style. He continued to rely on CDA, regardless of its modified format after October 1988. Like his military predecessors, Sarney did not take seriously the constitutional requisites of "urgency and relevance" which were intended to limit the use of the decree. Illustrative of his attitude was his first decree issued after the promulgation of the new Constitution (MP 10, of October 21, 1988),[12] which protected certain fishes from being captured during their reproductive cycle and imposed fines on the fishermen who violated the new rules. Why this regulation could not have been sent to Congress as an ordinary bill is known only to the angler-in-chief, but the Assembly afforded him the benefit of the doubt and ratified the decree within the allotted thirty days. One may object to the presentation of this example as trivial, but that is precisely the point. The first precedent set was one in which Sarney treated the constitutional language trivially, and Congress, perceiving a fait accompli, went along with him. This disregard for the "urgency and relevance" clause quickly became institutionalized, as Sarney stepped up the flow of MPs. Under the 1988 Constitution, he issued an average of 8.5 decrees per month, or about one every four days.[13] This was the most intensive deployment of presidential decree power since the military closed the legislature by force in 1968.

Another important precedent set by Sarney was the reissuing of expired MPs. Amazingly, the Constitution had nothing to say about this question, and it was unclear as to what the president could do if Congress did not act on an MP within thirty days. Therefore, on the advice of his chief legal adviser, Saulo Ramos, Sarney imposed his own interpretation and began consistently to re-decree every *medida provisória* that Congress did not expressly reject.[14] This decision was not inconsequential, because the increasing flow of MPs meant that Congress was facing a backlog of decrees that it had to review.

Several months after the promulgation of the new Constitution, the National Congress, recognizing that President Sarney was intent on using Article 62, set out to design procedures whereby presidential decrees could be reviewed by the legislature in an orderly and timely fashion. These procedures were set out in Congressional Resolution No. 1 of May 1989, which remains in effect as of this writing in late 1997. The resolution prescribes that the President of the Congress, upon the publication of any MP, will designate a select joint committee to study the decree and then report it out to the full Congress, attaching specific recommendations on its admissibility, constitutionality, and merit.[15] If the decree is ruled admissible (i.e., if it is found to observe the language on "urgency and relevance" in Article 62), then legislators – by virtue of a paraconstitutional innovation of Resolution No. 1 – are given a period of five days in which to present amendments to the MP.[16] Any challenges to the admissibility ruling in committee must be decided with a floor vote. If the MP survives this step, the joint committee has fifteen days to rule on the aspects of constitutionality and overall merit. The final committee report may take three forms: recommendation for approval of the MP as it was originally issued, recommendation for approval of an amended version (which is technically no longer an MP but a *projeto de lei de conversão,* or "conversion bill"), or recommendation for rejection. Should the committee decide in favor of rejection, the MP automatically loses the force of law, and the committee must draft a special bill which corrects the effects the decree had while it was in force.[17] If the committee decides in favor of approval in whole or in part, either the original MP or the substitute conversion bill goes to the floor for a roll-call vote. From that point the decree is treated like any other piece of legislation. If the president of the Republic does not accept the version of the decree which eventually emerges from Congress, he or she may veto it (Horta 1990:14–15).[18]

Insofar as Resolution No. 1 demonstrated that Congress – not only the president – was capable of interpreting the new Constitution and of defending institutional prerogatives, it was an important first step taken by the legislature. However, as an internal legislative resolution, it had no binding effects on the president. The passage of the resolution caused no lasting decline in the rate of publication of MPs (see Figure 7.1), nor did it force President Sarney to take more seriously the criteria of "urgency and relevance." Consider two examples: MP 77 of August 1989 set the number of military police in the territory of Roraima, and MP 105 of November 1989 inscribed the names of two historical figures in the official registry of national heroes. In accordance with Resolution No. 1, Congress was required to install committees, prepare opinions and rulings, consider amendments, and vote on them, even when the decree's importance was minor. In 1989 many legislators began to complain publicly that the National Congress was saturated with *medidas provisórias* that were arriving from the president's desk; they also claimed that the legislature could rarely attend to other business. On the other hand Congress itself could be considered partially to blame, inasmuch as nearly every decree, including the absurd examples cited here, was found to be admissible by the special joint committees. In other words Congress frequently went along with the president's interpretation of urgency and relevance.

Congress also failed to use Resolution No. 1 to end the debate about whether an expired MP could be reissued. The resolution states that if an MP reaches the expiration limit of thirty days without final deliberation by Congress, then the legislature will automatically begin consideration of a bill which addresses the effects of the lapsed decree. However, to date (mid-1997), Congress has never actually acted on this. Instead, the practice, begun by Sarney, has been for the presidents to reissue the expired decree and for Congress to tolerate multiple submissions of MPs (Ferreira Filho 1992:25).

Under the terms of the 1988 Constitution Sarney produced a total of 147 MPs in 525 days. Nineteen decrees were reissued after Congress failed to rule on them within the prescribed thirty days. With the failure of Congressional Resolution No. 1 of 1989, consensus was emerging that something more had to be done in the way of reformulating decree power. By the time Sarney stepped down in March 1990, a number of bills regulating the use of MPs were already circulating in both houses of Congress, and many more were being drafted. Sarney, however, escaped a full-scale legislative backlash, not only because his term was ending but also because political energies were largely concentrated on the presidential elections of November 1989 (the first free elections in twenty-nine years) and on the specter of hyperinflation (when Sarney stepped down, inflation was running at 84 percent monthly). Therefore, the anti-MP movement in the legislature fell largely on the man elected to succeed Sarney: Fernando Collor de Mello.

THE EXPERIENCE WITH DECREE POWER
SINCE 1988: COLLOR

In an early glimpse of his presidential style, president-elect Collor visited Sarney several days before his inauguration, and he asked the outgoing president to issue a decree on behalf of the incoming administration. Sarney's last act as president was to decree a bank holiday in preparation for Collor's impending economic package, the contents of which were completely unknown.

Assuming the presidency on March 15, 1990, Collor quickly surpassed his predecessor in the use of the *medida provisória*. Within hours of being sworn in, he signed the twenty-two decrees which laid out his long-awaited anti-inflationary measures, the so-called Collor Plan (*Plano Brasil Novo*). The most controversial measure was a freeze on bank accounts in excess of $650 – which was said to remove 80 percent of liquid assets from circulation – but the plan also included other steps such as the firing of public employees, the selling off of federally owned real estate, a crackdown on tax evaders, and a new currency (the third in four years). In the days and weeks that followed, many more supplementary decrees were signed by the president; most of them corrected and refined the shock measures, but some of them were designed to head off public, legislative, and business opposition to the plan.

The reasons for Collor's liberal use of the MP were different from those of Sarney. The late Sarney relied on decree power because he was weak; the early Collor relied on the MP because he was strong. Unlike Sarney, Collor was an elected president, who enjoyed the legitimacy conferred by 35 million votes. Although his party controlled less than 3 percent of the seats in the legislature, his strong campaign and initial popularity in office allowed him to forge (at least temporarily) a multiparty coalition in Congress. This coalition, preoccupied with congressional and gubernatorial elections only seven months after Collor's inauguration, was content to leave the legislative initiative up to the president and his advisers. Second, the economy had disintegrated to a point where the electorate was willing to afford the president considerable latitude in attacking inflation. Public morale had sunk considerably in the late 1980s. Sarney's administration had failed to stabilize the economy, and Collor, who had campaigned as a political outsider, had carte blanche to try something new.[19] The telegenic young president understood this well, and he was initially successful at using the media to go over the heads of Congress and generate public support for his economic plan. Finally, Collor relied on decree power in part because Sarney had done so and gotten away with it. As he began to follow Sarney's example of reissuing expired decrees, he even cited the legal opinions broached by the Sarney government on this subject.

Although both presidents were criticized for their heavy reliance on the MP, Collor's decrees were generally seen as more controversial – that is, they were more dubiously grounded in legality – than Sarney's. The first batch of MPs surrounding the Collor Plan were not all anti-inflationary measures: Some of them

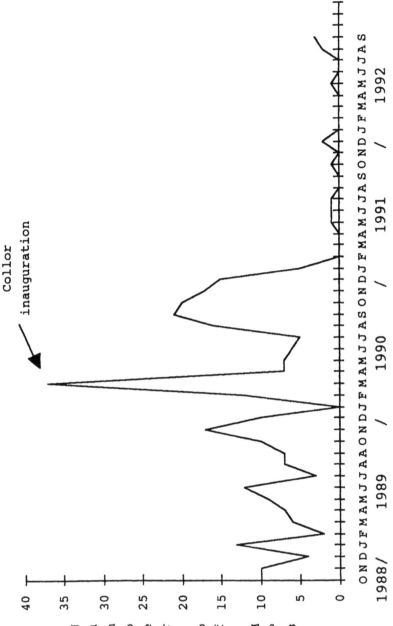

Figure 7.1 Use of decree power by Presidents Sarney and Collor, 1988–92 (number of MPs issued by month)

were intended to discourage legal challenges to the economic package, whereas others tried to expand the capacity of the executive branch, allowing it to crack down on individuals and firms that did not comply with various new regulations.[20] MPs 153 and 156, for example, defined new crimes against the public treasury and the *economia popular* (the people's patrimony). These two decrees were clearly unconstitutional, because only the legislature has jurisdiction over the penal code – that is, the executive branch is not permitted to invent a new crime. Amid a public outcry and pressure from Congress and distinguished jurists, Collor was forced to withdraw these two measures in April 1990.

After Collor completed thirty days in office, it became apparent that Congress would not be able to keep pace with the decrees emanating from the Planalto Palace. Unwilling to place any element of the economic plan in jeopardy, Collor issued explicit instructions to his aides to proceed automatically with the republication of any decree that Congress did not consider within thirty days. Furthermore, he authorized his spokesperson to announce this policy to the press (*Jornal de Brasília*, April 18, 1990). With his decree pen on automatic pilot, it is no surprise that Collor's presidential style led to renewed polemics in Congress about Article 62 of the Constitution and its silence on the renewability of MPs. What is surprising is that Collor purported to discover even more latitude in Article 62 than had his predecessor, and this led directly to another confrontation over constitutionality – this time with the judicial branch.

On May 4, 1990, Collor decreed MP 185, which authorized the president of Brazil's highest labor court to suspend any wage hikes won by unions in class-action suits that the government regarded as dangerously inflationary. On May 31, the Chamber of Deputies voted to reject the decree.[21] The following morning, Collor issued MP 190, whose text was almost identical to that of the rejected MP 185. While both Sarney and Collor had reissued many decrees not definitively ruled upon by Congress, this was the first time a president had reissued an MP that the legislature had expressly rejected. The reaction from civil society was swift, with nearly unanimous condemnation by political parties and eminent jurists. The *Procurador-Geral da República* (the independent public prosecutor and an ombudsman in constitutional matters), Aristides Junqueira, immediately sought a Supreme Court injunction to stop Collor's action. Five days later, on June 6, the Supreme Court struck down MP 190 by a vote of nine to zero. The written opinion made it abundantly clear that Collor had overstepped the bounds of presidential authority (*Supremo Tribunal Federal* 1990). It is notable that in the two-year struggle over the interpretation of constitutional decree authority, when push came to shove, it was the judiciary and not the National Congress which defined the outer limits of presidential power in this area.

Although the Supreme Court defeat seemed to have an immediate deterrent impact on Collor's use of the MP (Figure 7.1 shows a mild dropoff in June and July 1990), the latter half of 1990 saw an increased output of decrees. Once again, legislators introduced supplementary laws[22] and constitutional amendments which sought either to abolish all presidential decree authority altogether or to rewrite the ambiguous language of Article 62. One bill of the latter type, introduced by none other than Nelson Jobim, eventually succeeded in forcing Collor to back down on his use of MPs, but he did so only as the result of the protracted struggle and a political standoff.

The Jobim Bill, an idea which dated from the Sarney period, sought to codify the conditions under which the president could use decree power. It was heavily amended, and it became a composite bill backed by a broad spectrum of legislators concerned with Article 62. By the time it came up for a floor vote in March 1991, it contained several important innovations. Upon issuing an MP, the president would have to attach a message justifying the decree's compliance with the constitutional language on "urgency and relevance." The president would be forbidden from issuing decrees on the subjects of supplementary laws and constitutional amendments, political and electoral rights, nationality and citizenship, individual liberties, budgetary issues, taxation, and the penal code, among others. The most controversial provision of the bill – and the one that the Collor government most vociferously opposed – was its Article 9, which would allow the president only one renewal of an MP not expressly approved by the National Congress. In practice this would have meant that the president would have sixty rather than thirty days to form a majority around some satisfactory version of his original decree. But failure would be costly: If the president failed to get a satisfactory version of the MP passed by Congress, the issue would have to wait until the next legislative session.[23]

Because many of Collor's most important initiatives rested on his ability to re-decree them repeatedly (a presidential power which, I stress again, is not found in the Constitution but which rests entirely on paraconstitutional precedent and the acquiescence of Congress since 1988), consideration of Article 9 of the Jobim Bill immediately became politicized. Planalto Palace did not view this particular provision as a fine-tuning of the Constitution; rather it saw it as a frontal attack on Collor. However, the president's legislative leaders recognized that the general thrust of the Jobim Bill was widely supported in Congress, and thus they focused their energies only on deleting Article 9 (*Jornal do Brasil*, March 7, 1991). Pro-government legislators forced a separate vote on the controversial provision. Collor then attempted to negotiate a compromise on the language of Article 9, in which the president would be allowed to reissue an MP twice rather than once (*Folha de São Paulo*, March 13, 1991). The opposition declined to negotiate, believing it had the votes to pass the original version of the clause. But when Article 9 came up for a vote in the Chamber of Deputies on March 20, it garnered only a simple majority of 247 in favor to 178 opposed, thus falling 5 votes short of the absolute majority needed for passage. Similarly, Collor's allies were also successful in killing Article 5 of the Jobim Bill, which would have prohibited decrees dealing with matters of taxation. Later, the watered-down Jobim Bill was passed by the Chamber, but without its most potent provision – namely, the limitation on multiple publications of MPs.

The Jobim Bill then went to the Senate, where the opposition PMDB party controlled 25 of the 81 seats. Immediately, the PMDB leadership amended the bill and reattached the two controversial provisions defeated in the lower house. In an extraordinary move the PMDB's National Executive Committee voted to impose party fidelity on the party's senators in a last-ditch attempt to get a stronger version of the Jobim Bill passed. (Interestingly, one senator was released from party fidelity: former president José Sarney, the originator of iterated decrees.) But on two occasions in April 1991, Humberto Lucena, the PMDB leader in the Senate, failed to put the bill into play: Walkouts by pro-Collor forces deprived the upper house of a quorum. When Lucena failed even to get the necessary signatures on a petition requiring an immediate floor vote, the Jobim Bill fell into legislative limbo (*Correio Braziliense,* April 24, 1991). According to Nelson Jobim, the only recourse left to the PMDB party – the largest in the National Congress, with about 22 percent of the seats – was to come to an understanding that all future MPs issued by Collor would be considered within the terms of the Jobim Bill even though it was not law. The PMDB would simply consider the defeated bill as a binding framework for executive–legislative relations. President Collor was informed of this understanding (Jobim 1993).

Although Jobim and his allies did not succeed in redefining Article 62 of the Constitution, their efforts seem to have resonated among Collor and his advisers. While the Jobim Bill was being considered by Congress in February, March, and April of 1991, Collor did not decree a single MP (Figure 7.1). In contrast to his first year in office, his restraint was astonishing. It is difficult to avoid the conclusion that the president imagined his good behavior might save him from having his decree power reduced by an act of Congress. It is also likely that Collor was further deterred by the Jobim Bill's strong showing in the Chamber on March 20, when 58 percent of the Deputies who were present – including many in the pro-government coalition – opposed his expansive interpretation of decree power. Finally, the PMDB's strong endorsement of the Jobim Bill in the Senate, including the imposition of party fidelity, could only have led Collor to conclude that future abuses of the MP would have invited repeated confrontations with Brazil's largest political party. It was clearly in the president's interest, then, to back down and accept the "understanding" promoted by the PMDB leadership. If Collor would not abuse presidential decree power, the PMDB would not attempt to curtail it.

The events of early 1991 clearly had a deterrent effect on the president, because for the remainder of his term he resorted only rarely to the institution of the *medida provisória.* From his inauguration in March 1990 through January 1991, Collor averaged 14 MPs per month, but from February 1991 through the end of his term, he averaged only 0.6 decrees per month. By late 1991 Collor, under pressure from international financial institutions and a new bevy of more pragmatic advisers, had come to the conclusion that long-term structural adjustment in Brazil could only be achieved by major changes to the 1988 Constitution. This realization marked a shift from confrontation to negotiation with key elites, and the administration began work on a wide-ranging package of constitutional amendments for presentation to Congress (the so-called *Emendão*). The *Emendão* strategy was interrupted in May 1992, when Collor's brother Pedro revealed the existence of a massive corruption scheme within the government (see Weyland 1993). This was the beginning of the end for Collor. The president was subsequently impeached and removed from office on September 29, 1992, and he was replaced by his reclusive vice president, Itamar Franco.

Collor's two successors in the presidency are not analyzed in this chapter, because most of the relevant precedents and debates surrounding CDA were already set in place by Collor and Sarney before them. However, a few comments are in order to illustrate how the unresolved battles of the Sarney and Collor years continue to haunt executive–legislative relations. Immediately after taking office in late 1992, Itamar Franco was pegged as a weak and inept president, and he was frequently compared to José Sarney. Much like the later Sarney, the early Itamar relied on CDA to promote an ill-defined legislative agenda, and he ran headlong into the wall of inflation: His first three finance ministers had an average life span of only eighty days due to economic difficulties. His fortunes began to change in May 1993 when he appointed his fourth finance minister, Senator Fernando Henrique Cardoso, and effectively withdrew from most day-to-day decision making. A congressional insider functioning as a de facto prime minister, Cardoso spent the next year laying the groundwork for the *Plano Real*, a currency reform implemented in July 1994. With its early success at reducing inflation, the *Plano Real* served as the launching pad for Cardoso's successful campaign in the presidential election of October 1994; Itamar Franco, ironically, retired as the most popular Brazilian president in the history of opinion polling. This remarkable turnaround in the fortunes of both Franco and of the Brazilian economy was propelled by Cardoso's crack economic team, which prepared literally hundreds of MPs for the president's signature in the 1993–94 period. Itamar Franco surpassed both Sarney and Collor in the use of decrees, issuing 505 MPs in his brief interregnum.

Cardoso's accession to the presidency on January 1, 1995, was seen by many as the beginning of a new era of energetic reformism driven by an activist executive. The same was said of the "outsider" Collor in 1990, but most – even his most implacable opponents – believe that Cardoso's greater experience, prestige, and pragmatism will serve him better than the confrontational and aloof populism of his ousted predecessor. In terms of policy objectives, however, there is no mistaking that Cardoso's neoliberal reform agenda strongly resembles Collor's. What elements of presidential initiative should be employed to pursue this agenda? In contrast to Collor, who learned on the job, Cardoso came to office with an ambitious program of long-term economic reform through constitutional revision. Through the amendment process, several state monopolies were ended in short order, but other proposals – concerning social security, state employment, and tax reform, to name only a few – languished in congressional committees in 1995 and 1996. But for the day-to-day management of the stabilization plan which he had instituted as Finance Minister in 1994, Cardoso relied on CDA even more than his predecessors.

As Itamar Franco's economic czar, Cardoso had experienced vicariously the immediacy and flexibility conferred by decree power, and as president he shattered all previous records in the use of MPs. By August 1996 he had already issued more than 700, or approximately 1.2 decrees for every day of his presidency (see again Table 7.1). The actual number of initiatives is far smaller than the number of MPs suggests, because hundreds of these decrees were actually re-issues intended to renew the key provisions of the *Plano Real* (for example, the new currency itself was finally codified into law by Congress in June 1995, after twelve months of being continuously reinstituted by decree). In one important sense the need to renew decrees works to the advantage of the president: Rather than introduce a policy in one fell swoop, the executive can fine-tune it every month by making modifications, as necessary, when the decree is renewed.[24] Renewability of decrees thus grants the executive an important space for policy improvisation, which may explain why presidents have fought so hard to maintain this paraconstitutional privilege.[25]

Clearly, Franco did not feel bound by Collor's earlier commitment to restraint in the use of decree authority, and neither did Cardoso. Because to date no supplementary law or constitutional amendment has been passed to redefine Article 62, executive–legislative relations in Brazil remain poorly defined and potentially explosive.

COMPARING THE DECREES OF SARNEY AND COLLOR

Further insight into the institution of the *medida provisória* can be gained by a brief comparison of the decrees issued by Sarney and Collor, using aggregate data that was obtained from the on-line legislative database of PRODASEN (Senate Data Processing Center, Brasília) and was coded by the author. Table 7.2 compares the subject matter of the MPs issued by the two presidents. When taken together, nearly half (45.6 percent) of all decrees were miscellaneous presidential orders directed mostly at the executive branch itself. The vast majority resulted from the presidents' efforts to split, rejoin, and rename elements of the executive branch (ministries, secretariats, administrative agencies, and state-owned enterprises). The next largest category was that of anti-inflationary measures (27.1 percent), followed by a catch-all category for economic restructuring (liberalization and privatization initiatives, totaling 17.3 percent). Collor's neoliberal orientation is clearly visible in the data: More than a quarter of his decrees entailed economic reforms. Overall, economic crisis (inflation) plus restructuring were responsible for nearly half of all MPs. The remaining MPs were dedicated to the updating of old *decretos-leis* (many of which are still in force, some dating from the 1930s) or were unclassifiable.

Table 7.2 *Substantive content of presidential decrees*

Subject	Sarney %	Sarney (N)	Collor %	Collor (N)	Total %	Total (N)
Old decree-law	16	(23)	1	(2)	8	(25)
Miscellaneous executive regulation	57	(84)	35	(56)	46	(140)
Anti-inflationary	20	(29)	34	(54)	27	(83)
Liberalization/privatization	8	(11)	26	(42)	17	(53)
Other/miscellaneous	0	(0)	4	(6)	2	(6)
Total	100	(147)	100	(160)	100	(307)

Because percentages were rounded to whole numbers, columns may not add up to 100.
Source: Coded by author from PRODASEN data.

How did the two presidents' decrees fare in Congress? The first two rows of Table 7.3 demonstrate a major shortcoming of Congressional Resolution No. 1 of May 1989, which instituted "admissibility committees" to determine if presidential decrees met the constitutional requisites of urgency and relevance. These are revealed as low-viscosity committees, permitting more than 90 percent of all presidential decrees to circulate in the National Congress. Given that many of Collor's decrees violated the separation of powers, one must either question the ability of these committees to rule on constitutional issues or consider whether they are too easily neutralized by pro-government forces.

In one-third of all cases, the National Congress did not reach a decision on a presidential decree within the prescribed thirty days. It is difficult to ascertain whether this is due to legislative inefficiency or to the "fait accompli" complex – that is, the de facto awareness that the president would reissue the decree anyway (one of Collor's MPs survived for eight months in this fashion). A review of the formal *apreciação* (legislative consideration) of MPs shows that in 31 percent of the cases, consideration of the decree was interrupted at least once (and often more) by the inability to achieve a quorum in Congress. This is a complex issue, because some legislative delays were due to the normal lassitude of the Brazilian Congress, whereas others were due to obstructionist tactics on the part of the government and opposition. My own view is that the two tendencies at work here – Congressional inefficiency and presidential abuse of decree authority – are mutually reinforcing. I return to this theme in the conclusion.

The data also illustrate that – contrary to the widespread impression – Sarney's decrees were much more successful than Collor's. Sarney saw 44.9 percent of his MPs made directly into law, whereas Collor's figure was only 13.1 percent. Looking only at decrees that were allowed to expire by Congress, these figures are almost perfectly reversed: Sarney's MPs expired 17 percent of the time, and the equivalent rate for Collor was 49.4 percent. Once again, this may be partially

Table 7.3 *Legislative consideration of presidential decrees*

MPs that were . . .	Sarney % (N)	Collor % (N)	Total % (N)
ruled admissible by Joint Committee[a]	91 (119)	91 (123)	91 (242)
ruled inadmissible by Joint Committee	9 (12)	9 (12)	9 (24)
final congressional decision within the 30-day time limit[b]	83 (120)	54 (84)	68 (204)
no final decision within 30-day limit	17 (25)	47 (73)	33 (98)
made directly into law	45 (66)	13 (21)	28 (87)
amended and transformed into "conversion bills"[c]	30 (44)	31 (49)	30 (93)
expressly rejected by full Congress	5 (8)	6 (10)	6 (18)
expired after 30 days ran out[d]	17 (25)	49 (79)	34 (104)
tabled or returned by Congress	2 (3)	0 (0)	1 (3)
rescinded by the President	1 (1)	1 (1)	1 (1)
reissued once	13 (19)	16 (25)	14 (44)
twice	NA	11 (17)	6 (17)
three times	NA	8 (12)	4 (12)
four times	NA	3 (4)	1 (4)
five times	NA	2 (3)	1 (3)
six times	NA	1 (1)	0 (1)
seven times	NA	1 (1)	0 (1)
N	147	160	307

Because percentages were rounded, columns may not add up to 100.
[a]Total N of cases = 266. The Joint Committees did not exist prior to Congressional Resolution No.1 of May 1989 (see text).
[b]Total N of cases = 302. Five missing cases in PRODASEN data.
[c]Conversion bills did not exist prior to Congressional Resolution No.1 of May 1989.
[d]Includes some decrees that were reissued one or more times but which had lost their validity prior to June 1993.
Source: Coded by the author from PRODASEN data (June 1993).

due to the congressional learning curve. Because the multiple-decree practice was thoroughly ingrained by the time of Collor and because Collor's policy of automatic renewal of MPs was publicly announced, there was little incentive for Congress to spend time and energy on the less controversial decrees.

After the passage of Congressional Resolution No. 1 in May 1989, many MPs were amended and became conversion bills. As one would expect, conversion bills have a much better chance of becoming law (72.1 percent) than do unadulterated decrees (28.3 percent). Again, Sarney outperformed Collor in getting his conversion bills passed (80.4 percent success versus 66.2 percent). Sarney exercised the line-item veto on 22 percent of his converted MPs, and Collor on 32 percent of his. Collor also vetoed outright three of his own decrees as amended by Congress (data on veto overrides were unavailable). The PRODASEN data also show that on average a Sarney decree attracted about 5 amendments from legislators, whereas Collor's mean was an impressive 33 amendments per MP. This is further evidence that under President Collor, it was not only the frequency of his *medidas provisórias* but also the programmatic content of his decree agenda that met with resistance from the National Congress.

HOW BRAZILIAN POLITICIANS PERCEIVE DECREE POWER

Research for this chapter involved interviews with some of the principals in the decree drama since 1988. In this section I provide a contextual understanding of the political battles, as well as some tentative predictions about the future of decree power, by comparing executive versus legislative perceptions of decree authority.

An executive view. In an interview with the author, Fernando Collor de Mello reaffirmed his position as a supporter of parliamentarism for Brazil (Collor 1993). At the same time he argued that while presidentialism remains in force (and this is likely to be for a long time, given that presidentialism was overwhelmingly victorious in a plebiscite held in April 1993), its current Brazilian variant cannot survive without some form of CDA. According to Collor, "the *medida provisória* is a permanent focus of tension in the relations of the executive branch with the legislative and judicial branches, and in the relations of the executive with society more generally. At the same time, it is the only instrument of governability which the President of the Republic possesses" (ibid.). When he was asked to imagine what his presidency would have been like *without* the use of decree power – that is, if in 1990 he had had to submit an ordinary legislative package to Congress – Collor responded,

> I couldn't have done it. I couldn't have done it, because how could we have frozen all liquid assets (*ativos*)? How could we carry out all these measures by saying, "Listen, we need to call in all the *ativos* for a year and [a] half or so, in order to reduce the amount of money in circulation, and thereby get rid of inflation!"? These were measures that would have been impossible to adopt without the use of the MP. As was the *Plano Cruzado*, as were the other plans – the Bresser Plan, the Summer Plan. Every heterodox economic plan here in Brazil made use of the *medida provisória*. Without the MP, they would never have passed. That doesn't mean that I am defending the *medida provisória*: I am against it. But it is the only instrument of governability and of administration that we have available to us today. That's it. There is no

other way. However, that the MP is a permanent focus of tension in the politics of the country . . . of this there is no doubt.[26]

While clearly rationalizing his own actions as president, Collor is also alluding here to a very real problem. A towering challenge to the consolidation of Brazilian democracy is a situation of permanent minority presidentialism in which the executive must constantly form and reform ad hoc coalitions in the legislature. (In the most extreme example of this, Collor's own party, the PRN [Partido Reconstrusão Nacional], controlled only 3 percent of the seats in Congress.) Even in situations where the leadership of a party is committed to supporting the president, factors such as the weakness of parties, the individualism of legislators, and what Scott Mainwaring (1992; 1993) termed "the irresponsible nature of much of the Brazilian political class" mean that the president cannot really depend on anyone for support.[27] Moreover, the National Congress itself is a notoriously inefficient institution (Novaes 1994). Collor argued that the *medida provisória* aggravates these problems, allowing legislators to use presidential decree power as an excuse for fence-straddling and the abdication of congressional authority. He said,

> I believe that the MP aggravates greatly (*inflama muito*) the separation of powers, because the legislature, which recovered most if not all of its prerogatives, feels threatened and intimidated at any moment by the publication of an MP which conflicts with the interests of the parties ideologically arrayed within the National Congress. And at the same time, the *medida provisória* is used to provide political cover for various positions in the Congress. Let's imagine the people who say they're against something: "No, I'm against a decree on wages, I'm against the president's veto, I'm against a wage policy that does not give workers full restitution of the inflationary losses that they are suffering." Well, when a decree comes down modifying all this, this person is covered, because he says, "Well, I was against it, but the decree came along, and it's already in force, so let's forget about it." Do you follow? It [the MP] allows the less responsible sectors in the National Congress to find a commodity with which to change their positions and their political discourse vis-à-vis society. (Collor 1993)

What Collor fails to mention, of course, is that this abdicant behavior on the part of legislators is encouraged by the practice of multiple reissues of decrees, a practice which allows the Congress to postpone decision making. As president, Collor fought desperately to maintain this privilege, which he sees as implicit in the constitutional text. In the interview he argued that Congress has no authority to restrict the power of the executive as written into Article 62 ("*se a Lei Maior não restringe, uma lei menor não pode restringir*").[28] Collor cites as evidence for this view the fact that more than 200 articles of the 1988 Constitution were non–self-executing and called for supplementary laws to elaborate them, but Article 62 was not one of them. This is an interesting argument which cannot easily be dismissed, and it illustrates two things: first, that the Constituent Assembly showed little foresight in its crafting of Article 62; and second, that attempts to modify decree authority may require a constitutional amendment rather than a supplementary law like the Jobim Bill.

Views from the legislature. As related earlier, former federal deputy Nelson Jobim (PMDB-Rio Grande do Sul) was the principal defender of the MP in the Constituent Assembly of the 1987–88 period. When presidential abuses became routinized in 1989, Jobim, as the Father of CDA, became a lightning rod for criticism. However, through 1994 Jobim worked the hardest to curtail abuses, especially in his initiative to limit the reissuing of MPs.[29] Other legislators, such as Adylsson Motta (PPB-Rio Grande do Sul), argued that such efforts are misguided and that the best solution is to abolish CDA altogether (which Motta himself tried to do in the ANC). According to Motta, the current MP is worse than the authoritarian-era *decreto-lei*, which was restricted to three areas of policy. The current MP has no such restrictions: It can apply to anything. Motta believes that decree power is not necessary, given that the president already has the power to request urgent consideration of any legislation that he/she sends to Congress (Motta 1993).[30]

Other legislators continue to fight for Nelson Jobim's position – that is, to maintain the MP but to reformulate the constitutional language on "urgency and relevance." When asked in an interview why it was worth the trouble, Jobim, a longtime advocate of political democracy and the rule of law, responded with astonishing frankness: "You *need* a mechanism like the MP to avoid having the government act illegally. If you do not have a legal way to decree, then the government will have to invent one" (Jobim 1993).

The future of the MP. A survey conducted by the author in June 1993 found that there was considerable consensus among the congressional members that presidents have misused decree authority but that legislators differed on what to do about the problem.[31] Some 85 percent of the legislators agreed ("strongly" or "somewhat") that "Under the Constitution of 1988, the Presidents of the Republic have abused the power of *medidas provisórias.*"[32] When asked a more daunting question – whether Brazil *needs* presidential decree authority – the legislators split evenly (Table 7.4). Ideology as measured by party identification was an important variable here. Some 60 percent of conservative legislators agreed on the need for the MP; conversely, 60 precent of progressives disagreed. Among legislators who support the presidential system of government, 65 percent agreed, whereas only 43 percent of self-described parliamentarists concurred. Interestingly, another important variable was prior experience in the executive branch. Members of Congress who had served as governor, mayor, minister, etc., said that decree authority was necessary (by a 56–44 percent margin). In contrast members whose political experience was entirely in legislative bodies said that the MP was unnecessary (by a margin of 58 to 42 percent).[33]

A parallel survey was conducted in the 1992–93 period by DIAP, a parlia-

Table 7.4 *Perceived need for CDA among Brazilian federal legislators, June 1993*

STATEMENT: "In Brazil, it is necessary to give the President of the Republic the power of *medida provisória.*"

	Left of center[a] % (N)	PMDB % (N)	Right of Center[b] % (N)	Congress % (N)
Agree (strongly or somewhat)	40 (23)	43 (16)	61 (52)	50 (91)
Disagree (strongly or somewhat)	60 (35)	57 (21)	40 (34)	50 (90)
Total	100 (58)	100 (37)	100 (86)	100 (181)

[a]Left of center parties: PSDB, PDT, PT, PSB, PPS, PC do B, PSTU.
[b]Right of center parties: PFL, PPR, PP, PRN, PTB, PL.
Source: Author's survey of Congress (June 1993).

mentary lobby maintained by labor unions. Some 418 legislators were asked specific questions on how they planned to vote in a special assembly scheduled to revise the Constitution in 1994 (see below), and they were made aware that their responses would be published in a book (DIAP 1993). DIAP found that on the subject of MPs, only 14 percent saw no need to change Article 62. Another 55 percent of the legislators endorsed what was essentially the position held by Nelson Jobim: that Article 62 should be maintained, but that the language on "urgency and relevance" should be rewritten. Factoring in the 8 percent who favored the addition of more rigorous criteria to Article 62, DIAP (Departmento Intersindical de Assessoria Parlamentar) found that in the 1992–1993 period there was a coalition of 77 percent of the Congress in favor of retaining *some* form of CDA. Only 20 percent of DIAP's respondents said they were entirely opposed to decree authority. This was a puzzling finding, not only with regard to the distribution of opinion in Table 7.4, but also in light of the tremendous political battles of the preceding five years. The only plausible explanation was that the majority in favor of retaining decree power was convinced that the impending 1994 constitutional revision, the *Congresso Revisor*, could successfully reform Article 62 and effectively put an end to the ambiguities and acrimony of the recent past.

The 1988 Constitution had stipulated that five years after its promulgation, the National Congress would meet in an extraordinary session to revise the constitutional text. The long-awaited *Congresso Revisor* convened in March 1994 and immediately began a slow, agonizing death. Despite a promising start with the election of Nelson Jobim as its chief legislative officer, the constitutional revision was paralyzed by a major corruption scandal involving twenty-nine members of Congress (Fleischer 1994; Krieger, Rodrigues, and Bonassa 1994). Investigations dragged on into the middle of the year, by which time the election campaign of 1994 had already begun to heat up. Finally, congressional leaders pulled the plug on the comatose special assembly, putting to rest five years of hopes for constitutional reform. Of 30,000 proposals presented, only five were enacted as constitutional amendments. None addressed CDA.

When the legislature elected in 1994 convened for the first time in February 1995, new constitutional amendments limiting CDA were once again introduced both in the Senate and in the Chamber of Deputies. Despite the relative simplicity of constitutional amendment procedures in Brazil, it is as yet unclear whether these initiatives will fare any better than the Jobim Bill in 1991 or the special assembly in 1994.

CONCLUSION: TOWARD A POLITICAL AND THEORETICAL UNDERSTANDING OF THE MP

This chapter has reviewed the travail of presidential decree power in Brazil since 1988. The task of this study was primarily empirical, focusing on constitutional and institutional arrangements, the legal production of decrees, and the politics of executive–legislative relations since the promulgation of the new Constitution. In the concluding remarks in this section, I first review the empirical evidence before placing the findings in political and theoretical context.

The evidence on Brazilian presidential decree authority. From an unabashedly formalistic perspective, by focusing only on the legal and constitutional aspects of contemporary Brazilian decree power, we can clearly see that Article 62 of the 1988 Constitution is an invitation to chaos. In three striking ways, the article is a lesson in how *not* to draft a constitutional provision. First, on the issue of who is to define "urgency and relevance," its language is ambiguous. Second, Article 62 places no restrictions on which policy areas are subject to presidential decree. Third, on what emerged as a central theme in our empirical discussion – whether a president may renew an expired MP – the Constitution is silent altogether.

The unfortunate wording of Article 62 derives from its unsuccessful importation from Italy, where a parliamentary system exists. In 1987 the Italian *provvedimenti provvisori* was selected for a "transplant" to Brazil, but at the last moment, the host "body" was switched. The Italian-style CDA was grafted onto a presidential constitution, where it does not belong. In a pure parliamentary system, one in which the government – by definition – commands a majority in the assembly, a "provisional measure" does nothing more than speed up what is (usually) a more predictable legislative process.[34] Abuses of decree authority are deterred by the principle of executive responsibility to the assembly. If a prime minister, when signing an emergency decree that invoked dramatic constitutional language on "urgency and relevance," were then to have such a decree rejected by the assembly, there is a high probability that he or she would lose the confidence of parliament – and with it, his or her job. In contrast, in a presidential system like Brazil's, no comparable constraint exists on the executive, because the executive and the legislature have "separate origin and survival" (Shugart and Carey 1992). The assembly's main weapons against the abuse of decree authority by the president (constitutional amendment or the more remote possibility of impeachment) either require extraordinary majorities or are politically unrealistic – or both.[35]

Tellingly, even in early 1991, when there existed considerable consensus in the Brazilian Congress that CDA should be partially restricted, the legislature confronted serious collective action problems in attempting reform. A sitting president needed only to *aggravate* these ongoing collective action problems in order to avoid a legislative defeat. It is true that it was the Brazilian legislature that gave the president extraordinary powers in the first place, but it is also true that what is given is not so easily taken away. Presidents are more efficient and agile actors than legislatures. When an activist executive already holds the high ground, he or she is unlikely to be dislodged by a disorganized and divided assembly.

If Brazilian decree authority is as dangerous as I have implied – if Article 62 is really a fault line running under the *Praça dos Três Poderes* (Plaza of the Three Powers) – then the question persists: Why would a rational assembly delegate such tremendous power to a president? One should not entirely discount the chaotic and disappointing performance of the 1987–88 Constituent Assembly, which left much unfinished business in its wake.[36] But in accord with hypotheses suggested by the editors of this volume, there likely was some method in the apparent madness of the constitutional convention. In their theoretical account of why assemblies delegate decree authority to executives, Carey and Shugart derive two initial hypotheses from collective action theory. The first is that legislative decision making is generally a slow process and that delegation to a unitary executive could be an attractive option; the second is that legislators seeking policy change have a difficult time deciding among various acceptable alternatives to the status quo, and thus they may choose to assign the final decision to the executive. Evidence supporting both of these hypotheses emerged in the debates from the 1988 ANC and from interviews with legislators. A third hypothesis suggested by Carey and Shugart is that legislatures may delegate decree authority on issue-areas in which information and policy expertise are concentrated in the executive branch. This is highly plausible, because the majority of presidential decrees in Brazil are dedicated to macroeconomic policy, a subject on which the understaffed National Congress is notoriously underinformed.[37] But here it is necessary to recall that the decree authority enshrined in Article 62 does not single out any area of public policy for its appropriate use – that is, the delegation of authority was never issue-specific. Finally, Carey and Shugart suggest that assemblies may delegate authority to the executive to avoid responsibility for policies that they believe to be necessary but expect to be widely unpopular. Fernando Collor argued for this very view (albeit somewhat self-servingly) while evincing frustration with abdicant legislators' rhetoric against his decrees. However, although the evasion-of-responsibility hypothesis explains conjunctive strategic behavior on the part of legislators, it does not explain why they would *permanently* enshrine decree power in a constitution, thus writing a blank check for unknown future presidents. In the language of this volume, the evasion-of-responsibility hypothesis explains DDA but not CDA.

Carey and Shugart's hypotheses explain delegation largely in terms of political process; and they frame their insights against the ongoing game of executive–legislative relations. However, it is possible to suggest an additional hypothesis, one that is not process-oriented but that is rather a "genetic" account of delegation by a legislature to an executive. Here I refer to the external environment impacting constitutional conventions. Constitutions are not written in a vacuum, and the 1988 Brazilian Constitution was written in a maelstrom. Inflation, foreign debt, the collapse of the public sector, increasing poverty and social dualism, and a parade of failed economic stabilization plans were the specters haunting the Brazilian framers. Had the crisis of the 1980s not confronted them so overwhelmingly, perhaps they would not have delegated the *medida provisória* to the chief executive. In his account of the delegation, Nelson Jobim (1993) specifically cited the perceived need to overcome the crisis. One could object to such an argument by remarking that Brazil is *always* in crisis, but this in itself is revealing. Since 1937, Brazil has had presidential decree power for about 70 percent of the time.[38]

Toward a political understanding of the MP. Beyond a formal understanding of the MP, it is important to place presidential decree power in the context of *politics.* How exactly does decree authority affect the exercise of political power in Brazil? Three simple observations are advanced here.

First, the *medida provisória* creates a tremendous temptation for presidents. Given the way CDA is currently configured, both strong and weak presidents are attracted to its use. A very strong president with a popular mandate can implement entire programs through decree, as Collor showed in his first two months in office. Congress ratified his MPs in large batches. A weak president with little support in the legislature can attempt to legislate using the MP by placing Congress on the defensive through the renewal of expired decrees: This was the presidential style in the late Sarney period. This perverse situation, in which both honeymoon and disgraced presidents will resort to CDA, rests largely on the premise of the renewability of the MP. If decrees were not renewable, then weak presidents would have less of an incentive to issue them. Failure to get the decree ratified would impose unacceptable costs on the president, for reasons outlined earlier in this paper.

Second, the *medida provisória* ensures the continuity of one Brazilian political tradition: The executive acts and the legislature reacts. During the authoritarian regime of the 1964–85 period, some 75 percent of all Brazilian laws resulted from executive initiatives – either decrees or proposals (see Table 7.5). After the

Table 7.5 *Output and origin of Brazilian legislation, 1964–92*

Presidents(s)	Number of new laws during presidential administration(s)	Percent of new laws that originated in executive branch[a]
Total for five military presidents, 1964–85	2,981	75
Sarney, 1985–90	705	64
Collor, 1990–92	464	76
Franco, 1992	148	83
Total for three democratic presidents, 1985–92	1,317	71
Total, 1964–92	4,298	74

[a]Includes laws that originated as presidential decrees.
Source: Câmara dos Deputados 1993.

introduction of the democratic Constitution of 1988, in the three-year 1990–92 period, the equivalent figure was 77.9 percent. This seems to belie the conventional wisdom about the role of the legislature in Brazilian politics – that is, that under military rule the National Congress was merely a rubber stamp but that since 1988 it has won back significant powers. Admittedly, these aggregate data conceal one important innovation since 1988: Congress can now amend *any* legislation, even presidential decrees. But this does not change the basic conclusion: that under democracy, the Brazilian National Congress has made virtually no progress at all in becoming an *initiator* of legislation. It remains a reactive and not a proactive legislature. An adequate explanation for this situation would require attention to such issues as the party system, the electoral laws, and the internal organization of Congress, all of which are beyond the scope of this chapter.[39] But I am convinced that one cause of congressional inefficiency is the assembly's continual saturation with presidential decrees. Decrees are not the *only* reason for this, but clearly they detract from the legislature's capacity to advance its own reform and revitalization. And perversely, legislative disorganization leads to a perceived need for more decrees, creating a vicious circle. These observations echo those made by Della Sala (1988) in his study of the Italian Parliament under Craxi. The elective affinity between inefficient legislatures and decree-dependent executives is a promising avenue for further research.

A third way in which the MP affects Brazilian politics is by changing the nature of the debate over public policy. Much like other cases discussed in this volume, in this decree-dependent environment public policies are debated *after* rather than *before* their enactment into law. Therefore, the assembly's reaction to the policy is determined not by an anterior analysis of its positive and negative points (as in legislative consideration of an ordinary bill), but by an appreciation of its real-world and real-time effects since its enactment by decree. The assembly's decision is made not on the basis of the wisdom of *enacting* the policy in the first place, but on the basis of the costs and benefits of *repealing* it now that it is already in force.

Perhaps the best example of this phenomenon in Brazil came in the wake of the Collor Plan in April 1990. Many legislators were outraged that Collor had seized control of practically every banking account in the country, and they opposed the policy in principle. But they also recognized that to revoke the MPs in question and "unfreeze" liquid assets would mean immediate capital flight and a return to hyperinflation – and very likely, it would lead to a collapse of the banking system. Even for many politicians who opposed this aspect of the *Plano Brasil Novo*, the costs of repealing the policy were higher than the cost of maintaining it. Not surprisingly, Congress acquiesced. The nature of the debate over public policy was altered; in essence there was little deliberation at all. Presidential decree power is destructive of debate, which is something that presidents may not want but which democracy normally requires.

Moreover, in the cases when a decree is rejected by Congress, the legislature is actually imposing "cleanup costs" on itself. The 1988 Constitution grants the National Congress the power to invalidate MPs *ex tunc*, and it commits the legislature to correct all of the legal, social, political, and economic ramifications of a rejected decree. As Rosenn (1990:785) correctly notes, this aspect of Article 62 is "a feature fraught with [the] potential for [the] creation of juridical chaos." It is also unreasonable to expect Congress to dedicate much energy to these cleanup costs, especially when new decrees are arriving at a pace of one every three or four days. It is possible that a desire to shirk these costs – and the immense political responsibility they carry with them – may be partially responsible for Congress' timidity in rejecting presidential decrees.

Toward a theoretical understanding of decree power. The editors of this volume correctly challenge the facile "usurpation interpretation" of presidential decree authority.[40] Carey and Shugart are explicitly skeptical of claims that decree authority *alone* is what gives Latin American legislatures their rubber-stamp reputations. In the literature on Latin American politics, there are few case studies in which the balance of power between presidents and assemblies is a dependent rather than an independent variable. Whether presidents actually usurp authority remains an *empirical* question.

This chapter has attempted to contribute to the theory-building process by looking equally inside the executive and legislative branches in Brazil. In it I explored the origins of decree power and demonstrated that this power resulted from an essentially carte-blanche delegation by Congress to the executive. I also showed that when given a blank check, Brazilian presidents promptly cashed it (and nearly broke the bank in the process). Executives took what was already a broad delegation and tried to expand it even further, arrogating to themselves the right to renew expired decrees (and in one case, a rejected decree). Whether this constitutes usurpation is a semantic question, one which arises out of the nebulous wording of Article 62 of the Constitution. This aggressive presidential behavior is probably better described as "abuse."

One theme of this volume concerns the extent to which legislatures abdicate law-making authority to executives. Did the Brazilian Congress abdicate its constitutional responsibilities? No and yes. No, because the 1988 framers seemed sincerely to believe that the *medida provisória* was a real improvement over the universally hated *decreto-lei*; and yes, because by their own admission they were proved wrong. Did Brazilian presidents wrest law-making authority from the hands of Congress? No: the National Constituent Assembly awarded this authority to presidents by legal means. Did presidents later use decree power to run roughshod over an elected assembly? Yes – but the legislature's inability to respond to executive abuses is due partially to its own internal problems and partially to external factors connected to the wider Brazilian institutional environment, including the party and electoral systems. None of these very important factors could be discussed in these pages.[41]

The case study presented in this chapter pointed to a tremendous imbalance in executive–legislative relations in Brazil, one that has proved troublesome for the consolidation of democracy. Whereas the greatest threat to parliament in Brazil once came from bellicose generals and their "exceptional acts," today it is presented by a democratically elected civilian president acting in the exercise of his constitutional authority. The source of much of this travail is presidential decree power as codified in Article 62 of the Brazilian Constitution. In 1988, by virtue of its own decision, the Brazilian Congress changed its master from the sword to the pen.

NOTES

1 The author would like to thank Jales Ramos Marques of PRODASEN for data collection, Valéria Power for transcribing interviews, and Nelson Jobim and his staff for providing copies of many important documents. Earlier versions of this paper were presented at various seminars in 1994, including those of the Latin American Studies Association, the Council for a Viable Constitutionalism, the Federal University of Pernambuco, the University of Brasília, and the University of Buenos Aires Law School. I am grateful to the participants in those seminars and to the editors of this volume for many insightful comments.

2 Collor's impeachment process had little or nothing to do with executive–legislative relations. In fact, as is demonstrated in this paper, when the Collorgate scandal broke in May 1992, executive–legislative relations were less contentious than they had been two years earlier. Collor essentially brought about his own downfall. His impeachment is best explained by a combination of three factors: the aggressive role of the media in exposing official corruption, the high degree of popular mobilization against Collor and in favor of congressional action to remove him (mobilization which Collor unwittingly invited and which may have

swung the military to favor his removal), and the incredible ineptness of corrupt presidential aides in covering their own tracks. See the analysis by K. Weyland (1993).

3 In a series of acts which foreshadowed the authoritarian centralism of the twentieth century, the first provisional government used decree-laws to intervene in the states (then known as provinces), dissolving assemblies and naming new governors. In fact modern Brazilian federalism, in its first incarnation as the United States of Brazil, was created in this way: by an unelected government using decree power.

4 Article 180 of the authoritarian Constitution of 1937 declared that until Congress met again, the president could use the decree-law to legislate on any and all matters in the jurisdiction of the Union. Congress was never called into session, nor were elections ever held under this constitution (Santos 1991:178).

5 With the resignation of President Jânio Quadros in August 1961 and the military's subsequent refusal to permit Vice-President João Goulart to assume the full powers of the presidency, a constitutional amendment was quickly passed which instituted a parliamentary system. Goulart won back his powers in a plebiscite in January 1963, and then another amendment was passed, which revoked the 1961 amendment and returned the Constitution to the status quo ante.

6 According to information provided by the *Subchefia para Assuntos Jurídicos* of the Presidency of the Republic (telephone communication, August 2, 1993), between 1964 and 1988 Congress rejected only 33 decree-laws. This represents only 1.3 percent of the 2,481 decree-laws issued during this period. Legislative rejection occurred only five times before 1983. In fact, not a single decree was rejected between 1968 and 1983, a period in which 1,662 consecutive presidential decrees became law.

7 If a law is struck down under the doctrine of *ex tunc* ("from then"), then its effects are retroactively voided. In contrast the principle of *ex nunc* ("from now") invalidation holds that the nullification of a law is henceforth (i.e., *not* retroactive) and that the past effects of the invalid law remain.

8 The data in Table 7.1 show that the Médici administration, considered the most repressive and authoritarian of the five military governments, issued a relatively modest 253 decree-laws in five years. The rate of publication of decrees increased under General Ernesto Geisel, the initiator of political liberalization in 1974, and it increased again under the six-year administration of General João Figueiredo, who continued in a democratizing direction and eventually handed over power to the civilian opposition in 1985. This seeming paradox – a positive association between political liberalization and the use of executive decrees – can be explained by the fact that the electoral strength of the pro-military party (first known as ARENA, later as Partido Democrático Social or PDS) began to diminish after 1974. With shrinking majorities in Congress, Geisel and especially Figueiredo resorted increasingly to authoritarian CDA to pursue their legislative agendas.

9 Sarney feared that a move to premier-presidentialism would reduce his powers and/or shorten his term in office, and he therefore used the considerable powers of his office to pressure the Assembly to maintain the ongoing presidential system. In this effort he was supported by the military ministers, who saw in Sarney a reliable civilian ally.

10 During the authoritarian regime, even members of the pro-government ARENA/ PDS party expressed opposition to the *decreto-lei*. When the institution was incorporated into the authoritarian Constitution of 1967, more than 100 ARENA legislators publicly declared their opposition (*Estado de São Paulo*, March 15, 1975, p. 4).

11 Sarney was a longtime supporter of the authoritarian regime of the 1964–1985 period. As late as June 1984, he was the national president of the pro-military PDS party. At the time of his last-minute break with the regime, he was selected as a vice-presidential running mate by opposition candidate Tancredo Neves (PMDB) in the indirect election of 1985. Tancredo's unexpected illness on the eve of his inauguration and his subsequent death in April 1985 catapulted Sarney into the presidency.

12 As noted in Table 7.1, MPs 1 through 9 were actually DLs 2,473 through 2,481, they were issued prior to the promulgation of the new constitution, and they were transformed into MPs following a special transitional protocol.

13 Throughout this paper I follow Brazilian conventions in counting the number of MPs. An MP that expires and is later reissued is assigned a new number and is legally considered a new decree. I attempted to correct for this practice of multiple counting but soon abandoned the idea when I found that renewed MPs are frequently combined with others or with new decree legislation. The reader should recall this when interpreting the quantitative and tabular data presented in this chapter.

14 Saulo Ramos' legal opinion is reprinted in *Gazeta Mercantil* (June 27, 1989), p. 33.

15 The joint committees, known formally as *Comissões Mistas* and informally as *Comissões de Admissibilidade*, are comprised of seven members from each house, who are selected from the various parties in accordance with the proportion of seats held by the party. The two most important positions on the joint committee are the presidency and the *relatoria* (which refers to the rapporteur, who proffers the principal analysis and ruling on the MP). These positions are routinely rotated among the parties represented in Congress. See Szklarowsky (1991).

16 The constitutional language concerning the *medida provisória* (Article 62) says nothing about the possibility of amendments to an MP. However, elsewhere in the Constitution (Article 59), the MP is expressly referred to as an element of the "legislative process." Congress interpreted this to mean that it was exclusively a congressional prerogative to decide on how the MPs would be considered in the legislature, and this is the constitutional basis for Resolution No. 1 of 1989. That Congress would claim the right to amend the MPs was perfectly predictable; recall that under the previous constitution, the legislature was prohibited from amending the *decreto-lei*.

17 The act of Congress which retroactively corrects the effects of a rejected MP is called a *decreto legislativo*.

18 This has actually happened: President Fernando Collor vetoed three conversion bills (data from PRODASEN).

19 The decline in public expectations about government performance was spectacular. José Sarney had decreed the 1986 Cruzado Plan when inflation had reached the "emergency" level of 14 percent monthly, but by March 1990 prices were rising that fast in a single weekend.

20 To show his commitment to prosecute tax evaders, Collor appointed Romeu
   Tuma, the longtime federal police chief who enjoyed a reputation for efficiency,
   as head of the Brazilian equivalent of the IRS. Several MPs were clearly intended
   to make it easier for Tuma to proceed with a crackdown.

21 Like MPs 153 and 156, this particular decree was another attack on the separation
   of powers, and therefore it was unconstitutional. However, the Chamber agreed
   to vote on it, therefore implicitly endorsing its constitutionality. According to
   Saulo Ramos (former Justice Minister under Sarney), if the Joint Committee on
   admissibility of decrees had ruled MP 185 unconstitutional and returned it to
   Collor, the president would not have dared to reissue it (*Jornal do Brasil*, June 5,
   1990).

22 A supplementary law (*lei complementar*) is the Brazilian term for implementing
   legislation – that is, a law that enables or activates a provision of the Constitution.
   Few articles in the 1988 Constitution were self-executing; rather, many stipulated
   that "Congress will regulate this provision with a supplementary law," etc. The
   prevalence of non–self-executing provisions in the Constitution can be attributed
   in part to the political right, which saw this maneuver as a way to delay or enfeeble
   the *conquistas* won by progressive forces in the ANC of the 1987–88 period. Even
   by 1996, many constitutional articles had yet to be enabled.

23 According to Article 67 of the Constitution, if a piece of legislation is rejected
   by Congress, its subject matter cannot be brought up again in the same legislative
   session unless the absolute majority of one house requests this reintroduction in
   a special resolution.

24 I benefited from a discussion with Kurt Weyland on this issue.

25 Recognizing Cardoso's tendency to fine-tune the fine print in his iterated decrees,
   Senator Josaphat Marinho (PFL-Bahia) in mid-1996 introduced a bill along the
   lines of the Jobim proposal which was killed in 1991. Under Marinho's plan,
   presidents would have sixty rather than thirty days to get their decrees approved
   in Congress, but renewals would be prohibited. If Congress did not consider the
   MP within sixty days, the decree would automatically be transformed into an
   ordinary bill introduced by the president (Jânio de Freitas in the *Folha de São
   Paulo*, June 13, 1996, p. 5).

26 Collor's comments are strikingly similar to those of Argentine Economy Minister
   Domingo Cavallo, as cited in Delia Ferreira Rubio and Matteo Goretti's contribution to this volume.

27 Recent research by Figueiredo and Limongi (1995, 1996) questions this portrayal
   of executive–legislative relations, arguing instead that Brazilian presidents consistently get what they want in Congress. They claim that "parties matter, and
   presidents negotiate with parties and not with [individual] legislators and/or
   supraparty groups" (1996:29); that "behavior on the legislative floor (*plenário*) is
   predictable and consistent" (1995:516); and that "minority presidents possess the
   means to obtain legislative support through negotiations with the parties" (1996:
   33). These conclusions are derived from a roll-call methodology that examines
   the final disposition of legislation on the floor of Congress and thus does not
   capture the notorious foot-dragging, blackmail, and brinksmanship (on the part
   of both parties and individuals) that is characteristic of Brazilian legislative politics. A decree-driven agenda suggests presidential awareness of these problems.
   Heavy reliance on CDA may be interpreted either as an indicator that presidents

are uncertain of the results they will obtain if they pursue legislative goals through more routine channels, or as an attempt to improve their bargaining position in an environment of unpredictability. For a fuller review see my essay in Kingstone and Power (forthcoming).

28 "What the Great Law [the Constitution] does not restrict, a lesser law [ordinary legislation] may not restrict."

29 Jobim did not seek reelection in 1994, and he was subsequently named Minister of Justice in the first cabinet of President Fernando Henrique Cardoso in January 1995.

30 Article 64 of the Constitution stipulates that the president may attach a *pedido de urgência* to any bill. If at the end of forty-five days the Congress has not yet voted on it, the bill goes automatically to the top of the legislative agenda.

31 The survey was a mail questionnaire distributed to all 584 members of the Brazilian Congress. Total (*N*) responding was 185, or 32 percent of the membership. The sample was highly representative of Congress in terms of legislators' party identifications and regional origins. The last responses were received in September 1993.

32 The possible responses in Portuguese were: *concorda, plenamente; concorda, em termos; discorda, em termos; discorda, plenamente.*

33 These cross-tabulations were statistically significant at the .05 level.

34 In a classic parliamentary system, in the case of most bills submitted by the government, the assembly's majority (barring extraordinary circumstances) will eventually ratify some version of the legislation. In this context the purpose of decree power is merely to ensure that the bill has the force of law on Day 1 rather than on Day 100. According to the Italian Constitution, such authority should only be used in cases of "necessity and urgency" (see Appendix).

35 The fact that Collor resigned during impeachment proceedings does not weaken my argument here, nor should it be interpreted as a sign of congressional power vis-à-vis the presidency in Brazil. See note 2 earlier.

36 See Rosenn (1990) for an appropriately wide-eyed look at the ANC and the constitution it produced.

37 Virtually all economic indicators in Brazil are generated by agencies under the control of the executive branch, and the few that are not are produced by the private sector or labor groups. In Brazil there is no analog to the Congressional Budget Office in the United States. Independent economic analyses practically never emerge from Congress, except when they are provided by the economists-turned-politicians who have been elected to parliament (Roberto Campos, Delfim Netto, Francisco Dornelles, José Serra, Aloísio Mercadante, Eduardo Suplicy, etc.). To my knowledge, not a single prominent economist in Brazil has ever served on the staff of the legislative branch, whereas virtually all have worked in the executive branch. Of course, this is largely true throughout Latin America as a whole.

38 Constitutions written in crisis environments are likely to enshrine extraordinary executive powers, which may then prove difficult to expunge from the charter after the original crisis has passed. In this volume some examples of "crisis constitutions" promulgated in extraordinary political moments are those of France in 1958 (Chapter 8), Peru in 1993 (Chapter 4), and especially Russia in 1993 (Chapter 3).

39 See Baaklini (1992) for attention to some of these variables, especially legislative
    organization (information systems, staffing, leadership, and committees).
40 Along these lines, the editors argued in *Presidents and Assemblies* that "Congress
    cannot abdicate what it does not have and the executive cannot usurp what it
    legally has" (Shugart and Carey 1992: 133).
41 For analysis of the general weakness of political institutions in Brazil, see Ames
    (1995). Figueiredo and Limongi (1994), Mainwaring (1991, 1993), Novaes
    (1994), Power (1991), and Souza (1989).

PART III

ABSENCE OF CONFLICT OVER DECREE

8

EXECUTIVE DECREE
AUTHORITY IN FRANCE

John D. Huber

INTRODUCTION[1]

Influenced by the frequent inability of the government to act decisively during the Fourth Republic, Charles de Gaulle and Michel Debré, in crafting the institutional arrangements of the Fifth Republic, sought to create a strong executive, one that could bring efficiency and responsiveness to political decision making in France. To this end, the French Constitution of 1958 creates two executives, a president and a prime minister. For both of these executives, decree authority is an important ingredient in de Gaulle's and Debré's recipe for executive control.

The French president is directly elected by the voters, which gives substantial political authority to the office. In addition the president has the power to dissolve the National Assembly (although this power can be exercised only once a year). Aside from dissolution, however, the president has few institutional means for influencing legislative outcomes: The president has no formal opportunity to propose policies, alter the agenda, or amend policies in Parliament.[2] And in contrast to the United States, the French president cannot veto bills that have been adopted by the legislature.

Article 16 of the Constitution, however, gives the president the right to declare a state of emergency. Upon making such a declaration, the president obtains virtually unlimited power to take measures by decree in response to the emergency. In principle this constitutional decree authority represents one of the most important weapons that the president can use to influence policy outcomes in France.

The prime minister, as leader of the government, has significantly more institutional prerogatives than the president for controlling policy making in France. The government sets the legislative agenda in the National Assembly, can offer amendments on the floor of the legislature, and can effectively eliminate the French Senate from policy-making influence. In addition the Constitution grants the prime minister four different flavors of decree authority, The first two – rule making on regulatory matters and delegated legislative authority – fit squarely into the typology of decree authority defined in Chapter 1 of this volume. The second two forms of decree authority – the confidence vote procedure and the package vote – illustrate the connection between decree and agenda-setting authority. Through the confidence vote procedure, the prime minister can set policy in lieu of parliamentary actions, but neither procedure permits the executive to impose a new policy automatically as the result of a government decision. Each of these procedures permits the prime minister to make a "take-it-or leave-it" policy proposal to the legislature, forcing the legislature (in one fashion or another) to vote yes or no. Given the important proposal power these procedures give the French government, they are also included in the analysis.

This chapter examines the role of the five forms of decree authority in France through the lens of the argument in Chapter 1. The analysis has two objectives. One is to describe the precise institutional structure of the various forms of executive decree authority, and to use these descriptions to assess the comprehensiveness of the typology outlined in Chapter 1. The other objective is to test hypotheses about the circumstances under which the various types of decree authority should be used. The analysis supports one of Chapter 1's central arguments, which is that decree authority does not imply abdication of policy-making power by the legislature to the executive.

ARTICLE 16: THE EMERGENCY DECREE AUTHORITY OF THE PRESIDENT

I will examine the five forms of decree authority in turn, beginning with the only *presidential* decree authority in France: Article 16 of the Constitution. Emergency decrees have not played a prominent role in the politics of the Fifth Republic, insofar as only one emergency has been declared since 1958. This one instance occurred in 1961, when four senior military officials engineered a revolt by portions of the army in Algeria – the so-called revolt of the generals. President Charles de Gaulle responded quickly, invoking Article 16 on April 23.

The actual *putsch* lasted only four days, but de Gaulle's state of emergency lasted much longer, concluding on September 29, 1961.[3] Presumably, the emergency was maintained for so long because de Gaulle wanted to crush the OAS (*Organisation de l'Armée Secrète*), an underground army that formed following the military revolt and that fomented violence in Algeria and France in an effort to overthrow the Fifth Republic. During the emergency de Gaulle demonstrated the power of Article 16 by issuing sixteen substantive decrees, including decrees that enlarged police powers, enlarged the powers of the courts, banned certain publications, dismissed military and civil service personnel for encouraging subversion against the state (and eliminated their pensions), established two special military courts to try crimes against the state, revoked the permanent tenure of judges in Algeria, and circumvented the normal rules for promotion of personnel in the army

The procedural structure of Article 16. The conditions under which French presidents can invoke a state of emergency (*les conditions de fond*) are narrowly defined in the Constitution. Article 16 states that the president can declare an emergency only when there is a "grave and immediate threat" to any *one* of the following:

- the institutions of the Republic;
- the independence of the nation;
- the integrity of the nation's territory, or
- the fulfillment of France's international agreements.

According to this article, before a president can invoke emergency decree authority, it must also be the case that "the regular functioning of the constitutional public authority be interrupted." And if an emergency is declared, Article 16 states that the measures taken by the president "must be inspired by the purpose of securing for the constitutional public authorities, in the shortest time, the means of carrying out their mission."

In order for the president to declare an emergency, several procedural hurdles must be climbed (*les conditions de forme*). The president, for example, is required to meet with the prime minister, the President of the National Assembly, and the President of the Senate prior to declaring an emergency. On April 23, 1961, de Gaulle met with each one of these individuals at the Elysée Palace, and all three individuals agreed with de Gaulle that the conditions warranted the declaration of an Article 16 emergency (Debbasch, Bourdon, Pontier, and Ricci 1988: 316). The president must also consult the Constitutional Council, a body that adjudicates conflicts concerning the authority of different constitutional entities.[4] According to a law passed in 1958, the president must seek the opinion of the Constitutional Council in writing, must express his or her motivations, and must publish the written request in the *Journal Officiel*. The Constitutional Council's opinion is then made public. In 1961 the Constitutional Council, in its opinion to de Gaulle, acknowledged that the generals in Algeria were in "open rebellion against the constitution" and that their actions posed "a grave and immediate threat to the institutions of the Republic."[5] Thus, there was no question of usurped presidential authority in de Gaulle's response to the Algerian crisis.

In addition to requiring consultation with other political entities, the Constitution requires the president to inform the nation of a decision to declare an emergency under Article 16. The president can do so in any manner he or she wishes. In 1961 de Gaulle delivered an address that was carried on television and radio on April 23. The text of this address was then published in the *Journal Officiel* on April 24.

During an emergency period the Constitution creates two (related) political checks on the president. First, Parliament meets "by right," ensuring that France's elected deputies have an opportunity to educate the French people about the president's emergency decrees. Second, during an emergency the president cannot dissolve the National Assembly. Thus, in declaring an emergency, the president relinquishes a most powerful institutional weapon.

The Constitution, along with the precedent of the 1961 events, establishes a limited role for Parliament during an emergency. On April 25, 1961, de Gaulle sent a letter to the National Assembly outlining his view of Parliament's prerogatives during the Algerian crisis. On matters unrelated to the problem in Algeria, de Gaulle stated that the legislative powers of Parliament, as well as the relationship between the National Assembly and the government, would be unaffected. On matters related to the crisis, however, Parliament was to defer completely to the president (and, in fact, would have to support him in his efforts) (see Debbasch et al. 1988: 317).

De Gaulle's view of parliament's role only applied, however, if the Parliament was meeting in a regularly scheduled session. When Parliament's spring session ended in July of 1961, Parliament could still meet by right (as guaranteed under Article 16) but only in a special session convoked because an emergency was in effect. Conflict about Parliament's role during a declared emergency came to a head in August, when several deputies pressed to consider a law concerning agricultural price supports. At that time the Conference of Presidents of the Senate and the National Assembly scheduled a special meeting of the chambers, one that was to take place on September 5 in the Senate and on September 12 in the National Assembly.

On August 31, de Gaulle wrote a letter to the prime minister (which was communicated to the presidents of the assemblies) stating that it was contrary to the Constitution for members of Parliament to consider ordinary legislation during a special session of Parliament if that special session existed only because of an Article 16 emergency. During such special (rather than ordinary) sessions, de Gaulle argued, the National Assembly met by right only to handle any exceptional circumstances occasioned by the crisis.

It turns out that de Gaulle's attitude toward Parliament's prerogatives during the special session never became directly relevant to the agricultural issue, because on September 4 the government declared the private members' bills "irreceivable" (because they violated Article 40 of the Constitution, a provision requiring all private member bills and amendments to be revenue neutral). After the government declared the agricultural prices' support legislation irreceivable, the Socialist group in the National Assembly submitted a motion of censure, raising a constitutional question of a different sort – namely, can a majority in the National Assembly censure the government during a crisis under Article 16?

Since the Rules of Procedure for the National Assembly were silent on this issue and since the Constitutional Council determined that it did not have jurisdiction to settle the question (*Journal Officiel*, September 19, 1961), the President of the National Assembly, Jacques Chaban-Delmas, drew on de Gaulle's August 31 letter and on Article 49 of the Constitution to make the ultimate decision. Article 49 (discussed shortly) permits the government to "engage its responsibility" on a specific piece of legislation, forcing a majority in the National Assembly either to censure the government or to accept the government's policy. Invoking de Gaulle's argument that Parliament could not legislate during a special session of Parliament under Article 16, Chaban-Delmas argued in a letter on September 19 that the government could not engage its responsibility on a bill during such times. Chaban-Delmas therefore reasoned that in order to maintain the balance between the government and the National Assembly envisioned by the Constitution, Parliament could not submit or vote a motion of censure during a special session that existed only because of an Article 16 emergency. During an ordinary legislative session, however, the National Assembly could submit and vote on a motion of censure when an Article 16 emergency was in effect.

In sum the events in 1961 established two important constraints on Parliament. On the one hand, Parliament could not adopt legislation on topics related to the events that provoked the declaration of an emergency. On the other, outside normally scheduled legislative sessions, Parliament could not undertake normal legislative activities and could not censure the government.

The use of emergency decree authority. Although there exist several procedural prerequisites for declaring an emergency, in actual fact there is little to constrain French presidents from invoking presidential decree authority. The Constitution, for example, narrowly defines the circumstances that could lead to emergencies. But the Constitution also gives the president the sole power to determine the circumstances under which an emergency actually exists – all the opinions that are obtained during the consultation process, even those of the Constitutional Council, can be ignored. If the president, for example, interprets the absence of a supportive majority in Parliament as a threat to the nation, nothing in the Constitution prevents the declaration of emergency decree authority. In fact there was speculation preceding the legislative elections in 1967 that if the elections did not return a majority for de Gaulle, then he would use Article 16 to govern.[6]

The Constitution also guarantees that the Parliament has the right to meet during an emergency. But the Parliament cannot legislate on matters that are within the scope of the emergency, a condition which is defined by the president. Thus, the Parliament's right to meet does little to constrain the scope of decisions that a president can take during a declared emergency.

So if Article 16 is such a powerful weapon, why is it almost never used? The answer lies in the analysis of other constitutional arrangements. Since the president and the deputies in the National Assembly are directly elected by the voters, each can legitimately claim popular authority. If the majority in the National Assembly and the president agree on policy goals, there will be no policy conflict and the president will not be tempted to declare an emergency for the purpose of controlling policy outcomes. But if the parliamentary majority and the president disagree, then it may be tempting for the president to declare an emergency to maintain policy control.

In fact, if the president and the majority disagree, the president has three options: He or she can

1. dissolve the National Assembly.
2. let the prime minister and the cabinet govern.
3. declare an emergency.

Dissolution is desirable if the president believes the voters will return a majority that supports the president. President de Gaulle, for example, called for new elections during the student riots in 1968, when the conservative parties held a slim one-seat majority in Parliament. The ensuing election returned a huge Gaullist majority. Similarly, Socialist President François Mitterrand dissolved the National Assembly and called for new elections following both of his presidential election victories (in 1981 and 1988), each of which occurred while there was a conservative majority in Parliament. The legislative election in 1981 resulted in a large Socialist majority, whereas the election in 1988 resulted in a Socialist plurality and the formation of a Socialist minority government.

At times it is clear that dissolution will not advance the president's policy goals. This may occur, for example, when legislative elections during the middle of a president's term return a majority opposing the president. In such situations, since the president has virtually no institutional means for influencing policy, he or she must either leave political responsibility with the government and National Assembly or invoke emergency decree authority to maintain policy control.

Since the beginning of the Fifth Republic, it has been clear that the president's only real alternative in such situations is to leave policy-making responsibility with the government and the National Assembly. One reason is political. If the voters express a preference for parties that oppose the president, then the president's political future – as well as that of his or her party – would be seriously jeopardized if the president usurped emergency decree authority to attack the policies of the legislative majority.

Another reason is institutional. The framers of the Constitution included a provision aimed at precluding usurpation of presidential emergency power: impeachment by members of the National Assembly and Senate. Article 67 of the Constitution creates a High Court of Justice, which is composed of members "elected in equal numbers and from their own membership by the National Assembly and the Senate after each general election or partial election of those assemblies." Article 68 states that if an absolute majority of the National Assembly and Senate so vote, a motion to impeach the president is heard by this court. The working group that drafted the Fifth Republic Constitution made it clear that impeachment could be used to end usurped emergency decree authority. It wrote,

It would be erroneous to attribute fundamental importance to Article 16 of the Constitution. Rather, this Article will play a role only in situations where it would be impossible to question the intentions of the President. If the President's intentions are questionable, then Parliament could, given its right to meet, either use its power to impeach the President for treason in the High Court of Justice, or force the President to resign.[7]

There have been two situations in which elections have failed to resolve conflict between the president and the National Assembly. On both occasions, called *cohabitation*, legislative elections returned conservative majorities while the president – in both instances, François Mitterrand – was a Socialist. Not surprisingly, on both occasions, the possibility of declaring an emergency was never considered a serious option. Instead, President Mitterrand allowed the conservative government to govern.[8]

Thus, one lesson from cohabitation is that presidential decree authority in France is limited to genuine emergencies – such as internal revolts in the army or invasions from Germany. More generally, the French case illustrates that the role of emergency decree authority in democratic systems depends fundamentally on the nature of seemingly unrelated institutional arrangements. In France the president's right of dissolution is a much more important procedure for controlling parliamentary activities than is emergency decree authority. And the possibility of impeachment by members of the legislature sharply constrains the possibility that French presidents will abuse their right to declare an emergency.

REGULATORY RULE MAKING: PASSIVE DECREE AUTHORITY IN FRANCE

Given the limited importance of presidential emergency decrees, a clear understanding of decree authority in France must focus on the four different types of decrees the government can issue. First, consider a provision that was widely held to be one of the most important innovations in the Constitution of the Fifth Republic. This innovation is Article 34, which explicitly defines issues falling within the "domain of law." Article 34 contains two lists. The first list defines those issues on which the law must fix the "specific rules." Examples from this list include civil rights, nationality, marriage, inheritance, crimes and misdemeanors, criminal penalties, tax collection, electoral systems, the nationalization of industries, the rights of military personnel, and the issuance of money. The second list defines issues on which the law fixes the "general principles." Examples include education, property rights, employment, unions, and social security.

The framers of the Fifth Republic Constitution carefully delineated the domain of law in Article 34 so that it would be possible to establish broader authority for the government, allowing it more leeway to issue regulatory measures by decree than had been possible in the Fourth Republic. The government's rule-making authority emerges from Articles 34, 37, and 41. Article 37 states that everything which is not within the "domain of law" is considered to be in the "domain of regulation." Article 41 guarantees that only the government can take actions on matters falling within the domain of regulation. Thus, the Constitution, in these three articles, attempts to increase the powers of the government at the expense of Parliament by permitting the government to take measures in the regulatory domain by decree.

Government decree authority in the regulatory domain was not a new innovation when the Fifth Republic was drafted in 1958. A law voted by Parliament on August 17, 1948, permitted the French government in the Fourth Republic to take measures by decree in the regulatory domain. But the legal basis for decree authority in the Fifth Republic is significantly different from the legal basis for decree authority during the Fourth Republic. First, in the Fifth Republic the government's decree authority is enshrined in the Constitution, and hence, it cannot be eliminated by elected deputies through the normal legislative process. Second, during the Fourth Republic the organic law creating decree authority carefully defined the specific areas falling within the regulatory domain, and it left all residual matters in the legal domain. In the Fifth Republic the Constitution specifies the legal domain and leaves all residual matters in the regulatory domain. Thus, at the outset of the Fifth Republic, the scope of government decree authority was believed to be much larger than the scope of government decree authority in the Fourth Republic.

The scope of rule-making authority. The government makes regulatory decrees on an almost daily basis, making it impossible to examine whether utilization of this decree authority is consistent with hypotheses in Chapter 1 of this volume. French legal scholars widely argue, however, that the government's authority to take measures by decree in the regulatory domain has been much more limited than was anticipated by the framers of the Constitution. In fact, Jean-Louis Pezant, upon reviewing French jurisprudence on the issue, goes so far as to argue that an examination of the government's decree power in the regulatory domain reveals perhaps the greatest gap between the intentions of the framers and the actual functioning of the Fifth Republic's institutions (Avril 1981; see also Debbasch et al. 1988; 431–41; Maus 1988a;326–7; Pezant 1984).

One reason the scope of the government's regulatory decree authority during the Fifth Republic has been very limited is that the two lists in Article 34 give enormous scope to the domain of law. It is in fact quite difficult to name significant issues on which parliaments normally legislate and which are omitted from these lists. But a more important reason for the limited importance of decree authority focuses on the role of the Constitutional Council.

The last sentence of Article 34 leaves open the door for the courts to shape the actual scope of the government's rule-making authority. The sentence reads, *"The provisions of the present article may be developed in detail and amplified by an organic law"* (emphasis added). Given this rather vague phrase, can Parliament, through an organic law,[9] add new areas to the domain of law? Is the domain of law in fact defined by organic laws adopted by Parliament rather than by the Constitution itself? Can Parliament use organic laws only to "amplify" those subjects that are already found on the two lists in Article 34? The answers to these questions can be provided only by the Constitutional Council, the French court with the constitutional authority to determine whether specific matters fall within the domain of law or the domain of regulation.

The role of the Constitutional Council has been absolutely crucial in defining the actual scope of the government's decree authority in the regulatory domain, and its rulings provide the most important reason that this decree authority has been much less significant than originally envisioned by the framers.[10] The Constitutional Council has established, for example, that Article 34 does not circumscribe the domain of law. Instead, drawing on the last sentence of Article 34, as well as on other articles in the Constitution (especially the Preamble and Arts. 72–74), the Constitutional Council has ruled that the domain of law can be established only by the adoption of the laws themselves. In ruling that only Parliament can determine the scope of the domain of law, the court has given Parliament the right to circumscribe the regulatory decree authority of the government and to tread in areas that traditionally might be viewed as regulatory matters.[11]

Viewed through the lens of the arguments in Chapter 1 of this volume, the experience with rule making in the Fifth Republic is interesting in several respects. On the one hand, the role of the Constitutional Council in limiting the scope of the government's rule-making authority – and in ensuring parliamentary sovereignty – underscores Carey and Shugart's arguments about the important role that judiciaries can play in determining the actual impact of executive decree authority on policy outcomes. On the other hand, the French case refines the arguments in Chapter 1 in two respects. First, the French case illustrates that the judiciary plays an important role beyond that of resolving specific disputes between the legislature and the executive. In fact, courts play a major, ongoing role in defining the boundaries that constrain the executive's decree authority in the regulatory domain.

Second, the French case brings into sharp relief the distinction between "defined" and "residual" rule-making authority. In the Fifth Republic the courts have ensured that Parliament can pass laws that limit the government's rule-making authority. But because the domain of regulation is the "residual" category in France, Parliament must act if it wishes to constrain the government. This is quite a different situation from that which exists when parliamentary acts positively define the domain of regulation, leaving the domain of law as the residual category. When the domain of regulation is defined, it will clearly be easier for members of Parliament to circumscribe executive rule-making activities. The French case therefore suggests that arguments about the impact of executive rule-making autonomy on policy outcomes must be fortified by precise explanations of how the law establishes – and the judiciary interprets – the regulatory domain.

ARTICLE 38: DELEGATED LEGISLATIVE AUTHORITY

The previous section explored the constitutional provisions by which the French Parliament delegates *regulatory*, or rule-making, decree authority to the government. This section describes the process by which Parliament delegates *legislative* authority to the government under Article 38.

The delegation process begins when the government submits a bill to Parliament ("*projet de loi d'habilitation*") specifying the scope and duration of the government's decree authority. Because this enabling law must go through the normal legislative process, members of Parliament, through amendments, can define the precise scope of the government's legislative authority under Article 38. In practice it is often the case that enabling laws specify rather narrowly the types of legislative decrees that the government can issue. In 1986, for example, the newly-elected conservative majority in Parliament adopted a bill delegating to the government the authority to privatize French industries. The bill specifically named the sixty-five industries that could be privatized (manufacturing or service industries that compete with private companies in free markets), but it left to the government the details of how quickly the privatizations should be accomplished, of how the prices of the privatized industries would be protected, and of how the participation of foreigners would be regulated.

Sometimes, however, the scope of delegated legislation is rather general and vague. The first time the procedure was used, for example, was in February 1960, following the "revolt of the barricades" in Algeria – a revolt by French settlers against de Gaulle's Algeria policy. Parliament adopted a bill giving the government the power to take measures "necessary to ensure order," and the limits placed on the government were political rather than policy-specific. The bill stated, for example, that (a) only the present government could make decrees, (b) the duration of decree authority would be one year, and (c) the decree authority would end if the National Assembly was dissolved (see Pierce 1968: 81–3).

The duration of the government's decree authority, something which is specified in the enabling law, varies a great deal. The average number of days for decree authority in enabling laws is 402 (with a standard deviation of 371 days). The median number of days is 290.5. The minimum number of days ever granted to the government was 80 (on a law in 1976 that delegated to the government the authority to redefine the tax code), and the maximum number of days given to the government to take measures by decree was 1,275 (on a law in 1966 that delegated to the government the authority to take measures related to changes in the Common Market).

After Parliament adopts bills, the cabinet (Council of Ministers) can begin the process of adopting decrees. Before any decree can be adopted, however, the Council of State must give its opinion on its constitutionality. The Council of State, the members of which are appointed by the cabinet, is both a legal adviser to the government and the highest administrative court (which means that the

Council of State adjudicates cases that contest the legality of actions taken by the state administration). Thus, although the government is not obliged to follow the Council of State's opinion (and sometimes does not), it risks subsequent nullification of its laws if it ignores this opinion.

Once the cabinet adopts a decree, it must receive the signature of the president. Whereas the Constitution obliges the president to sign bills adopted by the normal legislative process, it permits him to refuse to sign ordinances adopted by the cabinet under Article 38. This is precisely what occurred during the 1986–88 period of cohabitation, when Parliament was controlled by a conservative majority and the presidency was held by the Socialist François Mitterrand. The conservative majority adopted three laws delegating legislative authority to Gaullist Prime Minister Jacques Chirac's cabinet. The bills related to the privatization of French industry, changes in the French electoral law, and changes in laws that established the length of the work week. After Chirac's cabinet adopted a series of measures under this delegated authority, Mitterrand refused to add his signature, forcing Chirac to return to Parliament to adopt the measures through the normal legislative process (see Duverger 1987; Pierce 1991; Troper 1987). Parliament, then, cannot effectively delegate legislative authority to the cabinet without the consent of the president.

After the president signs a decree, it becomes effective immediately. The cabinet, however, must return it to Parliament for ratification before the expiration of the decree authority. If the cabinet fails to seek timely ratification of its decrees, the decrees become void. Similarly, of course, if Parliament refuses to ratify the decrees, they also become void. Parliament, then, not only narrowly defines the scope and duration of decree authority, it also determines which decrees ultimately become law.

The utilization of delegated legislative authority. Figure 8.1 provides annual data on the utilization of Article 38 from 1959–92. During that time laws delegating legislative authority to the government were adopted twenty-six times, or less than once a year; and the propensity to delegate has been sporadic over time, with basically the same level of delegations occurring in the early 1960s and in the more recent period. The topic of legislation for these twenty-six bills is given in Table 8.1. The most frequent topic is France's overseas territories, a topic that is neither unusually complicated nor of particular importance to most of the deputies in the National Assembly. One of these bills concerns Algeria; the rest deal with governing processes in places such as Mayotte, New Hebrides, New Caledonia, French West Africa, and St. Pierre and Miquelon. The second most frequent topic is various economic and social issues. This category includes delegation on agricultural issues, privatization of industry, the protection of workers' salaries, and the maintenance of social order, to take several examples.

Why does Parliament delegate legislative authority? I examine three hypotheses. The first hypothesis, H4 in Chapter 1 of this volume, is that as the level of urgency increases, delegated decree authority should also increase. To test this

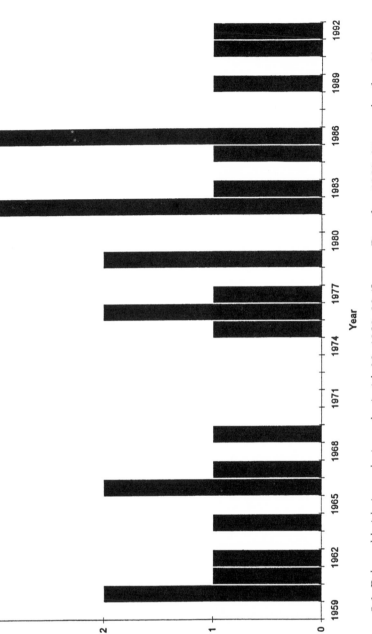

Figure 8.1 Delegated legislative authority under Article 38, 1959–92 (Source: Data from 1959–87 are taken from Maus (1988b); data from 1988–92 were provided by the staff of the National Assembly)

Table 8.1 *Types of legislation on which Parliament delegates to the government under Article 38*

	Topic of Legislation				
	Economic and Social Measures	Common Market	Electoral Law	Overseas territories	Total
Number of bills delegating authority under Article 38	9	3	1	13	26

Source: Data from 1959–87 are taken from Maus (1988b). Data from 1988–92 were collected by the author from the National Assembly.

hypothesis, I examine the timing in the legislative session with the expectation that when time on the legislative calendar is most precious – near the end of the legislative term – delegation should be most likely to occur. The data support this expectation. Of the twenty-six bills that delegated legislative authority under Article 38 from the 1959–92 period, twenty-five were adopted when time on the legislative agenda was extremely precious, either in the last week of a legislative session or during a special session of Parliament. Thus, delegation is most likely when time constraints are most pressing. It is important to keep in mind, however, that delegation under time constraints is not abdication, because members of Parliament define the scope and duration of delegated authority, and they can veto any decrees adopted by the government under this authority. It is also important to keep in mind that the number of times that delegation is used to address time constraints is quite small and often occurs on rather unimportant legislation.

The second hypothesis, related to H5 in Chapter 1 of this volume, concerns the level of majority support in the legislature. In a parliamentary system the majority status of the government could influence delegation in two respects. First, the size of the majority may be important. In periods where majorities are very slim, a small number of defections can torpedo legislative efforts, making it more difficult for the majority to legislate by the normal process. Small majorities therefore might lead to increased delegation if members of the government parties fear an inability to push legislation through on the floor. Second, the status of the government might influence delegation decisions. During minority government, the government party (or parties) in Parliament must receive the votes of opposition deputies in order to delegate legislative authority. Because parties in opposition may fear agency loss from delegating to ministers from another party, they may be unwilling to support delegation bills. Minority governments should therefore use delegation less frequently than majority governments. During majority government, on the other hand, no parties in the government's majority need fear agency loss from delegation (because presumably such losses are minimized through the process of government investiture). There might nevertheless be differences in the propensity to delegate during single-party majority governments and during coalition majority governments. These differences are due not to agency problems; rather, they are due to bargaining problems. If a single party has a majority of seats, bargaining problems will be minimized. During coalition government, however, bargaining will be more complicated, because more than one party must agree before any policy change can occur, and different parties generally care about different dimensions of particular policy issues. Given the problems inherent in choosing policies under open amendment processes with heterogeneous preferences, it might be beneficial for parties to delegate legislative authority rather than to enter into open conflict on the floor of Parliament (see Huber 1992). Thus, delegation should be less likely to occur during single-party majority government than during coalition majority government.

Table 8.2 presents some crude tests of these expectations. Before we consider the results, it is important to acknowledge that France has only had slim majorities for three years since 1959, and, strictly speaking, France has only had two years with single-party majority governments. It is therefore unwise to make strong assertions based on these data. It is also important to note that from 1968 to 1973, the Gaullists controlled a majority of seats (although they formed a surplus coalition with other parties on the right), and that from 1981 to 1986, the Socialists controlled a majority of seats (although they formed a coalition with the Communists for three of these years). During the periods of surplus majority governments, the parties enjoying solid majorities could have voted to delegate under Article 38 without worrying about their coalition partners. It might therefore be appropriate to classify these surplus governments as single-party majorities. Of course, if the single-party majorities ran roughshod over their coalition partners, these partners could have responded by leaving the coalition (as the Communists did in 1984), which for electoral reasons may be bad for the majority party.[12] Thus, it might be best to classify these surplus governments as coalitions. Rather than trying to sort out whether surplus majority governments should be classified as coalitions or single-party majorities, I report the data both ways.

As expected, the data show that during periods of majority government, delegation is most likely to occur when the majority is very small. Given the small number of cases with slim majorities, however, the relationship between the size of the majority and the use of the two procedures is not statistically significant. We also find that majority coalitions delegate more often than other types of governments, but again, these relationships are not statistically significant. Surprisingly, minority governments tend to delegate slightly more often than single-party majorities. It may be worth noting, however, that the three bills delegating legislative authority to the government during the five years of minority govern-

Table 8.2 *The relationship between decree authority and government composition, 1959–92*

	Size of majority (excluding minority governments)		Government status		
	1–2 deputies	At least 20 deputies	Minority	Majority coalition	Single-party majority
Delegations under Article 38				.8	.5
per year	1.3	.7	.6	.9ᵃ	.6
Package votes	17.3	5.6	16.4	7.2	1.0
per year				*9.4*	*1.9*
Confidence vote procedures	3.7	1.0	7.8	1.2	3.0
per year				*1.4*	*1.1*
Number of years	3	26	5	27	2
				(19)	*(10)*

ᵃFrom 1968–73 and 1981–84, a single party controlled a majority of seats, but a surplus coalition government was in office. In columns four and five, the first number categorizes these surplus governments as majority coalitions. The italicized number categorizes these governments as single-party majority governments.
Source: Data from 1959–88 are taken from Maus (1988b). Data from 1989–92 were collected by the author from the National Assembly.

ment all concerned the organization of the territory of Mayotte, a rather unimportant issue to most deputies.

In sum the decision to delegate occurs less than once a year, and generally – but not always – on issues that are not of widespread concern (such as the management of France's overseas territories). Delegation under Article 38 seems to be a procedure used to manage time (because delegation laws are most likely to be voted on at the end of special sessions or during ordinary sessions). Delegation does not seem related to the composition of the government or the size of the majority.

CONSTITUTIONAL DECREE AUTHORITY: THE PACKAGE VOTE AND THE CONFIDENCE VOTE PROCEDURES

Two procedures that permit members of the government to make "take-it-or-leave-it" policy proposals in Parliament comprise the last two forms of decree authority in the Constitution of the Fifth Republic. The package vote (Article 44.3) and the confidence vote procedure (Article 49.3) both permit members of the government, at any time during the debate on a specific bill, to propose a precise policy package to the members of the legislature (by specifying which articles and amendments are included in the government's package and which are not). When either procedure is used, the members of the legislature must decide whether to accept the government's policy package or reject it; in the latter case, they retain the status quo. Both procedures therefore grant the government substantial policy proposal power while limiting the opportunities for members of the legislature to amend or otherwise alter legislative outcomes.

Although the package vote and the confidence vote procedure share important structural similarities, they also involve a very important difference. When the government invokes a package vote, there is a simple up or down decision on the government's policy package. When a prime minister invokes a confidence vote procedure on a bill, there is no vote on the bill itself. Instead, a majority in the National Assembly can defeat the bill only by submitting and adopting a motion to censure the government. If such a motion is adopted, the government must step down and the status quo policy remains in force. If such a motion is not adopted, then the prime minister's bill is considered to be adopted.[13] Thus, if the legislature takes no action, the government's proposal becomes law. The confidence vote procedure therefore forces a much more difficult decision on the members of the legislature than does the package vote, for defeat of a government bill under a confidence vote procedure not only defeats the government's policy, but it also defeats the entire government, thus potentially triggering an election.[14]

Utilization of the package vote and the confidence vote procedure. Prior to an examination of patterns in the usage of these two forms of decree authority, it is important to note that data on utilization is only a small part of the story about how the package vote and the confidence vote procedure influence policy outcomes. In contrast to the case of delegated decree authority, members of Parliament must always anticipate the possibility that the government could use the package vote and the confidence vote procedure. These two procedures can therefore have an important effect on policy outcomes even when they are not actually used. More generally, for any type of decree authority that is not delegated, one must be sensitive to important institutional effects that occur, often subtly, through the mechanism of anticipated reaction.

It is also important to understand why and under what circumstances the procedures are actually used, as well as to compare utilization of these nondelegated forms of decree authority with utilization of delegated legislative decrees. It turns out that there are several important differences between utilization of the package vote and of the confidence vote procedures, on the one hand, and delegation under Article 38, on the other. First, both the package vote and the confidence vote procedure are used more frequently than is delegated decree authority (under Article 38 of the Constitution). From 1959 to 1992, the French government used the package vote 279 times and the confidence vote procedure 76 times.[15] For the package vote this amounts to just over 8 times a year, and to utilization on about 8 percent of all bills adopted by Parliament. For the confidence vote procedure this amounts to about 2.25 times per year, and to utilization on about 2 percent of all bills adopted. During this same period a decision to delegate under Article 38 was made only 26 times.

Second, unlike many of the bills which are the object of delegated decree authority, the bills subjected to the package vote and the confidence vote procedures have often been extremely important, and the subject matter of these bills have been diverse. One or both of these two procedures have been used, for example, to adopt legislation dealing with the establishment of France's nuclear energy policy, its nuclear weapons program, the level of state aid to Catholic schools, the adoption of national budgets, the privatization of French industries, and the reform of the electoral law. Thus, the package vote and the confidence vote procedures have played a much more visible role in French policy-making processes than have other types of French executive decree authority.

What leads the government to use these two procedures?[16] Hypotheses regarding agency considerations are not relevant to an understanding of the use of the package vote and the confidence vote procedures because these constitutional provisions are invoked by the government, not delegated to the government. But the hypotheses in the previous section (on Article 38 and delegation) regarding bargaining problems should also apply to the package vote and confidence vote procedures. We should expect, for example, that constitutional "decrees" using either the package vote or the confidence vote procedures will occur most often during small majorities and coalition governments (as tools for the government to preserve policy bargains on the floor of the government). However, because agency problems are not relevant to an understanding of nondelegated decrees, expectations about the government status and the incidence of the package vote and the confidence vote procedures are somewhat different from exceptions for delegation under Article 38. In particular, if multiple parties in government increase bargaining problems, we should expect an increase in the use of the package vote and the confidence vote procedures during minority (over single party majority) government, because during minority government, both the governing party and at least one opposition party must be able to maintain policy outcomes on the floor of Parliament. This situation contrasts with the expectation of less delegation during minority government (because of fear of agency loss).

The first two columns of Table 8.2 indicate that in contrast to the case of delegated legislative authority, the utilization of both the package vote and the confidence vote procedures is related to the *size of the government's majority*. Compared with periods of large governmental majorities, the government is much more likely to use both the package vote and the confidence vote procedure during periods of slim majority government. Again, with only three years of small majorities, it is important to be careful when interpreting these results. Government status is also related to utilization of the package vote and confidence vote procedures, with both procedures used most often during minority government, and the package vote used much more often during coalition government than during single-party majority government.

An interesting difference between patterns of utilization of the two procedures is that (as expected) coalition governments lead to increases in the use of the package vote (over single-party majority government) but do not lead to increased use of the confidence vote procedure. Similarly, use of the package vote procedure is basically the same during both minority government and slim majority government, but the use of the confidence vote procedure is dramatically higher during minority government. In fact, 54 percent of the time that the confidence vote procedure has been used since 1959 was during the five years of minority government (41 of 76 times). The confidence vote procedure therefore seems particularly important in the resolution of the peculiar bargaining problems inherent to minority government, when the government must find opposition support for its policies.

These differences are consistent with differences found in Huber (1992, 1996a). Those studies show that the use of the package vote procedure increased substantially on dimensionally complex issues (bills considered by more than one committee in Parliament) and distributive issues (bills for which the Finance Committee had primary jurisdiction). The same findings did not hold, however, for the confidence vote procedure. The evidence therefore suggests that the package vote procedure is a form of decree authority that is used to resolve bargaining problems when majorities are thin, when there is more than one party in government, or when policy issues are multidimensional. The most important factor affecting the use of the confidence vote procedure is the presence of minority government.

If one considers the electoral implications of parliamentary behavior in conjunction with the unique parliamentary strategies created by the confidence vote procedure, one finds that an especially strong relationship between the presence of minority government and the use of the confidence vote procedure makes sense. Consider the electoral implications of parliamentary behavior. In multiparty government, parties often must cooperate with each other in the legislature while competing in the electoral arena. Consequently, a fundamental problem that parties face in periods of multiparty government is communicating information to voters about policy positions and about the responsibility for policy outcomes. During minority government – especially when there exist no formal support parties – this is a particularly difficult problem, because opposition parties must give their consent for legislation to pass. Parties therefore need strategies that will permit the adoption of legislation while they communicate information to voters about issue positions and political responsibility.

Now consider the parliamentary strategies made possible by the French confidence vote procedure. Since the procedure permits passive enactment, a majority of deputies can announce opposition to a bill without *actually defeating the bill*.

During the 1988–93 period of minority government, the opposition parties often would announce their intention to defeat a particular bill, and the government, seeing that it did not have the necessary votes on the floor, would invoke the confidence vote procedure before the final vote on the bill. In fact, sometimes opposition parties actually defeated bills without preventing the legislation from becoming law. This occurred when a majority voted against the bill on the floor, the government asked for a second deliberation, and the prime minister invoked the confidence vote procedure during the second deliberation. In such a case, the only existing public vote on the adopted legislation is negative.

Thus, the confidence vote procedure is not strictly a tool used by the government. It is also an institutional arrangement that permits parties in Parliament to adopt "position-taking" strategies by forcing prime ministers to adopt policies by means of the confidence vote procedure. In adopting this strategy, the parliamentary parties distinguish their policy positions from those of the government without destabilizing the government or obstructing policy-making processes. The confidence vote procedure is an important institutional arrangement for influencing how parties communicate information to voters about policy preferences and political responsibility during minority government.

CONCLUSION

The analysis indicates that the various forms of decree authority arise under different circumstances and for different reasons. For each of the five forms of decree authority, however, there is a common element: They do not result in executive dominance of policy making. The French president cannot, for a variety of reasons, use emergency decree authority to influence normal legislative processes. The courts have ensured that Parliament can establish the scope of the government's rule-making autonomy. Members of Parliament rarely delegate legislative authority to the government, and when they do, it is often on minor legislation and under important time constraints. The package vote and the confidence vote procedures are probably the most powerful weapons at the prime minister's disposal, but Parliament can defeat proposals using either procedure. Thus, we find that the package vote procedure is used to preserve bargains between political parties during coalition and majority government, especially on dimensionally complex issues. And the confidence vote procedure is used primarily as a tool by which parties can communicate issue positions and political responsibility during minority government.

An important lesson from France, therefore, is that the various types of decree authority should not be viewed as mechanisms that transfer power from one branch of government to another. Instead, they should be viewed as mechanisms that enable political parties – especially those that share the power of government – to overcome many of the standard problems associated with collective decision making in multiparty systems.

NOTES

1 I am very grateful to Roy Pierce for numerous helpful discussions on the issues discussed in this paper. John Carey and Matt Shugart provided constructive criticisms of a previous draft. This research is supported by the National Science Foundation.

2 Limits on the legislative powers of the French president are discussed in detail by Huber (1996a: ch. 1) and Shugart and Carey (1992). On July 31, 1995, France amended the Constitution so that the president can, on the proposal of Parliament or the government, pose a referendum to the French people on ordinary policy issues. Before the change, the president could only request referendums on institutional questions. The president cannot, unilaterally, demand a referendum.

3 The following discussion draws heavily on Debbasch et al. (1988: 313–20) and Pierce (1968: 63–5).

4 The Constitutional Council, for example, rules on the regularity of elections, the constitutionality of referendums, organic laws, rules of procedure for the National Assembly and the Senate, the jurisdiction of Parliament, and (if asked by the president, the prime minister, or the president of either chamber) on the constitutionality of laws and international commitments. There are nine members of the Constitutional Council. Three are appointed by the president, three by the President of the National Assembly, and three by the President of the Senate. All serve nine-year terms. See the Constitution, Articles 56–63.

5 See *Journal Officiel* (April 24, 1961).

6 See Maurice Duverger's article, "L'Article 16," in *Le Monde* (November 19, 1966).

7 *Documentation française*, notes et études documentaires, n° 2530 (11 avril 1959). Cited in Maurice Duverger's, "L'Article 16," *Le Monde* (November 19, 1966), p. 1.

8 The first instance of cohabitation occurred from 1986–88. For an excellent discussion, see Pierce (1991), and for a view from the inside, see Balladur (1989). The second period of cohabitation occurred from 1992–95.

9 Organic laws implement provisions of the Constitution. There is only one difference between the adoption of ordinary legislation and the adoption of organic laws. If the National Assembly and the Senate cannot reach an agreement on the final text of a bill, the government can ask the National Assembly to make the final decision (Art. 45). On ordinary legislation in this situation, the National Assembly can adopt laws by a majority of those voting. Organic laws considered by the National Assembly under Article 45 (after no agreement with the Senate) can only be adopted by a majority of all the National Assembly's members (so that abstentions count against adoption).

10 See in particular Debbasch et al. (1988) and Pezant (1984).

11 There are exceptions. Certain areas remain within the regulatory domain and cannot be placed in the domain of law by an act of Parliament. These include the organization of the civil service and certain issues related to the police. See Debbasch et al. (1988: 440).

12 Under France's two-round electoral laws system, the parties of each left–right *tendance* must typically cooperate with each other (through withdrawals of candidates for the second round) to maximize electoral success.

13 Because in this case there is never a vote on a bill, this method of passing legislation is sometimes called "passive enactment." Almost all parliamentary democracies have confidence vote procedures, but the French procedure is unique with respect to the possibility of passive enactment (Huber 1996a).

14 See Huber (1996b) for a comparative discussion of confidence vote procedures in other parliamentary democracies.

15 On no occasion has use of the confidence vote procedure led to the fall of the government.

16 A more comprehensive analysis than is possible here is given in Huber (1992 and 1996a).

9

IN SEARCH OF THE ADMINISTRATIVE PRESIDENT

PRESIDENTIAL "DECREE" POWERS AND POLICY IMPLEMENTATION IN THE UNITED STATES

Brian R. Sala

It is in the shadow-land between policy and its implementation – between the motion and the act – that the literature on the presidency is thinnest.
RICHARD P. NATHAN (1975: VIII)

I. INTRODUCTION[1]

The U.S. president lacks most of the explicit decree authorities available to chief executives discussed elsewhere in this volume. Nonetheless, conventional wisdom identifies the presidency as the dominant branch of the U.S. national government, with broad influence over policy outcomes. Furthermore, there are theoretical reasons to expect that an American president could use decree authorities to produce an impressive effect on policy. In Chapter 1 of this volume, Carey and Shugart argue that proactive executive tools will be formidable whenever the executive also holds some substantial reactive powers (e.g., a veto power) and/or whenever legislators find it *collectively* difficult to take action – independent of the executive – on salient policy questions. Both of these latter conditions are conventionally accepted as prevailing in U.S. national politics.

Carey and Shugart's argument applies to *executives* in general, not solely to presidents. However, although the U.S. Congress often delegates *foreign affairs* responsibilities to the president, it rarely delegates substantive policy-making authority directly to the president in *domestic* policy. Instead, it typically delegates to cabinet secretaries and agency heads. I focus in this chapter on the president's role in domestic affairs. In this arena, I argue, one key to understanding the president's influence on policy implementation is his or her constitutional mandate to ensure that the laws are "faithfully executed" by government agents. This mandate could be seen as an authority by which the president interprets statutory intent for bureaucrats. The hardest job facing a president, in the view of the U.S. presidency scholar Clinton Rossiter, is "not to persuade Congress to support a policy dear to his political heart, but to persuade the pertinent bureau or agency – even when headed by men of his own choosing – to follow his direction faithfully and transform the shadow of the policy into the substance of the program" (1956: 2; quoted in Nathan 1975: viii). I address this problem of persuasion within the context of U.S. politics.

American bureaucrats possess delegated rule-making authorities within the bounds of statute. Such rule-making authority can imply broad policy-making discretion. However, those bureaucrats are subject to presidential oversight and sanctions. Hence, bureaucrats need to *learn* what actions the president would likely punish. Moreover, both the president and Congress send signals to the bureaucracy about legislative intent. Presidents issue executive orders and "presidential signing statements" in order to shape bureaucrats' beliefs about intent and about the consequences of not fulfilling that intent. These presidential signals can, under narrowly defined conditions, help bureaucrats.

Congress likewise tries to signal bureaucrats about legislative intent and about the conditions under which bureaucrats would be punished by the president. In many cases Congress and the president will have conflicting incentives vis-à-vis policy choice. In these cases, I argue, bureaucrats will see congressional signals as credible when Congress' interests agree with the bureaucrats' own policy goals. In other cases, however, Congress and the president will have similar policy goals. When this situation arises, bureaucrats often will lack reasons to believe signals from either. Consequently, presidential actions to reject bureaucratic policy initiatives or to dismiss a president's own appointees for policy differences can occur in equilibrium.

The chapter is organized as follows. In Section II, I place the U.S. presidency in the perspective of Carey and Shugart's theoretical framework and show why Congress rarely delegates substantial authority to the president in domestic policy, but more often does so in foreign policy. I narrow the focus of my argument in Section III to the president's role in writing legislation. Presidents bargain with Congress over both the policy goals of delegations and the personnel to whom authority is to be delegated. I suggest that the president cannot credibly commit to legislators that he or she will refrain from reinterpreting legislative intent during the implementation process. In Section IV I present and discuss a model of bureaucratic policy choice in which the agent lacks complete information about presidential preferences but in which the president and Congress can send cheap-talk signals about a law's true intent. I present some concluding remarks in Section V.

II. THE U.S. PRESIDENCY IN
COMPARATIVE PERSPECTIVE

In this section I discuss the conditions under which the U.S. Congress likely would acquiesce to presidential initiatives, and I explain why the U.S. president holds some measure of DDA in foreign affairs but almost none in domestic affairs. I show why this is the case in order to motivate my focus in Sections III and IV on the president's constitutionally-based powers to interpret legislative intent for bureaucrats.

CONGRESSIONAL TOLERANCE FOR
PRESIDENTIAL POLICY INITIATIVES

Legislatures may well tolerate executive decrees for any of the three important reasons cited by Carey and Shugart. First, if presidents can easily change the Constitution when their goals are thwarted by the legislature, they can deter legislator opposition. Second, if the president's goals are very similar to those of a large majority of legislators, his or her actions will tend to mirror the actions that the majority would have chosen for itself. Third, if legislators have very divergent interests from one another, they may suffer from such legislative dead-lock that they would prefer presidential initiatives to no action at all.

The U.S. president has *no* formal role in amending the national Constitution, nor can it be changed easily.[2] Hence, the first condition for legislative acquies-cence to executive decrees cited by Carey and Shugart does not apply to the U.S. case. The Constitution did, however, provide both *proactive* and *reactive* powers to the president, and, as I shall discuss, Congress has made numerous delegations to the president, particularly during this century.

The second condition – agreement of interests between the president and most legislators – undoubtedly applies to the United States. Particularly during times of national crisis, members of Congress (MCs) are hesitant to express any signif-icant opposition to presidential leadership. During the American Civil War (1861–65), President Abraham Lincoln took numerous actions without clear, prior authorization from Congress. Lincoln's party held majorities of more than two-to-one in both chambers, and these majorities tended to support his policy choices. For example, in April 1861 (during a congressional recess),

> he [Lincoln] issued proclamations calling forth the state militia, suspending the writ of habeas corpus, and placing a blockade on the rebellious states. . . . Instead of claiming that he had full authority to act as he did, he ad-mitted that his actions were legally suspect. . . . After extensive debate, Congress passed legislation "approving, legalizing, and making valid all the acts, proclamations and orders of the President, etc., as if they had been issued and done under the previous express authority and direction of the Congress . . . " (Fisher 1993: 160, quoting *12 Stat. 326* [1861])

President Franklin Roosevelt enjoyed similar congressional confidence during the early part of the New Deal in the 1930s. On his first day in office, he issued an executive order halting gold transactions and proclaiming a national bank holiday. He then called a special session of Congress to consider a banking bill (written by Treasury Department officials) that validated his prior actions and delegated to him additional authorities. "With a unanimous shout, the House passed the bill, sight unseen, after only 38 minutes of debate" (Leuchtenburg 1963: 42–4). According to one account of the legislative process during this period, "legislators were so docile that they accepted measures drafted at the White House without making the customary protests about the encroachment of the executive on congressional prerogatives" (Mayer 1967: 429–30).

Thus, at least in these cases of crisis management in which the president enjoyed large, partisan majorities in Congress, presidents have been able to exercise decree-like powers with little or no protest from the legislature. But it should be noted that the two examples cited here are exceptional cases. Such crises as the Civil War and the financial panic of early 1933 are rare, and modern U.S. presidents seldom have enjoyed supportive congressional majorities as large as those that backed Lincoln in 1861 and FDR in 1933.

The third condition for MC acquiescence to presidential initiatives states that legislators may have to solve a difficult collective action problem in order to oppose such initiatives. If the president possesses action-forcing, decree-like powers, the collective action problem would broaden the scope in which the president could exercise those powers. This has two effects. First, it enhances the authorities the president possesses. Second, *because* legislators know the president would be difficult to oppose if he or she were to receive new, delegated powers, they are less likely to extend those powers in the first place.

In sum, U.S. presidents may exercise decree-like powers relatively unopposed when their party holds large majorities in the House of Representatives and the Senate *or* when party control of the two legislative chambers has broken down completely. These conditions, however, beg the question of how the president might receive decree powers. In the next subsection, I present a simple model of the U.S. legislative process in order to suggest when Congress is likely to delegate authority to the president.

PRESIDENTIAL DDA AND CONGRESSIONAL INCENTIVES

In contrast to chief executives in many other presidential systems, U.S. presidents have no formal, constitutional authority to issue laws by decree – in the terms of this volume, they lack CDA. What, then, are the conditions under which Congress would delegate decree authority to the president? The answer can be found in a reconsideration of the spatial model of legislation first discussed in the introductory chapter by Carey and Shugart.

I first assume that MCs care about policy outcomes per se, not just about their

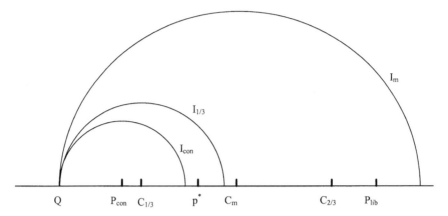

Figure 9.1 Agenda control and bargaining to sustain vetoes

ability to take positions on issues. U.S. legislators are strongly motivated to make names for themselves in the legislative arena.[3] But if MCs are as deeply divided as is often claimed, they face a daunting collective action problem in order even to propose a course of action in a given policy area. This generic barrier to making policy could motivate MCs to delegate proposal power to a central agent or even to *abdicate* their formal authority over a policy area by delegating decree powers to an agent.

Consider the situation depicted in Figure 9.1. The figure illustrates a stylized agenda-control game in one dimension, one in which the players are choosing an agent to implement policy on that dimension. There are four actors: a president, who is known to be either conservative (labeled P_{con}) or liberal (P_{lib}); and three members of Congress, representing the one-third quantile member ($C_{1/3}$), the median member (C_m), and the two-thirds quantile member ($C_{2/3}$). (For ease of exposition, I assume a unicameral legislature in this game.) Here, liberal and conservative refer only to the presidential types' relative distance from the status quo ante (labeled Q).

Suppose C_m has agenda power. In order to enact a policy change from Q (e.g., choose an agent who will implement a policy to the right of Q), C_m must gain the support of either *both* of the congressional players or the president and *one* of $\{C_{1/3}, C_{2/3}\}$. In the case of a conservative president, it seems plausible that he or she could bargain with the more conservative congressional player ($C_{1/3}$) to form a blocking coalition against proposals further to the right than some point p* between $C_{1/3}$'s indifference point (the point on the line intersected by the curve labeled $I_{1/3}$) and $C_{1/3}$'s ideal point. The *relative* utility loss suffered by the president and the conservative congressional player for failing to enact a new policy is in some sense smaller than that suffered by the more liberal players, thus adding an aspect of credibility to the bargain between president and conservative MC.[4] In contrast, should the president be a liberal (P_{lib}), the converse would be true – the president and his legislative ally at $C_{2/3}$ would seem to have more to lose if a policy change were not passed.

Conservative presidents (by which I mean those who seek only small changes in the status quo) tend to be better equipped to bargain concessions from congressional majorities than liberal presidents (who seek larger changes in policy; on the credibility of veto threats, see Kiewiet and McCubbins 1988; Carter and Schap 1987; Matthews 1989; for an alternate view, see Ingberman and Yao 1991). At the same time, however, legislative delegations to the president per se are more likely when he or she and legislative leaders share similar policy goals, which is most likely when they share the same party affiliation. This is because Congress lacks the ex post tools to punish presidents for failing to comply with congressional wishes and because presidents cannot easily bind themselves to implement any policy other than their most preferred ones (P_{con} for conservative presidents, P_{lib} for liberals).[5] A president's promises to Congress that he or she will deviate from his or her own ideal point are "cheap talk" unless he or she can be held accountable for his or her actions.

A bureaucratic agent, however, need not have preferences identical to the president's. By delegating to bureaucrats rather than to the president directly, MCs can move policy implementation away from the president's ideal point, even if they lack the ability or will to oversee bureaucratic implementation of policy. Thus, in the case of ordinary legislation, I argue that conservative presidents, relative to liberal presidents, are strategically advantaged to extract policy concessions from Congress, but that this advantage does not translate into an incentive to delegate directly to the president. Presidents cannot credibly promise to fulfill any policy agreements that would give them an outcome different from their own most-preferred policy, because Congress cannot punish them for noncompliance. But the president can nominate an agent whose preferences are such that he or she would willingly comply with any deal cut in a legislative bargain. This explains why Congress delegates to bureaucrats rather than to the president in domestic policy.

Foreign affairs and trade policy differ from domestic policy. The U.S. Constitution gives the president the sole authority to negotiate treaties with foreign powers, but it requires that treaties be ratified by a two-thirds vote of the Senate (the House takes no formal role in treaty making). In this case the president's ideal policy might actually be closer to the median preference in Congress than would be the preferences of the last few senators needed to ratify a treaty. The legislative majority can use direct delegation to the president (e.g., the Reciprocal Trade Agreements Act of 1934 [RTAA] and, more recently, the Fast Track proceedings for the U.S.-Canada Free Trade Agreement and for the North American Free Trade Agreement [NAFTA]; see Destler 1980; O'Halloran 1994) to bypass the constitutional requirement for treaty ratification by two-thirds of the voting members in the U.S. Senate.[6] O'Halloran argues that Congress's delegation to the president is best understood as an effort to "govern by creating procedures to control trade policy through, not despite, delegation" (1994:182).

For the most part O'Halloran's conclusions vis-à-vis trade policy extend to other direct delegations as well. Congressional majorities most often have used delegations to the president to enhance their control over policy, not to shirk responsibility for policy outcomes. The president's typical delegated role is as an oversight agent. The usual concern with oversight agents is that they will report strategically in order to promote their own private interests, which may be hidden from Congress (Lupia 1992). But because presidents are elected and are responsive to constituency opinions, Congress has strong prior beliefs about the interests that those presidents will try to promote. Hence, members of Congress often believe that presidential reports will help them manage the bureaucracy. In contrast Congress is much less sanguine about delegating either proactive or reactive powers to the president outside of the trade-policy area.

Having thus rejected the argument that the U.S. president should wield frequent and broad DDA, I turn back to the president's constitutionally mandated authorities. In the next section, I argue that the president does in fact hold an important proactive, constitutional authority that could be considered a form of constitutional decree authority.

III. PRESIDENTIAL SIGNALS AND THE POLICY IMPLEMENTATION PROCESS

In addition to their reactive veto power, U.S. presidents also possess two forms of proactive authority. First, as I noted in the previous section, presidents have accumulated numerous delegated powers, which range from the discretion to certify certain foreign governments' human rights records as a condition for extending their Most Favored Nation trade status to the requirement that they submit an annual budget and a budgetary report. Second, they hold several constitutional mandates: they nominate candidates for (nonelective) high executive-branch and judicial offices, they negotiate treaties, they command the military, and, most importantly for this chapter, they are responsible for seeing that the laws enacted jointly by the president and Congress are "faithfully executed" by governmental agents. In this section, I make the case for this faithful execution mandate as a potentially important form of constitutional decree authority.

THE LAST WORD AND LEGISLATIVE INTENT

The president's authority to see that the laws are executed faithfully could be and often is interpreted as a substantial, proactive constitutional authority over the actions of executive-branch bureaucrats. This mandate includes both instructions to agents about how he or she wants legislation implemented (ex ante influences) and ex post actions to reward and punish those agents for their behavior. In particular U.S. presidents have the constitutional authority to fire many of the agents they (or their predecessor) have appointed.

When presidents sign a bill into law, they often have the last word as to its meaning. In other words they have the last chance to frame legislative intent for bureaucratic action. Congress lacks the tools to punish a president who misrepresents presidential–legislative discussions about a law's intent. There is no "legislative veto" applicable to presidential rhetoric. The only real sanction against a president who reneges on deals with Congress in this way is controlled by voters, and even this sanction is lacking for second-term presidents because of the constitutional limit on how many times a person can be elected president. So, although a president can't necessarily take a law that says "Black" and credibly reinterpret it to mean "White," very little stands in the way of a president who would describe a law in shades of gray.

Presidents can accompany their signatures with a formal signing statement in which they propose an interpretive framework for the law. Similarly, they can issue an executive order detailing how the law is to be implemented. If the bureaucrats charged with implementing a legislative mandate find the president's interpretation credible, he or she may be able to alter the effective meaning of a law after he or she and Congress have agreed to its language.

PRESIDENTIAL RHETORIC AND CHEAP-TALK SIGNALING MODELS

In a 1974 committee print, the Senate Special Committee on National Emergencies and Delegated Emergency Powers wrote that "Nowhere in the Constitution is the President empowered to make law. Nevertheless, in the course of executing acts of Congress and of directing the executive branch, the President must issue numerous orders to the bureaucracy which have a binding effect on subordinate officials . . ." (U.S. Congress 1974: 6–7).[7] The actual legal force of each executive order and proclamation is an empirical question that can only be answered after the fact by the courts. The president's authority to issue law-like executive orders is not in question, but the scope of that authority is very much contested. So it is reasonable to assume that bureaucrats harbor some uncertainty as to how they should best respond to presidential demands that they dislike.

I assume that presidents can interpret legislative intent without any cost or risk to themselves (i.e., that the signal is cheap talk; see Crawford and Sobel 1982; Farrell 1987; Farrell and Gibbons 1989). This assumption is somewhat restrictive. Presidents may have valuable reputations that they put at risk by issuing executive orders that make policy demands on bureaucrats (Mueller 1970). The president also is engaged in an ongoing relationship with many bureaucratic units – otherwise costless actions vis-à-vis one agency could affect the president's credibility with other agencies on other matters.[8] In this chapter, however, I want to focus very narrowly on how presidential rhetoric affects individual cases treated in isolation.

What effect should we expect presidential rhetoric to have on policy outcomes? The standard, formal theory, cheap-talk result, one based on Crawford and Sobel

(1982), is that these signals can help two parties coordinate a mutually beneficial outcome when their interests are very similar. In agenda-control models such as mine, a cheap-talk stage that precedes stages in which the players take actions (e.g., the bureaucrat begins to implement a policy and the president fires/does not fire him or her) can be ignored entirely when the president (sender) and agency (receiver) know each other's preferences. This is because the point of the communication is to influence the other player's beliefs about the signaler's preferences – when these preferences are known, nothing can be gained by misrepresenting them.

More interesting is the case in which either the agency doesn't know for sure what the president wants out of it or it doesn't know just how much the president will let the agency get away with. Consider, for example, the case in which an agency head – say, the administrator of the U.S. Food and Drug Administration (FDA) – wants to take action on an issue. The August 1996 final FDA regulations governing tobacco advertising (*Federal Register* 1996: 44395–618) is one such case. The tobacco industry was traditionally an ally of the Democratic party in the southern United States. Since the 1960s, however, conservative southerners have become more likely to vote Republican, whereas Democrats in the White House and Congress have become more likely to take actions that hurt the interests of the tobacco industry.

Then-FDA Administrator David Kessler had been appointed by former President George Bush. The FDA's head, as is true of most top officials in the executive branch, can be fired by the president at any time. It stands to reason, therefore, that Kessler might have been concerned that President Clinton would fire him if he took a misstep on such a politically important initiative as the new tobacco regulations. Yet Kessler had no real way of knowing just what Clinton would be willing to accept. If Clinton acted more like a traditional southern Democrat, he would be fairly averse to strong, new regulations on tobacco advertising. On the other hand, if Clinton really were a "new" Democrat, he might be quite receptive to a sweeping regulatory initiative.[9]

In the standard, cheap-talk modeling approach, Kessler would expect, roughly, to know the difference between a very liberal president willing to go farther than the FDA head wanted and a moderate or conservative president unwilling to go as far as Kessler would prefer. But he couldn't expect to figure out exactly how far this latter type of president would be willing to go. Suppose Kessler's goal had been a total ban on tobacco advertising. In this case both a conservative president (on this issue) and a relatively moderate president would have sounded similar: Each would have threatened to veto Kessler's favorite proposal. This is the essence of Matthews' (1989) model of how presidential veto threats affect Congress' legislative proposals. Both the conservative president and the moderate president in this example would have accepted some modest change in tobacco regulation. But the moderate presidents would not want to reveal just how far they would want the policy to move, since Kessler would have responded by stretching his discretion to the maximum.

Thus, it would appear from the existing literature on cheap-talk models that presidential rhetoric could affect bureaucratic behavior on some issues and not others. When a president desires a greater change in a policy than does the agency head, critical rhetoric is unlikely to induce a greater change. Conversely, when the president wants a smaller change, critical rhetoric *can* induce a smaller change in policy, but the agent will find it difficult to tell the difference between a president willing to accept only a very small, incremental change from one willing to accept a moderate policy change.[10]

Standard cheap-talk models, however, only go so far. They cannot capture the full flavor of an agency's decision-making environment. This is partly the case because the standard models allow only two participants – a sender, such as the president, and a receiver, such as an agency. But agencies also receive signals from Congress. Do congressional signals matter? Do they affect presidential rhetoric?

CONGRESSIONAL RHETORIC AND POLICY IMPLEMENTATION

I argue in the remainder of this section that members of Congress do in fact have incentives to counteract presidential rhetoric with signals of their own. I then turn in section four to a model of bureaucratic response to presidential and congressional signals.

One argument vis-à-vis congressional signals, one popularized by Fiorina (1977), is that these signals are not intended to produce results so much as they are intended to help members of Congress shift blame for policy failures away from themselves. Fiorina argued that incumbent members of Congress have a strong incentive to disdain collective responsibility for policy outcomes and instead offer "ombudsman" services to their constituents who need assistance in dealing with the bureaucracy. Presidency scholars often imply that Congress exerts very little effort to control the bureaucracy, mainly because members of Congress see little profit in doing so. They prefer to *abdicate* to the president their formal authority to control the bureaucracy through very tightly crafted legislative delegations by instead writing very general legislation and then allowing the president to coordinate many of the specifics of implementation.

This perspective has recently been countered empirically by Aberbach (1990; see also Ogul 1976), who has shown that Congress actually devotes a great deal of time to oversight; and it has also been countered theoretically by numerous scholars, including McCubbins, Noll and Weingast (1987, 1989) and McCubbins and Schwartz (1984). The theoretical critiques have emphasized two points. First, theorists note that members of Congress prefer in many cases to employ "fire alarm" oversight techniques, which allow Congress to react to agency foul-ups only after constituents raise complaints, rather than "police patrols," in which MCs search for agency mistakes-in-the-making. Although these theories are broadly consistent with Fiorina's blame-shifting hypothesis, fire-alarm oversight likely provides Congress with similar or better information than police patrol oversight, and it does so at lower costs to MCs. Second, enacting legislative coalitions in Congress also prefer to design agency *procedures*, so that the coalition's policy interests are mirrored from the start in the constituency pressures brought to bear on agency decision making. This "autopilot" or "deck-stacking" approach also promises lower enforcement costs.

Thus, I would argue that there are good reasons to believe that MCs care about policy implementation and bureaucratic interpretation of legislative intent. Congress spends a great deal of its time on oversight proceedings and invests considerable effort toward designing agency procedures to shape bureaucrats' incentives. Although many individual efforts by MCs are consistent with the ombudsman thesis, committee oversight proceedings tend to be more broadly based than Fiorina's theory would require.

IV. A MODEL OF BUREAUCRATIC RESPONSE TO PRESIDENTIAL AND CONGRESSIONAL SIGNALS

Having established in the previous section that both the president and members of Congress have incentives to influence bureaucrats' reading of legislative intent, I turn in this section to a simple, stylized model of how bureaucrats interpret the signals they observe. My central goal is to characterize the conditions under which these signals affect bureaucrats' implementation choices. I present (informally) a series of examples in this section, each of which depends both on rather specific assumptions about presidential and congressional preferences and on how much the implementing agent knows about those preferences.

The basic concern motivating this model is whether or not the agent can learn the president's preferences before implementing policies. I ignore the possibility that Congress could exercise its own veto over an agent's choice. Congress' only role in this model is to choose rhetoric it hopes will influence the agent's behavior. The president, on the other hand, both can make a statement and exercise a veto on the agent's proposal.

There are three players in this game: an agency (whose ideal point is denoted A); the president (P); and a congressional oversight committee (C), which is treated as a unitary actor. Each player is assumed to have single-peaked preferences in a unidimensional policy space corresponding to the real number line. Both the president and the committee have complete information, but the agency has incomplete information about the president's preferences. The agency knows only that the president is one of two types ("high," denoted P_{hi}; or "low," denoted P_{lo}). A picture of this model is presented in Figure 9.2. The points P_{lo} and P_{hi} represent the veto points for a very conservative (or "low") president and a moderately conservative ("high") president, respectively. Here, "conservative" is

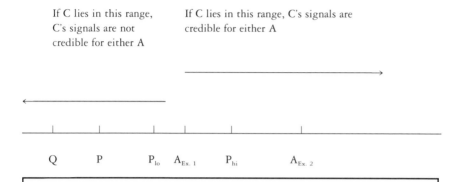

Key:

Q: reversionary policy, which results if A's proposal is vetoed by P

P: illustrative ideal point for president (not observed by the agent)

P_{lo}: veto point of low-type president; will accept any proposal between this point and Q

P_{hi}: veto point of high-type president; will accept any proposal between this point and Q

$A_{Ex.1}$, $A_{Ex.2}$: ideal points for agents in Examples 1 and 2, respectively

C: Ideal point for Congress

In Example 1, A implements either P_{lo} or $A_{Ex.1}$. If C's preferred policy outcome of this set is $A_{Ex.1}$, its signal is credible and helps A avoid a veto.

In Example 2, A implements either P_{lo} or P_{hi}. If C's preferred policy outcome of this set is P_{hi}, its signal is credible and helps A avoid a veto.

If both presidential types have the same ideal point, both always signal that they are "low" types. If, on the other hand, P_{hi}'s ideal point were sufficiently to the right of P_{lo}, that president would prefer either the agent's ideal or the point P_{hi} to P_{lo}, and so he or she would truthfully reveal his or her type.

Figure 9.2 Agency policy choice and presidential/congressional signals

merely a qualitative label that reflects the idea that the president's ideal policy is often closer to the reversion point than the other players'. The point Q represents the reversionary policy – the outcome that occurs in the event that the president vetoes the agency's proposal. Each presidential type is willing to accept any proposal to the left of his or her respective veto point and to the right of Q, but P_{lo}'s preferred-to set $P_{lo}(Q)$ is a subset of P_{hi}'s set $P_{hi}(Q)$.

The game is played as follows. First, the president signals his type (high or low). Next, the committee *verifies* the president's signal with one of its own (true or not true) (Lupia 1992). Third, the agency proposes a policy. Since the agency knows the president can be only one of two possible types, it can restrict its offer to one of three points – P_{lo}, P_{hi} or A. Finally, the president accepts or rejects the policy proposal and payoffs are distributed. Payoffs in this game derive from the utility gains (losses) implied by the enacted policy relative to the reversionary policy. At this point I am ignoring the president's ability to punish an agency above and beyond the utility gain that is foregone by the agency when the president vetoes a proposal. This has no affect on the agency's ability to learn. It does, however, affect the agency's expected utility calculations, making implementations of A or P_{hi} more likely than would be the case if the president were allowed to punish as well. I also assume that the agency pays no cost to implement policy. Costly action for the agency would only affect its choice from {P_{lo}, A, P_{hi}} in the event that the cost were a function of the policy change.

This game is a fairly straightforward application of Lupia's (1992) model of learning from cheap-talk signals. Lupia extends the original cheap-talk results (learning occurs when the receiver knows that the sender has very similar preferences) to incorporate the possibility of third-party verification. He argues that signal-receivers can learn when one (or more) of four conditions is true: either signal-senders or signal-receivers have similar preferences (the cheap-talk criterion); the sender must pay a cost to signal (so that small lies – those that lead to small changes in outcomes – are not worth telling); the sender must pay a penalty for lying (again, so that small lies are not worth the expected cost); or the sender's signal can be verified or refuted by a third party who knows the truth and is motivated to reveal it.[11] In the following examples, I have ignored the possibility that either the president or the congressional committee could have to pay an ex ante cost or ex post penalty for lying. Hence, the agency's ability to learn from signals depends on whether there is a coincidence of interests either between the agency and the presidential types or between the agency and the committee.

An agency whose ideal policy choice lies to the left of P_{lo} knows it can implement its ideal point with impunity. In this case all players know that all signals would be ignored. Hence, I focus only on the cases in which A lies between P_{lo} and P_{hi} or to the right of both. In the case that A lies between P_{lo} and P_{hi}, all players know that the agency will choose between implementing policy at P_{lo} and implementing at A, because it knows (by construction) that a moderate president would prefer A to P_{hi}. In the case that A lies to the right of P_{hi}, the agency would know that its own ideal policy would be rejected. Its implementation choice thus boils down to P_{lo} or P_{hi}.

EXAMPLE 1: *The agency's ideal lies between presidential types*

Suppose A lies between P_{lo} and P_{hi}. If moderate presidents prefer policy at A to policy at P_{lo}, they would have an incentive to reveal their type truthfully, whereas conservative presidents would always signal that they were conservative. Alternately, if moderate presidents preferred policy at P_{lo} to policy at A, they would have an incentive to misrepresent their preferences. Therefore, the agency knows with certainty that it is facing a high type in the event that it observes a high signal from the president. Most of the time, however, the agency expects to observe a low signal, which could come from a low-type president or from a high type who prefers P_{lo} to A. In this case the committee's signal could provide useful verification of the president's type. Under what conditions would the committee help the agency learn the truth?

As I noted above, this question boils down to a simpler one: When does the committee want to help the agency avoid a veto of its policy proposal? If the committee prefers the reversionary policy Q over any of {P_{lo}, A, P_{hi}} (e.g., if C were to the left of Q), it would not help the agency. Likewise, the agency would have no incentive to pay any attention to the verification signal if sent. Therefore, the agency would ignore any signals from such a committee unless that committee (or its parent, Congress) had sanctioning powers of its own, in which case the committee signals would have nothing to do with presidential preferences per se. Again, I am ignoring the possibility of congressionally-imposed sanctions in this chapter.

Next, if the committee's preferences were similar to those of a president who prefers P_{lo} to A, the agency could not learn anything from the committee's signal either, because this committee would have an incentive to announce that the president's low signal was true even if it were not. If the committee prefers A's ideal point to P_{lo}, on the other hand, it has an incentive to help the agency learn the truth. Finally, if the committee prefers P_{hi} to the other alternatives but if it still prefers A and P_{lo} to Q (as implied by my assumption of single-peaked preferences), it would again want to help the agency.

In this case, therefore, the agency has an incentive to pay attention to congressional committee signals whenever the committee's interests are sufficiently more liberal than those of a conservative president, even if the committee has no power to sanction the agency. Presidential signals, on the other hand, are completely informative only when presidents are themselves sufficiently liberal so that they prefer that the agency exercises complete discretion rather than mistake them for more conservative types.

EXAMPLE 2: *The agency's ideal lies outside both presidents' ranges of acceptable implementations*

Next, suppose that A lies to the right of P_{hi}. In this case the agency most prefers a large change in policy but knows with certainty that such a proposal would be vetoed. The relevant choice for the agency, therefore, is between implementing P_{lo} and implementing P_{hi}. This case exactly parallels the first, substituting policy choice P_{hi} for A. In other words a high-type president reveals his or her type if he or she prefers P_{hi} to P_{lo} and lies otherwise, whereas the committee tells the truth only if it is sufficiently liberal. When the committee is very conservative, it prefers Q to either policy alternative, so it would try to mislead an agency about the president's type. In between it prefers the conservative alternative to the more liberal one, so it would always signal that the president was conservative.

How should we expect agencies to respond to presidential and congressional signals, given the expectations I have laid out in these two examples? If we assume that all players are risk-neutral, expected-probability maximizers, outcomes will depend straightforwardly on prior beliefs. For example, suppose it is known that the agency places a 0.5 prior probability on the likelihood of a low-type (conservative) president, a 0.25 probability on the president being a high type who prefers P_{lo} to A (or P_{hi}, depending on the case), and a 0.25 probability on him or her being a high type who prefers A (P_{hi}) to P_{lo}. In the event that such presidents reveal that they are high or if the committee is sufficiently liberal, the agency learns the presidential type with certainty. If the committee is not sufficiently liberal and these presidents do not signal that they are high, the agency can eliminate the possibility that such presidents are high types who prefer the more liberal policy alternative under consideration. Hence, if we update the agency's beliefs via Bayes Rule, the posterior probability that the president is a low type is 0.667 (given that the committee is not liberal and, therefore, not a credible verifier, a fact that is known a priori). Given these updated beliefs, a risk-neutral agency would be more likely to choose to implement the more conservative policy alternative, P_{lo}.

Presidential executive orders can affect agency implementation choices even when agencies cannot ex ante learn the president's type with certainty from observable behaviors. Bureaucratic agencies seek confirming evidence that they will not be punished for acting as they see fit. For the most part, presidents will tend *not* to provide credible signals. But because some presidents would provide such signals, their absence would allow an agency to update its beliefs about the world. Conversely, when a president does send a confirmatory signal (what Matthews [1989] would term an "accommodating" presidential type), it is credible. Likewise, congressional committee reports can credibly verify those executive orders when their interests are sufficiently aligned with the agency's. From this simple model, I conclude that American presidents are severely limited in their ability to persuade bureaucrats to do whatever the president prefers. Presidents, I argue, lack the credibility needed to convince bureaucrats of their sincerity when they seek policy changes that bureaucrats disfavor.

DISCUSSION

Largely missing from this chapter has been any in-depth discussion of specific cases of presidential rhetoric, for the simple reason that illuminative cases are difficult to identify. Consider, for example, the case of President Reagan's attempt to create a "central clearance" function in the Office of Management and Budget (OMB) for new regulations proposed by executive branch and independent agencies. Executive Order 12291, which was issued on February 17, 1981, sought to impose new procedural requirements on most executive branch and independent agencies. Namely, it ordered agencies to prepare a cost/benefit-based "Regulatory Impact Analysis" for every major rule, new or old, where the criteria by which a rule was to be judged "major" were to be defined by OMB.

Executive Order 12291 by itself raised little opposition. Indeed, in one of his first official acts President Bill Clinton issued a memorandum on January 21, 1993, to indicate that "existing Executive orders on regulatory management [including E.O. 12291] will continue to apply" (*Weekly Compilation of Presidential Documents* 1993:93). In 1982 Congress strongly considered new legislation (H.R. 746 and S. 1080) that would have incorporated cost/benefit analysis requirements for major new rules into law. The legislation passed the Republican-controlled Senate unanimously, but it stalled in the House Rules Committee.

But in 1985 President Reagan promulgated E.O. 12498, which required all executive agencies subject to E.O. 12291 to submit annually to OMB a draft regulatory program for the year and, in essence, to have these programs approved by OMB, which would rule them to be consistent with the administration's policy goals. The OMB, through its Office of Information and Regulatory Affairs (OIRA), could thus order an agency to add or delete from its plan an order to reach conformity with the administration's policy goals. Such a review process would have created a new agenda power for the president (through OMB) for agency activities.

Not surprisingly, the Democratic-controlled House objected, going so far as to threaten to eliminate funding for OIRA from the 1987 budget. According to the logic of my model, executive agencies should have taken this congressional response as proof positive that they need not stake too much credibility in E.O. 12498's implied restraints on their regulatory authorities. The effect of Congress's protest is difficult to discern from the administrative records of the mid-1980s, but Congress and President Reagan continued to fight over his appropriate role vis-à-vis policy implementation for the rest of his term (Kiewiet and McCubbins 1991: 180–2). A definitive settlement did not arise until after the Supreme Court ruled in 1990 (during President Bush's term) that OMB had no authority under the Paperwork Reduction Act of 1980 (which created OIRA) to block another agency's directives regarding the publication of certain data. This decision significantly narrowed the scope of OMB's authority to block new regulations.

Subsequently, congressional leaders and then-OMB director Richard Darman worked out an agreement that "would require [congressional] notification when OIRA was considering a new regulation, would require OIRA to explain any changes made in a proposed rule and would set limits on the amount of time the agency had to review regulations" (*Congressional Quarterly* 1993:869). The agreement was contingent on passage of a bill reauthorizing OIRA, which ultimately failed in the Senate. Finally, in 1993 President Clinton issued a new executive order superseding 12291 and 12498 that adopted much of the language of the 1990 agreement (Barr 1993).

President Reagan made two bold statements of policy in 1981 and 1985, directing agencies to develop and apply a new economic cost/benefit test to proposed rules. He based these new policy pronouncements on his inherent authorities as the chief executive of the U.S. government. Congress initially was solicitous of the new approach – as indeed it had been for much of the Carter administration (see West and Cooper 1985). But although Reagan succeeded in slowing down the regulatory process in the early 1980s, it is unclear whether he had any significant success in making regulators more sensitive to economic cost/benefit calculations.

V. CONCLUSION

Policy implementation generates conflict. Often, the policy process finds an implementing agency stuck between what Congress wants and what the president wants – the proverbial "rock and a hard place." But by and large, policy implementation is not a zero-sum game between Congress and the president. These two institutional actors often fight over how policy should be implemented, but just as often they agree that *some* policy must be put into place. In this paper I have sought to illuminate a portion of this view of the policy-making process.

I have argued in this chapter that the president's ability to extract obeisance from agencies is limited by the extent to which he or she can send credible signals about his or her preferences and by Congress' ability to counteract his or her rhetoric. Presidents should not expect to jawbone an agency into doing whatever they want. Conversely, Congress should not be expected to contradict everything the president says, even when its majority disagrees sharply with the president's program.

The point of this essay is to highlight the role that U.S. presidents play in the policy-making process through executive orders. What I have found is that context matters a great deal in interpreting executive orders. U.S. presidents lack the institutional tools with which to "make law" unilaterally. As a consequence, their influence over the bureaucracy depends a great deal on their persuasive powers – but the president's ability to affect agency choices is contingent on the relationship between his or her rhetoric and Congress' own rhetoric. To borrow language from informational theories of delegation, the U.S. president often requires the acquiescence of a "verifier" in order to persuade bureaucrats of his or her sincerity (Lupia 1992). Even so, bureaucrats may be suspicious of congressional motives when MCs agree with the president. Even an executive order supported by corroborating congressional committee evidence may not be conclusive proof that an agency would be punished by the president for failing to comply with his or her orders.

The model I presented in Section IV was positive, but its most important implications are normative. First, agencies must be aware of the *political context* in which presidential and congressional signals are situated in order to draw the correct inferences from their observations. Agency heads who operate on the belief that either Congress or the president is dominant in the United States may be setting themselves up for a short and painful tenure. Likewise, any president who believes the rhetoric of the Imperial Presidency is similarly in for a frustrating tenure. The influence that each can bring to bear on agency choices depends on the specific policy context in question – sometimes circumstances will favor the president, sometimes they will not. But even when the president's veto threat seems to have some bite, if Congress has good political sense, it will be able to anticipate the president's position and alert agencies even before the president can take action.

NOTES

1 Thanks to John Carey, Brian Gaines, Jim Kuklinski, Terry Moe, Paul Quirk, Robert Rich, and Matthew S. Shugart for helpful comments on previous versions of this paper. A version of this paper was presented at the 1996 Annual Meetings of the American Political Science Association (August 29–September 1, 1996) in San Francisco.

2 Under Article V of the U.S. Constitution, if two-thirds of the members of each chamber in Congress concurrently call for an amendment to the Constitution, that amendment then goes to the state governments. It must be ratified by three-fourths of the states' legislatures (or specially-called state conventions). Alternately, Congress can be required to call a general constitutional convention if requested to do so by the legislatures of two-thirds of the states (after which any amendments must again be submitted for ratification by at least three-fourths of the states). The president's exclusion from the amendment process reflected the general orientation of the so-called Federalists who composed the Constitution. Although the Federalists' common goal was to enhance the national government relative to that of the states, most were nonetheless wary of shifting too much authority into the hands of an executive, whether plural or singular. For a broad-ranging examination of the constitutional foundations of the president's role in the United States, see Cronin (1989).

3 Congressional scholar Richard Fenno argued that MCs are driven by three key motivations: (1) a motivation external to Congress per se – the desire to retain office; (2) a motivation vis-à-vis one's peers in the legislature – the desire to advance one's own career; and (3) a philosophical or ideological motivation – the desire to create "good public policy" as each individual MC interprets the phrase (1978:137).

4 The credibility of the bargain is the sticking point for this argument. Can the conservative MC in this case credibly threaten to sustain the president's expected veto if the liberal majority passes a bill at I_{γ}? In a single-shot, noncooperative, game-theoretic model of this sort, sustaining a veto in this case would be out-of-equilibrium behavior. The threat to sustain, however, could induce the agenda setter to modify his or her proposal if he or she lacked perfect information about the conservative's preferences (Matthews 1989).

5 Under the Constitution, the president's pay cannot be altered during his or her term of office, which is likewise fixed by the Constitution. The only recourses available to Congress are to remove the president from office through impeachment (and, possibly, to bar the president from holding any future federal office) or to retract the delegation via new legislation. Impeachment can follow only after the House has passed articles of impeachment and the Senate has conducted a trial. It further requires a two-thirds vote of participating senators to convict (and thereby remove) the president or other officer or high official. Passage of new legislation would require either the president's signature or a congressional majority large enough to override a presidential veto.

6 The 1934 RTAA was passed during the first New Deal Congress – which paired a huge Democratic majority with a Democratic president who, in some ways, may have been more conservative than his legislative majority. This act authorized the president to negotiate bilateral trade agreements with foreign countries to lower (or raise!) tariffs within certain bounds, but these agreements did not have to be ratified by a two-thirds vote of the U.S. Senate, as is required of formal treaties.

7 By "binding effect" the committee appears to have meant that an agent's failure to comply would constitute cause for (a) the dismissal of a classified civil servant (e.g., career bureaucrats, as opposed to political appointees, who often serve at the president's pleasure once confirmed); (b) the impeachment of members of an independent agency board (e.g., the Federal Trade Commission, Federal Communications Commission, etc.); or (c) the reversal of a bureaucratic decision by the courts.

8 We could think of the president and the various agencies as players in a chain-store paradox type of game, one in which the president tries to ward off noncompliance by developing a reputation for toughness (on the chain-store paradox, see, e.g., Morrow 1994:281–90). In the chain-store paradox, the chain store has identical interests in each of many markets and faces identical (or at least very similar) potential competing entrants in each one. In a chain-store interpretation of executive/bureaucratic relations, presidents would have similar interests and face similar challenges to their authority in many policy areas. They would signal their preferences to an agency, which would then implement a policy. The president would then have to take *costly action*, either to punish the agency or to accept its choice, before the game could turn to the next agency. Real presidents, however, face many parallel policy tracks with different political saliences. The president may simultaneously signal many different agencies, none of which would necessarily observe the president's reaction to other agencies' policy choices before each made its own choice. Thus, it may be too expensive to the president to build a reputation for toughness that carries over from one policy area to the next.

9 In retrospect Clinton appears to have played the "new" Democrat role vis-à-vis tobacco advertising.

10 Kiewiet and McCubbins (1988) tell much the same story with regard to presidential veto threats on congressional spending bills. Presidents can club spending down by threatening to veto an appropriation, but they cannot force Congress to spend any more than its favorite level of expenditure.

11 What motivates verifiers to tell the truth? The same conditions can be applied to this actor as well – similarity of preferences, costly signals, penalties for lying, or the presence of a verifier. Hence, the verifier's role could be made credible by a (potentially very long) chain of subsequent verifiers.

10

INSTITUTIONAL DESIGN
AND EXECUTIVE DECREE

John M. Carey and Matthew Soberg Shugart

The case study chapters have provided a wealth of information about the specific conditions in particular countries under which decree authority is present – or in some cases not present – and the degree to which it provides for executive discretion in policy making. In this chapter we test the hypotheses that were originally presented in Chapter 1 against a broader set of data. For expository purposes we present the hypotheses again, as follows:

H1: The greater the influence of the executive (or of those who expect to hold executive office) over constitutional design, the greater the CDA.

H2: The greater the level of party discipline, the less likely is either CDA or DDA.

H3: Both CDA and DDA are more likely in bicameral than in unicameral systems.

H4: The greater the urgency of a policy issue, the more likely is DDA on that issue.

H5: When the executive has partisan majority support in the legislature, DDA is more likely than when the executive does not.

H6: The stronger the executive veto, the less likely is either CDA or DDA.

H7: The more difficult it is for legislators to change the constitution, the less likely is CDA.

H8: The greater the independence from the executive of the court that adjudicates executive–assembly disputes; the more likely DDA is.

H9a: When the executive has partisan majority support in the legislature, DDA is more likely as the informational advantages of the executive relative to the legislature increases.

H9b: When the executive does not have partisan majority support in the legislature, DDA is less likely as the information advantages of the executive relative to the legislature increases.

CASES

We draw on data from twenty political regimes in fourteen countries – seven in Latin American examples (Argentina, Brazil, Chile, Colombia, Costa Rica, Peru, and Venezuela), three post-communist cases (Russia, Ukraine, and Poland), and three advanced industrial states (France, Italy, the United States). First, we should make clear the main criterion by which the countries included in this analysis were chosen: We know something about them. For the most part this is because we were fortunate enough to find scholars who could provide the excellent case studies that comprise most of this book. We are able to include a handful of other countries in the analysis in this chapter as well because we have conducted research in them ourselves and are familiar with their institutions and history. We do not claim to have selected a sample at random. On the other hand, we do not know of any particular bias in the sample that would generate problems in interpreting our results.

Some of our cases are countries with thirty or more years of continuous democracy (Chile '25, Costa Rica, Colombia, and Venezuela, in addition to the three advanced industrial cases), whereas others are new and uncertain democracies. Additionally, this set of countries gives us a mix of regime types, with one that is often considered the prototype of a parliamentary system (Italy), another that has been the paradigmatic case for developing models of legislative behavior (the United States). We have more presidential than parliamentary regimes, but seven of our cases with directly elected presidents (France, Colombia '91, Peru '79, Peru '93, Poland '92, Russia '93, and Ukraine) also provide cases in which the cabinet is responsible to the assembly. Moreover, we do not limit our analysis to cases in which we frequently observe CDA or DDA. In five of the cases considered here (Colombia '68, Colombia '91, France, Peru '79, and Peru '93), we observe both; in a larger number of cases we observe either one or the other, and in four cases (Brazil '46, Costa Rica, Poland '92, and the United States), we observe neither. In short our case selection is not biased according to the value of our dependent variables.

What the cases have in common is that the relative balance of executive and assembly authority over policy outcomes has been the subject of intense political conflict and equally intense academic debate. Apart from that characteristic, the cases are strikingly diverse historically, culturally, economically, geopolitically, and institutionally. To the extent that variation on noninstitutional factors might drive a regime's reliance on decree authority, it is possible that this diversity could confound our efforts at empirical analysis. On the other hand, to the extent that we can detect regular patterns in the use of executive decree across such a diverse set of cases, we increase our confidence that our understanding of the phenomenon is not the product of a region-specific quirk or a unique property of young democracies, but rather that our general hypotheses about delegation and bargaining among politicians have some bite.

SCORING THE VARIABLES

To test the hypotheses presented earlier, we first develop a set of variables to serve as indicators of the historical, electoral, and institutional elements of our hypotheses. We try to keep all the variables as simple as possible, so that they can be scored uncontroversially. This means we develop a blunt set of instruments, but we hope that in doing so we avoid any bias in scoring individual cases.

As dependent variables, we focus on CDA and DDA. CDA takes a score of 0, 1, or 2. We assign 0 if there is no provision for CDA. CDA is 1 if it is limited either by the policy area(s) in which it may be exercised, if decrees lapse after a certain time, or if decrees do not take effect until some other conditions have been met, such as approval by the legislature. Effectively, CDA=1 describes the lower-left and upper-right boxes of Table 1.1, as well as cases where CDA is constrained by policy jurisdiction. CDA=2 only if decrees are unconstrained by jurisdiction and immediately become permanent law.

DDA is scored 0 if the legislature does not delegate legislative decree authority to the executive, and 1 if it does so routinely. Obviously, this scoring system begs the question of what "not delegating" implies as well as what is "routine." First, we only consider cases about which we have substantial historical knowledge – or about which we have consulted area specialists regarding this question specifically. These cases are scored 0 only if we know of no cases of DDA. Cases are scored 1 only if we know of three or more separate instances of DDA across different governments.[1] We do not know of any cases that fit in between these two extremes of "routine" or "no" DDA. In the cases of the new Argentine Constitution of 1994 and the Russian Constitution of 1993, we know of no instances of DDA, but not enough time has passed for us to score the variable with confidence.

The independent variables are executive domination over constitutional design (EXECDOM), the executive veto (VETO), legislative control over constitutional amendment (AMDT), party discipline (PARTYDISC), the number of legislative chambers (CHAMBERS), partisan majority support for the executive (EXEC-MAJ), and the independence of the courts from the executive (COURTIND). Scoring rules are as follows and are summarized in Table 10.1.

- EXECDOM is scored 0 if the constitution was drafted by an assembly without executive intervention; 1 if both an executive (or aspiring executive) and an assembly were involved in drafting and ratifying a new constitution; and 2 if the new constitution was drafted by an executive and if there was no assembly involvement in drafting or ratifying.
- VETO is 0 if there is no executive veto, or if executive objections to legislation can be overridden by a majority in the legislature; 1 if overriding the veto requires an extraordinary majority.
- AMDT is 0 if changing the constitution requires an extraordinary legislative

Table 10.1 *Scoring the variables*

CDA	0	None
	1	Limited by jurisdiction, sunset provision, or delay
	2	Immediately becomes permanent law; unrestricted by jurisdiction
DDA	0	Legislative decree authority not delegated to executive
	1	Legislative degree authority regularly delegated to executive
VETO	0	None; or majority override
	1	Extraordinary majority required for override
AMDT	0	Requires extraordinary legislative majority and/or other actors
	1	By legislative majority
CHAMBERS	1	Unicameral
	2	Bicameral
PARTYDISC	0	Party leaders lack control over nominations or candidate list positions
	1	Party leaders control both nominations and candidate list positions
EXECDOM	0	Constitution drafted by assembly
	1	Both executive and assembly in drafting, ratification
	2	No assembly involvement
COURTIND	0	Executive-centered appointment procedure, justices lack life tenure
	1	Executive-centered appointment procedure, justices have life tenure
	2	Executive does not control appointment procedure

majority or the approval of some other actor besides the legislature (president, courts, the electorate through referendum); and 1 if the constitution can be changed by legislative majority alone.

- PARTYDISC is 0 if party leaders either lack control over which candidates can be nominated to run on legislative ballots under their party labels, or lack control over the order in which candidates from their party are elected, or both; and it is 1 if party leaders control both nominations *and* candidate lists (cf. discussion in Carey and Shugart 1995 on the BALLOT variable).
- CHAMBERS is 1 if unicameral or if upper chamber approval is not required for passage of normal legislation; 2 if symmetrically bicameral.
- EXECMAJ is 1 if the executive enjoys majority partisan (or, in systems with parliamentary confidence, coalition) support in all chambers; 0 otherwise.

• COURTIND is 2 if the executive plays no role in the appointment of justices to the court that arbitrates disputes between the assembly and executive over decree authority; 1 if the executive has the authority either to nominate justices or approve nominees, but where justices serve life terms; and 0 where the executive has authority over appointments, and the justices serve fixed terms and are subject to reappointment.

The scores of the political systems included in this chapter on these variables (except EXECMAJ, which varies within systems over time) are presented in Table 10.2.

EVALUATING THE HYPOTHESES

H1 stated that CDA should be greater as the influence of the executive in the process of forming a new constitution increases. In Table 10.3, the relationship between EXECDOM and CDA supports the hypothesis.

Ecuador, France, Chile '89, and Russia '93 are the only cases in which constitutions drafted by executives, with no formal review by assemblies, were passed by referendums. In the French case, Parliament initially delegated to the de Gaulle government the authority to draft a constitution that would be subject to ratification by plebiscite. But the constraints imposed on the government in the initial delegation were minimal, and they did not touch on the question of CDA. Moreover, Parliament did not reserve for itself any authority to review the document drafted by the executive. The charter drafted by de Gaulle's advisers was submitted directly to a popular vote without revision by an assembly. The Ecuadorian Constitution was drafted by advisers to a military government and ratified by plebiscite before the convening of assembly and presidential elections. The current Chilean Constitution, which was drafted by the executive during the military dictatorship of General Augusto Pinochet, was first adopted in 1980 in a plebiscite marked by voter intimidation and procedural irregularities. The Constitution was substantially amended in a 1989 plebiscite, shortly before the return to civilian rule in that country. In neither case, however, was an assembly involved in drafting constitutional language. In the Russian case the parliamentary leadership of what was meant to be a consultative assembly on constitutional design walked out of negotiations in the autumn of 1993, leaving the charter to be drafted by presidential advisers. Yeltsin subsequently jettisoned any plans to subject the new Constitution to assembly review and relied on the vehicle of a plebiscite for ratification. Not surprisingly, all three of these constitutions provide for CDA, including the most formidable CDA for which we have record (under Art. 90 of the Russian Constitution).

Of the six cases in which both executives and assemblies were formally involved in drafting constitutions, four – Chile '25, Peru '93, Argentina '94, and Ukraine – include significant CDA. The Peruvian case in 1993 stands as a noteworthy

Table 10.2 Institutional variables and executive decree authority

Country	Year of Constitution	EXECDOM	VETO	AMDT	COURTIND	PARTYDISC	CHAMBERS	CDA	DDA
Argentina	1853	0	1	0	1	1	2	0	1
Argentina	1994	1	1	0	1	1	2	1	—
Brazil	1946	0	1	1	1	0	2	0	0
Brazil	1988	0	0	0	1	0	2	1	0
Chile	1925	1	1	0	1	0	2	0	1
Chile	1989	2	1	0	1	0	2	1	0
Colombia	1968[a]	0	0	1	2	0	2	1	1
Colombia	1991	1	0	1	2	0	2	1	1
Costa Rica	1949	0	1	0	2	1	1	0	0
Ecuador	1978	2	1	0	2	1	1	1	—
France	1958	2	0	0	2	1	1	1	1
Italy	1948	0	0	1	2	0	2	1	0
Peru	1979	0	0	1	1	0	2	1	1
Peru	1993	1	0	0	2	0	1	1	1
Poland	1992	1	1	0	2	0	2	0	0
Russia	1991	0	0	0	2	0	2[b]	0	1
Russia	1993	2	1	0	0	1	2	2	—
Ukraine	1992	1	0	0	2	0	1	1	1
USA	1789	0	1	0	1	0	2	0	0
Venezuela	1961	0	0	0	2	1	2	0	1

[a] In discussing the provisions of the Colombian Constitution prior to 1991, we are referring to the provisions put in place by the constitutional amendments of 1968. These amendments were drafted and adopted by Congress alone (EXECDOM=0). Moreover, simultaneously with establishing CDA, Congress also *amended the amendment procedure* to abolish the requirement of extraordinary legislative majorities for subsequent constitutional amendments (AMDT=1). The Constitution so amended in 1968 was adopted in 1886. Our knowledge of decree use prior to 1968 is limited, however, so the discussion here refers to the arrangement from 1968–91.

[b] Although the Supreme Soviet was drawn from the Congress of People's Deputies (CPD), Parrish's chapter, as well as other work on Russian legislative coalitions in the First Republic (Sobyanin 1994), demonstrate that the preferences of the two chambers were not congruent. Moreover, the CPD was sufficiently active and powerful to consider the system bicameral.

Table 10.3 *Executive dominance over constitutional design and CDA*

		CDA 0	1	2
	0	Argentina 1853 Brazil '46 Costa Rica Russia '91 U.S.A. Venezuela	Brazil '88 Colombia '68 Italy Peru '79	
EXECDOM	1	Chile '25 Poland '92	Argentina '94 Peru '93 Colombia '91 Ukraine	
	2		Ecuador France Chile '89	Russia '93

example of the role of assemblies in moderating executive claims on authority. Both Fujimori's *autogolpe* in 1992 and Yeltsin's showdown with the Supreme Soviet in 1993 are our clearest examples of presidents "calling out the tanks" during conflicts with legislatures. In the wake of these events, both presidents set about establishing new constitutions. Yeltsin opted to bypass any consideration by an assembly, whereas Fujimori opted to turn responsibility for drafting a new charter to a new body that would serve both as legislature and constituent assembly. Fujimori expected, correctly, that his co-partisans would dominate the elections to the assembly. What the president may not have expected was that the Congress would disregard what Schmidt calls his "hyperpresidentialist draft" and that it would impose significant procedural restrictions on the use of both CDA and DDA. Like the Peruvian Constituent Congress, the Argentine Constituent Assembly of 1994 established procedures for legislative review of decrees. Among the constitutions drafted by assemblies, on the other hand, five do not provide for CDA and four provide for CDA subject to limitations of some kind. In short executives prefer CDA, and executives that exert more influence over the design of constitutions tend to secure more of it. Confirming this proposition is not particularly surprising. But establishing this relationship allows us to turn our attention to the more interesting cases – those in which we observe executive decree authority but in which assemblies played an active role in constitutional design. In examining subsequent hypotheses regarding the existence of CDA, we narrow our set of cases, excluding Ecuador, Russia '93, France, and Chile '89, because all the subsequent hypotheses posit interests of *assembly members* in explaining the existence of decree authority.

Table 10.4 *Party discipline and CDA*

		CDA	
		0	1
PARTYDISC	0	Brazil '46 Chile '25 U.S.A. Poland '92	Brazil '88 Colombia '68 Colombia '91 Italy Peru '79 Peru '93 Ukraine
	1	Argentina 1853 Costa Rica Venezuela	Argentina '94

H2 proposes that low party discipline implies bargaining problems for legislatures and that therefore legislators in that situation should find executive decree more attractive than when discipline is high. We initially suggested that this should be the case both for CDA, given that constitutional assembly members frequently anticipate the electoral system that will be in place after a constitution is adopted, and for DDA, given that low discipline in a sitting legislature could encourage delegation of decree authority. We use the control of party leaders in nominating legislative candidates and determining party list positions as indicators of party discipline. Empirically, we find a strong bivariate relationship between weak party discipline and the existence of CDA, but we find no clear correlation between weak party discipline and the incidence of DDA, as can be seen by comparing Tables 10.4 and 10.5.

It may well be the case that in weak discipline systems, the existence of CDA "trumps" the need for DDA. Once executives have the authority to initiate policy changes under CDA, they may neither need nor request DDA. Moreover, the very condition of weak party discipline by itself may impede even collective decisions within legislatures to pass enabling statutes for DDA. These conditions would appear to describe both the cases of Brazil '88 and Italy '48, as discussed by Power, on the one hand, and by Della Sala and Kreppel, on the other. However, for a couple of reasons, we are hesitant to endorse this conclusion without reservation. First, it is not the case empirically that the existence of CDA absolutely precludes the use of DDA. Indeed, in the two Colombian and in the two Peruvian regimes, as well as in France, we observe both CDA and DDA. In all these cases, of course, CDA is limited by jurisdiction, whereas in Brazil '88 and in Italy it is not. It may be more accurate, then, to say that where CDA is not limited by jurisdiction, it precludes DDA. The second reason for caution, however, is that, despite the bivariate correlation between weak parties and CDA, party discipline

Table 10.5 *Party discipline and DDA*

		DDA 0	1
PARTYDISC	0	Chile '89 USA Brazil '46 Brazil '88 Italy Poland '92	Chile '25 Colombia '68 Colombia '91 Peru '79 Peru '93 Ukraine
	1	Costa Rica	Argentina 1853 Venezuela France

does not stand out as a strong predictor of either type of decree in our multivariate analyses later. In short H2 is supported with regard to CDA; with regard to DDA, the results are barely suggestive – especially as modified to account for jurisdictional limitations on CDA – but not compelling.

The results with regard to H3 are less subtle and certainly less suggestive. We do not find any evidence of a relationship between the number of legislative chambers and decree authority, as suggested in H3.

A stronger version of this hypothesis might hold that the transaction costs of legislating (and therefore, incentives to rely on decree) should be higher in bicameral than in unicameral systems only when bicameralism is incongruent (Lijphart 1984). Incongruence means that the two legislative chambers are elected[2] in substantially different manners, such that the nature of majority coalitions in the two chambers could be expected to differ substantially. In congruent bicameral systems, conversely, electoral districts and the electoral formula may be quite similar for both houses, such that majority coalitions in one are near replicas of the other. Italy, Chile '25, Colombia, and Venezuela all fit this description. Nevertheless, Tables 10.6 and 10.7 show no more sign of a correlation between incongruent bicameralism and decree authority of either type than between bicameralism more generally and decree. In short we find no evidence that H3 is supported.

H4 says that the greater the urgency of a policy issue, the more likely is DDA on that issue. The country-study chapters in this volume provide an abundance of suggestive evidence in support of this hypothesis. Many of the most prominent instances of delegated authority occurred in times of acute crisis, when immediate action was widely regarded as imperative but impossible under standard legislative procedures. Ferreira Rubio and Goretti's account of the broad delegation of economic and administrative powers to newly elected President Menem by a lame-duck Argentine Congress to address hyperinflation in 1989 is a prototypical

Table 10.6 *Number of legislative chambers and CDA*

| | | CDA | |
		0	1
	1	Costa Rica	Peru '93
			Ukraine
	2	Argentina 1853	Argentina '94
CHAMBERS		Brazil '46	Brazil '88
		Chile '25	Colombia '68
		U.S.A.	Colombia '91
		Venezuela	Peru '79
		Poland '92	Italy

Table 10.7 *Number of legislative chambers and DDA*

| | | DDA | |
		0	1
	1	Costa Rica	France
			Peru '93
	2	U.S.A.	Argentina 1853
CHAMBERS		Chile '89	Chile '25
		Brazil '46	Colombia '68
		Brazil '88	Colombia '91
		Italy	Peru '79
		Poland '92	Venezuela

example. Even more dramatic is the grant of legislative authority to President Yeltsin by the Russian Congress of People's Deputies after the attempted coup against the Soviet government in August 1991. Confronting an economic crisis embedded in a crisis of state dissolution, the Congress of People's Deputies delegated even broader power to Yeltsin than the Argentine Congress did to Menem. Crisp's chapter suggests that urgency has played a role in all five Venezuelan instances of DDA as well. The enabling law granting authority to President Betancourt in 1961 was entitled "The Law of Urgent Economic Measures." President Pérez's request of DDA in 1974 was accepted on the grounds that extant economic institutions could not accommodate the sudden increase in export revenues generated by the oil price shocks of the previous year – an unusually pleasant sort of "crisis" for any government to face. Ten years later, however, falling oil prices and the corresponding pressure on the Treasury by government debt obligations served as justification for delegation to President Lusinchi's gov-

ernment. Finally, the crisis in confidence in the Venezuelan government following President Pérez's resignation in 1993 prompted a delegation of authority to
interim President Velásquez until new elections could be held; and the continuing uncertainty in the wake of those elections justified a very brief delegation
to newly elected President Caldera in 1994.

Despite these examples, there are severe methodological difficulties in evaluating H4 systematically. The main problem is how to determine relative levels
of urgency. In the Argentine and Russian cases, the severity of the crisis was
plain. On the other hand, politicians regularly justify their actions as responses
to urgent problems, and researchers would be well advised to take such claims
with a grain of salt. If we equate Argentina's hyperinflation in 1989 with Venezuela's "crisis" of windfall oil revenues in 1974, for example, then we shall find
ourselves struggling to identify any political environment not in crisis. The problem of defining urgency is compounded by a problem of data selection. In principle, for example, we could analyze all cases in which DDA was granted to
evaluate whether the situations tended to be urgent. To do so would be to select
entirely on the dependent variable – the existence of DDA – and we would need
to have some sort of implicit idea in mind of what a *non*-crisis looks like against
which to compare our data. Ideally, we would want to code *all* periods of time
across all our countries, coding them as "urgent" situations and "non-urgent"
situations, and then we would have to try to determine whether DDA is more
likely in the former than in the latter. Apart from the thorny issue of what unit
of time would be considered a "period," this would require a coding effort that
is far beyond our capacity here.

An alternative cut on this problem is to examine the time constraints on
legislative action on the grounds, for example, that DDA is more likely when
legislative sessions are close to expiring. The delegation to Venezuelan President
Velásquez is suggestive here. So is Schmidt's account of the delegation of authority to Peruvian President Belaunde to rewrite the tax code in the months
before the 1969 election. Huber provides the most comprehensive test of data
along these lines in his examination of executive decree in France. Examining all
twenty-six bills granting DDA under Article 38 of the Constitution of the Fifth
Republic, Huber finds that twenty-five were adopted either during the last week
of a legislative session or in a special session of Parliament, when time constraints
were most pressing.

In sum, our lack of a generalizable measure of urgency and of comprehensive
data across systems against which to test such a measure, limits our ability to
test H4 as systematically as we would like. Nevertheless, H4 captures a justification for DDA that is ubiquitous among politicians involved in delegation, and
the country case studies provide substantial piecemeal evidence to support the
hypothesis.

Turning to the hypotheses related to agency problems, the evidence is more
compelling, although in the case of H5 we run up again against one more difficulty with the empirical data. H5 holds that DDA is more likely to executives

Table 10.8 *Partisan legislative majorities and DDA*

		DDA 0	DDA 1
Ever Partisan Majority?	YES	Costa Rica U.S.A	Chile '25 Colombia '68 Colombia '91 France Peru '79 Peru '93 Venezuela
	NO	Brazil '46 Brazil '88 Chile '89 Italy Poland '92	Argentina 1853 Russia '91 Ukraine

with majority partisan support in the legislature than to those without. Only for France, Peru, and Venezuela, however, do we have exhaustive data on the incidence of DDA that allows us to know with certainty the number of enabling statutes and the specific partisan conditions of delegation. In other cases we have been able to confirm either the existence or nonexistence of DDA, but where the former is the case, we are not always certain we have identified *all* instances. Thus, we cannot identify the precise relationship between the specific existence of a partisan legislative majority for a president and DDA in all cases. To examine the relationship then, we take two approaches. The first is to show the simple bivariate relationship between systems that have *ever* produced partisan legislative majorities and systems that rely on DDA. Although the data in Table 10.8 are crude, the results are suggestive. Of eight systems that have never produced single-party majorities that controlled legislatures, we find no DDA in five. Of nine systems that have produced legislative majorities, we find DDA in seven.

The second approach is to examine the specific incidence of DDA in the countries for which we have comprehensive data. Here, the results are mixed. In France, in twenty-nine years of majority governments from 1959 to 1988, decree authority was delegated to executives under Article 38 twenty-three times; in four years of minority government from 1988 to 1992, it was delegated three times – an almost identical rate of DDA across majority and minority governments. In the twelve-year history of Peru's 1979 Constitution, DDA under Article 188 was exercised more frequently than Article 38 in France, but again with no apparent relation to partisan support for presidents in Congress. The Venezuelan case is more suggestive. Here we have a lower frequency of DDA under Article 190 than in either France or Peru, but there is a striking correlation with

majority support for the first seven presidential administrations (which correspond exactly with congresses) under the 1958 constitution. From 1958 to 1993
we find that each of three presidents who enjoyed partisan majority support in
both chambers also received DDA at some point during his term. Of the four
presidents who lacked such partisan support, none received DDA.

The pattern is confused somewhat more recently, corresponding to recent political volatility in Venezuela. After President Pérez's removal from office in 1993,
interim President Velásquez was granted DDA to deal with specific economic
issues. Velásquez was effectively a nonpartisan president, however, one selected
by a consensus vote supported by both of Venezuela's largest parties to serve the
remainder of Pérez's term. Thus Velásquez's experience may be moot to the
question of the relationship between partisan support and DDA.[3] Most recently,
in 1994, DDA was given to minority President Rafael Caldera for a period of
thirty days. The 1994 delegation came in the wake of a 1993 election in which
the traditionally stable party system was shattered and which produced a congressional party system much more highly fragmented than any that Venezuela
had seen in three decades. Overall, the Venezuelan case conforms with H5, although the French and Peruvian cases are indeterminate on this count.

H6 suggested that the stronger the executive veto, the less likely would we
be to observe either CDA or DDA. The combination of veto and decree should
be unattractive to members of a constitutional or legislative assembly, because
an executive could use decree to set policy objectionable to a legislative majority
– and then he or she could veto attempts to retract that policy by standard
legislative procedure. The implication is, then, that proactive powers (such as
CDA) and reactive powers (such as strong vetoes) would be alternative means of
organizing executive–legislative relations (Shugart 1997). Constitutions designed
primarily by elected representatives would be unlikely to combine both types of
executive authority, at least in the same policy areas.[4]

Table 10.9 shows a strong relationship between vetoes and the incidence of
CDA across systems in which assemblies were involved in constitution writing,
with fourteen of sixteen cases falling as expected. Of the seven systems in which
an extraordinary majority is required to overturn an executive veto, only Argentina '94 provides for CDA. Of the nine systems either with no veto or where the
veto can be overridden by a majority of the legislature, all but Venezuela (where
DDA is constitutionally recognized and used regularly) do provide CDA.[5] In the
case of Argentina '94, President Menem was instrumental in the process of calling
for and drafting the new constitution. If there is one case combining a strong
veto with decree, it is not surprising that this should be it. Moreover, the story
of the incorporation of CDA into the new Argentine Constitution is complex.
Decrees of "urgent necessity" had been issued under the Constitution of 1853
by presidents before Menem, but Menem vastly increased their frequency. Thus,
although the 1994 Constitution recognized CDA, by specifying limits on its use,
the new Charter may serve to restrain a previously unchecked paraconstitutional
practice (Jones 1997).

Table 10.9 *Executive veto and CDA*

		CDA	
		0	1
VETO	0	Russia '91 Venezuela	Italy Peru '79 Peru '93 Brazil '88 Colombia '68 Colombia '91 Ukraine
	1	Argentina 1853 Brazil '46 Chile '25 Costa Rica Poland '92 U.S.A.	Argentina '94

Table 10.10 *Veto and DDA*

		DDA	
		0	1
VETO	0	Brazil '88 Italy	Colombia '68 Colombia '91 France Peru '79 Peru '93 Russia '91 Ukraine Venezuela
	1	Chile '89 Costa Rica U.S.A. Brazil '46 Poland '92	Chile '25 Argentina 1853

Table 10.10 accounts for the veto and DDA across all the systems where we have good enough information about the incidence of DDA to be able to classify it as either routine or nonexistent.[6] The pattern is a weaker version of what we observed in Table 10.9, with thirteen of seventeen showing the expected relationship. Among the deviant cases, Brazil '88 and Italy '48 are not problematic,

if we allow that the existence in these constitutions of unrestricted CDA across policy areas means that the assembly is less likely to resort to DDA. However, the other two cases that are off the diagonal – Argentina 1853 and Chile '25 – are puzzling. In both countries the constitution was long silent about the practice of DDA. A constitutional amendment in Chile in 1970 and a new constitution in Argentina in 1994 established that it was constitutional to delegate decree authority. In both cases, however, these constitutional changes only codified existing practice.[7] From the standpoint of possible agency losses, it is surprising that congresses would delegate decree authority when the executive also wields a veto with which potentially to block legislative "corrections" of decrees. Except briefly in Argentina under Juan Peron, presidents' parties tended not to have two-thirds majorities; indeed, in Chile between 1925 and 1973 no president even had a majority in both houses. The resort to DDA in these two cases may be explained within our framework, perhaps, by the way in which presidents were selected. In Chile most presidents were ultimately elected by cross-party coalitions in Congress, insofar as the Constitution called for a congressional vote between the two top vote winners in the event that no candidate received a majority of the popular vote. In Argentina an electoral college was used. In both cases party politicians had much greater input into the selection of the chief executive than in most presidential systems. However, especially in Chile, the coalition that elected the president was not always the coalition that continued to support the president throughout his term. If an "agency-loss" explanation holds, we would expect that delegation would have been more common early in the president's term than later, after coalitional changes.

The bottom line on the veto is that when assemblies control constitutional design or when they control delegation, the combination of executive veto with decree authority is rare. When the executive is denied a veto, on the other hand, assemblies are much more likely to endow the executive with DDA. H6 is strongly supported.

H7 directly addresses the issue of the endogeneity of institutions by suggesting that where assemblies are involved in creating constitutions, they will not likely endow the executive with CDA unless they can easily take that power back.

Table 10.11 shows the relationship between CDA and the difficulty of amending constitutions. "Legislative Control . . ." is scored "1" only if the constitution can be changed unilaterally by a majority of legislators.[8] If extraordinary majorities or action by any other party (e.g., executive veto, ratification by federal units, or a plebiscite) is required, it is scored "0." The pattern is not as strong as with the veto, but it is clear. When assemblies anticipate that future legislative majorities will be able to revoke executive authority, they are inclined to provide CDA. When assemblies create "stickier" constitutions, they are much less likely to endow the executive so generously.

Brazil '46 is the only constitution in our sample with "easy" amendment procedures and no CDA.[9] Of the three cases of "sticky" constitutions with CDA, we have already noted the unusual case of Argentina in 1994. A similar story

Table 10.11 *Legislative control of the constitutional amendment process and CDA*

		CDA	
		0	1
AMDT	0	Argentina 1853 Chile '25 Costa Rica Poland '92 Russia '91 U.S.A. Venezuela Ukraine	Argentina '94 Brazil '88 Peru '93
	1	Brazil '46	Colombia '68 Colombia '91 Italy Peru '79

could be told about Peru in 1993: Although the Constituent Congress was convoked only after a presidential military coup that represented even more dramatic executive intervention than in Argentina, the Constitution nonetheless imposed new constraints on executive authority. It does, however, continue to provide for CDA even while establishing a more cumbersome constitutional amendment procedure than in the 1979 Constitution. The 1988 Brazilian Constitution provides for CDA and, although it must be scored "0" on our score of legislative control over amendments, it is an unusually assembly-dependent constitution. The majority required to amend is only 60 percent – significantly lower than in any of the other constitutions that receive the same score on this variable. Even more noteworthy is that despite federalism, amendments to the Brazilian Constitution do not require any involvement by the states.[10]

H8 posited that DDA would be more likely as the courts that arbitrate legislative–executive disputes became increasingly independent from the executive. Table 10.12 shows some empirical support for this hypothesis. Often systems in which courts are most independent according to our indicators, DDA is routine in seven. Of seven systems in which courts are only moderately independent, DDA is routine in only three. A more complete test of the hypothesis eludes us because we have only one case of a court highly dependent on the executive: Russia '93. As we would expect, there has been no DDA in this case since the Constitution was adopted, but it is too early to say with any certainty that this new constitutional order is one of no DDA (hence its inclusion in the table only in parentheses).

Two countries in which appointment procedures have changed over time suggest movement in a direction that is consistent with the hypothesis. In the case

Table 10.12 *Judicial independence and DDA*

		DDA	
		0	1
	0	(Russia 1993)	
	1	Brazil '46	Argentina 1853
		Brazil '88	Chile '25
		Chile '89	Peru '79
		U.S.A.	
COURTIND	2	Costa Rica	Colombia '68
		Italy	Colombia '91
		Poland '92	France
			Peru '93
			Russia '91
			Ukraine
			Venezuela

of Russia, the First Republic's Court was elected by the Congress of People's Deputies, there was DDA, the Court was called in to mediate, and it tended to favor the legislature. The 1993 Constitution established a far more executive-centered appointment process, and so far there has been no DDA. Under the 1979 Constitution, Peru's court appointment process provided the executive with a veto over nominations to the Supreme Court and unilateral power to appoint one-third of the members of the Tribunal of Constitutional Guarantees. With moderately independent courts, we saw routine DDA in Peru under the 1979 Charter, but in the wake of conflicts over the scope of DDA, the new Constitution eliminated the executive's role in the Court nomination entirely.

In an assessment of the validity of the hypothesis more fully, it would be helpful to know if there is any variation in the use of DDA in Argentina (under the 1853 Constitution) and Chile '25 with regard to the timing of appointments. For instance, is DDA more likely when a given president or a succession of presidents of the same party has nominated a majority of the court members?[11] We lack the information with which to assess this intertemporal variation in court independence, but we do know that there are contingencies under which a given president is able to nominate and win confirmation for justices of his choosing (cf. Ferreira Rubio and Goretti's chapter on the case of President Menem's packing of the Argentine Supreme Court). Further analysis of how courts are involved in political processes, such as delegation of authority to executives, is tremendously fertile ground for further research.

H9 concerned an interaction between bargaining and agency problems and the role of informational advantages. A central tenet of agency theory is that agents, in performing the tasks for which they were delegated authority, acquire information not readily available to the principals. Thus, informational asymmetries between principals and agents are ubiquitous; what varies is their severity. We hypothesize that the likelihood of DDA would vary with the interaction between the severity of information problems and majority support for the executive. Majority executives should receive DDA in increasing probability as their informational advantages increase; nonmajority executives should receive it with a decreasing probability as their informational advantages decrease.

It is suggestive that in requesting and exercising decree authority, executives frequently make reference to the advantage of locating discretion over complex policy matters in the executive branch, among technicians and experts, rather than among the politicians in the legislature. H9 proposes that relying on executive expertise through DDA should appeal to legislators whose co-partisans control the executive, but such reliance should be unattractive otherwise. In order to test this hypothesis, however, not only would we need comprehensive data on all instances of DDA and of partisan compatibility between assemblies and executives, but we would also need reliable estimates on the asymmetries between executives and legislatures with respect to policy expertise. We are a long way from having sufficient knowledge to test the hypothesis rigorously. Nevertheless, on the grounds that "anecdote" is actually the singular form of "data,"[12] we offer the following observation. Stefoi-Sava (1995) notes an apparently peculiar strategy on the part of the Romanian executive in revealing information to Parliament. Although parliamentary committees are constitutionally empowered to demand information on policy alternatives from the government, the executive "ignores this provision, feeding committees insufficient or irrelevant information" (p. 81). Stefoi-Sava attributes this to the fact that committee seats in the Romanian Parliament are not distributed in proportion to each party's seats in the assembly. As a result, many committees are controlled by majorities in opposition to the executive. "Understandably, the government prefers to confront legislators when they meet in plenary session, where it enjoys majority support" (p. 81). Although the rationale for establishing committees whose membership inaccurately reflects the composition of the Romanian Parliament remains unclear, Stefoi-Sava's account jibes nicely with both halves of H9. The obfuscation of the Romanian executive in confronting hostile committees, compared with its forthrightness in addressing supporters in plenary session, suggests that legislators who would delegate decree authority ought to consider both partisanship and the extent of the Assembly's reliance on the executive for expertise.

We have hypothesized that a number of different independent variables affect the incidence of CDA and DDA. Some of these (e.g., CHAMBERS) show no sign of affecting the dependent variables. For others (e.g., URGENCY, EXECMAJ), we have strong positive evidence from our case studies, but we also face substantial problems of incomplete data. Nevertheless, in order to untangle the relationships among the viable variables for which we *do* have reasonable measures, it is worthwhile to consider a couple of multivariate probit analyses. Table 10.13 shows the strong inverse relationship between the existence of a strong executive

Table 10.13 *Probit analysis of the effects of institutional variables on the existence of CDA among cases in which assemblies were active in constitutional design*

Dependent variable: Equal to 1 if CDA exists; 0 otherwise.

Independent variables	Coefficient	Standard error
Constant	−0.36	0.38
VETO	−1.72	0.82
AMDT	1.01	0.98
PARTYDISC	0.14	0.94
N = 16		

Table 10.14 *Probit analysis of the effects of institutional variables on the existence of DDA*

Dependent variable: Equal to 1 if DDA is routine; 0 if no observations of DDA

Independent variables	Coefficient	Standard error
Constant	1.06	1.49
VETO	−1.74	0.88
PARTYDISC	1.12	1.00
COURTIND	−0.20	0.83
N = 17		

veto and the probability of CDA. In weaker form it also supports the proposition that CDA is more likely when legislative control over the constitutional amendment process is stronger. It shows no evidence, however, of a relationship between the level of party discipline (at least as we have measured it) and the likelihood of CDA.

Table 10.14 confirms that the existence of a veto strongly discourages DDA as well. It further confounds the relationship between party discipline and decree authority by turning up a slight *positive* effect of party discipline on the probability of DDA, although this relationship falls far short of conventional significance levels. Moreover, the probit analysis does not turn up any clear relationship between the independence of the court and the incidence of DDA, despite the many specific examples from case studies that suggest the importance of this variable.

Given the small number of cases and crudeness of our variables, we are cautious about inferring much from the specific probit coefficients or conventional indicators of statistical significance. The results, however, allow us to consider somewhat more information simultaneously than do our series of bivariate tables, and they largely confirm the intuitions from the bivariate analysis presented here. They also illustrate that the hypotheses related to agency problems prove to be somewhat more potent than those related to bargaining problems as explanations for the reliance of legislators on executive decree authority.

The first task of this chapter was to subject the data set we have compiled to a test that uses the hypotheses originally developed in Chapter 1. Generating this sort of broadly comparative data, however, always involves a certain loss of the subtlety of analysis provided by case studies, studies in which specific political contexts of decree can be examined. Moreover, the events of the case studies bring to our attention some issues regarding the use and expansion of decree authority that are not addressed in our hypotheses. It is to these that we turn now.

DISTINCTION BETWEEN EMERGENCY AND DECREE POWER

We have tried to distinguish legislative decree, which we regard as the power of executives to make new law, from both emergency powers and rule making – powers that are granted to most executives in some form but that do not generally entail the ability to act outside the discretion of the legislature. The distinction is important, particularly where decree, emergency, and rule-making actions may all be identified by the same word (e.g., in the Spanish-speaking countries). In most cases the distinction is fairly clear, because what we regard as legislative decree is both subject to different procedural restraints and is used to address substantively different types of issues – from emergency to rule-making actions. This is not always the case, however, as is particularly evident in the Venezuelan case.

Much action referred to as decree in Venezuela does clearly fall outside our definition of legislative decree authority. For example, the ability of presidents to convoke special committees to study policy issues and to draft legislation is not a legislative power unless the recommendations of such committees were to be implemented without legislative action or were necessarily granted privileged procedural treatment by Congress, neither of which is the case. Regarding the ubiquitous restrictions and suspensions of constitutional guarantees described by Crisp, these overwhelmingly involved the suspension of civil and political liberties on the basis of claimed security threats and disturbances by the executive.[13] Even the actions taken under the suspension of Article 96 (economic liberty) focused mainly on specific adjustments of foreign exchange rates and public sector transactions – actions that in many political systems are the domain of executive rule making rather than statute. And as Crisp notes, the grounds for suspending constitutional guarantees could formally have been revoked by congressional majorities at any time.

Nevertheless, beginning especially in December 1993 during the second administration of President Rafael Caldera, the suspensions of both Article 96 and Article 99 (right to private property) have been used in ways that violate the distinction between emergency and legislative powers. Crisp describes a reform of the tax code and the creation of new government agencies under the suspension of Article 96 as well as the confiscation and later the sale of property under the suspension of Article 99, noting that these actions have implications beyond any temporary suspension of rights, because their redistributive effects cannot be expected to revert to the status quo ante once the suspension is over. Not surprisingly, Congress immediately rejected Caldera's confiscatory policies, which resulted from the suspension of private property rights. Were this the end of the story, the distinction between emergency and legislative executive power in Venezuela would have been preserved, and indeed the line would have been conclusively established by congressional action. However, Caldera's explicit disregard for the check imposed on him by Congress and Congress' acquiescence set a new precedent under which the line between emergency and legislative power has been blurred.

CONSTITUTIONAL DESIGN AND SUBSEQUENT ADAPTATION

The melding of emergency and decree power in Venezuela also points to another critical area in which our original framework for understanding decree is open to question. We initially posit that constituent assemblies craft CDA in order to address anticipated bargaining problems in the legislature, and they also do so insofar as they anticipate potential agency loss to the executive. These beginning assumptions are supported by considerable evidence here, but they say nothing about the ways in which constitutional designers fail to anticipate the manner in which their charters can subsequently be manipulated by executives to establish domains of legislative decree authority originally unintended by assemblies.

For example, the Venezuelan Constitution nowhere establishes CDA, but executive actions taken within the suspension of some rights *that are guaranteed* in the Constitution have recently been used in such a way as to make policy as though under CDA. Moreover, the expansion of executive policy-making prerogative under the suspension of rights has occurred slowly over the thirty-five years since the current Constitution was adopted, in ways that could not have been anticipated by the document's original designers. The Brazilian case offers another example. CDA was explicitly adopted by the Constituent Assembly, but the question of whether lapsed decrees could be reissued was not addressed, and it quickly became the subject of controversy. Yet as former President Collor points out, there is good reason for legislators to tolerate the executive's reissuing of decrees in policy areas in which Congress would prefer not to act. Congressional action, supported by the judiciary, has established that the executive may not reissue decrees over the declared opposition of the assembly majority; but legislative inaction is now established as sufficient grounds for the executive to sustain its policy initiatives. The same condition applies in Italy.

Constitutions are not static documents. Their initial provisions establish the grounds on which subsequent procedural struggles will be waged, and in doing so they affect the outcomes of those conflicts. But constituent assemblies cannot perfectly anticipate how the charters they produce will affect the relative capacities of executives and legisatures to initiate policy. Perhaps more importantly, the motivations of executive and legislative actors with respect to procedural powers are relevant to the evolution of constitutions long after their initial adoption. We began with the assumption that executives want as much decree authority as they can get and that constituent assemblies adopt the institutional interests of legislators, granting decree authority according to their expectations about legislative capacity and executive preferences. The chapters on specific countries in this volume show that executives can be expected to persist in their efforts to enlarge their power, but cases like Venezuela, Brazil, Argentina, and Peru also demonstrate that subsequent legislatures may accede to executive expansions. This may be the case because of partisan support for individual executives, because of collective action problems within legislatures, or because of the individual electoral incentives of legislators themselves. The first two of these conditions we have discussed at length. The third one deserves some comment. Legislators' electoral incentives may not always be such as to lead them to defend the prerogatives of the legislature in the policy-making realm. In many systems – especially in presidential regimes – legislators may not be elected in such a way as to give them the incentive to develop and defend the legislature as a forum for representing their constituents' policy preferences. Instead, electoral rules or the existence of party machines that control legislators' future career paths may lead legislators to be relatively unconcerned with voters' policy preferences or the legislative institution itself.[14] Whatever legislators' motivation for tolerating executive decree authority rather than defending the institutional prerogatives of the assembly, the precedents set can have a substantial impact on constitutional evolution and, specifically, on the abilities of executives to make policy by decree.

Of course, acceptance by legislatures of aggressive executive decree is by no means uniform, even within individual countries. Legislative resistance to executive expansionism prompted crises that generated entirely new constitutions in Argentina, Peru, and Russia within the past five years. Perhaps more importantly, the chapters in this volume provide numerous examples in which legislatures, through standard institutional procedures, curb executive initiative without crises. The cases suggest that executives' efforts to establish and expand decree authority can succeed and establish precedents that fundamentally alter our understanding of constitutions, but they also suggest that assemblies with institutional resources to prevent agency loss through decree can use these tools effectively.

CONCLUSION

One central conclusion we draw from this dissection of decree authority is that the conventional interpretation of executive decree – what we call the *usurpation interpretation* – has been overstated. Certainly, there are famous cases in which executives have acted beyond the constitutional limits on their offices under the name of decree or emergency power; and when they did so, they have marginalized legislatures in the process or have even taken direct action against legislatures. It is also the case that where executives exercise influence over the process of constitution building and amending, they tend to secure greater CDA than when assemblies dominate constitution building, and as a result, such executives institutionalize greater discretion over policy relative to legislatures. However, executive decree is not always – or usually – a case of "calling out the tanks," and what we observe as decree is as frequently based on authority delegated from legislatures by statute as on authority found in constitutions. Moreover, when we examine the institutional characteristics of systems where decree is observed, we find patterns consistent with the proposition that decree does not necessarily mean that legislative interests – either policy interests or institutional interests – are being marginalized.

There are good reasons to expect that within the right institutional format, executive decree can be attractive to legislators as a means of expediting action on policy, even without ceding control over policy to the executive. Overall, the empirical evidence here accounts best for the proposition that when assemblies provide decree authority, they generally do so in a manner that mitigates the ability of executives to use that authority to hurt legislative interests. In urging reevaluation of the usurpation interpretation, we do not intend this book to be an apology for executive decree. In other work (Shugart and Carey 1992), we argued that constitutional regimes that endow the executive with greater constitutional powers over legislation result in greater levels of legislative–executive conflict and tend to be less stable than regimes with relatively more prominent legislatures. Although our earlier argument about the perils of too-strong executive power was directed mainly at presidential systems, we believe it can be generalized to parliamentary and hybrid systems as well. Indeed, where executives appear strong or even dominant in parliamentary systems, it is almost always because of consistent, disciplined party support in the legislature. Where assembly support for cabinets has been less consistent, as in Italy, not only are cabinets more unstable, but also decree power becomes a means of coping with executive–legislative impasses.

If strong assemblies – and strong parties within them – are crucial for parliamentary democracy, we suggest that the importance of this variable has been overlooked in the case of presidential democracies. Even an argument that decree authority is universally "bad" would have to come to grips with conditions that promote the resort to presidential decree powers. In this chapter we have tried to call attention to those conditions. A prominent agenda for future research on new democracies is to seek to understand the conditions under which legislative and party leaders would eschew institutionalization of the legislative branch in favor of reliance on executive initiative. If informational advantages for the executive are a prominent cause of recourse to decree authority, it is within the reach of legislatures and parties to develop alternative sources of information by establishing more professional staffs and stronger committee structures. If bargaining problems are a source of reliance on decree authority, why are some rank-and-file legislators more capable of adopting – or more willing to adopt – intraparty and intralegislative devices for mitigating those problems? These are largely unexplored avenues of research in studies of democratization. In conclusion, then, we wish to emphasize the importance of the institutional context in which executive authority is exercised. It is important to know, first, whether executive action necessarily implies executive power; second, whether power is being taken by the executive or given by the legislature; and third, on what terms this is happening.

NOTES

1 In the cases of Colombia '91, Peru '93, Russia '91, and Ukraine, we regard DDA as routine despite the fact that fewer than three executives have existed since the adoption of new constitutions (or over the life of the constitution). In each case, DDA has been exercised on a massive scale by each of the governments that have served. In the Colombia '91 and Peru '93 cases, moreover, regular use of DDA is consistent with precedent from immediately prior constitutions.

2 Or, in the case where upper chamber members are delegates from state-level governments (as in Argentina until 1994, Russia, or the United States until 1913), they are *selected*.

3 Crisp argues that Velásquez was effectively a majority president, owing his presidency to support by both the AD and COPEI parties. On this reading, DDA to Velásquez is simply a continuation of the pattern of DDA to majority presidents and no-DDA to others.

4 That is, a constitution designed by elected representatives might grant the executive decree powers in some policy jurisdictions and veto powers in a separate set of policy areas. Such a combination would be compatible with the hypothesis H5, but we do not explore such complexities here.

5 The Russian constitutional amendments of 1991 established a somewhat similar format, but given the difficulties of convening the entire legislature and getting

it to retract DDA in that context, some analysts regarded DDA in Russia from 1991–93 as effectively equivalent to CDA. For more discussion, see Parrish's chapter.

6 In some cases, the absence of DDA might be explained by constitutional provisions explicitly prohibiting the practice. In both Brazilian constitutions discussed here, for example, the legislature was/is prohibited from delegating legislative authority to the executive. On the other hand, the Brazilian Constitution of 1946 was easily amendable by legislative majority, so that if the legislature found DDA attractive, the obstacles to pursuing this strategy were not insurmountable.

7 On the widespread use of DDA in Chile, see Faúndez (1997); on Argentina, we rely on personal communication with Delia Ferreira Rubio.

8 We include cases in which this majority must be returned in a subsequent legislative session, but with no requirement of intervening elections.

9 This constitution is also the only one in our sample where we have a clear case of an assembly changing the constitutional structure of powers upon the ascendance to office of a president whose policy preferences are very different from those of the assembly majority. Upon the resignation of the incumbent president in 1961, Congress sharply reduced the president's authority over cabinets and weakened the veto.

10 The only institutional protection states have is the requirement for concurrence of 60 percent of the Senate, where each state is represented equally.

11 In the Chilean case, it is especially interesting, insofar as the "court" that ruled on the conformity of decrees to enabling legislation was unipersonal: the Controller General of the Republic. Thus, there should be rather extreme variations in the tendency of the Controller General to support the president, and they should depend upon whether the incumbent president had nominated the incumbent Controller General. Unfortunately, we lack data to test this hunch.

12 For this insight, Carey is compelled to credit Sam Kernell and his graduate seminar in research methodology, although it is likely that Kernell would be far too modest to claim responsibility.

13 In no way do we mean to disregard the importance of the suspension of civil and political liberties. However, consideration of the use of emergency powers to restrict such rights is outside the scope of this book. Our purpose is to evaluate the ability of executives to shape policy by making law through decree.

14 For a discussion of features of electoral rules that inhibit legislators' interest in representing voters' policy preferences, see Shugart and Haggard (1997). For a discussion of how bans on immediate reelection affect legislators' incentives, see Carey (1996 and 1997) and Weldon (1997).

APPENDIX OF CONSTITUTIONAL PROVISIONS REGARDING DECREE

ARGENTINA

CDA

Article 99.3: The Executive Power shall never issue lawmaking decisions. These kinds of measures will be considered null and void.

Only when exceptional circumstances make it impossible to follow the ordinary lawmaking process established by this Constitution, the Executive can issue NUDs insofar as they do not regulate penal, fiscal, electoral or political party matters. NUDs must be decided by the Cabinet assembled and must be countersigned by the Cabinet Chief and the other Ministers.

Within ten days the Cabinet Chief will personally submit the NUD to a Permanent Bicameral Committee which will be composed proportionally according to the political representation of the House and the Senate. The Committee will send its opinion to the floor within ten days. The House and the Senate must immediately consider the opinion. A special act, passed by the positive vote of the majority of the members of the House and the Senate, will determine the proceedings and effects of the Congress intervention in this matter.

DDA

Article 76: Legislative delegation to the Executive is forbidden except in the case of matters of administration and public emergency, with a limited time period for its effectiveness and within the standards for the delegation of authority established by Congress.

The expiration of the time period mentioned above will not cause the revision of the legal relations born under the rules issued as a consequence of the legislative delegation.

RUSSIA

CONSTITUTION OF 1978 (AS AMENDED 1991)

Article 121(8): The President of the Russian Federation issues decrees and orders on questions falling within his competence, and monitors their implementation. The implementation of decrees of the President of the Russian Federation is obligatory on all the territory of the Russian Federation.

Decrees of the President of the Russian Federation cannot contradict the constitution or laws of the Russian Federation. If a presidential act contradicts the Constitution or a law, the Constitution or law takes precedence.

CONSTITUTION OF 1993

Article 90:

(Section 1) The President of the Russian Federation issues decrees and orders.

(Section 2) The implementation of decrees and orders of the President of the Russian Federation is mandatory throughout the territory of the Russian Federation.

(Section 3) Decrees and orders of the President of the Russian Federation should not contradict the Constitution of the Russian Federation or federal laws.

PERU

CONSTITUTION OF 1933

Of General Relevance
Article 166: The acts of government and administration of the President of the Republic are countersigned by the Minister of the [respective] Sector. Without [fulfilling] this requirement they are null and void.

Rule making
Article 154: The President of the Republic has the following competences:

(Section 8) To issue regulations for laws without transgressing or perverting them and, with this same restriction, to dictate decrees and resolutions.

DDA
Article 40: The State recognizes the freedom of commerce and industry. The law will determine the requirements to which its exercise is subject and the guarantees that it is accorded. When the public safety or necessity may require it, the law can establish limitations or exemptions to the aforesaid exercise, or au-

thorize the Executive Branch to establish these, but in no case may such restrictions have a personal nor confiscatory character.

Article 49: Under extraordinary circumstances of social necessity, it is possible to enact laws, or to authorize the Executive Branch to adopt provisions, tending to lower the price of basic goods. In none of these cases will goods be expropriated without the appropriate indemnification.

Emergency Authority

Article 70: When the security of the State may require it, the Executive Branch can suspend, totally or partially, in all or in part of the national territory, the guarantees proclaimed in Articles 56, 61, 62, 67 and 68. If the suspension of guarantees is decreed while Congress is in session, the Executive Branch will immediately give it notice of the action.

The period during which guarantees are suspended will not exceed thirty days. The extension requires a new decree.

The law will determine the powers of the Executive Branch during the suspension of guarantees.

CONSTITUTION OF 1979

Of General Relevance

Article 87, para. 1: The Constitution prevails over any other legal norm. The law [prevails] over any other norm of inferior rank, and so on successively in accordance with the position of each in the legal hierarchy. [Supremacy of Constitution. Supremacy of Laws Over *Decretos Supremos, Resoluciones Supremas*, and lower-level decrees.]

Article 213: Acts of the President of the Republic that do not have ministerial countersignatures are null and void. [Relevant for all presidential decrees.]

Rule making

Article 211: The President of the Republic has the following competences and obligations:

> (Section 11) To exercise the authority to issue regulations for laws without transgressing or perverting them; and, within such limits, to dictate decrees and resolutions.

DDA

Article 188: The Congress may delegate to the Executive Branch the power to legislate, by means of *decretos legislativos*, on the matters and until the deadline that the authorizing law specifies.

With regard to their promulgation, publication, scope and effects, *decretos legislativos* are subject to the same standards that apply to laws.

Article 211: The President of the Republic has the following competences and obligations:

> (Section 10) To dictate *decretos legislativos* with the force of law, following delegation of [legislative] powers on the part of Congress, and with the duty to give notice to the latter.

CDA

Article 104: The President of the Republic may, in matters of his (her) exclusive competence, contract or ratify international agreements with foreign states or international organizations or adhere to these without the prior requirement of approval by Congress. In any event s(he) must give immediate notice to the latter.

Article 132: In situations of grave crisis or of emergency, the State may intervene in economic activity with transitory measures of extraordinary character.

Article 198: If a vote is not taken on the budget bill before 15 December, the proposal of the Executive Branch takes effect, with the latter promulgating it by means of a *decreto legislativo*.

Article 200, para. 2: The audit of the executed budget is examined and approved or rejected in the same ordinary legislative session in which it is presented or in the following one, in accordance with the procedure indicated for the budget.

Article 211: The President of the Republic has the following competences and obligations:

> (Section 20) To administer Public Finance; to negotiate loans; and to dictate extraordinary measures on economic and financial matters, when so required by the national interest and with the duty to give notice to the Congress.
>
> (Section 22) To regulate customs duties.

Emergency Power

Article 211: The President of the Republic has the following competences and obligations:

> (Section 18) To adopt the measures necessary for the defense of the Republic, the integrity of its territory and its sovereignty in the case of aggression.

Article 231: The President of the Republic, with the agreement of the Council of Ministers, decrees the states of exception that are contemplated in this article for a specific period in all or part of the country, giving notice to the Congress or to the Permanent Committee:

> a. State of emergency, in the case of disturbance of the peace or of the internal order, of catastrophe or of grave circumstances that affect the life of the

Nation. In this eventuality, it is possible to suspend the constitutional guarantees regarding personal freedom and security, the inviolability of the domicile, [and] the freedom of assembly and of movement in the country that are contemplated in points 7, 9 and 10 of Article 2 and in point 20-g of the same Article 2. Under no circumstances can the sentence of exile be imposed. The duration of the state of emergency does not exceed sixty days. The extension requires a new decree. Under a state of emergency, the Armed Forces assume control of internal order when the President of the Republic so stipulates.

b. State of siege, in the case of invasion, foreign war or civil war or imminent danger that these may occur, with enumeration of the personal guarantees that remain in effect. The applicable period does not exceed forty-five days. Upon the promulgation of a state of siege the Congress convenes with its full rights. The extension requires the approval of Congress.

Judicial Review

Article 236: In the case of incompatibility between a constitutional norm and an ordinary legal one, the Judge gives precedence to the former. Similarly, s(he) gives precedence to the legal norm over any other subordinate norm. [Basis for judicial review in regular courts.]

Article 298: The Tribunal of Constitutional Guarantees has jurisdiction in all of the territory of the Republic. It is competent:

1. To declare, upon the petition of a party, the partial or total unconstitutionality of laws, *decretos legislativos*, regional norms of a general character and municipal ordinances that contravene the Constitution in form or in substance. And

2. To adjudicate as a court of review decisions denying the action of habeas corpus and the action of *amparo*, once all appeals are exhausted in the regular courts.

CONSTITUTION OF 1993

Of General Relevance

Article 51: The Constitution prevails over any legal norm; the law over norms of inferior rank, and so on successively. [Supremacy of Constitution. Supremacy of Laws Over *Decretos Supremos, Resoluciones Supremas*, and lower-level decrees.]

Article 120: Acts of the President of the Republic that lack ministerial countersignatures are null and void.

Rule making

Article 118: The following pertain to the President of the Republic:

(Section 8) To exercise the authority to issue regulations for laws without transgressing or perverting them; and, within such limits, to dictate decrees and resolutions.

Article 123: The Congress has the following authorities:

(Section 23) To exercise the remaining essential attributes of legislative power.

DDA
Article 101: The Permanent Committee of Congress has the following competences:

(Section 4) To exercise the delegation of legislative power that the Congress may grant it. It is not possible to delegate to the Permanent Committee matters regarding constitutional amendments, nor the approval of international treaties, organic laws, the Budget Law and the Law of the *Cuenta General* [executed budget] of the Republic.

Article 104: The Congress may delegate to the Executive Branch the power to legislate, by means of *decretos legislativos*, on the specific matter and for the stated term established in the authorizing law.

Those matters that are indelegable to the Permanent Committee [of Congress] may not be delegated [to the Executive Branch].

With regard to their promulgation, publication, scope and effects, *decretos legislativos* are subject to the same standards that apply to laws.

The President of the Republic gives notice (*dar cuenta*) of each *decreto legislativo* to the Congress or the Permanent Committee. [DDA]

CDA
Article 56: Treaties must be approved by the Congress before their ratification by the President of the Republic, if they deal with the following matters:

1. Human Rights.
2. Sovereignty, domain or integrity of the State.
3. National Defense.
4. Financial obligations of the State.

The Congress also must approve treaties that create, modify or suppress taxes; those that necessitate modification or repeal of any law; and those that require legislative measures for their implementation.

Article 57: The President of the Republic may contract or ratify treaties or adhere to these without the requirement of prior approval by Congress in matters not covered by the previous article. In all these cases, he must give notice to the Congress.

When the treaty affects constitutional provisions, it must be approved by the same procedure that applies to amending the Constitution, before being ratified by the President of the Republic.

The abrogation of treaties is a prerogative of the President of the Republic, who has the duty to give notice to the Congress. In the case of treaties subject to approval by the Congress, abrogation requires its prior consent. [Contrast with CDA for international agreements under Article 104 of the 1979 Constitution.]

Article 80: If the signed Budget Law is not sent to the Executive Branch by 30 November, the latter's Proposal, which is promulgated by a *decreto legislativo*, takes effect.

Article 81: The audit of the executed budget is examined and evaluated by a review committee [of Congress] within the ninety days following its presentation. The Congress [then] expresses an opinion in a period of 30 days. If there is not a resolution by Congress during the stated period, the report of the review committee is forwarded to the Executive Branch, in order that the latter may promulgate a *decreto legislativo* that contains the audit of the executive budget.

Article 118: The following pertain to the President of the Republic:

(Section 19) To dictate extraordinary measures, by means of *Decretos de Urgencia*, with the force of law, on economic and financial matters, when so required by the national interest and with the duty to give notice to the Congress. The Congress may modify or annul the previously mentioned *decretos de urgencia*.

(Section 20) To regulate customs duties.

Article 135: During this interregnum [between the dissolution of Congress and the convening of a new Congress after elections], the Executive Branch legislates by means of *decretos de urgencia*, about which it gives notice to the Permanent Committee of Congress so that the latter may scrutinize them and forward them to the Congress, once the latter is installed.

DDA + CDA

Article 74: Taxes are created, modified or repealed, or an exemption is established, exclusively by law or *decreto legislativo* in the case of a delegation of power, except for customs duties and rates, which are regulated by means of *decreto supremo*.

. . . .

Decretos de Urgencia may not include matters of taxation. . . .

Emergency Authority

Article 118: The following pertain to the President of the Republic:

(Section 15) To adopt the measures necessary for the defense of the Republic, of the integrity of its territory and of the sovereignty of the State.

Article 137: The President of the Republic, with the agreement of the Council of Ministers, may decree the states of exception that are contemplated in this article for a specific period in all of the national territory or in part of it, giving notice to the Congress or to the Permanent Committee:

a. State of emergency, in the case of disturbance of the peace or of the internal order, of catastrophe or of grave circumstances that affect the life of the Nation. In this eventuality, it is possible to restrict or suspend the exercise of the constitutional rights regarding personal freedom and security, the inviolability of the domicile, and the freedom of assembly and of movement in the country contained in points 9, 11 and 12 of Article 2 and in point 24, subpoint f of the same article. Under no circumstances can anyone be exiled.

The duration of the state of emergency does not exceed sixty days. Its extension requires a new decree. Under a state of emergency the Armed Forces assume control of internal order if the President of the Republic so stipulates.

b. State of siege, in the case of invasion, foreign war, civil war, or imminent danger that these may occur, with reference to those fundamental rights whose exercise is not restricted or suspended. The applicable period does not exceed forty-five days. Upon the promulgation of a state of siege, the Congress convenes with its full rights. The extension requires the approval of Congress.

Judicial Review
Article 138: In any [judicial] process, if an incompatibility exists between a constitutional norm and a legal norm, the judges are to give precedence to the former. Similarly, they are to give precedence to the legal norm over any other norm of inferior rank. [Basis for judicial review in regular courts.]

Article 200: The following are constitutional guarantees:

1. habeas corpus
2. *amparo*
3. habeas data
4. the action of unconstitutionality, which is directed against norms that have the rank of law: laws, *decretos legislativos, decretos de urgencia,* treaties, rules of Congress, regional norms of a general character and municipal ordinances that might contravene the Constitution in form or in substance.
5. the *acción popular,* which is directed, on account of violations of the Constitution and of the law, against regulations, administrative norms and reso-

lutions, as well as decrees of a general character, whatever be the authority from which they emanate.

6. the action of *cumplimiento,* which is directed against any authority or functionary unwilling to respect a legal norm or an administrative act, without prejudice to his legal responsibilities.

An organic law regulates the exercise of these guarantees and the effects of the declaration that norms are unconstitutional or illegal.

The exercise of the actions of habeas corpus and of *amparo* are not suspended while the regimes of exception, to which Article 137 of the Constitution refers, are in force.

When actions of this nature are interposed with respect to restricted or suspended rights, the competent organ having jurisdiction examines the reasonableness and proportionality of the restrictive act. It is not within the judge's competence to question the declaration of a state of emergency nor of siege.

Article 202: The following pertain to the Constitutional Tribunal:

1. To adjudicate, with exclusive jurisdiction, the action of unconstitutionality.
2. To adjudicate, as the court of last appeal, decisions denying habeas corpus, *amparo,* habeas data and the action of *cumplimiento.*
3. To adjudicate conflicts of competences, or of attributes assigned by the Constitution, in accordance with the law.

VENEZUELA

Rule-making Authority
Article 190:
The faculties and obligations of the President of the Republic are . . .

(Section 10) To regulate totally or partially the laws, without altering their spirit, purpose, and logic.

DDA

Article 190: The faculties and obligations of the President of the Republic are . . .

(Section 8) To decree extraordinary measures on issues of economics or finance when required by the public interest and having been authorized to take action by a special law.

(Section 11) To decree, in cases of urgency, during congressional recess, the creation and endowment of new public services, or the modification or suspension of existing services, as authorized by the permanent commission of Congress.

Emergency Authority

Article 190: The faculties and obligations of the President of the Republic are . . . (Section 6) To declare a state of emergency and decree the restriction or suspension of constitutional guarantees.

Article 240: The President of the Republic shall be able to declare a state of emergency in case of internal or external conflict, or when there exist reasons to believe one or the other will occur.

Article 241: In case of emergency, of disturbance that could upset the peace of the Republic or of grave circumstances that affect social and economic life, the President of the Republic shall be able to restrict or suspend constitutional guarantees, or some of them, with the exception of those established in Article 58 and in sections 3 and 7 of Article 60.

The decree shall specify the reasons on which it is based, the guarantees that are restricted or suspended, and whether it applies to all or part of the national territory.

The restriction or suspension of guarantees does not interrupt the functioning nor affect the prerogatives of the other organs of National Power.

Article 244: If there exist reasons to fear imminent disturbance of public order, which does not justify the restriction or suspension of constitutional guarantees, the President of the Republic in Council of Ministers, shall be able to adopt the necessary measures to avoid that such disturbances occur.

These measures are limited to the detention or confinement of the relevant individuals, and must be submitted to the consideration of Congress or its Permanent Commission within ten days after their adoption. If these measures are declared unjustified, they shall cease immediately; otherwise, they are maintained up to a maximum of 90 days. The law shall regulate the exercise of this authority.

ITALY

CDA

Article 77: The Government may not, unless properly delegated by the Chambers, issue decrees having the value of ordinary laws.

When, in exceptional cases of necessity and urgency, the Government issues, on its own responsibility, provisional measures having [the] force of law, it shall on the same day submit them for conversion into law to the Chambers which, even if they have been dissolved, are expressly summoned for that purpose and shall meet within five days.

Decrees lose effect as of the date of issue if they are not converted into law within sixty days of their publication. The Chambers may, however, approve laws to regulate legal questions arising out of decrees not yet converted into law.

BRAZIL

CDA

Article 62: In relevant and urgent cases, the President of the Republic may adopt provisional measures with the force of law and shall submit them to the National Congress immediately, and if Congress is in recess, a special session shall be called to meet within five days.

Provisional measures shall lose effectiveness from the date of their issuance, if they are not converted into law within a period of thirty days from their publication and the National Congress shall regulate the legal relations arising therefrom.

FRANCE (ENGLISH TRANSLATIONS FOUND IN PIERCE [1968; APPENDIX 1]).

CDA

Article 16: When the institution of the Republic, the independence of the nation, the integrity of its territory or the fulfillment of its international agreements are threatened in a grave and immediate manner, and when the regular functioning of the constitutional public authorities is interrupted, the President of the Republic takes the measures required by these circumstances, after official consultation with the Premier, the Presidents of the Assemblies, and the Constitutional Council.

He informs the nation of them by a message.

These measures must be inspired by the purpose of securing for the constitutional public authorities, in the shortest time, the means of carrying out their mission. The Constitutional Council is consulted concerning them.

Parliament meets by right.

The National Assembly may not be dissolved during the exercise of emergency powers.

Rule making

Article 34: Laws are voted by Parliament.

Laws establish the rules concerning:

- civil rights and the basic guarantees granted to the citizens for the exercise of public liberties; the obligations imposed by national defense on the person and property of the citizens;
- the nationality, status, and legal situation of persons, marriage, inheritance, and gifts;
- the definition of crimes and misdemeanors as well as the penalties applicable to them; criminal procedure; amnesty; the creation of new judicial systems; and the status of magistrates;

- the base, the rate, and the methods of collection of all kinds of taxes; the system of issuing currency.

Laws also establish the rules concerning:

- the electoral system for the parliamentary assemblies and local assemblies;
- the creation of categories of public organizations;
- the basic guarantees granted to the civil servants and military personnel of the state;
- the nationalization of enterprises and the transfer of the property of enterprises from the public sector to the private sector.

Laws determine the fundamental principles:

- of the general organization of national defense;
- of the free administration of local communities, their jurisdiction, and their resources;
- of education;
- of the property system; of property rights; and of civil and commercial obligations;
- of the right to work; of trade union rights; and of social security.

The finance laws determine the resources and expenses of the state under the conditions and with the provisos specified by an organic law.

Program laws determine the objectives of the economic and social activity of the state.

The provisions of this article may be specified and completed by an organic law.

Article 37: Matters other than those which are in the domain of the laws are in the domain of rule making *{ont un caractère réglementaire}*.

Legislative measures concerning these matters may be modified by decrees issued after consultation with the Council of State. Those legislative measures which may be passed after this Constitution has gone into effect may be modified by decree only if the Constitutional Council has declared that they are in the rule-making domain by virtue of the preceding paragraph.

DDA

Article 38: The Government may, in order to carry out its program, ask Parliament to authorize it to issue ordinances, for a limited period, concerning matters which are normally in the domain of the laws.

The ordinances are enacted in the Council of Ministers after consultation with the Council of State. They take effect upon their publication, but become null and void if the Government bill for ratification is not placed before Parliament before the date set by the authorizing law.

At the expiration of the period mentioned in the first paragraph of this article, the ordinances concerning matters which are in the legislative domain may be modified only by law.

CDA

Article 49: The Premier, after deliberation by the Council of Ministers, engages the responsibility of the Government before the National Assembly on its program or, possibly, on a declaration of general policy.

The National Assembly questions the responsibility of the Government by voting a motion of censure. Such a motion is admissible only if it is signed by at least one-tenth of the members of the National Assembly. The vote may not take place less than forty-eight hours after the motion has been introduced. The only votes counted are those favoring the motion of censure, which may be adopted only by a majority of the members comprising the Assembly. If the motion of censure is rejected, its signers may not propose a new one during the same session, except in the case described in the paragraph below.

The Premier may, after deliberation by the Council of Ministers, engage the responsibility of the Government before the National Assembly on the vote of a text. In this case, the text is considered adopted unless a motion of censure, introduced within the next 24 hours, is adopted in the conditions set forth in the preceding paragraph.

The Premier may ask the Senate for approval of a declaration of general policy.

Agenda Authority

Article 44: Members of Parliament and the Government have the right to move amendments.

After the opening of the debate, the Government may oppose the examination of any amendment which has not previously been submitted to the committee.

If the Government requests it, the Assembly considering a bill decides by a single vote on all or part of the text under discussion, retaining only the amendments proposed or accepted by the Government.

Judicial Review

Article 41: If it appears in the course of the legislative procedure that a parliamentary bill or amendment is not in the domain of the laws or is contrary to a delegation of power granted pursuant to Article 38, the Government may oppose it as inadmissible.

In the case of disagreement between the Government and the President of the Assembly concerned, the Constitutional Council, upon the request of either party, decides the question within a period of eight days.

REFERENCES

Abad Yupanqui, Samuel B. 1990. "La medida cautelar en la acción de amparo," *Derecho* 43–44 (December): 373–434.

Abad Yupanqui, Samuel B., and Carolina Garcés Peralta. 1993. "El gobierno de Fujimori: antes y después del golpe." *Del golpe de estado a la nueva constitución.* Serie: Lecturas sobre temas constitucionales 9. Lima: Comisión Andina de Juristas, pp. 85–190.

Abente, Diego. 1990. "The Political Economy of Tax Reform in Venezuela," *Comparative Politics* 22 (January): 199–216.

Aberbach, Joel. 1990. *Keeping a Watchful Eye: The Politics of Congressional Oversight.* Washington, DC: Brookings Institution.

Alfonsin, R. 1994. *La reforma constitutional de 1994.* Buenos Aires: Union Civica Radical.

Ames, Barry. 1995. "Electoral Strategy under Open-List Proportional Representation," *American Journal of Political Science* 39, 2: 406–33.

Assembléia Nacional Constituinte. 1988. Diárro da Assembléio Nacional Constituinte. Brasìlìa. March 18.

Avril, Pierre. 1981. "Le parlement législateur," *Revue française de science politique* 31: 15–31.

Ayala Carao, Carlos M. 1992. *El Régimen Presidencial en América Latina y los Planteamientos para su Reforma (Evaluación y crítica de la propuesta de un Primer Ministro para Venezuela).* Caracas: Universidad Católica Andrés Bello.

Baaklini, Abdo I. 1992. *The Brazilian Legislature and Political System.* Westport, CT: Greenwood Press.

Bacalao Octavio, Domingo Alfonso. 1973. *Notas Sobre la Potestad Reglamentaria.* Valencia: Universidad de Carabobo.

Badeni, G. 1990. "Los decretos de necesidad y urgencia," *El Derecho* 138:926.

Baglini, R., A. D'Ambrosio, and H. Orlandi. 1993. *Juicio a la Corte.* Buenos Aires: Editorial Austral.

Baldez, Lisa, and John M. Carey. Forthcoming. "Pinochet's Constitution and Exec-
     utive Agenda Control: Budgetmaking in Chile." In Mathew D. McCubbins
     and Stephan Haggard (eds.), *The Structure of Fiscal and Regulatory Policy*.
     Washington, DC: The World Bank.
Balladur, Edouard. 1989. *Passion et longueur de temps*. Paris: Fayard.
Barbagli, M., and P. Corbetta. 1981. "La Svolta del PCI," *Il Mulino* (January–Feb-
     ruary): 95–130.
Baron, David P., and John A. Ferejohn. 1989. "Bargaining in Legislatures," *American
     Political Science Review* 89: 1181–206.
Barr, Stephen. 1993. "White House Shifts Role in Rule-Making," *Washington Post*
     (October 1, 1993).
Barrientos Silva, Aurea Violeta. 1990. "Funcionamiento de la delegación de facultades
     legislativas del Congreso al Ejecutivo en el Perú desde la Constitución de
     1979." Bachelors Thesis, Catholic University.
Basadre, Jorge. 1983. *Historia de la República del Perú*, 7th Edition. XI Volumes.
     Lima: Editorial Universitaria.
Belin, Laura. 1995. "High Stakes at Russia's Ostankino TV," *Transition* 1, 28 (April):
     1–8.
Bernales, Enrique. 1971. "El derecho de observar las leyes en la Constitución de
     1933," *Derecho* 29: 20–51.
     1981. *Parlamento, estado y sociedad*. Lima: DESCO.
     1984. *El parlamento por dentro*. Lima: DESCO.
     1989. "El funcionamiento del sistema político de la Constitución de 1979." In
     La Constitución diez años después, pp. 137–166. Lima: Fundación Friedrich
     Naumann.
     1990. *Parlamento y Democracia*. Lima: Editorial Hipatia.
Bianchi, A. 1991. "La Corte Suprema ha establecido su tesis oficial sobre la emer-
     gencia económica," *La Ley* C: 141.
Bidart Campos, G. 1988. *Tratado Elemental de Derecho Constitucional Argentino*. Buenos
     Aires: Ediar.
     1991. "El fallo de la Corte sobre el 'Plan Bonex.' El amparo: airoso; la propiedad:
     desprotegida; la Constitución: entre paréntesis," *El Derecho*: 141: 519.
Boloña Behr, Carlos. 1993. *Cambio de rumbo: El programa económico para los '90*. Lima:
     Instituto de Economía de Libre Mercado.
Bresser Pereira, L., J. Maravall and A. Przeworski. 1993. *Economic Reforms in New
     Democracies: A Social-Democratic Approach*. New York: Cambridge University
     Press.
Brewer-Carías, Allan R. 1980. *Evolución del Régimen Legal de la Economía 1939–1979*.
     Caracas: Editorial Jurídica Venezolana.
     1985a. *Las Constituciones de Venezuela*. San Cristóbal: Universidad Católica del
     Táchira.
     1985b. *Instituciones Políticos y Constitucionales*. Caracas: Universidad Católica del
     Táchira and Editorial Jurídica Venezolana.
Brewer-Carías, Allan R. 1989. "Consideraciones sobre la suspensión or restrición de
     las garantías constitucionales," *Revista de Derecho Pœblico* 37 (Enero – Marzo):
     5–31.
Bush, Keith. 1991. "Yeltsin's Economic Reform Program," *RFE/RL Report on the
     USSR* (November 15): 1–2.

1992. "Russian Privatization Program Accelerated," *RFE/RL Research Report* 1 (July 24).

Bustamante Belaunde, Alberto. 1981. "Facultades legislativas: ¿Ocaso del Parlamento?" *La Revista* 6 (October): 47–51.

Caldera, Rafael. 1981. "El Regimen Presidencial en la Constitución Venezolana." In *Libro Homenaje al Profesor Antonio Moles Caubet*, pp. 17–24. Caracas: Universidad Central de Venezuela.

Camera dei Deputati. 1985. *La decretazione d'urgenza.* Roma.

1987. *Notiziario della Camera dei Deputati.* Roma.

1994a. *Notiziario della Camera dei Deputati: Compendio Statistico dalla I alla XI Legislatura.* Roma.

1994b. *Atti parlamentari dell'Assemblea – Discussioni.* Vol. 3. Roma.

1995. *Notiziario della Camera dei Deputati.* XII Legislatura. N. 10 (April–May). Roma.

Câmara dos Deputados. 1993. "Leis de 1964 a 1992," mimeo. Brasilia: Câmara dos Deputados, Seção de Sinopse.

Carey, John M. 1996. *Term Limits and Legislative Representation.* New York: Cambridge University Press.

1997. "Strong Parties for a Limited Office: Presidentialism and Political Parties in Costa Rica." In Scott Mainwaring and Matthew S. Shugart (eds.), *Presidentialism and Democracy in Latin America*, pp. 119–224. New York: Cambridge University Press.

Carey, John M., and Matthew S. Shugart. 1995. "Incentives to Cultivate a Personal Vote: A Rank Ordering of Electoral Formulas," *Electoral Studies* 14, 4: 417–439.

Carter, John R., and David Schap. 1987. "Executive Veto, Legislative Override, and Structure-Induced Equilibrium," *Public Choice* 52: 227–44.

Cassagne, J. C. 1991. "Sobre la fundamentación y los límites de la potestad reglamentaria de necesidad y urgencia," *La Ley* E: 1179.

Cassese, Sabino. 1980. *Esiste un governo in Italia?* Roma: Officina Edizioni.

Casu, A. 1986. "Voto segreto e voto palese nei regolamenti dal 1948 ai nostrigiorni," *Rivista trimestrale di diritto pubblico* 2: 553–593.

Chirinos Soto, Enrique. 1991. *Cuestiones constitucionales.* Lima: Fundación M. J. Bustamante de la Fuente.

Collor de Mello, Fernando. 1993. Interview with author, Brasília (July 29).

Comisión Presidencial para la Reforma del Estado. 1985. *Analisis de Los Decretos Sustentados en la Restricción del Derecho al Libre Ejercicio de la Actividad Económica a Partir de 1961.* Caracas: COPRE.

Congressional Quarterly. 1993. *Congress and the Nation*, vol. 8, 1989–92. Washington, DC: CQ Press.

Conaghan, Catherine M., and James M. Malloy. 1994. *Unsettling Statecraft: Democracy and Neoliberalism in the Central Andes.* Pittsburgh: University of Pittsburgh Press.

Conaghan, Catherine M., James M. Malloy, and Luis A. Abugattas. 1990. "Business and the Boys: The Politics of Neoliberalism in the Central Andes," *Latin American Research Review* 25, 1: 3–29.

Coppedge, Michael. 1994. "Venezuela: Democratic Despite Presidentialism." In Juan J. Linz and Arturo Valenzuela (eds.), *The Failure of Presidential Democracy:*

The Case of Latin America, 322–47. Baltimore: Johns Hopkins University Press.

Corte Costituzionale. 1988. *Raccolta ufficiale delle sentenze e ordinanze della Corte Costituzionale*. Vol. LXXXII. Roma.

Cotler, Julio. 1995. "Political Parties and the Problems of Democratic Consolidation in Peru." In Scott Mainwaring and Timothy R. Scully (eds.), *Building Democratic Institutions: Party Systems in Latin America*, pp. 323–53. Stanford, CA: Stanford University Press.

Cotta, Maurizio. 1991. "Il Parlamento Nel Sistema Politico Italiano: Mutamenti Istituzionali e Cicli Politici," *Quaderni Costituzionali* XI, 2 (August): 218–223.

 1994. "The Rise and Fall of the 'Centrality' of the Italian Parliament: Transformations of the Executive–Legislature Subsystem after the Second World War." In Gary Copeland and Samuel Patterson (eds.), *Parliaments in the Modern World*, pp. 58–84. Ann Arbor: University of Michigan Press.

Cova, J. A. 1993. *27-N: Cita con la Historia*. Caracas: Vadell Hermanos.

Crawford, Vince, and Joel Sobel. 1982. "Strategic Information Transmission," *Econometrica* 50: 1431–52.

Crisp, Brian F. 1994. "Limitations to Democracy in Developing Capitalist Societies: The Case of Venezuela," *World Development* 22 (October): 1491–1509.

Crisp, Brian F. 1997a. *El Control Institucional de la Participación en la Democracia Venezolana*. Caracas: Editorial Jurídica Venezolana.

 1997b. "Presidential Behavior in a System with Strong Parties: Venezuela, 1958–1995." In Scott Mainwaring and Matthew S. Shugart (eds.), *Presidentialism and Democracy in Latin America*, pp. 160–98. New York: Cambridge University Press.

Cronin, Thomas E., (ed.). 1989. *Inventing the American Presidency*. Lawrence: University Press of Kansas.

CSJN. 1990. "Peralta, Luis c/ Estado Nacional, Ministerio de Economía – Banco Central," *La Ley* C: 141.

 1993. "Video Cable Comunicación SA c/ Instituto Nacional de Cinematografía."

 1995. "Video Club Dreams c/ Instituto Nacional de Cinematografia."

Dahl, Robert. 1994. "A Democratic Dilemma: System Effectiveness and Citizen Participation," *Political Science Quarterly* 109, 2: 23–34.

Debbasch, Charles, J. Bourdon, J. M. Pontier, and J. C. Ricci. 1988. *La Vᵉ Republique*. Paris: Economica.

Delgado-Guembes, César. 1992. *Qué parlamento queremos*. Lima: Cultural Cuzco.

 1995. Personal communication with the authors.

Della Sala, Vincent. 1988. "Government by Decree: The Craxi Government and the Use of Decree Legislation in the Italian Parliament." In Raffaella Y. Nanetti, Robert Leonardi, and Piergiorgio Corbetta (eds.), *Italian Politics: A Review*, vol. 2. London and New York: Pinter Publishers.

 1993. "The Italian Committees," *Legislative Studies Quarterly* XVIII, 2 (May): 157–183.

Departamento Intersindical de Assessoria Parlamentar. 1993. *A cabeça do Congresso: quem é quem narevisão constitucional*. São Paulo: Editora Oboré.

De Soto, Hernando. 1989. *The Other Path: The Invisible Revolution in the Third World*. New York: Harper & Row.

De Soto, Hernando, and Orsini, Deborah. 1991. "Overcoming Underdevelopment," *Journal of Democracy* 2, 2: 105–13.

Destler, I. M. 1980. *Making Foreign Economic Policy.* Washington, DC: Brookings Institution.

Diamanti, Ilvo, and Renato Mannheimer. 1994. *Milano a Roma: Guida all Italia elettorale del 1994.* Roma: Donzelli.

Diermeier, Daniel, and Timothy Feddersen. 1995. "Coherence in Legislatures: Procedural and Policy Coalitions." Working Paper in Mathematical Economics and Decision Sciences. Evanston, IL: Northwestern University.

Di Palma, Giuseppe. 1977. *Surviving Without Governing.* Berkeley: University of California Press.

Di Scala, S. 1988. *Renewing Italian Socialism: Nenni to Craxi.* New York: Oxford University Press.

Djelic, Bozidar. 1992. "Mass Privatization in Russia: The Role of Vouchers," Radio Free Europe/Radio Liberty *Research Report* 1, 16 (October).

Djelic, Bozidar, and Tsukanova, Natalia. 1993. "Voucher Auctions: A Crucial Step toward Privatization," *RFE/RL Research Report* 2, 23 (July): 10–18.

Duverger, Maurice. 1987. *La cohabitation des français.* Paris: PUF.

Economist 17. 1994. "More Power to the Boss." (December): 45–46.

Eguiguren, Francisco. 1989. "El estado de emergencia y su aplicación enla experiencia constitucional peruana 1980–1988." In *La Constitución diez años después*; 261–287. Lima: Fundación Friedrich Naumann.

1990a. "Las situaciones de emergencia y su tratamiento en la Constitución Peruana de 1979," *Lecturas sobre temas constitucionales* 5: 15–47. Lima: Comisión Andina de Juristas.

1990b. *Los retos de una democracia insuficiente: Diez años de régimen constitucional en el Perú 1980–1990.* Lima: Comisión Andina de Juristas and Fundación Friedrich Naumann.

1994. "La legislación delegada y los decretos de urgencia." In *La Constitución de 1993: Análisis y comentarios*, pp. 177–191. Serie: Lecturas sobre temas constitucionales 10. Lima: Comisión Andina de Juristas.

Farrell, Joseph. 1987. "Cheap Talk, Coordination and Entry," *Rand Journal of Economics* 19: 34–9.

Farrell, Joseph, and Robert Gibbons. 1989. "Cheap Talk Can Matter in Bargaining," *Journal of Economic Theory* 48: 221–37.

Faúndez, Julio. 1997. "In Defense of Presidentialism: The Case of Chile, 1932–1970." In Scott Mainwaring and Matthew S. Shugart (eds.), *Presidentialism and Democracy in Latin America*, pp. 300–20. New York: Cambridge University Press.

Fenno, Richard. 1978. *Homestyle: House Members in Their Districts.* Boston: Little, Brown.

Fernandez, Eduardo. 1976. *La Batalla de la Oposición.* Caracas: Ediciones Nueva Política.

Fernández-Maldonado Castro, Guillermo, and Jorge Melo-Vega Castro. 1989. "Las propuestas de reforma constitucional." In *La Constitución diez años después*, pp. 359–427. Lima: Fundación Friedrich Naumann.

Fernández Segado, Francisco. 1994. "El nuevo ordenamiento constitucional del Perú: Aproximación a la Constitución de 1993." In *La Constitución de 1993: An-*

álisis y Comentarios, pp. 11–65. Serie: Lecturas sobre temas constitucionales 10. Lima: Comisión Andina de Juristas.

Ferreira Filho, and Manoel Gonçalves. 1992. "Fundamental Aspects of the 1988 Constitution." In Jacob Dolinger and Keith S. Rosenn (eds.), *A Panorama of Brazilian Law*. Miami, FL: North-South Center, University of Miami.

Ferreira Rubio, D. 1991. "La regulación ha muerto. ¡Viva el Gran Regulador!" Unpublished.

Ferreira Rubio, D., and M. Goretti. 1994a. "The Emergency and the Relationship Between the Executive and the Congress During President Menem's Administration in Argentina: Use and Misuse of Prerogative Powers," in Longley, L. (ed.), *Working Papers on Comparative Legislative Studies*. Appleton, WI: Lawrence University RCLS-IPSA.

1994b. "Gobierno por decreto en Argentina," *El Derecho* 158: 848.

1994c. "Governar la emergencia. Uso y abuso de los decretos de necesidad y urgencia," *Agora*, 3–75.

Ferrero Costa, Eduardo (ed.). 1992. *Proceso de retorno a la institucionalidad democrática enel Perú*. Lima: Centro Peruano de Estudios Internacionales.

1993. "Peru's Presidential Coup," *Journal of Democracy* 4, 1: 28–40.

Figueiredo, Argelina Cheibub, and Fernando Limongi. 1994. "Mudança constitucional, desempenho do Legislativo e consolidação institucional." Paper presented to the XVIII ANPOCS conference, Caxambu, Minas Gerais, Brazil, November 23–27.

Figueiredo, Argelina Cheibub, and Fernando Limongi. 1995. "Partidos políticos na Câmara dos Deputados: 1989–1994." *Dados* 38, 3: 497–525.

Figueiredo, Argelina Cheibub, and Fernando Limongi. 1996. "Presidencialismo e apoio partidário no Congresso." *Monitor Público* 3, 8 (January–March): 27–36.

Figueiredo, Moreira, D. 1989. "Interferências entre Poderes do Estado," *Revista Informacion Legislislativa Brasília*, 26:103.

Fiorina, Morris. 1977. *Congress: Keystone of the Washington Establishment*. New Haven, CT: Yale University Press.

Fisher, Louis. 1993. *The Politics of Shared Power: Congress and the Executive*, 3rd edition. Washington, DC: CQ Press.

Fleischer, David V. 1994. "Political Corruption and Campaign Financing in Brazil: The Distraction Finesse of Impeachment, Congressional Inquests, Ceremonious Sackings, and Innocuous Legislation." Paper presented to the XVI World Congress of the International Political Science Association, Berlin, August 21–25.

Floridia, G., and S. Sicardi. 1991. "Le Relazioni Governo-Maggioranza-Opposizione Nella Prassi e Nell Evoluzione Regolamentare e Legislativa 1971–1991," *Quaderni Costituzionali* XI, 2 (August): 230–6.

Florit, Alejandra. 1996. "Menem: En siete años, 398 decretos," *La Nación* (on-line edition). Buenos Aires (November 24), 1,332.

Furnish, Dale B. 1971. "The Hierarchy of Peruvian Laws: Context for Law and Development," *The American Journal of Comparative Law* 18: 91–120.

Gaceta Oficial de la Repœblica de Venezuela. Various Issues. Caracas: La Republica de Venezuela.

Gamarra, Eudardo. 1997. "Hybrid-Presidentialism and Democratization: The Case of Bolivia." In Scott Mainwaring and Matthew S. Shugart (eds.), *Presidentialism and Democracy in Latin America*, pp. 363–93. New York: Cambridge University Press.

García Belaunde, Domingo. 1989. "Funciones legislativas del ejecutivo moderno: El caso peruano," *Lecturas sobre temas constitucionales* 3: 18–39. Lima: Comisión Andina de Juristas.

———. 1991. "El presupuesto de 1991: Idas y venidas," *El Jurista* 3 (August): 43–55.

García Belaunde, Víctor Andrés. 1988. *Los ministros de Belaunde 1963–68 y 1980–85*. Lima: Minerva.

Garcia Lema, A. 1993. *La reforma por dentro*. Buenos Aires: Planeta.

García Sayán, Diego. 1987. "Perú: estados de excepción y régimen jurídico," *Síntesis* 3 (September–December): 274–96.

Geddes, Barbara. 1996. "A Comparative Perspective on the Leninist Legacy in Eastern Europe." *Comparative Political Studies* 29.

Gonzalez, J. V. 1983. *Manual de la Constitución Argentina*. Buenos Aires: Estrada.

Goretti, Matteo. 1991. "El 'decretazo,' un hábito que erosiona la credibilidad," *Ambito Financiero* (April 30), Buenos Aires.

Gualieri, Dominic. 1993. "Russia's New 'War of Laws.'" *RFE/RL Research Report* 2, 3 (September 1993): 10–15.

Hilliker, Grant. 1971. *The Politics of Reform in Peru: The Aprista and Other Mass Parties of Latin America*. Baltimore: Johns Hopkins University Press.

Hine, David. 1986. "The Craxi Premiership." In R. Leonardi and R. Nanetti (eds.), *Italian Politics: A Review*, vol. 1, pp. 106–10. London: Frances Pinter.

———. 1988. "Italy: Condemned by Its Constitution?" In V. Bognador (ed.), *Constitutions in Democratic Politics*. Aldershot: Edward Elgar.

———. 1993. *Governing Italy*. Oxford: Clarendon Press.

Hine, David, and Renato Finocchi. 1991. "The Italian Prime Minister," *West European Politics* 14, 2 (April): 79–86.

Horta, Raul Machando. 1990. "Medidas Provisórias," *Revista de Informação Legislativa* 27, 107 (July–September): 5–18.

Huber, John D. 1992. "Restrictive Legislative Procedures in France and the United States," *American Political Science Review* 86: 675–87.

———. 1996a. *Rationalizing Parliament: Legislative Institutions and Party Politics in France*. New York: Cambridge University Press.

———. 1996b. "The Vote of Confidence in Parliamentary Democracies," *American Political Science Review* 90: 269–82.

Humana, Charles, (ed.). 1992. *World Human Rights Guide*. New York: Oxford University Press.

Ingberman, Daniel E., and Dennis A. Yao. 1991. "Presidential Commitment and the Veto," *American Journal of Political Science* 35: 357–89.

Jobim, Nelson. 1993. Interview with author, Brasília (June 15).

Jones, Mark P. 1995. *Electoral Laws and the Survival of Presidential Democracies*. Notre Dame, IN: University of Notre Dame Press.

Jones, Mark P. 1997. "Evaluating Argentina's Presidential Democracy." In Scott Mainwaring and Matthew S. Shugart (eds.), *Presidentialism and Democracy in Latin America*, pp. 259–99. New York: Cambridge University Press.

Jurado Nacional de Elecciones (JNE). 1982. *Resultados de las elecciones políticas generales de 1980*. Lima.

Karl, Terry. 1982. "The Political Economy of Petrodollars: Oil and Democracy." Ph.D. dissertation, Stanford University.

Kelley, R. Lynn. 1986. "Venezuelan Constitutional Forms and Realities." In John D. Martz and David J. Myers (eds.), *Venezuela: The Democratic Experience*, pp. 32–53. New York: Praeger.

Kiewiet, D. Roderick, and Mathew D. Cubbins. 1988. "Presidential Influence on Congressional Appropriation Decisions," *American Journal of Political Science* 32: 713–36.

——— 1991. *The Logic of Delegation: Congressional Parties and the Appropriations Process.* Chicago: University of Chicago Press.

Kingstone, Peter R., and Timothy J. Power (eds.). Forthcoming. *Democratic Brazil.* Pittsburgh: University of Pittsburgh Press.

Konstitutsiya Osnovnoi (Zakon) Rossiiskoi Federatsii. 1992. Moscow: Izdatelstvo Verkhovnogo Soveta Rossiiskoi Federatsii.

Konstitutsiya Rossiiskoi Federatsii. 1993. Moscow: Yuridicheskaya Literatura.

Kornblith, Miriam. 1991. "The Politics of Constitution Making: Constitutions and Democracy in Venezuela," *Journal of Latin American Studies* 23 (February): 61–89.

Krehbiel, Keith 1992. *Information and Legislative Organization.* Ann Arbor: University of Michigan Press.

Krieger, Gustavo, Fernando Rodrigues, and Elvis Cesar Bonassa. 1994. *Os Donos do Congresso: a Farsa na CPI do Orçamento.* São Paulo: Editora Ática.

Kubicek, Paul. 1994. "Delegative Democracy in Russia and Ukraine," *Communist and Post-Communist Studies* 27, 4: 423–11.

Kuczynski, Pedro-Pablo. 1977. *Peruvian Democracy under Economic Stress.* Princeton, NJ: Princeton University Press.

Laakso, Markku, and Taagepera, Rein. 1979. "The 'Effective' Number of Parties: A Measure with Application to West Europe," *Comparative Political Studies* 12, 1: 3–27.

Larkins, Christopher M. 1996. "Judicial Independence and Democratization: A Theoretical and Conceptual Analysis," *American Journal of Comparative Law* 44, 4: 605–26.

Leonardi, R., and D. Wertman. 1989. *Italian Christian Democracy: The Politics of Dominance.* London: Macmillan.

Leoni, Raœl. 1968. "Suspensión de Garantías Constitucionales en el Estado Zulia," *Documentos* 32: 417–18.

Leuchtenberg, William E. 1963. *Franklin Roosevelt and the New Deal.* New York: Harper & Row.

Lijphart, Arend. 1984. *Democracies: Patterns of Majoritarian and Consensus Government in Twenty-One Countries.* New Haven, CT: Yale University Press.

Linz, Juan J. 1994. "Presidential or Parliamentary Democracy: Does It Make a Difference?" In Juan Linz and Arturo Valenzuela (eds.), *The Failure of Presidential Democracy*, pp. 1–87. Baltimore: Johns Hopkins University Press.

Locke, John. 1986. *The Second Treatise on Civil Government.* Buffalo, NY: Prometheus Books.

Longi, Vincenzo. 1994. *Elementi di diritto e procedura parlamentare.* Milano, Italy: Giuffre.

Lugones, N., A. Garay, S. Dugo, and S. Corcuera. 1992. *Leyes de Emergencia. Decretos de Necesidad y Urgencia*. Buenos Aires: La Ley.

Lupia, Arthur. 1992. "Busy Voters, Agenda Control, and the Power of Information," *American Political Science Review* 86: 390–403.

McClintock, Cynthia. 1996. "La volundad política presidencial y la ruptura constitucional de 1992 en el Perú." In Fernando Tuesta Soldevilla (ed.), *Los enigmas del poder: Fujimori 1990–1996*, pp. 53–74. Lima: Fundación Friedrich Ebert.

McCubbins, Mathew D., Roger Noll, and Barry Weingast. 1987. "Administrative Procedures as an Instrument of Political Control," *Journal of Law, Economics, and Organization* 3: 243–77.

1989. "Structure and Process, Politics and Policy: Administrative Arrangements and the Political Control of Agencies," *Virginia Law Review* 75: 431–82.

1992. "Positive Canons: The Role of Legislative Bargains in Statutory Interpretation," *Georgetown Law Journal* 80: 705–42.

McCubbins, Mathew D., and Thomas Schwartz. 1984. "Congressional Oversight Overlooked: Police Patrols versus Fire Alarms," *American Journal of Political Science* 28: 165–79.

Mainwaring, Scott. 1991. "Politicians, Parties, and Electoral Systems: Brazil in Comparative Perspective," *Comparative Politics* 24, 1 (October): 21–43.

Mainwaring, Scott. 1993. "Brazilian Party Underdevelopment in Comparative Perspective," *Political Science Quarterly* 107, 4 (Winter): 677–707.

Mainwaring, Scott. 1994. "Presidentialism, Multiparty Systems, and Democracy: The Difficult Equation," *Comparative Political Studies* 26, 4: 198–228.

Mammi, Oscar. 1987. *Fra Governo e Parlamento*. Firenze, Italy: Passigli Editore.

Mannheimer, Renato. 1991. *La Lega Lombarda*. Milano, Italy: Franco Angeli.

Manzella, Andrea. 1991. *Il Parlamento*, 2nd Ed. Bologna: Il Mulino.

Marienhoff, M. 1988. *Tratado de Derecho Administrativo*. Buenos Aires: Abeledo-Perrot.

Massai, Alessandro. 1992. *Dentro Il Parlamento*. Milano, Italy: Il Sole 24 Ore Libri.

Matthews, Stephen A. 1989. "Veto Threats: Rhetoric in a Bargaining Game," *The Quarterly Journal of Economics*, 104: 347–69.

Maus, Didier. 1988a. "La Constitution jugée par sa pratique. Réflexions pour un bilan." In Olivier Duhamel and Jean-Luc Parodi (eds.), *La Constitution de la Cinquième République*. Paris: Presses de la Fondation Nationale des Sciences Politiques.

1988b. *Les grands textes de la pratique institutionnelle de la V Republique*. Paris: La Documentation française.

Mayer, George H. 1967. *The Republican Party, 1854–1966*, 2nd edition. New York: Oxford University Press.

Mello, José Celso de. 1990. "Considerações sobre as Medidas Provisórias," *Revista da Procuradoria General do Estado de São Paulo* 33 (June): 203–25.

Morrow, James. 1994. *Game Theory for Political Scientists*. Princeton, NJ: Princeton University Press.

Motta, Adylsson. 1993. Interview with author, Brasília (June 23).

Mueller, John E. 1970. "Presidential Popularity from Truman to Johnson," *American Political Science Review* 64: 18–34.

Naim, Moises. 1993. *Paper Tigers and Minotaurs: The Politics of Venezuela's Economic Reforms.* Washington, DC: The Carnegie Endowment for International Peace.

Nathan, Richard P. 1975. *The Plot that Failed: Nixon and the Administrative Presidency.* New York: Wiley.

Nikitinskii, Leonid. 1994. "Kak Izbrali Sudei" ["How the Judges Were Elected"], *Ogonek* 48–9 (December): 6–7.

Novaes, Carlos Alberto Marques. 1994. "Dinâmica institucional da representação: individualismo e partidos na Câmara dos Deputados," *Novos Estudos CE-BRAP* 38 (March): 99–147.

O'Donnell, Guillermo. 1993. "Estado, democratización y ciudadanía," *Nueva Sociedad* 128: 62–87.

O'Donnell, Guillermo. 1994. "Delegative Democracy?" *Journal of Democracy* 5, 1:55–69.

Ogul, Morris. 1976. *Congress Oversees the Bureaucracy: Studies in Legislative Supervision.* Pittsburgh, PA: University of Pittsburgh Press.

O'Halloran, Sharyn. 1994. *Politics, Process and American Trade Policy.* Ann Arbor, MI: University of Michigan Press.

Olson, Mancur. 1965. *The Logic of Collective Action.* Cambridge, MA: Harvard University Press.

Orttung, Robert W. 1995a. "Yeltsin and the Spin Doctors," *Transition* 1 (May 26): 11–14.

    1995b. "A Politically Timed Fight Against Extremism," *Transition* 1, 23 (June): 2–6.

Palmer, David Scott. 1996. " 'Fujipopulism' and Peru's Progress," *Current History* 95, no. 598: 70–5.

Pareja Pflücker, Piedad. 1987. *Atribuciones constitucionales del presidente de la república.* Lima: Ediciones Rikchay Perú.

Parrish, Scott. 1995. "A Turning Point in the Chechen Conflict," *Transition* 1 (July 28): 42–51.

Pasquino, Gianfranco. 1986. "Modernity and Reforms: The PSI between Political Entrepreneurs and Gamblers," *West European Politics* 9, 1 (January): 121–40.

Pezant, Jean-Louis. 1984. "Loi/règlement. la construction d'un nouvel équilibre." In Olivier Duhamel and Jean-Luc Parodi (eds.), *La Constitution de la Cinquième République*, pp. 342–74. Paris: Presses de la Fondation Nationale des Sciences Politiques.

Pierce, Roy. 1968. *French Politics and Political Institutions.* New York: Harper & Row.

    1991. "The Executive Divided Against Itself: Cohabitation in France, 1986–88," *Governance* 4: 269–94.

Planas, Pedro. 1992. *Rescate de la Constitución.* Lima: Abril.

Power, Timothy J. 1991. "Politicized Democracy: Competition, Institutions, and 'Civic Fatigue' in Brazil," *Journal of Interamerican Studies and World Affairs* 33, 3 (Fall): 75–112.

Power Manchego-Muñoz, Jorge. 1989. "El modelo constitucional del régimen político peruano." In *La Constitución diez años después*, pp. 167–82. Lima: Fundación Friedrich Naumann.

Przeworski, Adam. 1991. *Democracy and the Market: Political and Economic Reforms in Eastern Europe and Latin America*. New York: Cambridge University Press.

Rae, D. W. 1971. *The Political Consequences of Electoral Laws*. New Haven, CT: Yale University Press.

Rahr, Alexander. 1991. "The Presidential Race in the RSFSR," *RFE/RL Report on the USSR* 7 (June).

Remington, Thomas F., Steven S. Smith, D. Roderick Kiewiet, and Moshe Haspel. 1994. "Transitional Institutions and Parliamentary Alignments in Russia, 1990–93." In Thomas F. Remington (ed.), *Parliaments in Transition: The New Legislative Politics in the Former USSR and Eastern Europe*. Boulder, Co: Westview Press.

Resumar Semanal. 1990–97. Añas xiii–xix, nos. 580–923. Lima: DESCO.

Rey, Juan Carlos. 1989. *El Futuro de la Democracia en Venezuela*. Caracas: Colección Idea.

1994a. "Polarización Electoral, Economía del Voto y Voto Castigo en Venezuela: 1958–1988," *Cuestiones Políticas* 12: 3–95.

1994b. Personal communication.

Roberts, Kenneth M. 1995. "Neoliberalism and the Transformation of Populism in Latin America: The Peruvian Case," *World Politics* 48, 1: 82–116.

Rodríguez Brignardello, José Hugo. 1993. "El fallo en la acción de inconstitucionalidad contra el Decreto Legislativo No. 650 sobre compensación por tiempo de servicios." In *Formas de gobierno: Relaciones Ejecutivo-Parlamento*, pp. 213–24. Lima: Comisión Andina de Juristas.

Roeder, Phillip. 1994. "Varieties of Post-Soviet Authoritarian Regimes," *Post-Soviet Affairs* 10 (January–March): 61–101.

Rosenn, Keith S. 1990. "Brazil's New Constitution: An Exercise in Transient Constitutionalism for a Transitional Society," *American Journal of Comparative Law* 38 (Fall): 773–802.

Rossiter, Clinton. 1956. *The American Presidency*. New York: Signet.

Rubio, Marcial, and Bernales, Enrique. 1988. *Constitución y sociedad política*. Lima: Mesa Redonda.

Rudolph, James D. 1992. *Peru: The Evolution of a Crisis*. Westport, CT: Praeger.

Ruiz Moreno, H. 1990. "Los llamados reglamentos de necesidad y urgencia. La emergencia comomotivación de las leyes y reglamentos," *La Ley* B: 1029.

Sagues, N. P. 1991. "Legislación del Poder Ejecutivo detraída del Poder Legislativo. Apropósito de los decretos 'delegados' y de 'necesidad y urgencia'," *Revista de Derecho Bancario y de la Actividad Financiera*. Buenos Aires: Depalma.

Sakwa, Richard. 1993. *Russian Politics and Society*. London: Routledge.

Salvadori, Massimo. 1994. *Storia D'Italia e Crisi di Regime*. Bologna: Il Mulino.

Santos, Brasilino Pereira dos. 1991. "As Medidas Provisórias no direito comparado e no Brasil." 2 vols. Master's thesis, Departamento de Direito, Universidade de Brasília.

Schmidt, Gregory D. 1996. "Fujimori's 1990 Upset Victory in Peru: Electoral Rules, Contingencies, and Adaptive Strategies," *Comparative Politics* 28(3): 321–54.

Servizio Informazione e Relazione Esterne della Camera dei Deputati. 1994. *Tavolariassuntiva dei decreti legge*. Roma.

Sharlet, Robert. 1993a. "The Russian Constitutional Court: The First Term." *Post-Soviet Affairs* 9 (Winter): 1–39.

———. 1993b. "Russian Constituional Crisis: Law and Politics Under Yeltsin," *Post-Soviet Affairs* 9 (Fall): 314–36.

———. 1995. "The New Russian Constitution and Its Political Impact," *Problems of Post-Communism* (January–February): 3–12.

Shugart, Matthew S. 1997. "The Inverse Relationship Between Party Strength and Executive Strength: A Theory of Politicians' Constitutional Choices," *British Journal of Political Science* 27:519–47.

Shugart, Matthew S., and John M. Carey. 1992. *Presidents and Assemblies: Constitutional Design and Electoral Dynamics.* New York: Cambridge University Press.

Shugart, Matthew S., and Stephan Haggard. Forthcoming. "Institutions and Public Policy in Presidential Systems." In Mathew D. McCubbins and Stephan Haggard (eds.), *The Structure of Fiscal and Regulatory Policy.* Washington, DC: The World Bank.

Sigel, Thomas. 1995. "The Dismally Slow Pace of Agricultural Reform," *Transition* 1 26 (May): 15–18.

Slater, Wendy. 1994. "Russia's Plebiscite on a New Constitution," *RFE/RL Research Report* 3 (January 21): 1–7.

Soares, Glaucio Ary Dillon. 1979. "Military Authoritarianism and Executive Absolutism in Brazil," *Studies in Comparative International Development* 14, nos. 3–4 (Fall–Winter): 104–26.

Sobyanin, Alexander. 1994. "Political Cleavages Among the Russian Deputies." In Thomas F. Remington (ed.), *Parliaments in Transition: The New Legislative Politics in the Former USSR and Eastern Europe*, pp. 181–216. Boulder, CO: Westview Press.

Souza, Maria do Carmo Campello de. 1989. "The Brazilian New Republic: Under the Sword of Damocles." In Alfred Stepan (ed.), *Democratizing Brazil*, pp. 369–93. New York: Oxford University Press.

Spisso R. 1992. *La consolidación de deudas del Estado.* Buenos Aires: Depalma.

Stefoi-Sava, Elena. 1995. "Romania: Organizing Legislative Impotence," *East European Constitutional Review* 4, 2 (Spring): 81.

Stein, Steve. 1980. *Populism in Peru: The Emergence of the Masses and the Politics of Social Control.* Madison: University of Wisconsin Press.

Stephens, O., and G. Rathjen. 1980. *The Supreme Court and the Allocation of Constitutional Power.* San Francisco: Freeman Co.

Sterpa, Egidio. 1990. "A Montecitorio si volta pagina," *Nuovi Studi Politici* XX, 2 (April): 126.

"Suspensión de las Garantías Para Qué?" 1994. *Referencias: Boletín de Derechos Humanos y Coyuntura* 6 (July): 1–2.

Szklarowsky, Leon Frejda. 1991. *Medidas Provisórias.* São Paulo: Editora Revista dos Tribunais.

Teague, Elizabeth, and Wishnevsky, Julia. 1991. "Yeltsin Bans Organized Political Activity in State Sector," *RFE/RL Report on the USSR* 16 (August): 21.

Thorson, Carla. 1991a. "Has the Communist Party Been Legally Suspended?" *RFE/RL Report on the USSR* 4 (October).

———. 1991b. "RSFSR Forms Constitutional Court," *RFE/RL Report on the USSR* 20 (December).

"The Fate of the Communist Party in Russia," *RFE/RL Research Report on the USSR* 1, 18 (September).

Tolz, Vera, and Julia Wishnevsky. 1994. "Election Queries Make Russians Doubt Democratic Process," *RFE/RL Research Report* 3 (April 1): 1–6.

Torre, J. C. 1993. "The Politics of Economic Crisis in Latin America," *Journal of Democracy* 4, 1: 104–16.

Torres y Torres Lara, Carlos. 1991. *Los decretos de urgencia*. Lima: Librería Studium.

———. 1994. *Preguntas y respuestas sobre la nueva constitución*. Lima: Desarrollo y Paz.

Troper, Michel. 1987. "La signature des ordonnance: Fonctions d'une controverse," *Pouvoirs* 41: 75–91.

Tuesta Soldevilla, Fernando. 1994. *Perú político en cifras: Élite política y elecciones*, 2nd ed. Lima: Fundación Friedrich Ebert.

Urban, Michael. 1994. "December 1993 as a Replication of Late-Soviet Electoral Practices," *Post-Soviet Affairs* 10 (April–June): 127–58.

Velásquez, Ramón J. 1976. *Venezuela Moderna: Medio Siglo de Historia 1926–1976*. Caracas: Fundación Eugenio Mendoza.

Verbitsky, H. 1993. *Hacer la Corte. La construcción de un poder absoluto sin justicia ni control*. Buenos Aires: Planeta.

Villegas Basavilbaso, B. 1949. *Derecho Administrativo*. Buenos Aires: Tea.

Weekly Compilation of Presidential Documents. 1993. Vol. 29. Washington, DC: GPO.

Weldon, Jeffrey. 1997. "Political Sources of *Presidencialismo* in Mexico." In Scott Mainwaring and Matthew S. Shugart (eds.), *Presidentialism and Democracy in Latin America*, pp. 225–58. New York: Cambridge University Press.

Wegren, Stephen K. 1993. "Rural Reform in Russia," *RFE/RL Research Report* 2, 29 (October): 43–53.

West, William F., and Joseph Cooper. 1985. "The Rise of Administrative Clearance." In George C. Edwards III, Steven A. Shull, and Norman C. Thomas (eds.), *The Presidency and Public Policy Making*. Pittsburgh, PA: University of Pittsburgh Press.

Weyland, Kurt. 1993. "The Rise and Fall of President Collor and Its Impact on Brazilian Democracy," *Journal of Interamerican Studies and World Affairs* 35, 1 (Summer): 1–37.

Wise, Carol. 1994. "The Politics of Peruvian Economic Reform: Overcoming the Legacies of State-Led Development," *Journal of Interamerican Studies and World Affairs* 36, 1 (Summer): 75–125.

Wishnevsky, Julia. 1992. "Antidemocratic Tendencies in Russian Policy Making," *RFE/RL Research Report* 1 (November 15): 21–5.

Wishnevsky, Julia. 1993a. "Russian Constitutional Court: A Third Branch of Government?" *RFE/RL Research Report* 2, 12 (February): 1–8.

Wishnevsky, Julia. 1993b. "Literal Opposition Emerging in Russia?" *RFE/RL Research Report* 2 (November 5): 5–11.

Zaffaroni, E. 1994. "La reforma cancela el parlamento," *Clarín* (May 20).

INDEX